Charity & Merit

TIMOTHY C. JACOBSON

Charity & Merit

TRINITY SCHOOL AT 300

TRINITY SCHOOL

New York, New York

Published by

UNIVERSITY PRESS

OF NEW ENGLAND

Hanover & London

Published by University Press of New England,
One Court Street, Lebanon, NH 03766
www.upne.com

© 2009 by Trinity School

Printed in the United States of America

5   4   3   2   1

Library of Congress Cataloging-in-Publication Data
Jacobson, Timothy C., 1948–
Charity & merit : Trinity School at 300 / Timothy C. Jacobson
    p. cm.
Includes bibliographical references and index.
ISBN 978-1-58465-748-4 (cloth : alk. paper)
1. Trinity School (New York, N.Y.)—History. I. Title II. Title: Charity and merit.
LD7501.N529J33 2009
373.22'2097471—dc22 2008044667

In Memory of

CLARENCE BRUNER-SMITH

1903–2001

Member of the Faculty 1927–2001

and

HENRY C. MOSES

1941–2008

Twenty-seventh Headmaster 1991–2008

Contents

Preface and Acknowledgments

In 1991 Henry C. Moses was named twenty-seventh headmaster of Trinity School in New York City and almost immediately began to ask questions about Trinity's history. Conversations soon began with The Winthrop Group, Inc., a consulting firm of business and organizational historians, and this book, a response to Moses's curiosity and published on the occasion of Trinity's 300th anniversary, is the result.

Trinity is one of the oldest schools of any kind in North America, and it is the oldest continuously operating school in New York City. It is not exactly what one might expect. Like all independent schools in today's fiercely competitive market, Trinity is expensive to attend, yet it is not a wealthy institution. It occupies a warren of unselfconscious buildings on West 91st Street that are far from fancy. It is an academically elite school but not one for the economic elite alone. It is called "Trinity," and a cross marks its logo, though only a minority of its students is Christian. It began its long life as the ward of Trinity Church in downtown Manhattan, but for the last century and more it has been an institution of the Upper West Side. This study of its history began in earnest in the early 2000s and as Moses wished is completed on the eve of the school's tercentenary, though he himself did not live to see the finished book. He wished only to learn from Trinity's past in order to gain perspective on his own times and lead Trinity more wisely. He set no instructions or limitations but for a book that spoke plainly and reached conclusions independently.

It is based on documentary research in a number of repositories, including Trinity School, Trinity Church, the Episcopal Diocese of New York, Trinity-Pawling School, the New-York Historical Society, General Theological Seminary, and the Library of Congress, and on interviews with Trinity people who have known the school firsthand from the 1930s until today. It has benefited from review by a committee of Trinity faculty, staff, alumni, and friends that included Myles B. Amend, Andrew Delbanco, Peter Donhauser, Justin Jamail, Paul Kerz '58, Barbara Lutz, Maxine McClintock, John Nichols, Brooke Palmer '00, Audree Pospisil, Kevin Ramsey, Thomas Roberts, Robert Stewart, and Deirdre Williamson. Sylvia Kollar, Winthrop Group archivist assigned to the Trinity School Archive, was an extremely knowledgeable and helpful guide to the collection.

The project was financed through special fund raising, and donors included The Loewy Family Foundation, Charles E. Albers '58, John P. Arnhold '71, Lawrence B. Benenson '85, Caroline Franklin Berry '75, Herbert Chen '78, Claude A. Chene '78, George B. Clairmont '66, John S. W. Dawson '78, Roanak V. Desai '96, William V. Fogg '84, Kenneth L. Greif '53, Frederic Haber '75, Murk-Hein Heinemann '68, Allan M. Keene '64, Paul J. Kerz '58, Melissa Franklin Keyte '77, William P. Lauder '78, David A. Lifson '68, Jeffrey Mass '58 *in memoriam*, Alissa Reiner McCreary '85, Eric Moscahlaidis '78, Richard B. Nye '57, Victoria A. Oliver '78, Thomas P. Peardon, Jr. '56, Douglas M. Polley '85, John Ryan '78, Nicholas and Julie Sakellariadis, Harry W. Segalas '78, Benjamin R. Shute, Jr. '54, Douglas T. Tansill '56, Scott F. A. Thiel '83, John F. Werner '58, and Joanne A. Zervos '78.

Special thanks are due to Davis Dyer of The Winthrop Group, Inc., for wise counsel and valued editing, and to Myles B. Amend, Director of Development and Alumni Relations at Trinity, and Suellyn Preston Scull, Interim Head of School at this writing, for warm welcome and friendship as we have striven to understand a very old and unique institution.

Summer 2008

Charity & Merit

ONE *Time, Place, and Purpose*

*I*n 1903, the Reverend Dr. Lawrence Thomas Cole came to Trinity School in New York City as headmaster, or "rector" in the old Episcopal usage, in a long line reaching back to William Huddleston and the school's founding 194 years before. He stayed on until retirement in 1937, Trinity's longest serving head thus far. Also in 1903 was born Trinity's best remembered and perhaps best loved teacher, whose name now adorns the yearbook: Clarence Bruner-Smith. Cole hired Bruner-Smith (hereafter "Bruner," as he was universally known to the Trinity community) to teach English at Trinity in 1927, and he stayed on in the classroom until 1970, Trinity's longest serving teacher thus far.

Cole died in 1956 and left no memoir. Few now are living who remember his tenure. Bruner never really retired at all. He kept an office at school until 1995 and continued in an alumni relations role until his death in 2001. He lived in an apartment in Trinity House, over the store. He corresponded in longhand with students, some for decades after their graduation; thousands still remember the man. He left copious memoirs and told several interesting stories. Few dwelt on Bruner himself. All intertwined with Trinity.

REMEMBERING TRINITY

The earliest of Bruner's memoirs had to do with Cole and, even though two-thirds of the way through the chronology, they are a good opening onto a history that reaches back over 300 years. Twenty-four when he arrived at the building on West 91st Street, Bruner brought, in addition to rookie teaching skills, an unpretentious middle-class biography. He was smart and, with the formal learning that a good bachelor's degree alone once conferred, well educated. He was not a native New Yorker but a Midwesterner, not exactly a refugee from the provinces (where far on into life he faithfully journeyed each year to visit family) but dazzled for sure at the happenstance that had landed him in the metropolis. His was a variant of the old country-boy-comes-to-big-city American story, though he did not come to New York seeking material fortune, fame, or romance, but to teach school. In teaching, he found his fortune, and in New York the love of his lifetime.

He was born in Decatur, Illinois, and shared the same name with his father, a salesman.[1] His mother, Louella Barnard, died when he was sixteen, and there was one sibling, brother Leonard, nine years his senior. Decatur was a prosperous downstate county seat and since the founding of Milliken University there in 1900 a college town. Bruner described himself as a bookish fellow from the start, and Decatur as a not-bad-at-all hometown. He had good teachers in the public schools, took piano lessons and learned to play the organ, served Sundays as a chorister at the local Episcopal church, big black bow and broad collar over his white surplice as was then the fashion. College material but with a newly widowed father, he started out at home at Milliken, pretty clearly an English major in the making. In his sophomore year, he headed-up Milliken's Elizabethan Society, which sponsored guest speakers, one of whom would turn him toward New York. Novelist, poet, and music critic John Erskine taught at Columbia and apparently was not above poaching promising talent for his employer, even from places as modest as Milliken. He urged Bruner to transfer. It was apparently an easy sell, and, Columbia aside, the prospect of life in the big city had a lot to do with it. Had Erskine hailed from Northwestern or the University of Chicago, Chicago probably would have cast the same spell and Francis Parker or Chicago Latin been the beneficiaries of his teaching gifts. As it was, the result was Clarence Bruner-Smith, A.B., Columbia class of 1925: avid concert and theatergoer, a regular at libraries and bookstores, early and lifelong enthusiast for a new magazine launched that very February and called *The New Yorker*.

At Columbia, just as he had back home, he excelled as a student and decided he wanted to become a teacher. Senior year, he took courses at Teachers College and student taught at Horace Mann School at 91st and Broadway. He looked for work through a teachers' agency, which landed him a first job, alas, back in the woods. Silver Bay School for Boys on Lake George disappeared long ago, an old-time proprietary outfit near the bottom rung of the boarding-school ladder. With no experience of boarding-school life but in no position to turn down the offer, Bruner left New York for an unpromising start in teaching.

Remoteness need not be a direct function of distance, as Silver Bay, not a hundred miles from Manhattan, proved to be for young Bruner, who traveled by train as far as Ticonderoga and then by steamboat from Lake George Village. He found there a sympathetic headmaster in Robert Carver French, and a "rather motley student body" that, as is the case with first-time teachers, taught him as much as he taught them.[2] The first year he earned $1,600 (minus $480 for room and board), but had it been twice that, he probably would have fit no better. He taught everything from *Silas Marner* to the life of Christ, took dorm duty, and endured all the rest of the boarding-school routine, seven days a week. "Afraid of hard work" was not a phrase ever associated with Bruner, and his discontent was probably an instance of the shock of the new coupled with youthful impatience at finding himself not quite where he wished to be. When he tried to resign after the first year, French simply told him he couldn't. French also increased his salary to $2,200, and the second year turned out better as the young man began to get the hang of it and gain confidence that he could in fact learn to teach.

Two years was enough, though, and French could not hold him. Bruner told the agency he would rather quit teaching than continue in boarding school. Then he got lucky. "*The best independent day school in Manhattan*," the letter put it that invited him to an interview with the Rev. Lawrence Cole, Rector of Trinity School, in the spring of 1927. At the end of May, Cole offered Bruner the mastership of English for the school year 1927–28 at a salary of $2,750. Without hesitation he took it.[3]

Two years out of college, Bruner had found his vocation and the right place to practice it—a fortunate man. He was not ungrateful, and in the years ahead returned to Trinity the fullest measure of devotion. At the time, he brought decent knowledge of his subject plus all of youth's energy and enthusiasm. He also hoped, no doubt, that Lawrence Cole, his second headmaster, would turn out to be as good a man to work for as had been Robert French, but in a more congenial setting.

Bruner remembered his nervous first dinner with Cole, in the winter of 1927. Unmarried, Cole lived in the brownstone rectory at 147 West 91st and, in those far-off times, kept a Filipino houseboy named Ito who slept in the cellar by the coal bin.[4] Churchman to the core, Cole liked his rituals. There was daily chapel at Trinity in those days (with the Litany, during which the boys all knelt, on Fridays), and at the rectory each evening there was the cocktail hour. "One is sufficient, two are too many, and three are not nearly enough," Cole cheerfully hosted his guests, Prohibition or not. Bruner, also a lifelong bachelor and known later in life to enjoy his own nightly martini, found Cole at first overwhelming, and though accustomed from his Illinois boyhood to grace said before meals was unprepared for Cole's added rubric of grace afterward. He was also at first additionally uncomfortable at the circumstances of his hiring, for the man he replaced was reportedly a fine teacher and popular in the school. The vacancy had come about, however, when Cole refused to renew the teacher's contract because he intended to marry a divorcée.[5]

For the ten years remaining before Cole retired, Bruner could not remember ever seeing Cole dressed other than in his clericals. As Bruner grew more comfortable in and continued to observe his setting, it became apparent to him what this meant. Cole, he later recalled, was "a kindly gentleman more interested in the church, really, than he was in education."[6] Bruner caught Cole two-thirds of the way through his Trinity tenure. When he first observed Cole midway through the 1920s it would have been perfectly reasonable for a young Bruner to conclude that the school over which this kindly priest presided was indeed the same solid concern as described in the agency's letter as the best independent day school in Manhattan. Cole certainly sent off no other signals.

Bruner, who went on to serve under five subsequent headmasters, remembered Cole as the last of his kind at Trinity. This was literal: Cole was the last of the headmasters in Holy Orders. It was also symbolic: Cole formally headed the school but did not quite lead it, as all his successors would try to do with one degree of success or another. His immediate predecessor, August Ulmann, had tried, too, imposing a German *gymnasium*-style regime on unwilling faculty and distressed parents who revolted and saw to his ouster. Cole came in to restore calm. He had the right touch, and Trinity was still calm in 1927 when Bruner made his appearance there: 300 or so boys in grades one to twelve, eighteen faculty, a happy, self-sustaining little crew. From his big classroom on the third floor, Bruner could look down onto the living room of the rectory to observe Cole, mid-morning with the school day in full swing, placidly turning the pages of the old *Herald Tribune*. Once a month, he appeared in Bruner's class where, as the boys rose politely, he ceremonially presented the English master his paycheck, adding with sparkle: "If Mr. Bruner doesn't want this I will be glad to share it with you."[7]

Cole did not hand out money to his teachers alone, but to a good many of their students too. He took seriously Trinity's ancient warrant as a charity school of the Anglican, then the Episcopal, Church, and to the extent that a modest endowment made possible, he subsidized students with little reference to financial need. Bruner often heard him remark that if the school made "one dollar in profit, it was not living up to the purpose of its establishment." The endowment had originated in a highly entailed bequest from the 1790s of farmland on the East River, which had it been handled differently might have made Trinity a wealthy school. It wasn't, and so Trinity wasn't, and much of the money it did have appears to have slowly seeped away during Cole's time. He had no head for numbers. As the stories came down to Bruner, Cole's standard question to the parents of boys applying for admission in those day was, "Do you want a scholarship?" If yes was the answer, then a scholarship was what they got.

An easygoing administrator and father figure around the boys, Cole presided at chapel, taught the required courses in sacred studies, liked to welcome "his boys" to school in the morning and shake hands as they left, sending each off with a hearty "play hard!" By benign default, the faculty ran the school then. This suited both greenhorns like Bruner and the veterans whose path he would follow, teachers who came to Trinity young and stayed on until they were old. It was then long before the days of elaborate orientations for new staff, and he remembered a sink-or-swim attitude that older faculty took toward beginners. He could not even recall an opening-of-school faculty meeting that autumn of 1927. He was given a schedule of his classes, was assigned a homeroom, and was left to figure it out for himself.

If Cole had a philosophy of education that he could be said to have applied at Trinity, "God will take care," in Bruner's phrase, summarized it. With those of other headmasters, his portrait hangs today outside the current headmaster's office. He looks rather like Bruner remembered him: kindly, low-key, content. He is dressed in clericals. Trinity's last "rector," he got on with his board, got out of his faculty's way, and spread scholarship largesse through a student body then still largely middle-class, homogeneous, and, as a ninety-something Bruner wistfully looked back on his own youthful Trinity days, a student body "with good manners and who were a pleasure to teach."8

Cole's Trinity sputtered during the Depression, which revealed financial weaknesses and the need for a different sort of leader. Bruner remembered him too. He was Matthew E. Dann, and he also had come to Trinity in 1927, to teach math and French. Dann's portrait hangs near to Cole's: headmaster from 1937 to 1955. He wears a business suit and carries a ledger. Dann was a banker with a master's degree in economics from Columbia, who turned to teaching after a brief stint on Wall Street. A more different character from Cole, who to his credit was unafraid to hire to his own weaknesses, it would be hard to imagine.

They got on, though, and with Cole's full approbation Dann became assistant rector in 1935 (the title was discontinued four years later in favor of "headmaster") and heir-apparent upon Cole's retirement. If Cole had little nose for business and was more churchman than schoolman, Dann was, as Bruner put it economically, "a businessman at heart." A good thing, too, for the school likely could not have gone on for much longer in Cole's God-will-provide mode of management. Part of his Christian duty, however, was to stay alert to fresh signals from on high: God worked in mysterious ways his wonders to perform and, who knew, maybe someone like Dann was one of them. Bruner accepted Dann as the man that the times demanded, pretty much leaving God out of it, and the times demanded a good deal.

Cole and Dann differed hugely as personalities, and those personalities dictated their attitude to the business of schooling in the circumstances where they found themselves. Cole was a conservative, ever faithful in the day-to-day, year-to-year operations of the school to his understanding of why Trinity had been founded. To Dann, relatively speaking a radical, founding pieties were of small interest compared to how Trinity responded, or failed to respond, to the challenge of changing times and markets. It was a question he bequeathed to all his successors.[9]

As Bruner perceived it, the distinction in this particular instance was between a headmaster (Cole) who understood Trinity primarily as a close community of teachers and students alone, and another one (Dann) who understood and began to manage Trinity as an institution with other constituencies as well. This meant at first trying to shore up the financial ship. "Penny-pincher," Bruner described Dann, and meant it. If Bruner's most indelible memory was of Cole genteelly presiding in chapel, or at cocktails, of Dann it was the memory of a sharp pencil. When the two men arrived at Trinity in 1927, the school's library contained all of 500 books, mostly on religion. Augmenting it became one of Bruner's pet projects over the years. The English teacher would make out his list, but the banker held the purse strings: "If any one of them cost over $5.00, he crossed it off." Like books, like teachers: "Matt had the philosophy that you paid a teacher what you had to."[10]

That was one reason why Dann proved a success. The Depression had left even fewer of Trinity's students paying the full, however modest, tuition. But to Dann anemic revenues signaled not just the need to cut costs and raise prices, but the need somehow to make the school more attractive to more students with parents prepared to pay, and to begin to address the problem of more places than applicants to fill them. Concepts not yet in vogue in independent education in the 1940s, marketing and self-promotion came slowly to Trinity, but it was Dann who planted the seeds.

To Bruner the academic (he became head of the upper school the same year Dann became headmaster), Dann the administrator took Trinity around the corner into an era more familiar from the 1990s, which was when Bruner wrote his memoirs—more familiar at any rate than Cole's old-time Episcopal prep school with its still heavy charity overlay. These two Trinitys—the Trinity of Bruner's first few years there and the Trinity of his remaining long career—shared, it is true, one general educational goal, to prepare young men for college, and one physical location. But if on West 91st Street Trinity seemed to have ended its long march up Manhattan and settled down for good, the city that surrounded it there certainly did not stand still, in two respects that Bruner found noteworthy. Literally, the neighborhood changed from a solidly middle-class, even fashionable Upper West Side of the late nineteenth century, to something so different by the 1950s as to demand comprehensive renewal and redevelopment. As its surroundings declined, Trinity and Trinity boys stuck out, and prickly relations between what appeared to be a fancy private school and its less-than-fancy neighbors required delicate management. External, community relations had not been an item high on Cole's agenda; thenceforth, they would be. Shifting markets for Trinity's educational services paralleled chronologically changes in its physical neighborhood and would pose challenges just as great. Bruner lived to see Trinity gets its arms around its new neighbors and become an active player in West Side redevelopment. He did not live to see solved an even tougher problem, centering on class and money, that was surfacing through the final years of his career.

What purpose, wondered Bruner from late in life, did Trinity serve anyway? The answer related directly to the people it served or, more clinically, the people who with other options chose to send their boys and, starting again in the 1970s, their girls to Trinity. The nature and number of those other options determined the relative place of a private school like Trinity in the educational marketplace of New York City. As long as poor, middling, and rich New Yorkers alike deemed the public schools to be adequate educational suppliers, then the pool of takers for Trinity's special brand of schooling was small and no more rapidly growing than the population. If and when enough New Yorkers judged the supply of public education less favorably, then the demand exerted even by a minority of them on private alternatives like Trinity would soar. This began to happen in the 1970s. Where once Matt Dann had worried over empty desks and too few applicants to fill them, Bruner lived to worry over the reverse dynamic, which bid up Trinity's value in the eyes of families whose own heated expectations drove up the prices the school had to charge in order to deliver on them.

Bruner was as happy with Trinity's academics and its overall educational program in the 1990s as he had been in the 1920s. In some ways he was happier: Girls, who reappeared in the 1970s after a long hiatus, he thought were a great addition. He was less happy over who more generally got the privilege of partaking of Trinity. "For the first twenty years that I was here, nine-tenths of the student body came from middle income or low income families." He may not have had the proportions exactly right, but he fairly set the question. "My great worry about Trinity School is the fact that it will become, and is becoming, a school for the very rich."[11] That was in 1992, when tuition was $14,500. In 2007, it crested $30,000.

A formal old-fashioned schoolmaster who wore crisp suits and jackets, well-knotted ties and polished shoes, who was proud that Trinity required Latin and offered Greek, who thought highly of fencing because it taught "many a boy [to] achieve poise and good bearing,"[12] Bruner did not mind at all that what Trinity had to offer was not for everyone. Even so, he believed that less-than-genius boys and girls when well taught and supported could rise to its standards, and he hoped that less-than-rich ones would continue to get their chance to prove it. He drew the distinction between an elite school—nothing wrong with that in his eyes—and a school for the economic elite. It was a distinction that Bruner feared Trinity might someday forget or fail to manage correctly.

THE LONG PAST

By the time he wrote all this down in the early 1990s, Trinity's longest serving teacher was over ninety, and Trinity some 280 years old. Bruner served through a good sixth of that long past, which was long enough to become the symbol of Trinity's continuity and to bear witness to a fair portion of Trinity's change. Any history as long as this comprises disparate stories. Trinity's beginning, which reaches back more than three centuries, seems so remote as to belong to a different world from our own. Past and present relate with difficulty, though key periods of transformation help connect the story. Trinity has experienced three: the first in the 1830s, from charity school to fee-charging preparatory school; the second as Bruner observed it starting in the 1930s, from Cole's aloof self-sufficient Trinity to Dann's more businesslike institution; the third in the 1970s, from Episcopal school for boys alone to pluralist independent school for girls and boys together. Both before and after the first period of transformation, long continuity marked Trinity's story. In more recent times, change of ever-increasing velocity has crowded in.

Each of these transformations was both authored from the inside and occurred against the backdrop of contemporary social and economic change. Across its long history, Trinity has had twenty-eight headmasters. From the late nineteenth century at least, we have record enough of who these men were to see the extent to which their identities impressed themselves upon the institution. Those impressions were deep and lasting, so this narrative puts their influence frankly to the fore. Trinity was and remains a relatively a small place, highly sensitive to the touch of those called to lead it. Every text has a context, however, and the actions of none of Trinity's leaders can be understood outside the story of New York, its schools, and its neighborhoods. Though Trinity was small and set apart, its story relates to the slow rise of a system of public education in New York City and, tangentially, to the city's "school wars" later in the nineteenth and twentieth centuries. Its story also illuminates in tight focus something of the evolution of New York City itself from colonial seaport to modern metropolis. Trinity's fitful migration northward up Manhattan, from the environs of Trinity Church to its current home on the Upper West Side where it arrived at the end of the nineteenth century, echoed the city's growth and development. The story of how Trinity's leaders in the mid-twentieth century struggled with the question of whether or not to stay on West 91st Street, long after the neighborhood had declined, and to participate in its redevelopment, links text and context more tightly yet.

In the beginning everything looked diminutive. Founder William Huddleston's Trinity was tiny and so, relatively, was the world in which he worked. New York City at the turn of the seventeenth century contained some 5,000 people, English subjects all since the Dutch in 1664 had surrendered New Amsterdam to King Charles II, who then renamed it for his brother and heir James, Duke of York. Born in 1662 in Cumberland and trained as a lawyer, William Huddleston came to New York probably in 1685, the year Catholic James acceded to the throne where he precipitated, three years later, the Glorious Revolution and the Protestant ascendancy. Huddleston arrived in a Calvinist town that still spoke Dutch. In the movement to make New York more thoroughly English he found his métier, not as a lawyer at all but as a schoolmaster. Making New York more English was problematic because of the diversity of the place even then, filled as it was, in addition to Dutch and English, with Germans, Danes, French, Indians, Africans, and Jews. By the standards of the age, New York was a tolerant trading city at the junction of a safe harbor and a rich hinterland, but with still pallid civic institutions, especially schools. Demand for schooling, if not exactly vigorous, was at least latent in a place where exchange was everything. Ever in need of paying work, Huddleston stepped up to meet and encourage it.

Huddleston started teaching in the 1690s, and when the vestry of Trinity Church, chartered in 1697, decided to establish a charity school under parish auspices, parishioner Huddleston's ambition met the opportunity. In 1709, partly at Huddleston's bidding, the Society for the Propagation of the Gospel in Foreign Parts (SPG), the missionary arm of the Church of England, granted a formal charter for "The Charity School of Trinity Parish" and with it a small subsidy. Huddleston was named as schoolmaster. With the Anglican charity school in the city of New York, the SPG appears to have been largely satisfied from the very beginning, when it "ordered that £10 for one year from this time [1709] be allowed to the said Mr. Huddleston in consideration of his being well recommended to the society & upon consideration that he shall teach 40 poor children and transmit certificate thereof to this board." From that distant point, the history of Trinity School formally got under way, in time even a modest historiography growing up around it.[13]

FROM THERE TO HERE

Founder William Huddleston had no idea where history in the early eighteenth century was heading, and Trinity's current leaders do not know now. Huddleston was concerned with survival for himself and his family, and running a school in colonial New York was means to that end. Henry Moses, Trinity's head during most of the writing of this book, presided over a more substantial and complex Trinity but where teaching and learning, or, for him, primarily the administration of teaching and learning, consumed his days as they did Huddleston's. Not all of them were good ones. The author encountered the harried headmaster in the Great Hall at 139 West 91st Street in February 2004 and asked how his school was going that particular winter afternoon. Came a weary, "You wanta trade jobs? Here, take her, she's yours!"[14] Moses was a man who could make, and take, a joke, and he spoke with a twinkle, hurrying on.

Three centuries separate Henry Moses and William Huddleston: centuries containing a revolution, a civil war, several depressions, and locally a good deal of change in the neighborhood, as New York grew from an Anglo-Dutch colonial seaport to, the locals today will tell you, the world's greatest city. Moses came to Trinity from a job at Harvard, one of the few schools in America at any level older than this one. Huddleston came from England, a poor man on the make. They both ended up in charge, but there, given the obvious differences in the place they were in charge of and the world it occupied, comparison might end. But for this: Both worried constantly about their respective societies' resources for training up the young and relating their training to the long portion of those lives that would be lived after school was over. For his time, Moses said two things above all filled his days and occupied, and sometimes troubled, his mind. How does Trinity attract, retain, and sustain the very best faculty: the masters who make the learning happen? And how does Trinity prepare the students they teach for citizenship?[15]

"Prep" as in prep school was a usage that would not gain currency for 150 years after Huddleston died in 1721. Today Trinity belongs to a pack of the best prep schools in the land. Ask students what Trinity preps them for, and they will say "to get into a good college." This is true but limited. Moses knew better, or more. The capability of today's Trinity to advance its students to good colleges frankly measures its advantage or disadvantage in an intensely competitive educational marketplace. It is a capability that, while Moses could not quite take it for granted, Trinity's faculty reliably sees to. No one, or virtually no one, went to college in or from New York in Huddleston's far-off day. Huddleston was not a university man himself. "Prep," if we could ask, conjured to him a different goal: life as a skilled manual tradesman, for instance, or as a wife who could read as well as sew.

What now looks small and modest then did not. The difference may not be as large as it first seems, however. Huddleston's humble hand-to-mouth charity school taught a few New York children skills that their society valued and that equipped an individual better to get on in this life and (for it was a school of the church) into the next. It taught boys and girls how to carry themselves toward others, in family and community: duties and responsibilities in addition to skills and knowledge. There were no citizens then but only subjects, and notions of civic space and individual freedoms were in that age rather more constrained than now. But the price of failure could be just as high, and so the urgency of training: Life offered abundant cracks to fall through, and fortune then as now favored the prepared. Moses's more sophisticated Trinity also taught a few New York children skills that their society values, the absence of which it discounted harshly. Trinity remains a school of the church, though oddly so, and Moses hoped still that it prepped students in ethical if not always religious ways to live better in community: what he meant by citizenship.[16]

Moses worried most about faculty, how to get and keep them. In the early twenty-first century, prospective students line up at Trinity's door. Not so for Huddleston, who fretted endlessly about students, how to get and keep them. In the early eighteenth century, there was no need for faculty without, as he called students, "scholars." Neither Moses nor Huddleston had much perspective on his own tenure (though Moses hoped to improve his by reading this history). But regard them again from some distance in the future, say a century from now, and they will appear kin after all, not that far under the skin. Chances are that both men, along with the twenty-five others who came in between, will appear to have been chasing the same thing, to have shared the same purpose, to have puzzled at the same questions. By what process do teachers best teach students and students learn from teachers and from one other? What does such teaching and learning impart beyond the classroom? What can we learn from their answers?

Set in the floor of the Great Hall in the old 139 building there used to be a mosaic rendering of Trinity's official motto: *Fides, Labore et Virtute*. Bruner reported that in 1958 someone (who, the record is silent) decided permanently to rearrange that grand space, and the mosaic disappeared. Thenceforth, the motto was simplified to *Labore et Virtute*, and so it remains today. Trinity itself was not so easily simplified, however, and *fides*—faith—variously interpreted continued to have something to do with it. Ask a weary senior, burned out in preparing for finals, SATs, and college applications. Ask a master teacher, who in students values curiosity over cleverness. Ask a headmaster determined to graduate not just smart students but virtuous citizens.

Another Latin fragment today intrudes even more sharply onto Trinity's consciousness. *Trinity Per Saecula*, title of the alumni magazine, fits and flatters an audience whose schooldays are now past but who carry, so the school hopes, something of Trinity "out there" into the world beyond 91st Street, beyond the Upper West Side, beyond even New York City. It sounds serious and is meant to be: Serious alums support their old school. This is good, for Trinity in 2009 is still not a wealthy school. Recent history suggests, though, that competition has made Trinity an ever more elite school.

Further history instructs us to regard this fact within an old debate, about the place and content of elite independent education in a democratic society. How to reconcile educational aristocracies, albeit aristocracies of talent, with the instinct of egalitarianism to level down not up? How to nurture the spiritual and intellectual lives of young people in a commercial, secular culture? How, in a metropolis ever filled with newcomers, to welcome strangers and yet transform them—how to be enriched by diversity but not overcome by it? How to help those who need a hand up? How to translate, *per saecula*, the richness of Trinity's virtues to schools less fortunate and starving for mentors to imitate? The chances increase that Trinity's leaders will arrive at better answers if they know their own inheritance and can connect present events with past experience by studying their history.

TWO *William Huddleston's School*

*T*rinity School dates its institutional beginning to the year 1709. The date marked the school's formal charter, so it is a good— or good enough—mark to use. But not unlike the dates of other long-ago foundings of schools, companies, hospitals, there are a couple of cautions. First: While such sharp dates are necessary, if only so later generations can celebrate them, real beginnings are gradual and unperceived by the people who at the time, we can now see, were getting things started. So the story here begins with a dip back a bit farther, into the 1690s. Second: If the thing we are marking the beginning of is, at the time of our marking, a very old thing, as is the case with Trinity School in 2009, then chances are the thing then and the thing now bear slight resemblance, if any at all. So for many decades after 1709, the story here is not the story of much of an institution at all but a story from a strange and foreign world.

Still, it is a story of schooling: of how in early New York a modest demand for the formal education of the young met a modest supply of educated men prepared, for a price, to meet it. The first of those was William Huddleston, the man remembered as Trinity School's founder. Precisely when he "founded" it is open to some question, which is probably best answered by saying that Trinity School had its origins in the evolving career-as-teacher of this man.[1] That evolution stretched over a period of many years, by the end of which it is reasonable to say we have reached the beginning.

Huddleston was English, an immigrant to America, and one small agent of the process whereby English ways gradually became American. He was born in Cumberlandshire in 1662 and probably by 1689–90 had found his way to New York. A migrant, he was part of that process of the settlement of America, and the unsettlement of Europe, that historians refer to as the general crisis of the seventeenth century, the great stirring up of people, ideas, and institutions that followed on the decline of feudal economies, the rise of mercantile capitalism, all the turbulence of Renaissance and Reformation, religious war on the Continent, and civil war in England.[2] The Huddlestons of the north of England are traceable back to the twelfth century and along several branches. William belonged to the Cumberland branch, middling farmers who had achieved some measure of independence but hardly affluence. Records identify William's father, Joseph, sometimes as "gentleman," but not always. He was most likely a literate man himself, and he certainly pursued literacy for his offspring. Designation in New York records of his son William as "gentleman" suggests the ambition for upward mobility and some accomplishment of it at least for the next generation.

In England, the son would have gone to a free grammar school, one of which is known to have been in the neighborhood of Monks Foss Farm where his father worked the land. In school, he would have learned first to read, then to write, a process that would have begun around age eleven or twelve. By seventeen, boys were thought ready to move on or out. Huddleston moved out, to clerk in the nearby office of Curwen Rawlinson. (When Huddleston petitioned New York Governor Benjamin Fletcher for permission to practice law in the colony in October 1694—the earliest such petition in New York history—he testified that he had been educated in the law in England at the expense of his father and under the tutelage of Curwen Rawlinson, Esq.) The Rawlinsons were a more prominent family than the Huddlestons—Rawlinson's father had studied law at the Inns of Court in London, and Curwen had gone to Oxford and married the daughter of a bishop and cousin of a duke. Association with them, for Huddleston father and son, must have been deemed highly valuable. The son apprenticed for three years.[3] To take up his studies, Huddleston had to move fifteen or sixteen miles from home, and in moving he joined a general social phenomenon of that time and place, a surge in geographical mobility symptomatic of social and economic change. Moreover, primogeniture still compelled younger sons of the landed classes, whether of grandees or modest holders like the Huddlestons, to turn to trade or the professions to make their way in the world.[4]

Beyond that, there is scant clue of why the young Huddleston chose law, nor any of what he thought about it, only that he studied with Rawlinson for three years, not the five usually required for aspiring barristers. In a learn-by-watching-and-gradually-doing atmosphere, however, Huddleston would have learned something about business, too, for the Rawlinsons were also involved in trade and shipping. What his education apparently did not do or promise to do to his satisfaction was to secure him a place, at home in England. For the next we hear of him is in America.

Where he left home from is not known, though it could well have been the port of Whitehaven, then one of England's busiest. Most migrants to America sailed early in the year from ports within fifty miles of where they lived, and Whitehaven would have fit Huddleston's profile, assuming he had remained in the North.[5] The westward transatlantic passage then took one to two months, and for the vast majority of migrants the trip was one-way. It was for Huddleston. With arrival as with departure: Exactly when he landed in New York (presuming it was in New York that he first landed) we do not know, but for his own testimony many years later that in the fall of 1691 he was active as a schoolmaster in the colony of New York.[6]

Huddleston then would have been close to age thirty when he started out afresh in the new world: a time of life older then than now in terms at least of expectations. Still, thirty was close enough to youth to leave a healthy man with ample energy, and it was old enough to give him some appreciation that time inevitably was short and that the job of getting on with life grew every year more urgent. Or so Huddleston's subsequent behavior in America would suggest: He was a man who would never stop running, and though he slipped frequently enough he ended up modestly ahead of where he had begun when he had decided to become an immigrant. There is both a literature and a mythology about why some people sail away and others stay home, and though part of a larger historical process of migration then at work, Huddleston's individual motives for migration bear at least this much speculation. If opportunity, however ill-defined, is what drove him, then he must have intuited or soon learned from experience that opportunity favored the prepared and the adaptable. Huddleston had prepared for life as a lawyer, which was good preparation for he soon became a lawyer of sorts, a minor official, and a trader in real estate. But he also became a teacher, a line of work about which he could have learned only by having been taught himself. His decision to take up teaching could have had philosophical or religious underpinnings; certainly it had opportunistic ones. It was something that it looked like he could probably do decently well and get paid for.

The record for the 1690s is richer, however, on Huddleston's life in real estate than it is on his life in the schoolhouse. The buying and selling of land and the attempt to establish a law practice went well together, and the real estate market in Manhattan, then fluid and inexpensive, afforded a medium even for starters-out to buy, sell, perhaps even do well.[7] Even so, much about Huddleston's activities here remains foggy: Some deals involved urban tracts, some rural or even wilderness. He was involved in some twenty-eight transactions, including one large parcel of over 500 acres in Orange County, and while no parcel seems to have stayed in his possession forever and while no sale ever made him rich, his activities suggest two themes.[8] On the one hand, he was probably trying to advance his status along the path followed in rural England and other agricultural societies for centuries, via landholding. On the other, he was almost certainly trying to supplement his own income, via land trading.

The deeds recording his land transactions crack the door, slightly, on what else he was doing and why: teaching to support a growing family. First mention of his wife, Sarah, appears in a land transaction from 1694; Huddleston and Sarah would eventually have a large family and never, it seemed, quite the wherewithal to support themselves without worry. Sometimes he did very well, for a time. In 1696, Huddleston realized a substantial profit of over £80 in just one month, enough apparently to alter his social status upward, almost permanently. At least, before these particular sales of three city lots, the deeds describe him as "William Huddleston, Schoolmaster." Thereafter, he would be called "William Huddleston, Gentleman of New York City."[9] Money linked to status then as now, and what went up could as easily come down. After 1718, when he encountered real estate reverses, the sobriquet reverted back to just plain "schoolmaster" and so remained until his death five years later: never the "gentleman" again.

At the same time as some of his busiest real estate dealings, the middle and late 1690s, Huddleston also worked to secure his place as a lawyer. Self-attestation that one had practiced law in London or clerked for an English lawyer was then commonly accepted for admission to the bar in the colonies, and so Huddleston attested to his training with Rawlinson. There is record that he pleaded a case first in 1696 and lost, and it is possible that his English training may still have been a disadvantage in colonial New York, where English law had yet to transfer perfectly. Which laws, which local precedents applied? English training could be small help.[10] Moreover, the practice of hiring attorneys at all to plead was still in its infancy, and the market for legal services would remain weak until society's overlay of laws became too complex for untrained laymen to manage. In 1698, Huddleston acted as attorney for Jamaican John Robinson, trying to collect debts in New York and Pennsylvania. Beyond that, however, Huddleston seems to have done less and less with the law as a means of advancement and enrichment, and to have left that particular part of his own formal education farther and farther behind.

CHURCH AND SCHOOL

Huddleston did not follow the same pattern with the two other, earlier parts of his education: church and school. He was an Anglican, though probably one of recent vintage and from a family that had remained Catholic for many years after the Reformation.[11] In New York, there is no indication of anything but a strong Protestant allegiance. This was a wise choice at a time of Anglican ascendancy in the colony, even though ascendancy would never mean dominance in a setting where competition among different versions of the faith remained as intense as the place itself was diverse. We do not really know what kind of Anglican he was, and we certainly have no light onto his conscience and cannot judge the fervor of his devotion to Christianity as interpreted by the Church of England. Yet something can be inferred from his behavior as a proselytizing agent for that faith. This is one way, anyway, of looking at his long career as a schoolmaster in New York. It is as this juncture that the story of Huddleston the ambitious English newcomer to New York (where still in the 1690s Dutch was heard as often as English), and who called himself a schoolmaster, intersects with the story of Trinity Church.

Anglicanization, as the process is referred to whereby Dutch domination gave way to English, accelerated in the 1690s after the Leisler Rebellion, ironically under the aegis of William III, a Dutchman.[12] Local dynamics mattered more than faraway monarchs, however. A Judiciary Act was passed in 1691 under Governor Henry Sloughter to begin to institute a uniform system of English common law to replace Roman-Dutch law. Sloughter's successor, Benjamin Fletcher, set out to extend the process of anglicanization to matters of church and state. This was no easy job, given the religious as well as the ethnic diversity of the place, which to the English was one of the troublesome legacies of the Dutch regime.[13] Ethnicity and religion typically reinforced one another. Ethnic groups worshipped largely within ethnic lines: Dutch were Dutch Reformed, the Huguenot church attracted the French. Anglicans then were a small minority, probably less than 10 percent of the city's then 2,100 white adults. Except for Roman Catholics, toleration was decreed by the Act of Toleration of 1689 guaranteeing the right to public worship, yet Fletcher in the wake of the Leisler episode determined that "a settled ministry" was essential to keep out further heresy and sedition and, for he believed these things were connected, to combat the low moral tone of New York society: a "sink of irreligion, drunkenness, cursing and swearing, fornication and adultery, thieving and other evils."[14] A Ministry Act in 1693 empowered county vestries to pay the salaries of "good and sufficient Protestant ministers," which to him meant Anglican ones. The Dutch, however, quickly forced a compromise, which exempted by charter the still dominant Dutch Reformed Church from ever supporting the Church of England. The English got their own charter a year later in 1697, and their first church outside the old chapel in Fort James—"Trinity Church"—opened its doors at Broadway and Wall Street in 1698 with the Rev. William Vesey in charge. For a time a sort of dual establishment prevailed, though under successive Anglican governors the presumption of Anglican establishment grew. The tension would not fully abate, however, for the rest of the colonial period, which meant that the Anglicans in fact, if not in theory, were forced in the context of heterodoxy and toleration to compete for the Christian faithful along with everyone else.[15]

Massachusetts-born, Harvard- and Oxford-educated William Vesey, who served as rector of Trinity Church until his death in 1746, symbolized Anglican militancy in the city of New York. Vesey forthrightly allied himself with equally zealous Anglican royal governor Edward Hyde, Lord Cornbury, and squared off in defense of the prerogatives of Trinity and its rector against the more moderate Robert Hunter, Cornbury's successor, in the 1710s.[16] William Huddleston entered the Trinity Church record at the very beginning, as one of the fifteen men who contributed to the subscription drive to erect a church building (he pledged £2 out of £35 raised) and then as one of the church's first ten vestrymen. He even helped oversee the construction site. Intermittently, he would serve as the salaried clerk of the parish and enjoyed status enough to merit his name on a pew (though one the Huddlestons shared with neighbors).

Establishment locally of Trinity Church in New York preceded by just five years establishment of another Anglican agency not local at all and militantly missionary in character—the Society for the Propagation of the Gospel in Foreign Parts (SPG)—which would also entwine the subsequent career of William Huddleston as churchman and schoolmaster. Founded in England in 1701 to evangelize for Anglicanism in the colonies, the SPG sprang from the mind of a young priest from Warwickshire named Thomas

Bray. Bray had written a book popular with the hierarchy, *Catechetical Lectures*, and served as commissary of the Church of England to parishes in Maryland, where he observed firsthand the obstacles to securing Anglicanism in the provinces. Back home, he launched a plan and a subscription for continuing clergy education through establishment of parochial libraries, and with friends founded the Society for the Propagation of Christian Knowledge (SPCK) in 1699 to promote his work. Soon the plan broadened to advocate, both in "the plantations" abroad and in rural regions of England, free catechetical schools for poor planters' children, conversion of the Indians, and charity schools for poor children at home. It was the colonies, though, that seemed in most need of evangelism, and two years later, in 1701, Bray oversaw creation of another society dedicated to spreading the gospel in "His majesties plantations, colonies, and factories beyond the seas," which it was feared were highly vulnerable to heresy, infidelity, atheism, and popish infiltration. This was the SPG, a unique, unprecedented agency, neither creature of the state nor quite of the church, but embracing the aura and authority of both, combining "imperial evangelism with philanthropic benevolence and the power of royal charter with the force of private initiative."[17]

Between 1701 when the first enquiries went out from London to colonial officials about needs and the first petitions for assistance began to come back, the SPG mounted the most ambitious, most unified program of education ever to be seen in provincial America. Until its activities there terminated with independence,[18] the SPG set up 169 missionary stations from New Hampshire to Georgia and at different times subsidized eighty schoolmasters and catechists; it distributed thousands of Bibles, prayer books, tracts, and school texts in English, but also in Dutch, French, German, and Indian dialects. Works like Richard Allestree's *The Whole Duty of Man*, William Wake's *The Principles of the Christian Religion*, and William Stanley's *The Faith and Practice of a Church of England-Man* were staples in its library, with their stern message of civility, piety, and obedience, respect for monarchy, and belief in bishops. Such cultural and religious doctrines were not always an easy sell among a polyglot people like the people slowly settling Britain's American colonies, but to the extent that Anglicanism sustained itself and grew modestly in its American setting, the SPG was probably the reason.

In the history of cultural transference that underlay English colonization in America, the SPG fills a curious double role. Bray's clarion call to mission rang with a proselytizing zeal not before manifest inside the established church and that, ever since, roosted uneasily among outer branches of a dignified denomination generally uncomfortable with evangelism. At the turn of the seventeenth century, however, with religious settlement at home safely secured but only after decades of turmoil, and with imperial expansion in the air overseas, the SPG launched what would become a worldwide missionary program to buttress the faith in those "foreign parts" where the church itself was seen to be weak and locally not up to the job. It is also possible to view the SPG ideologically, as a tool to fight nonconformity in the colonies. If it was, then New York, where there was probably more nonconformity than anywhere else, should have been rich ground indeed.[19] It may be better though to regard the SPG as symptom of the anxiety that triumph of the Protestant cause in Europe could not be taken for granted and that Catholic resurgence had ever to be guarded against. Overseas, among native peoples and slaves with whom empire was bringing English Protestants into new and constant contact, Christ's "Great Commission" as recorded at the end of St. Matthew's Gospel—"Go ye therefore and teach all nations, baptizing them in the name of the Father, the Son and Holy Ghost"—found virtually limitless new fields for application. One of the finest examples of this aspect of the SPG's work in New York was the career of the saintly Elias Neau, himself an Anglican convert and Huguenot refugee from France, who gave up a life in commerce to serve as the SPG's catechist among New York's slave population, teaching literacy and Christianity while prudently disavowing any link between evangelization and abolition.[20]

IN REAL LIFE

The grandest of enterprises invariably get used locally on the ground in ways and for reasons that, while not necessarily inconsistent with statements of grand purpose and subsequent adoring histories, are often less lofty. Thus was William Huddleston's interface with the SPG. The SPG employed workaday means to advance noble ends: To secure the true Protestant religion from papists and bring the heathen to Christ, it ran schools. Or at least it employed and subsidized others to run them. It gave grants and spawned over the years grantsmen to get them.

By the time the SPG set up shop in the colonies in the first years of the new century, William Huddleston had been in New York for about a decade, striving to make his way. He had neither found things easy nor done badly, and had turned to schoolmastering for a third income stream along with real estate and law. He appears to have kept very busy. Like real estate and the law, schoolmastering was a competitive affair where the balance of supply and demand sometimes wobbled. Between 1700 and 1705 there were several teachers like Huddleston in New York competing for enrollment, and the supply of students worried him. Huddleston claimed in 1709 to have been in the teaching business for twenty years, and again in 1715 to have been at it "almost thirty years in that green colloney [sic] where almost nothing was spoken but Dutch when I first came there."[21] At times he had done quite respectably too: Sixty students in the early 1700s brought him an income of close to £100, though competition was biting hard.[22]

We know what we do of this prehistory of Huddleston's teaching career because of what he later reported about it, personally and through others at Trinity Church, to the SPG, from whom he sought subsidy to supplement his fee-based income. Starting in 1705, the letters to London began to flow, from Huddleston and his supporters, petitioning his appointment as master of a charity school in New York City. These made reference to both his present and past services. He merited help in part because he was a known quantity: The SPG knew what it was getting and could rely on his piety and ability. "I entreat your Honr.," William Vesey petitioned the SPG on Huddleston's behalf in 1705, "to use your interest with the Society to grant an Annuall allowance to Mr. Huddleston who has been schoolmaster in this City many years and has instructed many Dutch, French and English children in the church catechism and excellently taught them the liturgy."[23] The record of his having been paid by the vestry in 1702 to teach the sexton's son establishes the first formal connection between Trinity Church and education, and in 1706 he received a one-time £10 gratuity from the SPG and another £10 for books for his students.[24] His subsequent request for copies of the Book of Common Prayer in Dutch and French conformed with the drive for anglicanization, and both Vesey and Cornbury supported him as an agent of that process.[25]

It took another three years to get the regular appointment he sought as the society's schoolmaster for New York City, which the society granted officially on December 2, 1709. Its letter awarding £10 per year reached Huddleston in January: "Ordered that £10 for one year from this time be allowed to the said Mr. Huddleston in consideration of his being well recommended to the society and upon condition that he shall teach 40 poor children gratis and transmit certificate thereof to this board." The letter said nothing about children Huddleston already taught, nor that he might not continue to teach them.[26]

Between what he got and why exactly he claimed to need it lies some murky ground. As an entrepreneurial schoolmaster of some experience, he had been able to command ten times the SPG stipend, and even under competitive pressure still attracted a varying stream of fee-paying students. He also had income from his clerkships of Orange County and of Trinity Church (£10 each), which in turned opened opportunity to charge fees for duties associated with those offices but not part of the regular stipend. At church, he supplied wine for communion and laundered the linens; he kept the building open for weddings, baptisms, and funerals and collected what were essentially users' fees for his trouble. Against this, his and Vesey's persistent claims of "mean circumstance" and large family obligation grate, though pleas of poverty were the daily bread of many colonial Anglicans currying support from home and were known often to succeed.[27] The behavior that led finally to Huddleston's 1709 SPG appointment makes added sense in context of the larger process of place and patron seeking characteristic of the period. Trinity Church was and would remain the heart of the Anglican establishment of New York; the sympathies of its Tory rector were the same as those of the proselytizing SPG; Huddleston's interest in financial security and advancement converged with both. The value of the SPG's £10 we can probably safely presume Huddleston calculated at the margin: welcome money but not essential. The value of his association with the premier agencies, one local, one metropolitan, of Anglican ascendancy we can presume he calculated at the very heart of the matter of enhancing his own place and reputation and that of his family. In time, much more time, this would have institutional consequences as the charity school that the SPG subsidized at Trinity Church to Huddleston's benefit slowly evolved. At that moment, the consequences were a very modest addition to the local educational landscape of New York City.

On that landscape, schools were as yet minor features. For colonists in seventeenth- and early eighteenth-century America, family, church and community carried the heavier burden in that process by which, in Bernard Bailyn's encompassing definition of education, "a culture transmits itself across the generations."[28] Certainly they did outside New England, and most certainly they did in New York. Or, taking Lawrence Cremin's refinement—"education as the deliberate, systematic and sustained effort to transmit, evoke, or acquire knowledge, attitudes, values, skills, or sensibilities, as well as any outcomes of that effort"—schools as instruments of education followed upon but did not determine broader social impulse.[29] New York (New Netherland) under the Dutch had witnessed very modest ventures into deliberate elementary schooling starting in 1638, with church-sponsored but town-supported efforts that were allowed to continue after the English conquest. The Duke's Laws of 1665, a first attempt to establish New York's first English legal code, were silent on matters of schools. While governors had the right to approve teachers, none did so, and before the appearance of William Huddleston in the 1690s, attempts at English schooling appear to have been informal, intermittent, and, as was Huddleston's effort, entrepreneurial.[30]

The story of Huddleston's school can be followed on two levels, one political and one operational. Huddleston was an Anglican who chose actively to align his fortune with the colony's Anglican establishment at the time of its ascendancy. Keeping these relationships in good repair required constant attention and, we imagine, made him a perpetually anxious man. No sooner had his SPG appointment been confirmed than regime change raised questions about his local patronage. In 1710, Robert Hunter, a Whig, replaced Cornbury, a Tory, as governor of New York, for a term that would about coincide with the balance of Huddleston's own career. Hunter is remembered as a moderate conciliator, in contrast to the abrasive Cornbury. Vesey, a Tory too and close ally of Cornbury, opposed Hunter from the start, and tension between the governor and rector of Trinity Church simmered constantly. Hunter, for instance, chose to refurbish the chapel at Fort James, complaining that Trinity was too small for both its congregation and his garrison, and he lowered pew rent there to attract parishioners away from Trinity. Vesey for his part never let up in his efforts to get Hunter recalled. Against this background of political sniping, Huddleston, whom Cornbury had supported financially but whom Hunter would not, learned to be careful.[31]

With SPG patronage came the requirement to report back twice annually to the patron, and it is largely through these letters that we know what we do of Huddleston's progress as schoolmaster against this political background. His first report went to London in July 1710 and established themes for most that would follow: His students were poor, and so was he, and so he needed ever more money. At the same time, he would confess that he saw his appointment as SPG's schoolmaster as an entitlement as he grew older, though an entitlement for which he was willing to work hard. He needed to because the association with his new patron came at the price of alienating old business. He had had for many years a following among families able to pay for their children's schooling, but now there was an image problem. Reported Hunter to London in 1712: "The People of fashion in the town having taken their children from him out of a senseless notion that they will not send them to a Charity School."[32] He had at that moment lost all but seven of his paying customers. That Huddleston continued with the SPG for the rest of his life, incurring apparently substantial opportunity cost, suggests the high value he placed on the relationship aside from money. Moreover, despite claims to the contrary, he never served the SPG exclusively, but in the tradition of English schoolmastering in the eighteenth century continued to supplement his teaching salary with other income streams: He gave up neither of his posts, as clerk of Trinity Church and of Orange County, which continued to yield mixed rewards. And he always took paying pupils.[33]

In 1712, the society increased Huddleston's grant to £15, where it would remain. This may or may not have been related to elevation by a new Bishop of London of Vesey to status as commissary in charge of all New York's Anglican clergy.[34] But it was on paper. Whatever the reason for his lobbying success, Huddleston had difficulty sometimes in even collecting from the SGP, itself ever overstretched financially, and his reports took on greater documentation as he tried to press his claims on its subsidy and his expectation that it pay what it had promised.[35] Perhaps to press his claims of pay due for real performance, he began in 1713 to list the names of students, here forty boys, enrolled in his school.[36] The list for two years later included, without comment, the names of two girls, Mary Finney and Elizabeth Crannell.[37] Until 1714, Huddleston had probably taught these children at Trinity Church, but that year, when he also seemed to be experiencing greater than usual financial stress and was not re-elected to the Trinity vestry, he moved school to city hall.[38] Vesey remained his faithful local patron, however, and when he returned in 1715 from London, where he had gone to bolster his own position as commissary, Huddleston's prospects for another post brightened.

This was the job of catechist occupied by Elias Neau, which paid a handsome £50 per annum. With the SPG rebuffing his pleas for direct raises (at £15 he was already receiving a third more than the thirty-two other society-supported schoolmasters in the colonies, though he claimed to have more students than any of them) and with the local authorities refusing added support, Vesey's idea to give Huddleston Neau's post seemed a solution. It took three years before he succeeded and the SPG abandoned Neau in favor of Huddleston. Alas, they also took the opportunity to economize and offered Huddleston only £10 additional. This precipitated a spat in New York Anglican circles, with arguments back and forth about which man was less distracted by other occupations—with Huddleston the charity school, with Neau his business affairs—and thus best able to meet the duties of catechist. When Governor Hunter weighed in on Neau's side, the society relented and brought the Huguenot back, a blow for sure to Huddleston, who had served just over a year in the added post. Vesey did not let go easily and still encouraged Huddleston to increase catechizing work among his own private students and with interested apprentices, and for his trouble did secure in 1722, the year before Huddleston's death, a gratuity for the schoolmaster of £10.[39] But that would be all, for if Huddleston nursed expectations that his long loyalty to Trinity deserved one final reward, he would be disappointed. When Neau died in 1722, opening up the catechist's post at last, Vesey denied Huddleston both the honor and the income. Vesey wanted, he said, a clergyman for the job, and probably a younger, fitter man. Huddleston died the next August (1723) anyway, and Vesey got his way. Yet, spreading the emoluments into the next generation and keeping it in the family, the rector also supported Huddleston's son, Thomas, to succeed him as schoolmaster and clerk of Trinity Church.[40]

AT SCHOOL

Challenges of patronage and struggles for support from the powerful sound familiar and strange. Though the SPG was steadfast, its benefactions could never be called munificent, and it operated at the mercy of political events. With Britain's loss of the American colonies in the 1780s, its activities there would end altogether. Even before then, its activities would come under patriot suspicion.[41] The results of its efforts were mixed. Judged against its own high standard, it largely failed in the time it had in the American context in both its professed aims: to convert the heathen and to create a regime of charity schooling to uplift "the poor." The American confrontation with the Indians proved generally too calamitous for schooling to play any mitigating part. Schooling and slavery mixed dubiously at best. And charity schooling, aimed at the poor as a clearly defined and fixed social class, while it may have fit the English setting, did not fit the American setting, where a chronic labor shortage, abundant land, and the ready availability of employment put an increasing premium on the development of human capital through various modes of education.[42]

How New Yorkers, in this case, actually used the SPG's charity school in their midst suggests a different more positive outcome of the enterprise. If Huddleston himself used it, with some success, to secure his place and position, then so did his students and the families who sent them there also use it. Schooling, then as now, meant getting another foothold in life and, who knows, maybe even getting ahead. What happened in this one? Where, what, who?

In his pre-SPG years as a purely entrepreneurial unsubsidized teacher, Huddleston had taught students in his home, and though there is no record, he could also have used rented rooms as was typical of the time in England. Nor is there record of any dedicated "school house" before 1714. There is record that he taught in Trinity Church, in pews on the north side of the west gallery. His report to the SPG for 1714 and then in 1717 described teaching in a room in city hall, rent free, and his to-ing and fro-ing with his students between services at Trinity Church and classes at school.[43]

The schooling that occurred there and the curriculum that formalized it were shaped by the proselytizing aims of the SPG from afar, and locally by demand for the practical advantages conferred by literacy. These aims connected but were not identical. The association of literacy with piety was a profound legacy of the Reformation and the spread of printing. Protestantism spurred the profusion of printed material, beginning with translation of the Bible into the vernacular (first German and then English), but extending to commentaries, tracts, devotionals of all sorts, all with their instructional uses. The increased availability of things to read, much of it religious, in the seventeenth century in England gave practice to those already literate and motivation to those who would become so. Reaching out from metropolis to the provinces in the eighteenth century, the SPG sent the same message: that literacy was the handmaid of holy living among the faithful and weapon for proselytizing those not yet in the fold.[44]

Its fourteen-article "Instructions for Schoolmasters Employed by the Society," which today we might we view as a sort of guidelines for grant-getters, asserted the primary goal for every teacher as "the instructing and disposing of Children to believe and live as Christians."[45] From this more or less everything else was thought to flow. Reading was the key instrument to this end, so pupils were taught to read the Bible and the Prayer Book, and by reading—this was the key distinction from pre-Reformation ways—to comprehend and internalize the texts in ways that did not come with rote memorization. The SPG instructions called explicitly for catechizing all those attending its schools, in the Anglican version of Protestantism according to the Thirty-Nine Articles of Religion contained in every copy of the *Book of Common Prayer*. In polyglot America, filled with dissenters who sometimes too availed themselves of SPG schools, this could be awkward. We do not know exactly how thoroughly Huddleston carried out this part of his charge, though there were other masters nearby who fudged rather than drive away from their classes families who were dissenters.[46] Huddleston never speaks of the issue in his reports to London, though logically he would not have. He did, however, teach Dutch as well as English children. Perhaps he told his patrons the whole truth; more likely, just part of it. The English he catechized. The Dutch he may well have let alone.

Others of the articles would have reinforced the proselytizing mode of the SPG venture and its New York chapter. Article Six enjoined the use of prayers: "A Morning Prayer for the Masters and Scholars," "An Evening Prayer for the Masters and Scholars," "A Morning Prayer to be used by every Child at Home," "A short prayer for Every Child when they first come into their Seats . . . and as they leave their Seats," "Grace before Meat," and "A Grace after." Article Seven called on teachers to be certain their charges attended public worship on Sundays and other feast days. Huddleston reported that his did, but he never said how many. It is certainly possible that he practiced some accommodation: He was a long way from London, and it was difficult for his patrons to check up. Other instructions dealt with non-doctrinal "good behavior" issues that could have been expected to stir no objection from anyone: Call it "character education." Kind but firm masters were to set the tone. In turn, pupils were expected to meet them with modesty, courtesy, truthfulness, and respect.

Article Four had nothing to do with religion whatsoever, but buttressed toward another end the general rubric for literacy. It directed SPG masters to teach legible penmanship and arithmetic in order to prepare students for gainful employment when school was over. Here was an example of the connection between literacy and broadening opportunity, even an imperative, for its practical use: what Cremin called the distinction between inert and liberating literacy. The minimalist definition of literacy implied technical capability, but weak motivation, to decipher language in written form and to some degree (perhaps no more than to write one's name) the ability to write something down. But why bother? The historical dividing line in England fell somewhere in the sixteenth and seventeenth centuries. Up to then, a yeoman might be literate yet have no occasion to read anything other than Bible and prayer book. After that, he had vastly more material available to read, which, moreover, connected more immediately to the conduct of practical affairs. With literacy rates probably as high in the American colonies as they were in England in the eighteenth century (and higher than in Ireland), the setting of Huddleston's New York almost certainly encouraged the growth of literacy in this liberating sense, where need and opportunity would plausibly have encouraged competence and sharpened motivation to learn to read, write, and figure. Education in literacy or anything else does not, however, require the presence of schools. Households and churches historically did the job for many, and literacy can be self-taught. But liberating, expansive literacy—of the sort that increased one's chances to reach beyond one's immediate ken—was most likely to be encouraged and transmitted in schools, even proselytizing ones like those of the SPG.[47]

"I teach in the morning reading and writing till eleven," Huddleston described the school's routine to London in 1716, "then the bell rings them to prayers, where they daily appear to the great growth of the Church. In the afternoon they spell, read, cipher from one to five, when they read the Psalms for the day, and every one answers that can read—then they sing a staff or two of the Psalms they have just read—then ends the day." Two or three times a week he reported that he explicitly taught the catechism, and on Sundays he expected students to recite graces and prayers by heart, as well as repeat something of what they had heard of Trinity Church sermons.[48]

Thus minuted, it sounds very orderly and would appear to cover all the specified ground. The source—Huddleston's report to his faraway SPG patrons, from whom he endlessly pleaded for more money—bids some caution, however. He had clear incentive to tell his patrons what they hoped to hear.[49] And in declaring how well it was all evidently going, he also surely meant to imply how much they undervalued his services. Yet he must fundamentally have told the truth. To have been able to stay in business for as long as he did, and then to have bequeathed the business to his son, the schooling that Huddleston dispensed must have satisfied well enough patrons and clients alike. Of what that schooling actually consisted, of what was taught and who learned it, we know what we do from Huddleston himself and two other sources.

Huddleston outlined the curriculum in his own yearly reports: a steady diet of reading, writing, and arithmetic with a strong and expected dose of religion. This pattern had Dutch precedent, which also had mixed secular with sacred instruction, so it would have appealed to Dutch as well as English parents, who would have been less put off by a curriculum that offered some other version of the Christian faith than by one that offered none at all.[50] He began teaching at eight o'clock in the morning, broke for morning prayers at eleven, then to lunch probably at home, then started up again at one o'clock and ran till four in winter, five in summer. He probably ran the school year-round, perhaps adjusting for his own other responsibilities, and students themselves probably worked spasmodically, not the whole year through. Some students' names appear on his roster and then reappear, years later. He taught from books ordered from the Society in London: the new version of Tate and Brady's Psalms, Anglican Prayer Books in both English and Dutch, Lewis's *Exposition of the Church Catechism*, Nicholls's paraphrase of the Prayer Book, the Psalms of David, Old and New Testaments, and assorted primers containing the alphabet, prayers, the order of service, and a catechism.

Lewis's catechism particularly exemplified the pedagogical union of sacred texts and secular learning then generally taken for granted. John Lewis (1675–1747) was an English schoolmaster turned clergyman and author of a catechism specifically for use in English charity schools. He had consulted some thirty other catechisms and the result was something of a compilation, but he clearly knew what kind of presentation would be useful in the classroom. He broke up the bigger catechisms into smaller pieces and made the list of questions (thus practice in reading) much longer than the stated answers, which were designed for easy memorization. Next he grouped the questions into numbered units matching the number of weeks a child might attend school. Four questions per day, for example, took up a six-day week over a thirteen-week term. Other combinations of course were possible. In addition to sections on the Christian covenant, faith, obedience, prayer, and sacraments, it contained age-specific (this in an era that customized hardly anything for children) "prayers for children" for use in specified places and occasions: "an evening prayer to be said at school by teachers and children," "a daily prayer for the child to say at home," prayers for children upon entering and leaving church, before and after meals. Not just practical, Lewis's book was also cheap compared with competing editions, something that no doubt appealed to the SPG and perhaps was why Huddleston, ever wishing to appear frugal, specified it.[51]

From Lewis's catechism, students would have graduated to regular 1662 *Book of Common Prayer* and the Psalter, in the new metrical version introduced by Nahum Tate and Nicholas Brady in England in 1696 and adopted by Trinity Church in 1709.[52] Tate was poet laureate to William III and Brady a royal chaplain. Their rhymed settings of all 150 psalms were designed specifically to be sung in church or in school, which was where Huddleston's students sang them. New York printer William Bradford produced the first American edition of the *Book of Common Prayer* in 1710, though the book did not make money and soon became unavailable. Huddleston reverted to the SPG in England for his supplies, including a large-print version for his own weakening eyes.[53]

All this had to do with the reading component of literacy as Huddleston purveyed it. Of the writing side we know less, except that writing meant penmanship more than composition and sometimes but not always followed on the teaching of reading. During this period, many readers never became writers at all.[54] Different forms of handwriting abounded, complicating things—round hand, Italian hand, Roman hand. According to his reports, Huddleston simply taught "writing," which probably meant that his students learned by imitating letter forms and composing simple sentences. This must have included some attention to spelling, although there is no record of actual spellers being used in the charity school until 1747. Nothing remains of what his students themselves wrote.[55]

Nor of how they figured, though arithmetic reportedly occupied them from one to five each day. This seems a heavy dose. It is possible that the demand for numeracy was especially sharp in New York: "The City is so conveniently situated for trade and the genius of the people are so inclined to merchandize," wrote the fort's Anglican chaplain John Sharpe in 1713, "that they generally seek no other education for their children than writing and arithmetick."[56] Moreover, England was just emerging from a 200–year period of great change in concepts to do with numeracy, which rendered the techniques of counting and figuring, and the application of those skills to practical tasks, more accessible, more easily transferable, and thus fit subject for education. Roman numerals gave way to Arabic ones; the abacus to paper as the medium for figuring; decimals, logarithms, mathematical symbols all appeared.[57] To the large extent that Huddleston was training up boys for trades, this emphasis made sense. We know that in England at this time apprentices routinely were taught simple arithmetic, and that a progression from addition to subtraction, multiplication, and then division was commonly practiced. Huddleston probably practiced it in New York. Giving the whole afternoon to "arithmetick," he perhaps tells us something of the demand.

The indentures that defined terms of apprenticeship are the other source for our knowledge of what went on—or what was expected to go on—in the Charity School. Huddleston's rosters sent to London during his tenure from 1710 to 1723—the lists for three years, 1714, 1718, and 1720 are missing, and he submitted only numbers but no names for 1710, 1711, and 1712—include 365 entries that described 189 different individuals. Of these, apprenticeship indentures exist for twenty-five. Because indentures remain only for the years 1718 to 1727, this number may be low, but from it a few things can be learned.[58] Most provided for some schooling. "Three months in every winter" for John Hitchcock. William Dobbs was to "learn fit and evening schooling so that he may learn to read and write English for the performance of all and every said covenants."[59] Bordonaro sorts these indentures into several categorizes. Twenty-two stipulated that apprentices receive some sort of schooling. Those for two girls, Mary Waters and Elizabeth Hartman, tended to be more vague than those for boys: Both were to learn to read during the course of their contract, though this may have been perfunctory because each could already sign her name and thus most likely could also read. Boys in another group were to receive teaching in unspecified subjects but for defined periods of three months per year for the length of their contracts, seven to eleven years. They were then bound, "put out" as the expression was, to trades: masons, shoemakers, blacksmiths. For yet others there was to be a defined curriculum, meaning reading, writing and arithmetic but no specification as to how or where instruction was to take place. Masters could do it themselves or outsource it to a school. And finally, there were those whose indentures provided for instruction to take place formally in a school setting.[60] With them all, emphasis fell on a practical combination of reading, writing, and ciphering. None called for specifically religious instruction or behavior education, so we must assume that the SPG-mandated emphasis on just those things at the charity school either caused no objection with parents or was deemed an expected part of training up the young, whether at school or at home.[61]

Networks of friendship, kinship, even neighborhood proximity determined who the families were who chose the charity school, managing to recommend themselves to the mayor, who recommended students to Huddleston, whose roster eventually found its way to the SPG. Bordonaro's analysis of attendance patterns during Huddleston's tenure indicates the importance of simple association: Numbers of students' families knew other families apparently satisfied enough with Huddleston's operation to recommend it. The school's reputation was conveyed by word of mouth: There was no testimony as trustworthy as experience.

Starting in 1716, the names of girls appear on all the rosters. The records contain no direct comment on this, though it is possible that Huddleston simply needed to bolster enrollment. Huddleston's wife, Sarah, taught these and other girls, and being literate herself had opportunity to teach them in more than needlework. The family of Philip and Cornelia van Gelder Dally (English father, Dutch mother) sent two daughters to the Huddleston's (but not their sons), and may have hoped thereby to avail them entry into the English world. It was characteristic when English-speaking men married women of Dutch background, as Philip Dally did, that the wife's culture prevailed at home. The English school may have offered opportunity, in an English father's eyes, to socialize his daughters (who went on to marry into English families) in his own language and culture. It is also possible that parents saw in attendance at the English school the prospect of broadened economic opportunity for their children. This may have been true with the Dutch family of Johannes Bant, who sent four sons to the English School between 1713 and 1725. Bant was a cooper and would have educated his sons for his own trade in the family setting but may have feared that coopering could not absorb them all and that the English school might open other doors. Only one son for sure followed his father's trade; another became a mason. The Hartman family sent daughters and sons to the school, and like the Bants may have had job training and apprenticeship on their minds. The older Hartmans all went off to apprenticeships with cordwainers and coopers, where requirements that they attend night school (the son) and be taught to read (the daughter) would seem redundant, as the children had attended school for several years, could sign their indentures, and were clearly literate already. The point is that school families often knew other school families. The Hartmans knew the Bants. The families of Pieter Sinkam, Joost Paulding, and Maria Cosyn all knew each other, and some were related by marriage. All sent children to the English school and probably recommended it back and forth among themselves, resulting in a student body filled with friends and relations. While no record remains of what any of these students said about their experience in this period, the fact that brother attended and then sister, then followed by a cousin, a nephew, a godchild, a neighbor, suggests consistent satisfaction with the service Huddleston provided as it related both to moral training (whether or not Anglican doctrine) and as a lever for finding a place in an English-speaking and writing world.[62]

Between such patterns and the professed purpose of Huddleston's school subsequent to its SPG association in 1709, as a school to educate New York's poor, there is less than perfect consistency. Families, many with trades already and who were not indigent, chose to use it for their own purposes. No one, it seems, was means tested. They placed their children there intermittently and at different ages—some children entered as young as five and six, others as old as fifteen and sixteen—depending on family circumstance. Huddleston was probably happy to have them all. He complained only of his own low pay, never of overcrowding.

PURPOSE AND USES

So obscure as individuals do all these characters remain however—Huddleston and the several hundred "scholars" he taught over the years—that best perspective comes only at the risk of generalizing about them together, as groups. It could be that Huddleston and company, opportunists all to one degree or another, represent the first ripples on a calm deep of assurance that up to then characterized education as it had evolved in early modern England, and in England-as-transplanted to the American colonies. The configuration of processes embodied in family, community, and church by which English culture for centuries had cast itself from one generation on to the next and by which the young had passed easily from family into the larger society would not for long, in the process of transatlantic transplantation and in the American environment, go unchanged. Yet to see the rapid expansion of instructional facilities partly in the form of schools that took place in England in the century before American settlement as progenitor of the growth of American schools in the eighteenth century can be deceptive. The English processs largely affirmed, and did not question, the settled and familiar needs of a still rural, homogeneous, traditional society. In the American world, shaped by the disruption of migration and the necessity of fashioning community life in remote provincial settings, things would be different, starting at the most basic building block. The family, so extended in the Old World, would start to contract to its nuclear core. As it did so, it made room for the rise of other agencies of cultural self-perpetuation, schools among them.

New York, in Huddleston's time still a modest seaport town with nature close at hand, was the opposite of homogeneous and was rapidly becoming an environment not conducive to any settled order of things. It was a setting to which schooling, however rudimentary, might have been expected to respond and adapt. What little else we know of him, we can confidently describe Huddleston as a ready adaptor. He adapted to teaching when he had trained to be a lawyer. He adapted from entrepreneurship in teaching to mixing entrepreneurship with currying patronage so he could sustain his school and protect his income. He adapted, in all likelihood, the religious part of his curriculum to the sensitivities of multiple sorts of Christians and bent his patron's purposes to his own. Moreover, he started out teaching at the beginning of the eighteenth century in the American colonies—the time and place where, in Bailyn's memorable understatement, the idea of education was about to be "dislodged from its ancient position in the social order" and transformed into something radically different, something more problematic and controversial.[63] In that process, schools were to become a primary agency of education and to take on responsibilities they had not carried before. This dislodgement took decades, and it is conjecture to wonder how the school that Huddleston ran at Trinity Church under SPG auspices may have embodied or resisted it.

Clearer is the fact that his school operated against a backdrop of social changes that unquestionably sped the dislodgement along. Economic growth and the prospect of social mobility, so characteristic of life in America, would endow schools with a new utility as vehicles for personal advancement. It is no retrospective criticism to say that much of what Huddleston did was in the cause of personal or family advancement, including his long effort to run a school for the SPG. The families who made that possible by sending their sons and daughters to him for schooling certainly were looking after their own advancement too. Teacher and learners, the vendor and the customers, in this sense shared similar interests.

The competitive nature of American Protestantism—weak church establishments and a gaggle of contending denominations in search of adherents—formed another part of the backdrop against which Huddleston's school operated. In schools, denominationalism found a workhorse for missionary endeavor. As perhaps the most militant of missionary endeavors ever visited upon America, the SPG single-mindedly used schools thus, even as the schools, like Huddleston's, themselves evolved in directions that sometimes diverged from founding purposes.[64] The interests of patron and patronized were similar but different, and as the eighteenth century advanced, and certainly by the time of the Revolution, they diverged decisively. Education in service to piety long remained a stated aim and central theme of the English charity school, but the market compelled Huddleston to interpret the aim loosely enough to accommodate the demands of his customers. The point looks forward to a subsequent theme. This was the tension between traditional definitions of education as embodied in schools as they were handed down from England—here so clearly laid out in the stipulations of the SPG for its schoolmasters—and the desires of those in America actively choosing to be educated. Where those desires met the talents of teachers like William Huddleston defined a marketplace that mediated supply and demand and where, throughout much of the unfolding eighteenth century, there would be few barriers to entry and much lively competition.

These first opening years of the history of what would become Trinity School also reveal a persistent tension, contradiction even, inherent in all schooling and that would play out at Trinity according to particular, changing social circumstances. Is schooling controlling, or is it liberating? Both, of course. Schooling by definition socializes: It implants and buttresses in those to be schooled the values, beliefs, and prejudices of those who sponsor and conduct the schooling. There is little question about what these values were in the case of the SPG. Schooling pulled two ways at once, like literacy, which was an initial primary component of schooling, and like education, of which schooling was but one expression. In the old-time Prayer Book language of the SPG, schooling helped discipline the naturally unruly wills and affections of sinful creatures—children with potential to grow up into obedient members of the commonwealth or to become dangers to it. The school schooled according to expectations, sanctions, incentives designed to protect civil order and promote acceptable behavior, and it aimed to inculcate practical skills necessary for students to find a productive place in society and economy.

In the process of doing so, the school also exposed the young to ideas and to other people, masters and other students, they would not necessarily have encountered at home, in church, or at the apprentice's bench. Even as it instructed the young in how to behave and what to believe and thus imposed order, it risked opening minds whether modestly or grandly to options and new possibilities. It brought to the surface of consciousness what had long been latent at best, that life offered alternatives and required the exercise of choice.[65] Schooling at the charity school under Huddleston and under all of his successors would hold these tendencies to control and liberation, authority and freedom, in a shifting balance.

About Trinity in its eighteenth-century "charity" manifestation, it is tempting to conclude that at Huddleston's school control surely overbore liberation. If we look at intentions, that after all is what the SPG guidelines *said*. Unlike grammar schools that aimed to select and train the few to excel and move ahead, English charity schools aimed to save the poor by insuring their obedience, "to breed them to Civility and good Conscience, in the Knowledge of Letters, and the Principles and Practices of Christian Religion."[66] This must remain speculation, though. Granted our limited ability to discern outcomes of Huddleston's school for Huddleston's students, we do know that not all of those students were poor or English and that some came from families who, like Huddleston himself, were eager to get on and get ahead. What now looks largely constraining may then have been seen as rich with possibility relative to the alternatives. Anglicanization itself, of which SPG schooling was such a deliberate instrument, should be similarly regarded both as a policy of control employed by a new ruling class, and as a key for others to access the larger, fuller metropolitan world that those new rulers represented. In a provincial world then still on the far fringes of empire, which defined New York in Huddleston's day, such a key would have been hard to overvalue, and so the education served up in William Huddleston's school.

THREE *The Eighteenth Century*
PIOUS AND PRACTICAL LEARNING

*T*hrough the eighteenth century, New York City, like most of the rest of Britain's territories in North America, grew and prospered, eventually making a dramatic break from Britain altogether. Schools, it is tempting to say retrospectively, must have rolled along on the same exciting current. Yet during the eight decades following the death of William Huddleston, the institution today known as Trinity School changed little under the leadership of eight different schoolmasters, none of whom left behind much surviving record or appears to have made much enduring impact. Had Huddleston lived to be a hundred, into the 1760s, he would have had no difficulty identifying the charity school of Trinity Church then with the one he had struggled to sustain as a middle-aged man. He would have been pleased by dedicated and relatively new quarters and noted a diminishing reliance on the SPG for income, as well as the formal oversight by the vestry of Trinity Church. The school's everyday life, though, was unchanged: It pursued the same purpose, served about the same number of students drawn from the same backgrounds, and provided them with essentially the same instruction and post-school prospects.

Had Huddleston somehow time-traveled into the 1790s, on the far side of American independence, he might again have stepped comfortably into place, hardly pausing for a brushup. The quarters were brand new after 1794, but the duties of the schoolmaster would still have been recognizable, along with the continuing tight relationship between the school and Trinity Church. Looking outward, though, the view from the school would have seemed very different. New York City was growing rapidly bigger, richer, more crowded, and more diverse. Under the fledgling American republic, the local Episcopalian (née Anglican) establishment was no longer ascendant but jostling for place with Christians of other stripes, including Roman Catholics, as well as Jews, and a burgeoning population more concerned with commerce and opportunity than with cultural and religious identity. Immigrants from England and elsewhere in the colonies were pouring into the city in search of fortune. The role and place of an Episcopal charity school amid the bustle and

turmoil of end-of-century New York City were plainly in need of new definition, although that definition would take still decades more to work out.

If the narrative of this school across these decades suggests slight internal evolution, this is because of the context in which it is both embedded
and helping to illuminate and not, in fairness to Huddleston's now-pale successors, because these men chose to be caretakers rather than innovators.
First, what happened, or didn't?

EVENTS

Huddleston's school, a little presumptuously it now looks, was something
of a family affair. His wife Sarah came aboard in 1716 to help him with the
female pupils and his son Thomas appeared as "usher," a cleanup designation for all-around assistant. Their qualifications, beyond kinship, are unknown, though both for sure had less formal education than Huddleston
himself. We know that Sarah Huddleston was at least literate, for she had
signed legal papers in the 1690s. We know nothing at all of Thomas's education and must surmise that he had been taught at home and in school by his
own father.[1] The senior Huddleston died, at about sixty, probably in August
1723. Sensing his "advanced years," he must have worked out with Trinity
Rector William Vesey and the Trinity Church fathers that Thomas should
take his place. The school was impossible at this point to separate from the
schoolmaster, who might well and with some justification have come to
think of it as his own. At any rate, when it came time to provide for the next
generation, he certainly acted that way, which was not unlike the acts of
other sorts of skilled tradesman of the era who bequeathed tools to their
first-born to carry on with the coopering or the smithing. So Huddleston
sought to pass on his school, his biggest "asset" if only a virtual one, and he
succeeded.

The school moved through its first succession, or at least its first succession-
within-the-family, without interruption as Thomas took the reins in advance of his official appointment by the SPG but with support of Vesey and
the mayor. Memoranda to London praised him for "sobriety, diligence and
learning as a person fit to be made schoolmaster."[2] The SPG concurred
quickly and bestowed the same salary as his father's, £20 per annum. The
Trinity vestry further made him clerk of the parish, with the attendant fees,
and in 1727 gave him on its own account additional salary of £15.[3]

This was the first time that the school/schoolmaster received regular subsidy from Trinity Church. The vestry minutes are silent as to the reason for this extended generosity, though we might deduce both approval of the school's operation and confidence in its future. Evidently it was adequate at least to keep son Huddleston from his father's constant supplication to the SPG for more money, though in 1727 he did call on the society to endorse his petition to the governor and the city for an "annual allowance" for the support of schooling for poor children.[4] The SPG ignored his request; perhaps he had overstepped.

Thomas Huddleston died young—how young exactly is a question, for the parish records that would have fixed his birth date were destroyed in the fire of 1776—dying probably early in October 1731. The next transition in leadership hints slightly more at institutional evolution toward a kind of governance, by church of school. On the younger Huddleston's demise, his mother Sarah, William's widow, still lived. She in fact then took charge of the school, and during a several-month interim, a party lobbied the SPG to have her named her son's and husband's official successor. William Huddleston, for all his money troubles, had not been poorly connected in New York Anglican circles, and his widow appears to have basked at least in some of her husband's reputation quite as much as she shared his financial distress. Huddleston's brother Thomas (likely Huddleston's son was this brother's namesake) was an Anglican clergyman on Long Island and probably known to another Anglican priest, Alexander Campbell, who in 1731 and 1732 led a movement to enable Sarah Huddleston to carry on in charge of the family schooling business. Campbell orchestrated a petition to the SPG signed by sixty-eight New Yorkers, including the mayor, council president, aldermen, justices, and merchants, promoting Sarah as her son's successor.[5] Its primary effect was to prompt a row with the vestry of Trinity Church and Vesey in particular, who, though they had supported the esteemed widow with a gift of £8 at the time of her husband's death, perhaps had decided now several years later that a third Huddleston was one too many and it was time for a change. At least, they were backing another candidate whom they had already named to the Huddlestons' other old sinecure as clerkship of Trinity Church: Thomas Noxon.

Again, the characters here are shadowy, if not the antagonism between them. Campbell may have acted from charity to promote his old friend's financially distressed widow. Or he may have wished a fight with the imperious Vesey (which he got). Or specifically he may have disliked (probably too mild a word) Vesey's choice of Noxon. Perhaps it was all three. In opposition to Mrs. Huddleston, the Trinity party carefully said only that because of her advanced age (which we do not have, though probably she was in her sixties) they doubted her "capable to discharge a trust of duty of such great importance to the City and the Church."[6] Campbell was less polite about Vesey and Vesey's man. But careful too, for the SPG sided with management and rejected the protesters' petition. It is impossible now to sort substance from noise, but the volume of the argument is intriguing for Campbell did appear to lay serious charges. In good knock-about pamphleteering style, in "A True and Just Vindication of Mr. Alexander Campbell" (July 20, 1732), he fairly tore into Vesey for "representing to them most falsely and perfidiously that Mr. Noxon is qualified to be their schoolmaster, whereas it is certain he does not know how to set a Psalm in the church, and can neither read nor write English. I have never heard that he had any other merit to support his pretensions to that school, but being a passive implicit tool to Mr. Vesey."[7] Campbell further objected that Vesey demurred at Mrs. Huddleston's candidacy because of her gender and that consequently she "was not qualified to teach that school, for that there were many grown boys in the school."[8]

The SPG from a far distance probably couldn't be sure of the truth any better than can we from a far time. It made the politic choice, however, and stayed out of the provincial New York fray, giving Vesey and Trinity benefit of the doubt and assuaging Sarah Huddleston with a grant of £20 or the equivalent of one year's salary (a solution recommended by the Trinity party).[9] Bad feeling may have lingered, and perhaps as an additional sop Noxon two years later gave up the lucrative Trinity clerkship so as, he testified, to make the "Society's school his whole business."[10] Foregoing such a plum surely would have made him look earnest about the school, whatever his qualifications were to run it. The flap makes us wonder, who was this Noxon, anyway, other than a favorite of Vesey? An earlier historian tried to track him down some distance, which was not very far: probably of Dutch ancestry, but anglicized in the 1710s and 1720s and by the time of the Huddleston family's fading from the picture, a vestryman of Trinity Church and, as their memorandum to the SPG put it naturally, "a person of exemplary piety and virtue."[11] Whoever he was, what mattered was that Vesey wanted him for the school mastership, and Vesey generally got what he wanted.

It is a reasonable deduction that whatever he really wanted, individual personalities aside, the effect of promoting Noxon and dismissing the Huddleston claim to the school was to assert the prerogative of Trinity Church over the SPG's charity school in New York as it had not been asserted before. Noxon took up his new post on April 22, 1732. The day before, Trinity's vestry established a standing committee to inspect it.[12] The rector and New York's mayor had paid periodic visits to Huddleston's operation for years and never found it anything but praiseworthy. Under the new arrangement, they continued to do so but with formal mandate. Trinity did not act unilaterally, however: The SPG petitioned it to step up its interest.[13]

Through the rest of the colonial period, while the committee remained permanent, it evidently exercised a light hand. Only a handful of references to it dot Trinity's vestry minutes. This could mean they were neglectful; it probably means only that the committee members had established a routine and that nothing much seems to have gone wrong ever to alarm them in their role as permanent overseers. The reasons that the SPG solicited Trinity's fresh involvement are lost to the record, though the move, taken at the time of regime change that ended the founders' long run, suggests a certain opportunism. The SPG, for all its grandeur in the history of Christian missions, was forever hard up. To Huddleston the SPG may have looked the fat faraway patron susceptible to clever blandishment, but from its own broader perspective ambitions always outran resources. Huddleston was one of many supplicants ever at its door.[14] By the early 1730s the SPG had been at it for thirty years, long enough to have learned that the job its members had set for themselves would never be anything but a long, hard, hand-to-mouth slog. Where they could, they moved from patron to partner, and there could hardly look to a better partner than Trinity Church. Trinity was not only the spiritual mother church for Anglicanism in New York. It was also becoming materially wealthy,[15] and its wealth from an early date impinged on the school that Huddleston and the SPG had planted under its wing.

Virtually all of the schoolmasters' reports sent back to London, from the 1730s onward, were attested by Trinity officials. The more specific record of their involvement in the school had to do less with what we would think of today as educational policy than with money. This no doubt was as the SPG would have hoped. It transpired gradually but steadily and mostly not on Noxon's watch but on that of his successor in turn, Richard Hildreth. Noxon lasted in the job for twelve years, leaving in all likelihood on account of advanced age. Once past the rancorous appointment episode, his tenure seems to have been uncontroversial, and he left behind a school operationally not much different from the one he had walked into—except that, and this is an important exception, it was thenceforth a school of Trinity Church as well as of the SPG. In the school, the interests of these twin sponsors converged and made them good partners: the SPG's "global" interest to advance the Anglican cause in the colonies, and Trinity's local interest to fulfill a Christian duty to the poor in their midst by making some provision for their pious practical schooling.

The partnership took at least a little working out, however, as could be seen when the time came to name Noxon's replacement. Vesey was not unprepared, and in the same communication to the SPG where Noxon announced his resignation the rector put forward his new man, Richard Hildreth.[16] Though destined for a very long run, Hildreth almost did not get out of the gate. This was because the SPG just then expressed its hope to give preference to a clergyman in the appointment of schoolmasters and catechists and had several New England-educated candidates in mind, though none was named. The abruptness of the SPG announcement, coupled with expression of doubt about the need for its support of a school in New York at all, where other schools were proliferating, must have given Vesey a start. But he did not give an inch. Nor was he above trying to scare the SPG into continuing its decades-long subsidy by linking it directly to the health of local church. As he fired back: "If the honorable Society will not be pleased to support this school any longer, it will be a vast obstruction to the growth of our infant church [a stretch], to which it has been a constant nursery for above forty years, and to the children of the poor who's [sic] parents can hardly give them bread, may be deprived of the opportunity of learning to read etc., of being instructed in those principles of Christianity which are necessary to save their souls."[17] Who knows? Hildreth, who had been doing interim service without appointment, joined in the protest, and again Trinity prevailed.

That it did marks the 1740s out. "Watershed" grossly overstates, yet it was then that a couple of things occurred that signaled the sprout of an institution, maybe. Hildreth and the vestry got on. Though his SPG salary was only £15, Hildreth too served as parish clerk for another £15, and later as catechist to the Negroes for £10. As important, the vestry began to award him, in its words, "gratuities" or what look now like performance bonuses ranging from £20 to £60 or, because they became regular, amounting to a second church-supported salary on top of the SPG allowance.[18] A nice enough situation: a schoolmaster with two paymasters who as far as we know never pulled in different directions. Had they, which way would he have jumped? As it was, he appeared to do well; in 1770 his vestry salary would be fixed at £40 and raised to £60 two years later—yet he had a wife and four children and claimed in later years that only his church clerkship enabled him to afford to live in New York.

The point is that having formalized at least the form of its inspections in the 1730s, the church from the 1740s also began to outspend the SPG in the form of additional salary to the schoolmaster. Recall, moreover, that Huddleston for years had begged money not just for himself but for everything else he needed to teach, holding up the extreme poverty of his charity charges (though this was not exactly true or at least not for all of them). The church after mid-century began to see to more and more of these things too and to maintain a separate Charity School Fund. The money had two sources. Between 1727 and 1789 Trinity Church received, specifically for the care of the poor and for the charity school (seldom was the distinction clear; most bequests were to the school directly and most came during Hildreth's time), gifts and bequests of over £5,000 to be put out at interest in perpetuity.[19] Additional money was earned, or at least donated, at sponsored fund-raising events, chiefly charity sermons. Charity school sermons were begun in 1755 and continued through the end of the century. Ordered annually by the Trinity vestry but in fact preached more often, they were a popular mode of public communication in an era still tuned to the spoken work for edification and entertainment.[20] Charity sermons were then the vogue in England, and in New York newspapers advertised them regularly.[21] Though sectarian in content, they were public in format, with the idea being to spread the net widely and so the contributor base. Whether from the appeal of the preachers' oratory or their cause, sermons worked and for years produced reliably generous responses.[22] More unusual, there is also record of two benefit theatricals in 1750 and 1762: plays performed by professionals who contributed the box office receipts to the school.[23]

PATTERNS

Then, unlike now, the word "school" signified more the exchange of teaching and learning in a group setting than the place where the exchange occurred. Schoolteachers, schoolchildren, school days, preceded schoolhouse. Our contemporary understanding of schools as hierarchical, bureau-cratic organizations with dedicated physical facilities where children are dropped off in the morning and depart in the afternoon does not describe this earlier time. The English charity school associated with Trinity Church in fact had no house to call its own for forty years (counting from 1709). Its early masters taught at home or in the church belfry or in rented rooms. There is no record of any of the Huddlestons or Thomas Noxon ever lobbying for a school building; perhaps they had their hands full just trying to be sure the schoolmaster got paid and that there were enough schoolchildren to justify their jobs. When a request did come, from Richard Hildreth in 1748, its timing probably related as much to the growth and prosperity of Trinity Church as it did to the state of the school. For that was the same year that the Trinity Vestry took up the matter of building its first chapel-of-ease, or satellite church, what would be St. George's Chapel and the second place of Anglican worship in the city.[24] Hildreth had made a note of his desire that the school should have a schoolhouse to the SPG about the same time. He could hardly have had much hope of tangible assistance from that quarter for a major capital project, and there is no evidence that the society helped fund the project in any way. It suggests, however, that Hildreth must have been as astute a politician as he was a schoolmaster, who saw value in getting his desire on the official record even if the substantive help would have to come from elsewhere. It certainly couldn't hurt, and the blessing of the faraway umbrella patron might even help move things along.

Hildreth formally petitioned the vestry in April 1748. It quickly assented, to the extent of assigning the same committee designated to deal with the new chapel to deal with the prospect of a schoolhouse, yard, and garden. A month later it recommended that church ground adjacent to the nearby Lutheran Church be set aside for the building site.[25] Financing the actual construction appears to have been left largely to Hildreth's own orchestration; on this, we have his continuing reports to the SPG. "This pious design," he wrote to London, " being a thing so absolutely necessary as 'tis at present ye only charity school in this city (except a Dutch one) surely will be a standing monument of the Society's bounty, who were the first promoters and for so long time supported the same, to the immortal honour of that truly charitable body."[26] Hildreth had to fund raise, and he started at the top, with Trinity's most prominent member and governor of the colony, George Clinton. Clinton not only permitted the subscription campaign but started it off with his own donation, as did the new rector of Trinity Church, Henry

Barclay. (Vesey died in 1746, after forty-nine years on the job.[27]) Other worthies dutifully lined up for a good and probably fashionable cause, so that
within a few months Hildreth had collected upward of £300 for his building
fund. We do not know how much the schoolhouse cost, only that it was
more than £300, because the vestry committed to top up the difference and
add to Hildreth's subscription "a sum sufficient to build a handsome school
and Dwelling house fore the use of the Societys schoolmaster."[28]

Apparently, they did not scrimp, and in November 1749 occupied a fifty-
by twenty-six-foot two-story masonry structure, its facade "entirely of hewn
stone." In Hildreth's eye anyway, it was "one of the most beautiful edifices in
this city."[29] The ground floor was set aside for the schoolmaster's apartment
with a kitchen adjoining, and upstairs one spacious room for the school. It
was topped with a cupola for a "smart bell."

But not for long: A fire in the wee hours of February 23, 1750, gutted the
whole thing and even spread to the nearby steeple of Trinity Church, where
church records were stored—and destroyed. The whole loss to church and
school was guessed at £2,000.[30] A strange rumor spread that Hildreth himself might have been responsible for the disaster, presumably by some care-
lessness, though it was confirmed that he and his family were absent from
the building that night, and in fact lost everything in the flames. He defended himself publicly, and nothing came of it. No one knows the cause.

Whatever it was, the vestry promptly determined to rebuild, and Hildreth appears to have emerged none the worse for wear in the vestry estimation on account of it. The school opened for business in a new building
on the same lot in October 1751. There was some argument about Hildreth's
ability to pay rent for his residence, but this was resolved and he and his wife
and four children moved back in two years later. They and the school remained there until 1768, when the vestry decided to turn the building into
the church rectory. They hoped to put up a third schoolhouse facing the
town commons, but difficulties with leases required a location on a lot behind Trinity Church, probably somewhere on Lumber Street, today's Trinity
Place, and which then was virtually at the Hudson's edge. A temporary structure was ready late in 1768, about the same size as the one that had burned
(and its replacement) and again of brick with a slate roof. Why exactly this
was described as "temporary" is unclear, unless it was seen to be in a temporary location; the building itself seems to have been as substantial as the
previous "permanent" ones, one of which had proved so dramatically not to

be.[31] It is possible that a proper second permanent schoolhouse went up around 1772 "on a piece of land in the outward of the city" but not further identified. This at least would account for two buildings, and the great fire of 1776 that scorched much of the city was reported to have destroyed "two Charity School Houses."[32]

If the details go murky, it is even harder to generalize about the pattern. It is a temptation retrospectively to say, for example, that a school with a school building is more of a school than a school without one and that therefore Hildreth's charity school, say in 1770, was more of a school than Huddleston's in 1720. It probably wasn't. It was, however, more tightly linked to Trinity Church. Buildings, then and now, were the easy and the perilous part: magnets for raising money and sinkholes for spending it. Trinity's vestrymen seem to have had no hesitation after mid-century or so in investing in buildings in the name of charity schooling. Why not before? This could be as simple as that they had not been asked, but again why hadn't they been? This is probably a matter of accumulating chronology. Enough years had gone by in the history of the charity school to suggest permanence or at least not transitoriness, enough "past" to permit observation of steady, unchanging need being met by reliable, beneficent response.

There is no record of anyone at Trinity Church ever asking "why are we doing this?" By Hildreth's time, two reasons obviated that question. One was history's momentum. We do it because we have always done it. Not that forty years (from founding to first building) is "always," but it is more than a generation and long enough a time that people in their own thirties, forties, or even fifties could not personally remember a time before it. It is a past long enough to have gotten used to, even to have grown comfortable with. A future flowing naturally from it could be easy to contemplate, and perhaps literally to build for. The second reason that made connection of school-and-buildings to parish church seem foregone was that this was what Christians were supposed to do, the way they were supposed to behave. Through the church—the body of Christ on earth or, as Archbishop Cranmer's *Prayer Book* then taught them, "the blessed company of all faithful people"—Christians did their duty. Through the church, faith acted. Not that the Bible speaks much about schooling—but it does have an endless lot to say about the poor, chiefly, as eighteenth-century Anglicans read it anyway, that they will always be with you. There is no evidence whatever that charity schooling was understood at the time in England or America as anything but a duty to assist poor individuals obtain skills to give them some better purchase on life, with perhaps the additional unstated reason that equipping young people with practical skills makes them less likely later to become troublemakers or public burdens. To see in such views seeds of social meliorism is anachronistic. Helping the poor was not the same as trying to reduce poverty. That charity schooling might slow significantly the stream of poor who needed it would have seemed strange to Hildreth and his contemporaries. Theirs was a business for which demand, by definition, was endless, if non-paying. Build it and they would come, always.

SURROUNDINGS

Biblical motivation, while it can look straight, leads down crooked earthly paths. So the building of school buildings, even more than the maintenance of a standing committee to inspect the school, involved Trinity Church in the business of schooling and introduced the issue of ownership in two respects. Trinity Church in the City of New York began life in the 1690s with a church building that schoolmaster William Huddleston, among others, had helped to fund and build. By the 1750s the bricks and mortar were multiplying, in keeping with the growth of the city around them.

New York prospered enormously during the twenty-odd years of world conflict marked first by King George's War which began in 1739, and then by the Seven Years War, which ended in 1763. Given New York's strategic proximity to French Canada, the British government made New York a focus of its continental defense and fortified it with thousands of troops and large fleets. Privateers, several score of which operated out of New York in the late 1750s, brought home fat prizes and paid rich returns to their investors. If defense spending was good for New York business, so was Britain's incipient industrial revolution, which enhanced the colonies' role as a market for British manufactures and as a source of foodstuffs, naval stores, and other raw materials. Granted that it was restricted largely to Britain and British West Indian colonies, for this was the age of mercantilism, seaborne trade boomed. Prices of agricultural products went up more rapidly than prices of manufactured imports, which meant that American purchasing power rose steadily and with it American standards of living. The city's population nearly doubled in this period to almost eighteen thousand, ahead of Boston and in the decade before the Revolution coming up fast on Philadelphia.[33]

Trinity Church rode the same wave of prosperity and probably attracted a higher concentration of wealth and refinement than any other public place in New York: "the most influence, and greatest opulence." The Governor, the King's Council, members of the colonial assembly "with numerous trains of affluent merchants and landholders belonged." The church building received extensive renovations in the 1740s and 1750s, and got its first pipe organ from England. The parish also spread out, first with erection of St. George's Chapel on Beekman Street in 1752, and then with the more elaborate St. Paul's at Broadway and Fulton between 1764 and 1766, designed by Christopher Wren disciple James Gibbs to be a reasonable likeness of St. Martin in the Fields in London.[34] Even greater than its mercantile wealth, though, was Trinity's yet-to-be-realized wealth in the form of real estate. While Manhattan Island at mid-eighteenth century was not yet exactly crowded, it was destined to be crammed. The centerpiece of Trinity's holdings in Queen Anne's Grant, also known as the Duke's Farm and the King's Farm, was destined to make the parish permanently wealthy in a manner indexed to the growth of the city around it, and on occasion (for wealth had a price) the object of jealousy and resentment as well.[35]

An additional motive for the church's expansion and displays of prosperity was its interest in preserving primacy of place in a city growing more diverse—and less Anglican—by the day. An influx of immigrants, relatively few of them Anglicans, were buying up property, renting houses, and pushing northward the community's frontier. Although the Anglican establishment remained in control of leading institutions, it was not always without a fight. The founding of King's College in 1754 offered a case in point. For decades, prominent Anglicans, Dutch Reformed, Lutherans, and Presbyterians (among other Protestant groups) had advocated the establishment of a college in New York to train clergy and prepare young men for careers in medicine or the law. Although there was shared interest in founding a college, there was sharp disagreement about who would lead it and what sort of training its incipient clergy would receive. In the 1740s, the chorus for a college was joined by evangelical enthusiasts from the Great Awakening, who had notable success in founding colleges in other colonies, especially Pennsylvania's Log College, the direct ancestor of Princeton. Amid this buzzing noise and competitive threat, the clergy and vestry of Trinity Church recognized that its leadership and control were at stake. Using a large gift of land as leverage, they persuaded the colonial government to accept two conditions on the new college: that its president must always be a member of

the Church of England, and that religious services at the college be conducted according to Anglican forms.[36]

In this context, Trinity's gradual assertiveness in matters of the charity
school becomes more plausible—especially because the first sessions of the
new King's College were held in the quarters of the charity school. When
precisely the school became Trinity Church's responsibility above and beyond the SPG's is a question. The earliest recorded use of the phrase "Trinity School" is Hildreth's from April 27, 1763.[37] Thereafter he addressed all his
communications to the SPG from "Trinity School, New York." The usage
probably somewhat trails the fact, and no one moment can be said to have
marked the change. Evolution, not takeover, is what occurred. Gradually,
the owners of Trinity Church (that is, pillars of the parish who paid the bills
and who were also some of the pillars of New York society) also "took ownership" of—in the sense of becoming emotionally or intellectually invested
in—the school. At some point, too, they obviously took ownership literally
and legally. This is trickier because until 1749 there was no physical place actually to possess. That first schoolhouse Trinity Church at least partly paid
for, and if the donations raised by Hildreth are counted as donations to the
church earmarked for the schoolhouse, then the church paid for it entirely.
It also had begun to subsidize the schoolmaster. At that point, and absent
any competing claim, there could be no doubt. While Trinity School dates
itself from 1709, what it is really dating is the addition of substance by an
outside entity (the SPG) to one solitary schoolmaster's up-to-then proprietary operation. The time when church and school can be said to have
merged into one unit came later, the result of gradual assumption by the
church of fiduciary responsibility for the school's operation and the dominant hand in its governance. The vestry never said this in so many words.
They just began de facto to act the part. So school grafted itself onto church.
It is a question whether Trinity Church would ever have sponsored a charity school had the SPG not initiated one. Quite possibly. It is probably less
of question whether the SPG would have sustained one without the church
to help out, though that is not a certainty either.

What is certain is that a partnership made it all more likely, and that by
the time of the Revolution, society and church had worked out a sturdy
though evolving relationship. Reports still went to London, but attention focused in New York. Hildreth was still in charge, as he had been since the
1740s. We know nothing of his political sympathies, but something of his

masters'. Trinity Church was a symbolic citadel of loyalism. Its assistant rector (rector after 1777) Charles Inglis belonged to a circle of conservative Anglican clerics in the middle colonies that included Samuel Seabury and
Myles Cooper, president of King's College. Their pamphlets, though usually
burned by enthusiastic patriot crowds as quickly as they were printed, expressed the British establishment view that constitutional liberty and mobs,
of which New York saw an abundance in the 1770s and that typically in Inglis's view were filled with dissenters, did not mix and that only people of
rank and distinction were fit to rule.[38] If Hildreth disagreed, he probably
knew to keep his head low. In any case, he died (in 1777) before the matter
was settled.

Had the wartime fate of New York City been any indicator, the whole
matter would be settled in Britain's way. The same strategic considerations
that had led the British to attend so closely to New York's security in earlier
wars of the eighteenth century, and that in the course of things helped enrich it, put the city once again in the cross-hairs of the contending forces. At
first, in 1775 and the first half of 1776, the patriot cause surged, and loyalists
fled by the thousands. William Tryon, who turned out to be the colony's last
royal governor, reported how within days of July 4 the symbols of royal authority disappeared, from the king's coat of arms at City Hall to the numerous trappings at Trinity Church and St. Paul's: "Every vestage of Royalty, as
far as [has] been in the power of the Rebels [is] done away." And another:
"The Episcopal Churches in New York are all shut up, the prayer books,
burned, and the Ministers scattered abroad. . . . It is now the Puritan's high
holiday season and they enjoy it with rapture."[39]

The Continental Congress dispatched no less than its best soldiers,
George Washington and Charles Lee, fresh from successes in New England,
to see to New York's defense, though they might just as well not have bothered. Until the Stamp Act crisis in the 1760s when it had moved to Boston,
New York had been Britain's North American military headquarters and
was familiar and valued territory. This time too the British prevailed in New
York and up until the very end. Militarily, the Americans failed miserably,
and despite Washington's famed fog-shrouded withdrawal from Brooklyn
Heights across the East River to Manhattan, they lost much of their army to
the vastly larger British force under William Howe, whose grand fleet arriving off Sandy Hook looked to amazed New Yorkers like "London afloat."
Occupied and fortified—"The Gibraltar of North America," it was called—

New York remained peacefully in British hands until after the war had been decided far away in Virginia in 1781 and a peace treaty signed in Paris two years after that.

The New York that the British occupied, very shortly anyway, was not exactly what they remembered: At least, there was literally less of it. Sometime after midnight on September 21, 1776, a fire started, probably in the Fighting Cocks tavern near Whitehall Slip on the far southeastern end of Manhattan. Strong winds sent it north and west, crossing Broadway just below Trinity Church, which was consumed in minutes. Only a hastily organized bucket brigade saved St. Paul's, six blocks north. From Paulus Hook across the Hudson in New Jersey, it was reported that patriot crowds watched, and cheered, when Trinity's steeple (atop the belfry where charity school scholars once had learned their letters and memorized their catechism) came down in "a lofty pyramid of fire."[40] The flames finally burned themselves out along Barclay Street, having consumed some 500 houses, a quarter of New York's total.[41]

The Great Fire of 1776, which left the school once again without a schoolhouse, could not be said, however, to have much disturbed the continuity of its operation. Such disturbance as there was came earlier, in the few months between the declaration of American independence and the British reoccupation of Manhattan. Going into the war, Hildreth's school served a full complement of eighty-six children, thirty of them girls. By the early autumn, he counted thirty-five. This suggests two explanations: that the level of social disruption was such that schooling in general stopped, or that as a Tory-associated institution this particular school fell under suspicion during the brief patriot ascendancy and parents thought it prudent to keep their children away. It was most likely the latter. Hildreth himself left town briefly, finding it "necessary for my own safety to retire" and reporting to the society a few months later "the persecution against Friends of Government most of whom were obliged to leave the city, to avoid being sent prisoners to New England as many already were for no other crime than that of being loyal subjects."[42] He returned a few days after Howe's redcoats took possession, just in time to see the fire do its work. Trinity Church calculated the value of its loss from the fire at a hefty £22,200, of which £17,500 represented church and organ, £2,500 the rectory (or the old schoolhouse), £2,000 two charity schoolhouses (the "temporary" ones), and £200 the library.[43] For the school, the fire meant temporary quarters, which in a sense was nothing new except that they were rented (we do not know their location), and with the American evacuation the school's business otherwise appears to have returned quickly to normal, with enrollment rising again to eighty-six.[44] Nor did Hildreth's death in May 1777 of "nervous fever" at age fifty-five much disrupt things. Rector Inglis promptly stepped in and until he could find a replacement farmed out the whole operation to two private schools, where he assured the SPG "the utmost care is taken of them, and under our inspection as formerly, and where they are to remain until a person whom I have engaged arrives and takes charge of them."[45]

It appears though that private maintenance was expensive and that the church cut back on enrollment in order to economize until a new schoolmaster took up the post. His name was Amos Bull, and he arrived in April 1778. Previously he had run a school for psalm singing in New York, but Inglis found him working for the army's commissary department in Rhode Island, where he had fled when the Americans held the city.[46] He stayed just four years, in contrast to the long-serving Hildreth, and his tenure pedagogically at least differed little from his predecessors': penmanship and reading, arithmetic and merchants' accounts for the boys; reading, writing, and sewing for the girls; catechism for all once a week. There was further echo, too, back to Huddleston: Bull constantly complained about money. The war brought inflation, and the numbers he asked for sound large compared with the school's early days. When he came aboard, the SPG allowed him £15. The church supplemented this with another £15 for the parish clerkship (a post that over the years seems to have merged with the school mastership), and £60 for running the school. A year later he petitioned for, and got, another £40. The church also allowed him the £10 previously paid by the society to a catechist but that apparently had fallen behind in its remittance. Then in 1780 he received a supplement of £100, "the Board [vestry] taking under consideration the extravagant prices of every article of living at this time."[47]

In all this pleading, the difference from Huddleston's was that the object was no longer the SPG, whose contributions to the school had progressively diminished as a proportion of the total. There is no record of why Bull left,[48] but when it came time to set his successor's pay, Ebenezer Street, a Connecticut Tory, received a £200 salary, in [depreciated] "New York currency." (It was now 1782, and the Americans had won.) Nor is there record that anyone on the vestry argued about doubling, nominally anyway, the schoolmaster's pay. There was argument, however, from the SPG, over its by then long-standing £15 stipend to the Trinity schoolmaster. At the changeover, Inglis implored the SPG to continue it. Perhaps he did so in anticipation that, with independence, the Society would soon be departing the scene. It might also have been in part pro forma, on the principle that supplications not kept fresh will be ignored. Whatever the explanation, the plea prompted a protest from London only partly, it seems, related to the society's imminent exit. The real issue was recognition that Trinity School, or better Trinity School plus Trinity Church, had outgrown the SPG. The relationship went back a long time and was now winding down. Had the Revolution never occurred, or had the war ended differently, it is probable that society sponsorship would have reduced to a name-only affair anyway. Trinity, the church and the school, could more than take care of itself. Moreover, the missionaries of Anglicanism had more pressing needs in far needier fields than Manhattan Island.[49]

Street, a loyalist refugee from Connecticut who had fled to New York, stayed less than a year, but seemed determined to make the most of it. He got the last £15 from the SPG, plus £200 from the vestry; plus the Trinity clerkship, plus a stipend for catechizing the Negroes (paid no longer by the SPG but Trinity), plus he got permission to take in up to twenty "private scholars, provided this indulgence shall not prevent their [he was probably assisted by his wife and son] attentions to the public school." There had been no private payers since before Hildreth's time, and the deal must not have set well with the vestry, who revoked it for Street's successor, Edward Haswell, who also dipped quickly in and out, serving only from September 1783 to April 1784.[50] We know nothing more about him, though both the Streets and the Rev. Inglis quit New York for Nova Scotia sometime ahead of the British evacuation on November 25, 1783.[51]

CONFUSIONS

Historians look for and try to explain change over time. They do not always find it or very much of it. So the history of Trinity School in the eighteenth century moves on two tracks. One, sketched already, suggests a slow but perceptible evolution in the institutional relationship among school, a far-away sponsor, and a close-at-hand host. Not much changed at all from Huddleston's day through the Revolution in the schoolroom itself, where the records of what occurred are monotonously the same year after year, for decades. Sixty to ninety poor children (and sometimes a few paying ones) received lessons in the rudiments of literacy and numeracy, leavened with a strong dose of Anglican piety. One schoolmaster at a time taught them, assisted sometimes by an usher and a woman assistant who helped out with the girls.

From even this modest baseline, however, it is important to respect the distinction from those informal agencies of education—family, church, and apprenticeship—that still through all of the eighteenth century trained up the vast majority of New Yorkers. That is, it is important to remember how puny, relatively, were the primary/secondary (in today's nomenclature) schools of the period. Trinity was one of only a handful that could be said to have had any kind of institutional identity, in the sense of sustained group sponsorship.[52] We know that probably never much more than 130 pupils were being educated in these schools in any one year, which amounted (in the 1770s for instance) to only about 10 percent of the white common education cohort. In a society where the evidence points to literacy rates higher than in most other places in the world, this means that most young New Yorkers were learning their letters and figures and so to some extent their manners and morals in other less formal educational venues.[53] Today we automatically speak the two words together, "school" and "system." In the eighteenth century we would not have. Schools there were, but no notion of a school system. And most of the schools there were would not look much like schools today, far less even than the Trinity charity school looks like one. It is better to say that most of these schools were actually teachers alone, who taught classes in an open market to students whose ages and needs varied widely and who could be as transient as the teachers (who often had other jobs than teaching) themselves could be. On the teaching side, there was as yet no hierarchy, no specialization, little prospect of upward mobility. Teachers were either entrepreneurs, like the abundance of schoolmasters who taught for fees, or salarymen like Trinity's charity schoolmasters, or the two in combination. For learners, the linkage between formal schooling (outside apprenticeship) and subsequent success in a world where occupational choices were hugely limited compared with our own day was still tentative.

Given there was nothing remotely resembling a system and barely any schools that had in them even the seeds of institutions, it is still possible to discern a range of possible school experience into which this early Trinity can be fit. It fit at one extreme, as by definition (if not purely in practice) a school for the children of the poor who received schooling there gratis. These were a population of youngsters dependent on the public purse, and until the Revolution throughout British North America it was the Anglican churchwardens on behalf of vestries whose job was to oversee the poor, typically binding them to apprenticeships that sometimes called for ancillary minimal schooling. It was to the charity schools that such schooling for the bound poor got out-sourced. At the other extreme, the wealthy in America, as in England, employed private tutors, boarding schools, travel abroad, though what they too might choose to do with their education was limited: army, church, medicine, law, commerce.[54] In the middle was education in the broader market, the so-called common pay schools, a term that refers not to dedicated school buildings but to classes taught by schoolmasters for a fee, typically sixteen to twenty-four shillings per quarter. They attracted a diverse range of customers, drawing children both boys and girls from different neighborhoods, parental occupations, and denominations. It is calculated that such pay schools, which were little different pedagogically from Trinity's charity school, enrolled over 50 percent of New York's five- to fifteen-years olds in any one year, but that because attendance was so informal and discontinuous this means that probably 80 to 90 percent of the population could spend time in such schools as part of their educational experience.[55]

We enter here into a minefield of words, four in particular: "common," "market," "public," and "private." Unlike "charity," which retains today the core meaning that also attended it in the Hildreth's time, and so renders the phrase "charity school" easily and correctly understandable as a free school for the poor, the meanings of these other words have slipped more with time. The tangle impinges on the subsequent nineteenth-century story of Trinity School but has roots here, in the context of its eighteenth-century story.

New York's "common" pay schools, which then shouldered most of schooling's burden, were common, first, in the sense that they were the most common, that is, the most prevalent, of such schools as then existed. They were also common in the sense that the schoolmasters who single-handedly constituted them, no different from Trinity's schoolmasters at the same time, taught a common, very basic program: reading, writing, ciphering, and some sort of moral deportment. Finally, they were common in the sense that they appealed to a wide market and that attendance was common across a diverse range of occupational backgrounds. This third meaning is the one that would rear up in the school reform debates of the nineteenth century, when advocates of a free "public" system touted social mixing as a central aim of any truly democratic educational policy.[56]

But here, up through the 1790s anyway, schooling in New York was a matter hardly thought relevant to public policy at all. This was not because of ideology, but because the "system," which was no system and had virtually no relation to government, seemed to work, schooling large numbers of subjects/citizens at a rudimentary but adequate level. That this particular kind of interchange between teacher and learner worked satisfactorily and in the absence of any guiding central policy suggests the presence of a market where the information symmetries were reasonably good. That is, it was relatively easy for buyers to make judgments about the price and quality of the services on offer. On the supply side, schooling was a highly competitive, risky business, and the barriers to entry to teaching were low and unregulated. On the demand side, consumers had lots of choices and could switch suppliers easily—or they could choose none at all and just study by the light of the fire at home. Schoolmasters advertised. In what was still a small provincial community, parents and no doubt their children talked. Word got around.

If schooling in New York then functioned largely through the market, this did not make it to eighteenth-century eyes "private." Indeed, it seemed the opposite in two senses. These other meanings went back to antiquity. One referred to schooling that occurred, literally, in a group or community setting and was thus "public," in contrast to that which occurred through individual lessons with a tutor and was thus "private." The first meaning spilled over into the second, which had to do with the intent or purpose of schooling. Was it meant primarily to enhance private pleasure and selfish gain, or to promote the public good?[57] Thus England's elite fee-charging secondary schools, meant as they were to stamp onto boys a sense of their future public responsibility, became "public" schools. The Anglican worthies on the Trinity vestry employed the word probably in the first sense. At least, when authorizing the building of Hildreth's first schoolhouse in 1749 they used the word: "that [churchwarden] Robinson furnish and pay such

moneys as shall be necessary (over and above subscriptions) for carrying on
and completing the building for the public school."[58] The tricky meaning of
these words would surface in a strange way in the first decade after American independence as the eighteenth century drew to a close.

SORTINGS

The Revolutionary War itself had marked no turning point in the affairs
of the charity school or of New York schools generally. It is true that the
Dutch and the Jewish schools closed down, and King's College was used by
the British as a hospital, but in general New York passed a peaceful enough
war once Howe's forces occupied the city. Trinity, though it lost two "temporary" schoolhouses to the 1776 fire, did not cease operations, but moved
to a private house, then for a time farmed its boys out to independent masters, then picked itself up again and carried on for the duration. Given that
schooling was still largely pre-institutional at the time of the Revolution,
there were few institutions for war to disrupt. Family, church, apprenticeship, all continued in their educational functions, while the common pay
schools run by independent masters and who educated the majority of
schoolgoers probably improvised in wartime much as they had to do in
peacetime. There were plenty of them: eighteen in 1770, twenty-five in 1774,
seventeen in 1777. Of course there was turnover of teachers as there was of
population, but it turned out to be a long, as well as a tranquil, occupation,
and schooling was just one part of getting on with life. Who knew who
would win, anyway?

In the 1780s and 1790s, Trinity schoolmaster John Wood presided over
an operation of eighty-six charity scholars in addition to tending an unrecorded number of private-pay pupils at a separate evening school.[59] He did
so at first in rented quarters, until in 1794 the church completed a new schoolhouse at 44 Lumber Street and today close to the intersection of Rector
Street and Trinity Place (Lumber Street would become Church Street), and
facing the compass west though liturgical east end of the new Trinity Church,
itself rebuilt in 1790. It was paid for through the sale of church lots southwest
of Chambers Street and with charity donations and cost about £2,200. When
the building opened, it bore a vestry-authorized stone-engraved inscription,
"The First Episcopal Charity School, 1794."[60]

At the same time, something more controversial than bricks and mortar was afoot. The schoolhouse on Lumber Street was the first dedicated

intended-as-permanent building since the early 1750s. Trinity School at mid-century could be seen as the provincial expression of a metropolitan impulse, as a symbol of Church of England missionary zeal exerted through the arm of the SPG and the local agency of Trinity Church. Across an ocean, interests and ideologies aligned, even as the source of subsidy slid gradually from London to New York. Forty years on, with its SPG ties history, this proto-institution found itself caught up in a different metropolitan web of entirely American making. This time, however, interests and ideologies would defy easy alignment, and eventually would settle out around altered meanings of "private" and "public" in education. This occurred in the unique political context of American democracy's infancy when many questions once thought settled were asked anew. Among them were questions about what education-as-schooling was for, whom it should serve, and who should pay for it. Tiny Trinity (along with New York City's other charity schools) played an odd role both at the center and at the periphery of this story.

In 1795 the New York state legislature passed and Governor George Clinton signed a new law to assist common schools. They followed here in the wake of New England states and were able to do so thanks to revenue from state land sales.[61] The intent was to push down to the "common" level the principle of state aid to schooling already in place, through the state Board of Regents, for colleges and academies. The law appropriated £20,000 per year for five years to be distributed to counties on the basis of population; to be eligible for the state money the counties had to match with local taxes half the amount of their share.[62] What seemed simple enough in intention grew quickly confused in operation. This was because New York City was different from rural New York State, where existing schools were thin on the ground, which made it easy for local citizens-as-school commissioners to know where to direct the public largesse. In urban New York where common schools (i.e., those that taught "common" subjects) were relatively thick on the ground, and included both the operations of nearly 100 teacher-entrepreneurs plus half a dozen charity schools, the law said the money could go both to charity schools and to others. The New York Common Council, to whom the legislature left the job of deciding who got what, faced a tangle of interests unknown in quieter country precincts.

Moreover, the city's schoolmasters had recently begun to organize and for the first time spoke with something of a collective voice. The words again bid caution: this was the 1790s and long before unions. That decade

did, however, witness in New York City a burst of "associations," some ethnic in basis, some occupational, some literary, some political. The Friendly
Sons of St. Patrick, the Society of Tradesmen and Mechanics, the Democratic Club, and the Drone filled the coffee houses with boisterous talk,
often as not talk with enough Democratic–Republican flavor to it to make
Federalists uneasy. Although the American party system had not yet coa-
lesced, and "faction" was still widely feared as subversive of liberty, the political atmosphere of the 1790s carried an increasing ideological charge. As
the news from revolutionary France polarized opinion, the danger of faction in America deepened, the menace of parties grew harder to avoid.

In 1794, fifteen of New York's teachers, several of whom were active Republicans or at least anti-Federalists, had a go at an association of their own:
the Society of Associated Teachers. They met weekly in the evening and
talked about shared problems; they tried to coordinate school holidays
among them, they made a stab at establishing group standards and at ac-
crediting certain textbooks, and they set up a small professional library.
Mostly, it seems, they debated matters of educational—and sometimes political—theory and practice: "Whether silence or studying aloud be the
most conducive to the improvement of scholars in a public school"; "might
not schools be well-governed without corporal punishment?"; "ought any
religion further than morality be inculcated in schools?" "Does the difference of ability, so apparent among mankind arise from a superior intellect
or from external causes?" "Whether a republican or monarchical form of
government is most advantageous in a school." Twenty-nine teachers signed
up in the first few months. Most were entrepreneur-masters, but not all.
Serving as vice-president in 1796, president in 1798: John Wood, schoolmaster at Trinity.[63]

The 1795 law stipulated that in New York City both charity schools and
"others" were eligible for a share of the money. The freshly organized schoolteachers did not hesitate to lobby the council that the funds should be theirs
because they were the ones providing common schooling to more than 90
percent of the New York youngsters who got it. Though such schools were
creatures of the private market where buyers paid sellers of schooling-
services, they were also deemed "common" because of what they taught and
"public" because of the open-to-the-public group setting it which they
taught it. Nothing in the law, moreover, suggested that charging tuition as

these schools all did was any barrier to public subsidy: Upstate common schools charged it until 1867 and received state aid too.

Yet the council pulled back from the prospect of payments to independent masters competing in the free market, rebuffing the teachers' organization and giving all of the funds raised from city taxes (£944; Trinity's share was £110), even before the state share was in hand, to the charity schools. At this level, the council took refuge in tradition: For the occasional public support of charity schooling there was ample English and colonial precedent. However, restricted as it was to salaries, the state share of the money when it did arrive raised another problem. Because "from the manner in which the private [common pay] schools in the said city are conducted it is impracticable to distribute the said monies according to the Direction of the Act," the council refused the teachers' bid for subsidy. Perhaps it was the whiff of Republican politics; perhaps it was the fact that subsidy handed out to a shifting array of individuals by a public body that had never had anything to do with education was simply hard to handle. So the council banked the money, and asked the legislature to amend the law to permit New York City to use the state funds for something more concrete: "the erecting and supporting of one or more public schools in the said city." The first gerund is the important one, and suggests a new understanding—to us the modern one—of "public school," as a school sustained by the public purse and as the building where that schooling took place. In 1797 the legislature complied: One-sixth would continue to go to charity schools, the rest to the anticipated public schools, bricks and mortar and all.

Only it didn't. For the five-year life of the law, the city paid the charity schools and continued to sit on the rest. Had there been urgent need for new schools beyond the common pay providers this would be hard to explain, and it rather suggests that there was as yet no pressing political reason for government to become more involved in common education. Reason for such involvement would indeed develop in the nineteenth century, when amid new waves of immigration a public, free-for-all school system would be put forward as the means to acculturate newcomers and shore up moral attitudes among New York's more numerous, potentially disorderly, certainly impoverished, and increasingly diverse populace. But it had not developed yet. New York City, at the start of the nineteenth century and based on the experience of the eighteenth century, had schools enough (though no school system) to satisfy the limited educational market for formal schooling. Education and schools were still far from synonymous; certainly they were not synonymous for the many young New Yorkers who learned the rudiments without help from schools at all.

The common school law expired in 1800 for budgetary reasons: Revenues from land sales had not been enough to support a statewide program, and a statewide property tax intended to fill the gap was short-lived. New York City meanwhile had saved up some $30,000 of the undistributed state appropriation since 1795. In 1800, the city won special dispensation again to take the prudent course and reject attempting to build a system of "free schools" for all (as they called the public alternative) in favor of spreading the money among the existing charity schools (themselves thence called "free schools," as they quite literally were, though not free for all). Common education in turn-of-the-century New York still seemed something that it was reasonable to expect users to pay for individually: It was not yet a public good. For those others who also deemed common schooling desirable but could not afford it, there was a charity (free to the poor) system, now partly state funded. The charity schools were certainly sectarian, but no sect in New York (no longer even the Anglicans) was established: no discrimination here.

It is in context of this controversy and prospective sustained subsidy of the school from public sources that we observe the first shift in its structure and formal governance since 1709. In 1800, when the city was backing away from experimenting with "free public schools," Trinity Church moved to reestablish its own free charity school. The right verb is a little hard to find here. "To establish on its own" captures awkwardly but closely what was happening. A combination of two reasons probably accounts for the action, though in what proportion it is hard to guess. To this point, and since the 1730s, the church related to the school through an oversight committee of vestrymen and of course the person of the rector, and as the burden of support gradually shifted from the SPG to the local parish it would be fair to say that school and church became a functional unity. (Another way to look at it would be to say that Trinity Church, whose "business" was Christian worship, prayer, and almsgiving, slowly diversified into education as an instrument of Christian charity in partial fulfillment of the second of the two "great commandments": "Thou shalt love thy neighbor [particularly poor ones] as thyself."[64]) In 1800, the church established a separate committee of trustees to control the school apart from but interlocking with its own vestry, thus keeping things still comprehensively "in-house." The first committee consisted of the rector and his assistant and five vestrymen. They were charged with reporting the school's finances annually to the vestry and with having vestry approval of all teacher appointments.[65] A hint of independence, perhaps, though at the same time the cement between church and school would seem to have hardened in one other respect, as the new arrangement spelled out priorities for admission. The first three categories favored Episcopalians (as American Anglicans had come to be called): "orphans belonging to the Episcopal Church, children of widows belonging to the Episcopal Church," and "children of parents of reputable character, belonging to the Episcopal Church, who have been reduced to indigence."[66]

And yet a slip of separation had occurred. Since the 1750s, the school had been maintained largely through specific bequests from Trinity parishioners and from charity sermon appeals (fund raising). The largest of these, potentially anyway, had at the time of the re-establishment come quite recently in the 1796 bequest of John Baker of real estate on the upper east side of Manhattan. Possibly, by the 1790s, it might have seemed advisable that a separate entity exist to receive them, which could have been one reason for the church's decision. A second is that it might also have seemed advisable that a separate entity exist to receive the public benefaction spun out of the 1790s common schools legislation. Whichever was the case, the church conveyed to the school existing gifts and legacies held in trust as well as the Lumber Street school house, and in 1805 petitioned the state legislature for an act of legal incorporation that would formally establish, in 1806, the First Protestant Episcopal Charity School in the City of New York.[67]

There is the sense of trying to have it both ways. The school henceforth was a distinct legal entity but tied to the church. After incorporation it no longer had to seek approval to appoint teachers, though it did for new trustees, and its reporting requirements on operations and finances to Trinity remained very much in place. Yet it was not long before the vestry appeared to emphasize the school's independence from Trinity Church, if only to keep the gifts coming from Episcopalians who were not Trinitarians.[68] It would have been difficult, however, to dilute the school's fundamental sectarianism. Between them, its missionary and its charity history hemmed it in. In retrospect, conflict between that powerful dual heritage and the fact of the school's newfound public subsidy looks inevitable. Church–state issues seem to shout. They did not shout then, not yet. But given the settlement of 1800 that left the city's charity schools with sole access to the public spigot, there remained those on the old "private" side of schooling and those who still sought to become its "public" (and in time universal) side, whose interest it was to stoke the conflict. They founded, the same year as Trinity's petition to incorporate, the Free School Society of New York City and set to work getting their money back.

FOUR *Nineteenth-Century Incarnation*
CHARITY TO EPISCOPAL SCHOOL

*D*uring its first century, Trinity School performed a valuable public service in New York by giving impoverished boys and girls a foundation of practical education and a boost in life. During its second century, the school's mission would change, and it would evolve from a church-affiliated charity school into something else, a kind of hybrid between a charity school and a private Episcopal school for middle-class boys, most of whom were supported on scholarships and headed for college or careers in business. This evolution was unplanned and unfolded gradually and in stages, and at the end of the nineteenth century it was ongoing.

Trinity first began to reconsider its traditional mission in the 1820s, when the nonsectarian Free School Society persuaded city officials to terminate financial support to church-affiliated charity schools. This was a key step on the path toward the emergence of the modern, secular public school system in New York City. With children from all walks of life, including the poorest, educated in publicly supported schools, there was little need for traditional church-affiliated charity schools. So Trinity reassessed its position, choosing to emphasize its Episcopal identity in schooling and supporting boys and girls of all ages from toddlers to teenagers, and headed not only into the trades or business but to college or seminary and the professions. The Panic of 1837 prompted Trinity to scale back its ambitions and refocus as an Episcopal school for boys only between the ages of eight and eighteen. During the remainder of the century, the school quietly pursued this mission, educating sixty to 120 Episcopalian boys per year, mostly from the middle class. At the same time, Trinity adhered to its charity-school origins by drawing on income from its landed endowment to provide scholarships for a significant majority of the students.

During much of this period, Trinity lived modestly and operated out of a sequence of temporary sites as it followed the moves of successive generations of middle-class Episcopalian families from downtown up the island. At the very end of the century, using the proceeds finally realized from a major eighteenth-century bequest, Trinity occupied handsome new quarters on W. 91st Street next to St. Agnes Chapel, a new Trinity Church chapel of ease. This location on the Upper West Side, in the latest resting place of the middle-class Episcopalian migration, symbolized more than continuing strong connections between the school and the church; it was also a statement, an affirmation of traditional religious values in an environment of fast-paced, nearly incomprehensible change in the world around it.

Trinity School's quiet evolution could hardly have occurred in more dramatic circumstances, as the city of New York experienced spectacular growth and constant, dramatic change. Between 1800 and 1890, the population exploded from 75,000, most of it Episcopalian, to 2.5 million, most of it foreign-born, very little of it Episcopalian. New York evolved from a regional port to one of the world's greatest cities, the dominant center of American economic and cultural life. Development largely colonized Manhattan and spilled over into Brooklyn, Queens, and the Bronx, across the Bay to Staten Island, and across the Hudson to a host of communities in New Jersey. Massive waves of immigrants arrived successively to participate in a diverse, rapidly industrializing economy: from Ireland and Germany before the Civil War, and thereafter from southern, central, and eastern Europe and Russia. Late in the century, more newcomers hailed from the American South as freed slaves and their descendants migrated by the thousands to the city. The new arrivals contributed much to civic life, but the pace and scale of social and economic change, locally and nationally, produced friction and conflict in the contest for control of the city.

Trinity School stood apart from this turmoil and in fact consciously sought shelter from it—physically in the long migration, with stopovers, from downtown to an enclave on the Upper West Side; and philosophically, in adhering to a traditional approach to education with strong Episcopal overtones. At the end of the nineteenth century, the school modestly offered an alternative to families seeking an explicitly religious component in the schooling of their sons or who were uncomfortable with the public schools or the latest trends in public education.

TWILIGHT OF THE CHARITY SCHOOL

During the first half of the nineteenth century, New York City grew from a town at the foot of Manhattan, where territory north of City Hall was sparsely populated and rural in character, to a vast, diverse metropolis—

Gotham, in the title of the recent authoritative history of the city before 1900.[1] In 1800, most of the 75,000 residents lived within a mile or two of the Battery and moved about town on foot or by carriage. Indeed, New York still had the feel of a village, albeit an increasingly crowded one. The population drew water from the rivers or from wells scattered across Manhattan. By 1830, the population surpassed 200,000 and by 1860 was on its way to 800,000, more than a quarter of whom had been born in Ireland. By the latter date, many citizens routinely traveled long distances across the city on horse-drawn rail carriages or journeyed still farther by steam-powered trains that linked Manhattan with the West, as well as along the traditional North–South trade routes, or by steamships that carried them up the Hudson to the Erie Canal or across the Atlantic. Many New Yorkers drew water from a public aqueduct and increasing numbers of them used gas light to labor or party through the night.

Huge, rapid growth in numbers and new technologies stressed and stretched the physical environment of the city. After 150 years of haphazard development, city and state officials sought a more orderly pattern. In 1811, the city adopted a master plan laying the territory north of 14th Street to Washington Heights into a master grid that still defines modern Manhattan: a dozen great avenues plus Broadway running North and South, with 155 cross streets cutting East and West, each divided into building lots. The grid began to fill in almost immediately, not only with the modest homes and establishments imagined by the planners, but also with multistory town-houses and tenements, large commercial structures and warehouses, impressive civic buildings and churches, and a multitude of shops, schools, theaters, and taverns. Culturally and commercially, the city began to sort itself into distinctive neighborhoods and districts defined by the national or ethnic origins of residents or a characteristic type of economic activity such as finance, trade, manufacturing, or merchandising. This was a city teeming with people, alive with activity, and full of events, including occasional crises ignited by wars and national politics, ethnic and economic tensions, financial panics, natural disasters, and unruly mobs.

The city's physical and economic and social transformation during the first half of the nineteenth century is the backdrop against which Trinity School underwent a significant change—from a church-affiliated charity school to a private religious school with a majority of scholarship students.

THE DISCOVERY OF POVERTY . . .
AND LEARNING TO DEAL WITH IT

To the genteel and pious Anglicans (thence Episcopalians) responsible for the Charity School of Trinity Church in the eighteenth century, poverty was understood not as a social problem to be ameliorated but as the natural condition of a sinful world to be ministered unto. Trinity in the eighteenth century had aimed to give boys and girls largely but not entirely poor basic tools of literacy and numeracy and so some modest step up in life, to make of them loyal citizens, productive contributors to society, and better Christians. Charity, in schooling or almsgiving, was done at heaven's command, not society's bidding.

Throughout the eighteenth century, this Christian message conformed comfortably enough to the social and economic realities of New York life, yet untested by massive waves of immigration. "Poverty" as an urgent, even threatening urban problem for society to address reared up only when there were many more of the poor. There soon enough were, with the city's exploding population, many of whom, for a time anyway, struggled to subsist.[2] The city's changing ethnic and economic composition also soon enough reshaped understanding about the purpose of schools and the policies and structures necessary to advance them. As the number of impoverished inhabitants soared, new voluntary organizations such as The New York Association for Improving the Condition of the Poor and The Children's Aid Society sprang up to deal with them. Some did so in the spirit of Christian charity and drew from the same ancient well as the old charity school of Trinity Church. Others acted more in the belief that massive immigration would spawn social challenges of a magnitude that could not be extrapolated from the colonial experience and thus could not be solved in a traditional manner.[3]

The discovery of poverty as an urban social condition in America dates from the early decades of the nineteenth century, as immigration changed what had been a chronic labor shortage into a chronic labor surplus. Real wages fell and with them the prospects for a generation and more of the newest New Yorkers. As old trades and apprenticeship patterns of learning them gave way to industrialism, labor was progressively deskilled and class lines grew more visible and hardened.[4] Periodic panics and depressions left many thousands of New Yorkers living on the margin. The poor concentrated in slums at the bottom and sides of the island, while the better off, including most Trinity Church parishioners, moved up and north, geographic distance amplifying economic separation.

Yet there were also natives who, even as they abandoned old neighborhoods, stepped up to help out. The special vulnerability of children, and the dire prospect that today's deprived and ignorant youth, if left unreformed, would become tomorrow's vagrants or troublemakers, invested the moral earnestness of reformers with political urgency. New attention focused on the role of schools in uplifting or at least controlling the masses of children whose socialization through the old informal means of family and church seemed suddenly so inadequate. Starting in the early nineteenth century, schools became an important battleground where this clash of old and new cultures in New York would play out.[5]

This seemed natural enough, given the long heritage of New York's religious (chiefly Protestant) diversity and the traditional association of education with religion. In New England, where one brand of the faith, Calvinism, was dominant, a sense of community (public) responsibility for schooling developed much sooner and more strongly.[6] In heterodox New York, the old pattern of charity schools for the poor and private pay schools for others (with some overlap) was etched just as deep, as the problematic implementation of the 1795 Common Schools law particularly in New York City demonstrated.[7] While it had continuing advocates, the old system seemed to many to be increasingly inadequate to the task. The efforts of a few leaders toward the end of the eighteenth century signaled the start of what would shortly become a wider campaign to build publicly supported "free schools."

Backed by John Jay and Alexander Hamilton, the Manumission Society opened a school for black children in 1787, a school that grew quickly and in 1794 was incorporated at the African Free School, the city's first free school unaffiliated with an existing church or sect. Then in 1801 a group of Quaker women established the Female Association, a second free school, this one for impoverished white girls.[8] What flowed from this, in the context of the debate over the use of public funds as made available in the 1795 law, was an effort to reach out yet more broadly to the ever larger number of poor New York youth not served by the church-affiliated charity schools and who consequently received no education at all. Wealthy Quakers again led the way, when John Murray, Jr., and Thomas Eddy organized a small group in support of a new philanthropy on behalf of the education of poor boys not belonging to any religious denomination. This became the Free School Society, chartered in 1805, and would appeal for and receive public funds under the Common Schools as applied to New York City. De Witt Clinton, then mayor, was the society's first president.[9]

The Free School Society believed that opening up educational opportunity to more of the city's poor would help prevent development of a large pauper class as was common in Europe. Rather than punishing the antisocial behavior of the poor with harsh laws and more prisons, its members preferred to use schools to attack mischief's causes, chiefly, as they saw them, irreligion and troubled families. The poor were not in their view innately inferior, just ignorant and disadvantaged. When homes and churches fall down, schools could and should step in.[10]

But the leaders of the Free School Society also were afraid. The stability of society as they knew it was threatened by the ignorance of the poor or, as we would put it, by the behavioral consequences of their faulty socialization.[11] Therefore, they fixed upon schooling as a tool to redeem the consequences of ignorance and to re-form in the poor proper morals and industrious habits. In the process, they moved a step closer to an understanding of education as a democratic right of all free people and the responsibility of the public to provide.

To deal with the large and ever-growing numbers of children in poverty, the Free School Society embraced a new pedagogy, the Lancaster system of monitorial instruction, which was demonstrating effectiveness in England.[12] Joseph Lancaster was an English Quaker who in 1798 had opened a school for poor children in Southwark in London that employed a system that enabled a single teacher to oversee the schooling of several scores of students. The system relied on a pyramidal, hierarchical structure, with the teacher at the apex directing assistants, usually older students, who in turn supervised student monitors responsible for particular tasks such as teaching writing or arithmetic to small, homogeneous groups of students. Lancaster supplemented this structure with detailed instructions and procedures for performing particular tasks, with "a place for everything, and everything in its place."[13]

The system seemed marvelously efficient and successful. Between 1798 and 1805 when he gained the patronage of George III, Lancaster increased his enrollment from sixty to nearly a thousand pupils. From there, rapid growth continued: by 1809, he had twenty schools, whose 10,000 pupils were being educated for the attractively low sum of four shillings per child per year (approximately $20 today).

Eddy and others from the Free School Society visited Lancaster's English operation and became quick converts.[14] In 1807, the society secured state funding at first from a licensing tax on inns and taverns and in 1815 from the common school fund established under the 1795 law. The city donated land next to the almshouse near the intersection of Broadway and Park Row for the first dedicated schoolhouse, which opened in 1809 with capacity for 500 pupils in one enormous second-floor classroom. At the dedication, Mayor Clinton lauded both society and system as the perfect match:

> . . . when I perceive the extraordinary union of celerity in instruction and economy of expense and when I perceived the one great assembly of a thousand children under the eye of a single teacher, marching, with un-exampled rapidity and with perfect discipline, to the goal of knowledge, I confess that I recognized in Lancaster the benefactor of the human race. I consider his system as creating a new era in education, as a blessing sent down from heaven to redeem the poor and distressed of this world from the power and dominion of ignorance.[15]

The Free School Society, which originally had envisioned just a single school for boys ultimately found itself with many.[16] The second school opened in 1811 on land donated by Trinity Church. By 1825 there were eleven free schools in the city operating on the Lancasterian model. Meanwhile, in 1808, the state legislature had expanded the reach of the society to include all poor children, not just unchurched ones, which was important as it both increased competition with the church-affiliated charity schools and edged the society toward the principle of free schools open to many if not yet all New York City children. Though the old common (i.e., entrepreneurial or private pay) schools continued to enroll more children, the schools of the society enrolled thousands of poor ones, all regimented, disciplined, and modestly educated under the machine-like Lancasterian system. It seemed a marvel of the time and just the right marvel for the place—and it was the beginning of what would become a true public school system for New York.

TRINITY ADAPTS

Trinity of course was a charity school, too, though one focused on serving poor children primarily from Episcopalian families in the neighborhood. In the enlarging picture of schools in New York after 1800, Trinity (or The First Protestant Episcopal Charity School as it was known legally after incorporation in 1806) began to reexamine what and how it taught—a process that played out over several decades.

The first step was to ensure that teaching at the school was up to date. In January 1808, a special committee of Trinity's trustees was authorized to visit the Free School Society to learn more about the Lancasterian system, which was already being embraced by other church-run charity schools, including the Dutch Reformed Charity School (Collegiate).[17] The surviving record is silent as to whether Trinity adopted the new system, though ten years later, the Trinity board, then headed by John Henry Hobart, Bishop of New York, met to consider a proposal from William Cooper, a training teacher from England who had come to New York via the Bahamas where he had successfully instituted a large monitorial school for white children, followed by another for blacks using "Bell's [monitorial] system." Cooper must have been persuasive, and two weeks later the trustees committed to introducing Bell system at Trinity. They voted Cooper a fee of $300 evidently to get things started, this at a time when schoolmaster John Young received a yearly wage of just twice that. In addition, student John Cameron was appointed monitor at $50 per quarter.[18]

There is an irony in the preference of Bell to Lancaster, because it was Lancaster who probably had learned, if not stolen, the fundamental method from Andrew Bell, whose name is remembered little outside scholarly circles while Lancaster routinely makes his way into high school texts and American history surveys. The chief difference between their systems seems to have been that Quaker Lancaster's was nonsectarian, though scripturally based, while Anglican Bell's advocated teaching doctrine specific to the Church of England.

Bell was an Anglican clergyman and missionary in Madras in India in the 1780s. There he had worked out, for the soldiers' orphan asylum where he was employed, a monitorial approach to schooling fit for large or small numbers of pupils and requiring just one master plus assistants. Bell returned to England in 1789 and published his ideas as *An Experiment in Education Made at the Asylum in Madras, Suggesting a System by which School or Family may Teach Itself under the Superintendence of the Master or Parent*.[19] He followed with a revised and expanded version in 1805, but meanwhile, Lancaster had published the initial version of his system and then went on to prove his genius as much as promoter as innovator, from George III to De Witt Clinton.[20]

Bell designed his system to operate on a smaller scale than Lancaster's, stipulating a maximum enrollment of 200, a limit well beyond Trinity's size at the time (c. 125 students). The method began by arranging a school into classes and then into groups of the appropriate size. Next, the schoolmaster selected his monitors or "ushers," as they were sometimes called, from among the best and most senior students. Bell even recommended that boys themselves, by "elective voice," should best choose who these leaders were to be. Each class was then to be paired off into tutors and pupils, the best tutors getting the worst pupils. Who ranked where depended on daily performance, and new arrangements occurred regularly:

> The tutor often falls below his pupil, where, if he remain for any length of time, he becomes in turn pupil, and his pupil, tutor. In those lessons of writing, arithmetic, etc., where the tasks are performed individually, each inferior boy or pupil in the class sits by a superior or tutor, who sees that he is busy, and assists him when necessary; while himself is instructed by his teacher or assistant.

Among younger students, no lesson was to last longer than fifteen minutes, and no more than thirty minutes for older ones. Under no circumstances was a lesson to be passed over, Bell commanded, "till it be well said." He rejected coercive forms of behavior control and encouraged "emulation"—essentially competition among peers, student-to-student for places in the hierarchy—as the best discipline.

At the end of every school day, everything was toted up and marked down in a book—the number of lessons read, pages gone over, hours employed, in three adjoining columns according to subjects: catechism, religious instruction, writing, ciphering. At the back of his own copy book, each student kept an individual record on himself or herself, which was then compared by the teacher with what he had done the day before and with what others had done.[21]

Bell described the subject contents of his "system" in nine chapters. "Jesus stooped down, and with his finger wrote on the ground" (John 8:6) started off his chapter on teaching the alphabet by writing the characters in sand. Then one proceeded to reading monosyllables; the best book for beginners he thought was "Mrs. Trimmer's Charity-school spelling book, Part First," which accounted for all the syllables that most usually occur in English. Next followed syllabic reading, spelling and writing (penmanship). "Let the elementary parts be perfectly learnt in classes by short, easy, and frequent lessons, repeated as often as necessary." The same sort of division of labor, or learning in short and frequent stages, applied to arithmetic and to "the most important branch of instruction, the Catechism, morality and religion.[22]

At Trinity under Masters Cooper, Young, and Cameron, the Bell system grouped students by ability into six classes at the elementary level, though there is no detail as to exactly how it was applied. Boys and girls in the first, or most senior, class (today's sixth and seventh graders) were put to work answering drills from religious books like Robert Nelson's *Festivals and Fasts* and the *Abridged Institutes of Religion*. The next class down worked from selections of such texts and in arithmetic did multiplication and division problems. They also, for the first time, were permitted the use of writing paper and ink. Next down, students read from the New Testament and parts of the Catechism, and did simpler math but using only slates, not paper. The beginning classes would have used Bell's own books, published in England under the auspices of the Society for the Propagation of Christian Knowledge.[23] Reading content began with simple sentences: "He is in." "Go by us." "It is so." "Do ye it."

The tools were simple, and in the course of mastering them pupils learned a relentless moral message: "A bad man is a foe to God. We may not go in the way of a bad man, for it has a sad end." Or there was the illuminating tale of poor boy "Tom Bowles," who had a bad home life and consequently knew nothing of church and what it was for: "He had no thought of God, and yet he took the name of God in his mouth, but it was to swear and curse by. In this sad way Tom Bowles went on till one of the good friends of the poor said to him one day, do you know who God is, my lad?"

In both Bell and Lancaster systems, structure followed strategy. In order to socialize the poor and deter their delinquency, the method of their schooling aimed less to open minds than to develop basic skills and discipline habits. Learning the monitorial way did just that.[24] "Tom Bowles" may have been made up, but he stood for a real enough type: the poor child who so worried the founders of the Free School Society, the child whom poverty and perhaps a bad home had left unchurched and thus especially susceptible to moral error and dangerous behavior.

To modern sensibilities, the system may seem mind-numbing, imagination-deadening. But even with its relentless emphasis on order and discipline, it was not static. Bell believed that children responded to competition, and students were encouraged to vie with one another and when they excelled were rewarded. Learning may have been achieved mechanically, but rank in a class and promotion from it were based on performance solely, not social distinction or the length of time one had spent in school. Within its narrow bounds, the system was meritocratic, even democratic.

We have no further picture of its precise operation at Trinity. We know only the context for its adoption there and one probable consequence. Because the monitorial system was cheap, it made possible increased enrollment at little increase in cost. In 1820, enrollment was 124; in 1822 the trustees decided to double it. In between, in 1821, they also decided on seeking larger accommodation and petitioned Trinity Church for help in relocating. This would lead to the school's first move outside the Church's neighborhood, though not outside its influence—the first of many such moves during the next seven decades.

NEW LOCATION, NEW COMPETITION

Trinity's new location was five lots on an irregularly shaped block at the corner of Varick and Canal streets, not far from the Hudson River in a fashionable neighborhood known as St. John's Park or Hudson Square.[25] The park took its name from the adjacent St. John's church, an Episcopal "chapel of ease" built by Trinity Church in 1807 on the east side of Varick Street and a block south of Canal Street to accommodate the growing number of parishioners moving up the island from the old neighborhood. The term "chapel" is something of a misnomer, as the building had a capacity of more than a thousand people and the steeple rose to 214 feet and could be seen from (and the bells heard) all over the city. The park itself was modeled after the elegant residential squares in London's West End, with handsome and substantial dwellings around its flanks. The nearby land across Canal Street was available for Trinity School because the development had not met expectations, and though some residents were Episcopalian families, it had not served to anchor a growing population of Trinity parishioners.[26]

The new schoolhouse was ready for occupancy in 1822. A three-story hip-roofed structure, it featured two chimneys and a simple classical facade. There was a small schoolyard for outdoor games, though nothing like playing fields (this was still decades before organized athletics); there were outdoor privies and iron stoves for heating. For the first five years, the Episcopal Church's recently consolidated General Theological Seminary leased two rooms on the ground floor. In 1827, the seminarians left for their own new quarters in Chelsea on land donated by Trinity Church member Clement C. Moore, today remembered as the author of *'Twas the Night before Christmas*.[27]

On Varick Street, a fresh location filled with "monitored" students betokened more than another application of Bell's (or Lancaster's) genius for educating large numbers of urban poor on the cheap. Trinity School's actions, in adopting the pedagogy it did and in its expansion, related to the larger controversy in New York City over the nature and extent of public responsibility for schooling and what role religion should play in it. Moreover, the charity school model of which Trinity by now was the oldest in continuous operation and in which mold the Free School Society originally conceived itself shifted decisively in the 1820s. As it did so, Trinity at first found one source of its income threatened, and then found itself considering an entirely new set of challenges.

Trinity's records of early 1824 note the appointment of a committee to "consider the propriety of applying to the legislature on the subject of the Free School." It is a cryptic reference that came near the end of a long controversy.[28] The "subject" referred to money and dated to the odd disposition in the first years of the century that the New York City Common Council had made of the funds under the 1795 common school law: disposition to the city's charity schools and not to the masters of its common schools. Under that arrangement, Trinity's share based on enrollment had ranged from just over $300 to just over $400 in a given year, in the range of a tenth of its total budget. When chartered in 1805, the Free School Society at first received no public funds, though two years later the legislature relented, with financial support to build its new schoolhouse and with the promise of $1,000 per year in operating funds to be raised from licensing fees on city inns and taverns.[29] The society also won access to its per capita share of the common school fund, up to then shared only by the church-run charity schools, and in 1817 secured an amendment permitting it to apply its share of common school funds, after paying salaries, to school construction.

In 1820, controversies arose over the issue of the society's effective monopoly of publicly supported nonsectarian free education, when the Bethel Baptist Church opened a charity school without reference to the faith of its scholars and secured funding from the common school fund not just for salaries but also for new school buildings. Until then, construction funding had been a privilege of the Free School Society alone and one that had enabled it to grow quickly. The Baptists, who had built three schools by 1824, threatened competition in the nonsectarian market; more alarming, other churches too joined in with their own free but nonsectarian schools for the poor.

Trinity's trustees regarded this trend warily but took time to settle on an appropriate response. Having just constructed a new building without public assistance, the trustees for a moment allied themselves with the Free School Society to try to repeal the new Baptist building privilege on fairness grounds, arguing that one sect should not be favored over another. When the society attempted to have the legislature restrict the church charity schools from receiving any but children from their own parishes (Trinity had for years drawn from many), the alliance foundered. Then, more radically, the society took the position that all sectarian schools should be denied any public funds whatever, thus overturning the 1805 settlement. The church schools banded together for the cause of saving public funding. Trinity trustee Rev. Benjamin Onderdonk, an assistant rector at Trinity Church and later Bishop of New York, led in pressing the case, but ultimately to no avail. As it had done decades earlier, the legislature tossed this unique New York City controversy back to the city's Common Council, which in 1825 sided with the society and ended all public funding of church-affiliated schools.[30]

Several factors were at work here, and it is anachronistic to fix on the church/state issue that today fairly leaps off the page. The schools of the Free School Society, though nonsectarian, had not been and never would be secular schools. This was still a world where the chain linking religion to morality to desirable behavior was unbroken, and as poverty and associated problems appeared to threaten the city, there seemed more reason than ever to strengthen it through the schools. Constitutional niceties were less the issue than competition. In the 1820s the Free School Society's schools enrolled about 6,000 students, compared to 4,000 in the church schools. The society by this time also had a certain momentum and rationalized the desire to eliminate subsidies, not just on the sectarian issue but also on the basis of efficiency.[31] So they argued that money from a common school fund designated for the civil education of youth was less well spent when spread over several groups than it would be if concentrated through a single agency—theirs.

The end of public funding for church-affiliated schools and the Free School Society's achievement of monopoly status as the city's only publicly subsidized educational purveyor signaled a momentous change in public policy. With it, the ground shifted under those church-affiliated schools that had enjoyed subsidy but were now cut off, while the Free School Society attempted to build on its newly expanded position. In 1826 the legislature granted it a new charter and a new name—the Public School Society—with its schools to be open to all children, with reference to neither sect nor income. All its buildings were to be conveyed to the city, which then granted them back on perpetual lease presuming their continued educational use, and the mayor and city recorder were made ex officio members of the society's otherwise still entirely private, self-perpetuating board.

Plans for a public high school to be conducted on Lancasterian lines were also drawn up, and a nominal tuition was instituted for those who could pay. This at first sounds odd (for no one who could not pay was to be refused admission) but was an indication of the hoped-for broadening of the evolving "public" model implicit in the name change. Today, tuition and public schools are antithetical; then, at their inception in New York City, it was hoped to employ tuition to smooth over the public schools' rough charity-school origins and perhaps attract students from more affluent families. If this were to happen, the mixing of social classes in the schoolroom might prove an antidote to increased class alienation outside it, and the public schools would have quickly demonstrated their new democratic and socializing worth. That the presence in the classroom of middle-class children, advantaged supposedly with superior home life and therefore, presumably, better behavior, might additionally help to uplift poorer ones seemed plausible too.

The tuition plan flopped, however, and quite the opposite from attracting a "better element" who might not otherwise go near a "free" school or were simply too proud to stoop to a charity school, it drove enrollments temporarily down. It would take more time and better quality instruction to attract middle- and upper-class families who had other options to the society's public schools. Better quality required more funding, which came in starts toward the end of the decade, and after the early 1830s from a city real estate tax.[32]

Even as the reborn Public School Society established itself as the quasi-official agent of primary and secondary education for New York, the religious question thought to have been settled in 1825 reignited with the coming of the Irish and German Roman Catholic immigrants in the second quarter of the century. Leaders of these immigrant communities viewed the Public School Society as an essentially Protestant organization and agitated for more balanced handling of religious topics and observances in the schools. After more than a decade of controversy, in 1842, the state legislature sought to put an end to it by establishing a new public school system to replace the Public School Society schools. The new system featured elected ward trustees and a central board of education. It also prohibited religious instruction in the schools. This solution was not to everyone's liking. As alternatives, the Roman Catholic diocese of New York began building a system of parochial schools, while many Protestant denominations, including the Episcopalians, kept their older church-affiliated schools going or established new ones to offer schooling with an explicitly religious component.[33]

As the modern model of a secular public school system with private alternatives was emerging, the older model of church-affiliated charity schools became obsolete. The traditional paternalistic view of the poor also was fading away. Whether understood as the moral responsibility of the church or of society, the poor had been seen as objects of paternalistic benefaction through education, which promised to relieve their condition and protect the benefactors. In the tumultuously democratizing New York of the nineteenth century, such condescension was fast becoming politically hazardous and ultimately irrelevant.[34]

New York's evolving public schools did not become models of class mixing overnight. They did, however, embody, from the 1820s onward, the principle of public provision in education as every child's democratic right. This principle wholly displaced the older, once equally pervasive principle under which schooling was left to individual initiative and provided by the market or philanthropy. Beginning in the second quarter of the nineteenth century, "public" became public as we have ever after understood it in education, and "private," private.[35] "Charity" largely drops from education's vocabulary. The charity schools that lived on, Trinity among them, did so in a strange in-between land, and in this setting Trinity began afresh to work out its own future.

Given its Episcopal identity, independent endowment, and new school building, there was no reason for Trinity to abandon its mission after losing the modest support it had received from the public purse. There was still need to provide for "the education of poor children in piety and useful learning," in the phrase of the 1806 act of incorporation. At the same time, though, Trinity, like other church-affiliated charity schools, interpreted the end of public funding as the end of an era.[36] Henceforth, such schools would no longer be responsible for educating all of the poor in their parishes. They could selectively teach whom they wanted, as long as the students (or their parents for them) also wanted to be taught by these institutions. Admission and financial assistance became not duties to be performed but privileges to be granted. The recipients of these privileges might be poor children without means to pay for school, or they might be children from families with greater, though still modest, resources who could benefit from a subsidized Episcopal education.

EXPANSION AND RETRENCHMENT

In the mid 1820s, Trinity School and its sponsors made several adjustments to the new reality. The long-standing tradition of raising money through annual charity sermons at Trinity Church and other Episcopal chapels and churches came to an end. Henceforth, the school would admit some students for pay, though it would also continue to subsidize many with "benefices" or scholarships. In 1827, the school secured a revised charter from the state legislature that officially changed its name, from the New York Protestant Episcopal Charity School to the New York Protestant Episcopal Public School. The charter also allowed the school to expand its scope by admitting some pay students and permitting the establishment of one or more additional "schools or departments for instruction in English Literature, Mathematics, Philosophy and Classical learning."[37]

During the next decade, Trinity School launched a number of new initiatives and programs to fulfill its broader mission. It cast a broad net for students: at one end down, to the very young barely out of infancy, and at the other up, to seventeen- and eighteen-year olds preparing for college or seminary. In the middle it maintained its male and female elementary schools. At all levels, the school continued to welcome most pupils free alongside a few who could pay. And it continued to profess, in the words of one trustee, "the great importance, in our city, of uniting religion with education." This meant daily chapel and instruction in the Bible and Episcopal doctrine.[38]

The elementary school admitted students at age eight and girls could remain there until fourteen. Its curriculum for both boys and girls promised a common English education including grammar, arithmetic, geography, reading, and writing—not much different from eighteenth-century charity school times. The primary or infant department, which was started in 1832, was an innovation, however, in the spirit of thinking present in the Public School Society at that time, that even two- or three-year-olds were not too young for the "inculcation of moral, ideal and literal knowledge." At Trinity, space was made for this primary department in the basement at 76 Varick Street, remodeled with the funds saved when Trinity Church remitted the rent on its five lots there. Whether schooling of the very young amounted to much more than mere supervision is unclear. But such numbers as we do have—269 registered primary students in 1832—suggest a need at least.

Such high enrollment figures, however, conceal what probably was a high rate of turnover. At the elementary level, far more students were registered than actually attended: 283 girls and 441 boys were signed up when the school had capacity for only 144 each, and just 80 and 138, respectively, registered present. Such numbers indicate a substantial churn in attendance as children came and went during the school year—schooling could still be an intermittent affair.[39] Many who began never finished, and the pressure to quit school and work was always high. The occupations of the school's parents then—for example, twenty-four carpenters, thirty shoemakers, twelve laborers, eight clerks, seventeen seamstresses, three musicians, a sailor, a fisherman—are suggestive. Many children attended Trinity to prepare themselves to be bound to a trade. They probably left then not after completing a course, or at the end of the year, but whenever a suitable apprenticeship opening occurred.[40]

For older students in the Upper or Collegiate School, the trustees apparently had in mind an alternative to the fledgling public high school in the city as well as something like the offerings of the New England academies, which encompassed "all principal branches of English education and also in classical learning."[41] Students were divided into two tracks, with an "English" curriculum to train literate and numerate graduates and a "classical" curriculum to prepare students specifically for college or seminary. A principal but not exclusive goal of the Classical Department was to channel students toward the Episcopal ministry.[42]

The plan to bolster the Upper School was less ambitious than may at first appear, though it did result in 1832 in building a separate, dedicated facility on an adjacent lot at 160 Canal Street. The second and third stories of the new building were devoted to classrooms, while the ground floor was rented to dry goods merchants who helped pay for the investment. For "English scholars," who would complete their schooling at Trinity, the curriculum featured composition and elocution, bookkeeping, and reading and writing. All this was taught and learned in a school year divided into quarters and running from September to the end of June.

The curriculum of the Classical Department was tied to the admission requirements of fellow Trinity Church offspring Columbia College, and "in special cases," General Theological Seminary.[43] Columbia, for example, declared:

> No student shall be admitted in the lowest class unless he be accurately acquainted with the grammar of both the Greek and the Latin tongues including such rules of prosody as may be applicable to such of the Poets as he is to be examined upon . . . shall be well-versed in the first four rules of arithmetic, divisions of weights and measures, the theory and practice of vulgar and decimal fractions, the use of algebraic functions and negative exponents, and with modern geography.

According to a recent authoritative history of Columbia, however, not too much should be read into these requirements: They "were not higher than elsewhere; they were likely lower." At the time Columbia itself was tiny, with approximately 100 students, smaller than Trinity, and it had a traditional and unchanging curriculum and a narrow conception of its potential market.[44]

Only a handful of pupils—twenty to thirty each year—enrolled in the Upper School, a mixture of scholarship and paying students. Most students fell in the former category, while the latter paid tuition ranging from six dollars per quarter in the English Department to twice that in the Classical Department. There is no information about how these fees were set or how scholarships were valued, but it seems unlikely they were tied to the costs of providing an education; rather, they appear to be roughly equivalent to the public school tuition, itself probably a reflection of the fees paid traditionally to masters of the common schools. The enrollment figures at Trinity were consistent with the larger pattern of schooling in New York: In 1830, the city's population was about 250,000. About 25,000 children were registered in schools, including 1,200 under age five, 23,000 between five and fifteen, and just 766 older.[45]

Not surprisingly, Trinity experienced difficulties in accommodating so many programs and initiatives at once. In the attempt, the school ran through a lot of personnel. Between 1827 and 1838 nine men and three women filled the leadership roster.[46] John Young, master in the charity school since 1803, remained as head of the new boys elementary department, which probably continued the Bell curriculum and methods. The Rev. William Henry Hart, an Episcopal priest from Virginia and a Columbia graduate, became first principal of the upper school in 1827. John W. Curtis, a priest trained at General Theological Seminary, took over in 1830. Apparently sickly, he lasted just a year.[47] Francis Windsor followed John Young in charge of the boys' elementary school; he was the son of the principal of a Free School Society school where he had worked as a Lancasterian monitor. He was replaced by his brother Lloyd, an 1834 Columbia graduate and an Episcopal deacon.[48] Henry Elwell followed in Curtis's place in 1832, and T. W. Battin for the year 1834–1835. Joshua Harrison, another clergyman, dipped in and out even more quickly, appearing in 1835 alone, and finally there was F. A. Streeter, a layman, who filled in the three years to 1838. Looking after the girls in the elementary school, Ann Jones, an aging widow, was replaced in 1832 by Eliza Windsor, sister of Francis and like her brother and father a Free School Society veteran.

The official records we have of their service, sparse as they are, do not permit much association between the school's progress in these years and any of their particular personalities. Under Streeter, however, discipline in the Upper School may have been allowed to slip, as complaints lodged with the trustees noted "the little attention paid to religious instruction" and "the neglect of attendance at Divine Service." The trustees attempted to correct these problems by appointing an Episcopal chaplain, who served without pay.[49]

Meanwhile, economic conditions forced the school to sharpen its focus. The Panic of 1837 hit the city hard. In March, a leading trading house collapsed after falling cotton prices prompted southern merchants to default on repayment of loans. Within weeks, more than ninety brokerage firms, commission houses, and jobbers, all linked and now trapped together in a web of financial ties, went under. With the cash supply dwindling dangerously, the crisis rippled outward, to banks, real estate speculators and developers, railroad investors, manufacturers, and general merchants. Misfortune spread quickly to the laboring classes, where four in every ten lost their jobs. These extremely depressed circumstances persisted more than a year, with a return to precrisis conditions taking several years more.[50]

In these circumstances, the school's trustees called for sharp retrenchment. The Primary Department for children under seven and the "Female Departments" were closed and eliminated. A new leader, the Rev. William Morris, took charge and school opened in the autumn of 1838 a month later than usual. He would preside over a smaller institution with total enrollment below 100 and consisting of an elementary school and upper school, for boys alone, with the latter continuing its divide into English and Classical Departments. Religion, and specifically Episcopal doctrine and discipline, remained required subjects at all levels of the school and were the responsibility of the "rector," as the head of the school was henceforth called and who, it was stipulated, was to be an Episcopal clergyman.

EPISCOPAL SCHOOL FOR BOYS

The Rev. Morris was thirty-three years old when he came to Trinity School. The son of an Anglican priest in England, he was educated there and at Trinity College, Dublin. He emigrated to the United States by the mid-1830s and served as an assistant minister of an Episcopal church near Albany before relocating to New York City and coming to the attention of Trinity School's trustees.[51]

Morris would remain at Trinity for nearly two decades and, though he would break the string of short-termers who had preceded him, he would leave little lasting impression on the school. At the outset, he was paid a handsome salary of $1,600, plus lodging. He also received half the tuition fees collected, which he in turn used to compensate faculty members. This arrangement gave him tight control over operations, an especially important factor during the financially troubled years early in his tenure.[52]

With the rector, two committees of the board helped run the school: the Standing Committee, which dealt with financial matters including rental income from the landed endowment; and the School Committee, which oversaw admissions, the program of instruction, and, when it came to it, suspensions and expulsions—for "immoral conduct, contumacy, or neglect of studies." The Rev. John McVickar headed the School Committee, which visited the school periodically to monitor and report on progress.

McVickar would remain an important figure at Trinity for many years, the most active trustee and a champion of "uniting religion with education" there and elsewhere. An 1804 graduate of Columbia, he had rejoined his alma mater in 1817 as professor of moral philosophy and "of the evidences of Christianity." A restless, hard-working man, he taught one of the earliest courses in the United States on political economy—the "the moral instructor of nations," he called it—and he was intensely interested in religious education as a means to bring youth out of poverty or aimlessness and into productive society. He helped to establish a wide range of educational institutions, most of which were affiliated with the Episcopal Church, including the grammar school attached to Columbia College, an Episcopal school of Trinity Church offshoot Grace Church, and St. Stephen's (later Bard) College. He also presided over the Society for the Promotion of Religion and Learning, which funded scholarships for students planning to enter the Episcopal ministry, including some at Trinity School.[53]

One of McVickar's aims was to revise again the official name of the school, which would require another amendment to the 1806 act of incorporation. The school was popularly called Trinity School, though legally it remained The New York Protestant Episcopal Public School. When the trustees approached the state legislature to approve the legal name of "Trinity School," however, they encountered resistance. Rep. Clark of the Committee on Charitable and Religious Societies believed that the popular name would not accurately portray the nature of the school as a religious foundation established to manage a landed endowment for the purpose of educating poor children. Clark also pointed out that if the charter were to be reopened it would necessary to look again at language in Section I that limited the school's annual income from real estate to $15,000. This was not much more than the school presently received and would be exceeded once the school gained full control of the Baker Farm bequest (see later discussion). Given these circumstances, the trustees withdrew the name-change request.[54]

Meanwhile, the shape of the restructured school emerged over a period of several years. The record suggests at least some admissions requirements at the school: The board minutes a few years later, for example, stipulated that "no boy be admitted as a scholar in the English Department who cannot read."[55] Applications were to be submitted by the last Monday in January, April, or October and had to be signed by the party making it and "accompanied by the full documentary evidence on all the points required by the existing plan of the school." It had to be documented that a boy had been baptized in the Protestant Episcopal Church, had received Holy Communion (and thus been confirmed), and had parents of "good moral character and religious habits" who were connected with a parish in the diocese. Children of deceased clergymen, widows, or communicants were to receive preference if otherwise qualified, and, except by unanimous consent of the board, no more than one scholarship could be awarded to the same family. Every applicant was required to appear personally before the School Committee or some individual member for examination as to his qualifications. On approval, all such "papers," as these admissions materials were called, were to have been "filed, tied up together and endorsed by the secretary as the papers of such beneficiary, and placed in the permanent archives of the board."[56]

Benefices meant slightly different things in the two departments. In the Classical Department a free scholarship entitled a boy to tuition, books, and stationery without charge and, after a probationary period of half a year, a stipend paid in two installments to his parents or guardians for clothing and general support, of between $20 and $50 per year. In the English Department, boys got less, only up to a $30 maximum.[57] Presuming good behavior, scholarships ran for four years, provided that if a boy in the English Department was capable of promotion to a scholarship in the Classical Department before the expiration of his term he would still be entitled to the full run of support as a classical scholar. The minimum age for admission to the English Department was eight, and in the Classical twelve.[58]

The number of scholarships in the school's gift were determined each May, with boys recommended from several sources, all of them affiliated with the Episcopal Church. The Bishop of New York nominated five classical and three English scholarships, as did the vestry of Trinity Church; Grace Church and St. George's were allotted two classicals each. Six others belonged with the vestries of the remaining parishes in the diocese of New York in the order of their dates of incorporation, one to each in annual rotation. And any other parish in the city might endow a scholarship in perpetuity on payment to the school of $1,000, or it might support a boy for up to four years a year at a time, for $80 per year. For a brief period in the 1840s, Trinity Church also supported sixteen partial scholarships for boys in the church choir. These arrangements fell apart, however, because the school,

TABLE 4.1 Enrollments at Trinity School, Selected Years, 1840–1885

Year	Total	Scholarship	Paid
1840	NA	31	NA
1845	108	48	60
1850	123	65	58
1855	73	62	11
1860	NA	NA	NA
1865	74	65	9
1870	80	70	10
1875	85	72	13
1880	82	72	10
1885	75	72	3
1890	116	100	16
1895	202	125	77

Source: School Committee and Trustee Minute Books, Trinity School Archive.
Note: NA = not available.

according to Edward Hodges, the church choirmaster, "does not furnish musical talent enough" to meet the church's needs.[59]

The full scholarships obviously were attractive, more so than the tuition. After a deceptive opening burst, the proportion of pay students trended steadily downward from 1850 through the 1880s (see Table 4.1). The record is unrevealing of the reasons for this, except that in 1858 the trustees ruled— quite optimistically, in retrospect—that "pay scholars may equal in number but shall never exceed the number of free scholarships."[60] The school wanted and perhaps needed some paying students, but it took great pride in continuing its charity tradition through scholarships. It is possible that the school's leaders viewed opportunity to pay as a way to attract more middle-class families averse to the aura of charity-for-the-impoverished perhaps still clinging to the place; as noted earlier, this was the thinking behind the forlorn attempt of the Public School Society to charge tuition in the 1830s.

Even as Trinity reincarnated as an English/Classical school, so sharpened and narrowed its market, few paying customers lined up to attend. Enrollment appears to have peaked around 1850 but then slid gently downward, with paying scholars soon all but vanishing. The Panic of 1857 probably contributed to this pattern, but it was clearly evident before then. The school's competitive environment was ever more crowded by the spread of now tuition-free public schools as well as other private schools being established or undergoing reorientations similar to Trinity's.[61] Another problem was location. As the city continued to expand and immigrants, most of them Roman Catholic, poured in, an Episcopal school at the corner of Varick and Canal seemed to be in the wrong place for middle-class Episcopalians. Commerce also encroached on the neighborhood, especially after the completion in 1851 of the Hudson River Rail Road linking the west side of Manhattan with Albany, and with the rising volume of steamships docked in the nearby Hudson. By the mid-1850s, the neighborhood of St. John's Park was crowded with warehouses and bristling with commercial activity. Just a decade later the park and adjoining land were sold to Commodore Cornelius Vanderbilt, who erected an enormous freight depot on the site.[62]

That it would be "expedient to remove the school to the upper part of the city" was something the board considered for several years before finding its next address in October 1857: 181 West 14th Street at the corner of Eighth Avenue. The facility was a four–story house, of which the school took the top three floors. It stood several blocks west of Union Square, at the time another (temporarily) affluent neighborhood filled with mansions, theaters, and concert halls, including the recently opened Academy of Music. For the first time in its century and a half, the school was not juxtaposed to Trinity Church or one of its offshoots, though it was within easy walking distance to General Theological Seminary and St. Peter's Episcopal Church on Ninth Avenue.[63]

That same month, Rector Morris, pressed by the board over a simmering and embarrassingly public divorce scandal, resigned. There may have been other tensions between him and the board, however. As noted, in the early years of his term, Morris received in addition to his salary one-half of tuition fees, with which he was to pay additional teachers. This nudged up to two-thirds in 1846 and then all of it in 1852. These changes probably reflected declining enrollments of paying students, but the trustees probably also came to regret ceding too much authority. When a new rector came aboard in 1857, the trustees pushed back to a 50–50 arrangement, but also committed to paying all teachers from corporation funds, and to the principle of hiring "the best talent according to their means" as faculty. The board also stated its commitment to the principle of raising salaries in proportion to both merit and service.[64] A reasonable inference from these measures is that the trustees were concerned about the dwindling amount of tuition fees and their use, as well as about the relationship between these and the quality of teaching at the school.

TRINITY AT 150

In 1859 Trinity turned 150 years old, taking the formal SPG grant in 1709 as its official date of birth. The school marked the anniversary at a triumphal church service at Trinity Church just before Christmas, an occasion that left at least one observer skeptical going in. "It seems the school proposes celebrating its 150th anniversary—in the usual way, I suppose," wrote tough-minded attorney and school trustee George Templeton Strong: "—by boring an assemblage with gab and speechification."[65]

The main address of the day was delivered by seventy-two-year-old Rev. John McVickar, whose long, eminent career had by then included more than three decades as a trustee of the school. Speaking to Trinity's students, McVickar took note of "the antiquity of the school" as a source of pride and inspiration: "Remember that you are scholars of no *mushroom* school, here to-day and gone to-morrow. . . . You should therefore feel on this day, as in foreign lands does the youthful heir of some old Baronial line, looking back with honest pride, and forward with a noble courage, eager to show, in the self-denying duties of life, that he is worthy of his blood."[66]

Looking ahead, McVickar believed the school's major challenge would be to overcome the strictures of its present—"the narrow bounds and inadequate accommodation of its actual location" in a rented facility. He anticipated this challenge would be met soon enough through prudent management of the school's landed endowment, including Baker Farm (see below), which would yield more than enough income to build new quarters. Once firmly established, he asserted, nothing would stand in the way of Trinity's "raising her head to a level with the great ancestral schools of England, Harrow, and Eton and Westminster and Winchester, and will then, we trust, prove to *our* Church and *our* land, what they have so long been to theirs, the prolific nurseries of Christian Teachers, Christian Statesmen, Christian Scholars, and Christian Gentlemen!"

Such optimism had foundation not only in the school's longevity and endowment but also in new leadership. Two years earlier, the trustees had hired Trinity's most credentialed schoolmaster yet. Thirty-year-old Charles D'Urban Morris (no relation to William) filled his beleaguered predecessor's shoes with a flourish, though he came at a relatively high cost. Another Englishman, well bred (the son of an admiral, albeit one born in New York City), possessor of two degrees from Oxford, Morris received an annual salary of $3,000 plus housing and half of tuition payments. He not only bore an impressive educational pedigree but was an author of two textbooks, *Principia Latina* and *Principia Graeca*, to which he soon subjected Trinity's classical scholars. He presided over a faculty of six, plus an Episcopal chaplain.[67]

As it happened, Morris would not be at Trinity for long, nor would McVickar's ambitious hopes come close to being realized anytime soon. Less than a year after the anniversary celebration, the election of Abraham Lincoln as president of the United States triggered the secession of seven Southern states, events soon followed by the formation of the Confederate States of America and the outbreak of the Civil War. New York City embraced the Union cause, but it did so with mixed feelings, reflecting prewar politics and circumstances. Lincoln had not carried the city in 1860 due to widespread opposition to war among cotton merchants with strong financial ties to the South as well as among many Irish immigrants, who feared, with justification it turned out, that they would pay a disproportionate price if war should come. This same ambivalence was evident among New York's Episcopalians, who corporately had not embraced abolitionism, in part out of respect to their southern co-religionists. Vignettes of three New Yorkers at the (national) General Convention of the Episcopal Church in Philadelphia in 1862 are revealing: One rose to condemn "the rebellion"; another opposed any motion to censure the South; and a third insisted that seats be left open for southern delegates lest anyone believe they had been expelled. Rev. Horatio Potter, who was consecrated as bishop of New York in 1861, seldom mentioned the war publicly except to honor the bravery and sacrifices of the combatants, remarks carefully crafted to offend no one.[68]

The war proved a boon to the local economy, though it also caused periodic disruptions and upheavals in daily life. At Trinity School, teaching and learning continued without interruption, but several incidents in its neighborhood surely disturbed it. The school's proximity to Union Square, which supplanted City Hall Park as the center of civic life during the war, must have enhanced the excitement and apprehension of teachers and pupils following the course of events. A week after the firing on Ft. Sumter, for example, a rally in support of the Union attracted "somewhere between 100,000 and 250,000 people" to the square, making it "reputedly the largest demonstration ever seen on the continent." Some local incidents surely were scary, too. Although the major clashes in the anti-draft riots of July 1863 flared up in distant neighborhoods and perhaps took place when the school was not in session, a particularly nasty set of incidents occurred just two blocks away, at Sixth Avenue and 14th Street, where atrocities included murders of black men, looting and burning of homes of black families along Sixth Avenue, and attacks on Republican mansions and Protestant missions.[69]

Amid such circumstances, the optimism of the 150th anniversary celebration quickly dissipated. Enrollments, particularly of paying students, remained low throughout the war, while efforts to gather more endowment income were put on hold. In 1863, Charles Morris resigned to become headmaster of another private school near Peekskill, New York. It turned out his years at Trinity and at the next job were stepping-stones on a path leading eventually to a significant academic career. Later in life he taught classics at the University of the City of New York and published numerous articles and books on classical topics. In 1876 he became one of the original six faculty members at Johns Hopkins University, where he is credited for introducing to U.S. higher education a system of faculty advising of students.[70] At Trinity, Morris was remembered as a stern taskmaster. Repeated failure to recite correctly was likely to trigger the command, "Hold out your hand, Sir!" and a thwack on the palm. Other misdemeanors might result in a box on the ears or a visit to the rector's quarters for thumps on the backside. The rector was not entirely mean-spirited, however. He sometimes said to the students, smiling, that he was designing "a flexible, double-acting ruler" that would enable one swing to deliver two blows.[71]

Morris's successor, thirty-six-year-old Rev. Robert Holden, was the first Trinity School graduate to become its head. Like his predecessor, Holden bore a noteworthy pedigree. His father was a doctor in England and his mother a niece of W. E. Gladstone, the great politician who would serve three of his four terms as England's prime minister while Holden was rector of Trinity School. Holden's parents emigrated to New York by the mid-1820s and he was born in the city. He entered Trinity School the age of eleven in 1838, thus becoming an "original student" of the newly restructured Episcopal boys' school. Evidently good at school, he graduated from the Classical

TWO MID-CENTURY "ALUMS"

The number of "graduates" or "alumni/ae" of Trinity School during the nineteenth century is difficult to estimate for the obvious reasons that only occasional lists of such people survive and that many students attended the school for a time and did not seek, much less earn, a certificate or diploma. A rough guess is that something between 2,500 and 3,000 students passed through the school during the century.[73] These "alums" include a few well-known people and at least one very famous person but most apparently led quiet lives that later generations little noted. For all Rev. Dr. McVickar's soaring rhetoric at the 150th anniversary celebration, Trinity was far removed from being or becoming a school to train political, economic, social, or cultural elites. That said, the school surely helped and encouraged many along their way, whether they proceeded on to the trades or to business, to college or to seminary. Brief sketches of two prominent alums, one on the collegiate track, the other on the "English" track, illustrate how students experienced Trinity in the mid-nineteenth century.

Charles Todd Quintard was born in 1824 in Stamford, Connecticut, into a family of Huguenot descent. His parents were wealthy and probably well educated, and they arranged for the boy to be sent to Trinity School sometime in the late 1830s. The exact years of his attendance, whether he received a scholarship or paid (probably the former), and where he lived while at school are unrecorded. We do know he was taught classics by the rector, the Rev. William Morris, who came to the school in 1838. Quintard may have been a classmate and was probably a friend of Robert Holden, later rector of the school, who entered Trinity at about the same time. Much later in life, Quintard recalled his school lessons as a strict "diet of Latin and Greek roots." He also remembered "how they were made to stick in his memory by well directed appeals to his physical senses."[74]

After leaving Trinity, Quintard attended Columbia before deciding to become a doctor. He earned a medical degree at the Univer-

sity of the City of New York in 1847. Following a year of training at
Bellevue Hospital, he moved to Athens, Georgia, where he practiced
medicine and married into a socially prominent family. In 1851, he
moved to Tennessee, taking up a position as chair of physiological
and pathological anatomy at the Medical College of Memphis. While
there, he became fast friends with the Rev. James H. Otey, the first
Episcopal bishop of Tennessee. With Otey's encouragement, Quintard entered holy orders and was ordained to the priesthood in 1856.
He served successively as rector in churches in Memphis and
Nashville before volunteering in 1861 as a chaplain and surgeon in
the Confederate Army of Tennessee. He was at or near numerous
battles on the Western front, including Shelbyville and Chicka-
mauga, which he described vividly in a diary published after his
death in 1898. He also took time to compile *The Confederate Soldier's
Pocket Manual of Devotions* (1863). After the war, he succeeded the
Rev. Otey as Bishop of Tennessee. Quintard was consecrated at the
General Convention of the Episcopal Church in Philadelphia, an occasion to which he invited his old schoolmaster, the Rev. Morris.[76]

Quintard was a fervent proponent of Episcopal schools in his
diocese. He also served as vice-chancellor of the University of the
South, an Episcopal institution in Sewanee, Tennessee, which he
helped to organize in the late 1860s and supported indefatigably with
fund raising. At one point, he preached 250 sermons in 180 days to
benefit the school.[76]

In the year that young Dr. Quintard left New York, Edward
Henry Harriman was born in nearby Hempstead, the fourth child of
the Rev. Orlando Harriman and his wife, the former Cornelia Neil-
sen. Both families were well-to-do, and numbering among Cornelia's
ancestors were Stuyvesants, Bleeckers, and Livingstons. Orlando,
however, had a difficult nature and seldom served a church for long.
The family relied heavily on relatives to make ends meet, as well as
for social connections. By 1858, the Rev. Harriman was rector at an
Episcopal church in Jersey City, New Jersey. At this point, the Rev.
William Berrian, rector of Trinity Church, stepped in to help, nomi-

nating young Henry (as he was called in his youth, though he was later known to the world by his initials) for a scholarship in the English Department at Trinity School. And so, at the age of ten, Henry undertook the daily commute from Jersey City, beginning at or before dawn: a trudge to the dock, ferry across the Hudson, and another mile of walking to school, then reversing the trek at the end of the day. During much of the academic year, both commutes took place in the gloom or the dark.

Young Harriman was an honor student—the best in his class in 1860—though also, apparently, a challenge to manage: "the worst little devil in his class," according to one report. Though probably present for the Rev. McVickar's anniversary speech, Harriman was not dazzled by visions of the school's future. He had no intention of staying there any longer than necessary. In 1861, after three years of commuting across the Hudson, he announced to his parents that "I have become convinced that there is something else in life for me besides school and books. I am going to work." He joined the world of business as an office boy with a Wall Street broker, and from there, his toughness, talent, and industry took him far, though marriage to the daughter of a bank president also helped. By the 1880s and 1890s, Harriman was a titan in the railroad industry, one of the wealthiest men in New York, and scion of a prominent and accomplished branch of the family.[77]

Department in 1844, subsequently earning both B.A. and M.A. degrees at Columbia. He then taught at Burlington College in New Jersey, and at Churchill's Military School in Sing Sing, New York, before returning to Trinity in 1857. Back in the city, he entered Episcopal orders, being ordained as a deacon in October 1861 and as a priest two years later—just after becoming rector of the school. Happily married, he fathered ten children, including Robert Holden, Jr., who later taught music at Trinity.[72]

THE PROMISE AND PROBLEM OF BAKER FARM

Rector Holden kept Trinity School functioning during the war and afterward expected to preside over its move to permanent quarters at the earliest possible time. This ambition was to be thwarted during the entirety of his twenty-seven-year tenure. As the Rev. McVickar had divined, the school's future was indeed linked to the endowment of Baker Farm, but realizing its value would prove to be a daunting and protracted challenge.

In the 1850s, Baker Farm had a tangled past and a litigious future. The thirty-acre parcel along the East River above East 76th Street had once been part of a larger estate owned by the wife of Capt. William Kidd, the famed pirate hanged in 1695. During the next century, it passed through several hands before Dr. John Baker, a surgeon-dentist and Trinity Church parishioner, acquired it in 1790.[78] When Baker died in 1796, he bequeathed the property to the as-yet-unincorporated charity school of Trinity Church. Baker's will forbade the sale of the property in parts and also, because he did not wish to dispossess the tenants, provided that the property would revert to the school after the eventual demise of certain designated beneficiaries. By the mid-1850s, all but one of these had died or surrendered their claims. One difficult tenant remained, however. James Hogg, who leased about a third of the property, not only rejected being bought or forced out, but he also disputed the school's claims to ownership. He was prepared to defend his interests aggressively.[79]

For Trinity, Baker Farm represented both an enormous future asset and a significant present-day liability. The burden was not only an impending legal battle with Hogg but also sharply rising costs of ownership. As development pushed inexorably northward in Manhattan, land values soared but at the same time landowners found themselves paying higher taxes as well as assessments for improvements such as roads and sewers. As early as 1855, Trinity's trustees investigated the possibility of selling parts of the property to pay the bill for grading and paving of East 79th Street, only to be blocked by the terms of Dr. Baker's will.[80]

In 1857, the trustees turned to one of their newest members for assistance. Thirty-seven-year-old Trinity Church vestryman George Templeton Strong, name partner in the city's oldest law firm of Bidwell & Strong (today Cadwalader, Wickersham & Taft), was well practiced in real estate. Even by the standards of a city that was full of grand characters, Strong cut an exceptionally broad swathe at the top end of New York civic and business life at mid-century. He was a member of the artistic and literary Century Association, president of the Philharmonic Society, trustee of Columbia, and (during the Civil War) secretary of the United States Sanitary Commission. But it was publication many years later of the diary kept from 1835 to 1875 that assured his historical reputation. Among his many interests, Trinity School was certainly well down on the list. When the involvement demanded commitment, however, he invested the time.

Strong had joined the Trinity board in 1857, in the waning days of the Rev. William Morris's tenure, and he viewed the school with a clear eye, though he also recognized potential. "At present a very debilitated institution," he described the school after taking a first look, one that for "some time . . . has been in a very paralytic state under the rectorship of the Reverend Mr. Morris." However—and this is what interested him—it was "seized of some thirty acres of land at or near Hell Gate [Baker Farm], now productive only of taxes and assessments, but destined to constitute a most beneficent and glorious endowment for future generations if wisely managed."[81]

Strong made a personal inspection of Baker Farm, and his account vividly portrays problems for Trinity as a landlord of property under economic development:

> We took a Third Avenue car to 79th Street and waded about through the abysmal mud of divers newly opened and nominally "regulated" streets and avenues. . . . Some souvenirs of faded rurality and respectability still survive in the old mansion, with its lawn sweeping down to the East River—formerly called "Sans Souci" but now "Baker's Retreat," as the testator described it in 1796; the Delafield country seat for the succeeding half-century; all the rest is shabby and seedy and dilapidated; horrid with shanties and newly excavated trenches (that will be streets hereafter), with unwholesome, water-soaked fields between; pigs and stramonium and mouldy old tottering fences. Country in the first stage of morbid organic change of structure, ossifying into city, a process that is purulent and gangrenous and most unlovely while it lasts, but which will result in city lots and leases and a rent-roll, if we can but hold the property long enough and are not rooted up by our Hogg.[82]

The challenge of realizing more income from the property began with a murky title. The Baker bequest preceded the school's formal incorporation. If the title could be shown in any way doubtful and the property shown to have escheated rightly to the state, then James Hogg as tenant-in-possession stood to benefit and might even have been able to purchase the property from the state for a nominal amount. Despite Hogg's protests and objections, Strong managed to satisfy the courts that Trinity School existed prior to incorporation and thus was a rightful owner. The legal battle had just begun, however. For the school to sell parts of the property, the title had to be proved not only good but also marketable, which required an act of the state legislature in Albany.

Strong's father-in-law Samuel B. Ruggles, a wealthy and well-connected lawyer then serving in the state assembly, was engaged to see the legislation through. He promptly ran head-on into a ghost from Trinity's distant past in the shape of State Senator James Noxon, arch-enemy of Trinity Church and great great grandson of Thomas Noxon, Trinity School's schoolmaster in the 1730s. Hogg had led James Noxon to believe that the Trinity School bill was just a disguise "to enrich the coffers of Trinity Church." Not until Strong could persuade him that it wasn't was any progress made, though Hogg remained obdurate to the end of the debate.[83]

Eventually Ruggles and Strong prevailed, and a legislative act in 1859 authorized the school to sell the estate, in its entirety or in parts, under the direction of the state supreme court. Notices then went out for service on the life tenants, the Hogg family, which a sarcastic Strong found deeply satisfying: "My personal apprehension is that we shall be unable to effect personal service on all of them. If we can, I think we shall put a ring in their snouts."[84] It still remained to buy out Hogg's lease: He wanted $75,000, which Strong thought outrageous but his fellow trustees accepted to be rid of Hogg quickly and finally.[85]

Two subsequent court cases in the early 1860s confirmed the legislature's action, though by then plans to exploit the property were complicated by the war.[86] The school managed to stay ahead of the tax collectors and assessors but not to profit much from the property for many more years. Meanwhile, as the war hastened to conclusion, the school's landlord announced new plans for the 14th Street property and asked Trinity to leave. The school trundled 20 blocks north on Eighth Avenue, settling at No. 451 on the West Side, between 33rd and 34th Streets. The new digs did not differ much from the old: another four-story house, notable for the fact that it came with potable piped-in water from the Croton reservoir.[87]

The school met in a large room on the second floor, but it was not so large as to permit enrollments to climb beyond eighty students, the vast majority of whom remained scholarship boys. The trustees continued the search for a permanent home in the late 1860s and early 1870s, repeatedly looking at Baker Farm as a likely resting place. At one point, they blocked out "the entire block of ground bounded by Avenue A and First Avenue and 79th and 80th Streets." At another, they investigated the possibility of erecting an Episcopal church on the property to afford the school "a religious nursery and home." At still another they considered selling off waterfront property so that developers could construct a bridge across the East River.[88] Some projects—the church, for example—failed because of conflicts with the requirements of the ownership trust "for the education, support, and maintenance" of Trinity scholars. Others foundered because the school or aspiring developers never had quite enough cash on hand to fund them.

Rental income from the property was relatively modest, at least as compared to rents collected on the school's assets downtown. Trinity's rent rolls on Greenwich Street, Rector Street, William Street, and Broadway always exceeded income from the Baker Farm.[89] In collecting rents, moreover, the trustees remained mindful of the provision in the 1806 act of incorporation that limited total rental income to $15,000, though there were indications the state would consider adjusting the total upward while not insisting on strict compliance.

Meanwhile, there remained the two costs of ownership. One was continuing taxes and city assessments. Taxes on the Baker farm in 1885 were $7,300 (downtown, which was less property though productive of higher rents, $1,350). Avoiding or mitigating assessments for municipal improvements as development moved north appeared an endless, and losing, battle. For ten years, the school litigated an 1875 assessment for grading on 77th Street—unsuccessfully—and was finally forced to pay the city with interest $27,308, which was more than three times what the property produced in rents. The second cost was investment in improvements made in hope of pushing rents up. To obtain better income from the Baker Farm, the school hopefully erected buildings at the corner of First Avenue and 80th Street for, to start, $5,000. But at the same time, the school continued to sell land, finding it difficult to get what it wanted in rent: In 1885 five lots on the corner of Avenue A and 80th were offered for $27,500, efforts to lease it for long terms having proved unsuccessful.[90]

Consider these numbers in context. At the time, the school was educating about 100 boys on an annual operating budget of about $20,000. The biggest single expense item was the tax bill on Baker Farm. Faculty salaries came in second at $6,100. Whatever the Baker farm earned about equaled what it cost, not counting the headaches of managing it.

STEADY STATE

In 1873, Trinity moved once again: to 648 Seventh Avenue, on the west side of the convergence of the Avenue and Broadway between 44th and 45th Streets at the north end of Longacre (later Times) Square.[91] This was another four-story walk-up made for trade, or for living, but probably never imagined as a school. The third floor in fact still went to a tenant, the fourth to the school's janitor, who took living space in lieu of pay. The building was owned by Trinity Church parishioner William Astor, however, and the rent was modest. Development in the neighborhood was controlled by the Astors and there were many elegant houses in the vicinity. The school was not far from St. Chrysostom's Chapel, yet another Trinity Church chapel of ease, recently opened at 39th and Seventh Avenue. Another sister institution, Columbia College, stood within easy walking distance at 49th and Fifth Avenue.

The school's new lodgings continued to hinder its operations and constrain its ambitions. In 1869, the Trustees fixed the number of scholarships at seventy-two, consisting of thirty-two each in the Classical and English departments plus eight nominated by the Society for the Promotion of Religion and Learning. Cramped quarters permitted only a few additional pay students to attend each year.

Meanwhile, there is about the academic character of Trinity, at least since the time of William Morris in the 1840s, and for the rest of the century, the steadiness of well-settled intentions. Year to year, and we suspect day to day, from Morris and through the tenure of alumnus Robert Holden, Trinity went quietly about its work. It seemed a bystander in the major school controversies that roiled through New York in the mid and late nineteenth century, controversies to do, first, with Roman Catholic challenges to the public schools in the 1840s and 1850s, then with school centralization in the 1890s; at least Trinity's records are silent on these matters. Rather, the school continued to focus on conservative and thorough teaching of an unchanging curriculum.

Under Holden, a faculty of five taught between seventy-five and eighty-five boys, about 90 percent of them on scholarship, from ages nine to seventeen. Religion, Latin, Greek, mathematics, and French in the Classical Department, and reading, spelling, writing, grammar and composition, arithmetic, geography, and history in the English Department made up the curriculum. The school year began the first Monday of September and was divided into four quarters, ending November 15, January 31, April 15, and June 30. There was a Christmas vacation and time off for major church feast days and legal holidays. The school day ran from nine to two-thirty with a half-hour recess at noon. Public examinations were conducted twice a year and report cards went home monthly, grading boys by subject as "Very Good," "Good," "Pretty Good," "Tolerable," and "Bad." Grading was also numerical, with 10 the greatest credit for each daily lesson, and each month totaled up for all subjects into a number then dubbed acceptable or not. There were credits for punctuality and good behavior, deductions for unexcused absences and tardiness.[92]

For those few boys whose parents paid, tuition scaled up as a boy got older: $15 per quarter for beginnings (Class V) in the English course, $20 for Classes IV and III, $25 for II and I. The classical course commanded a small premium, starting at $20 per quarter at the bottom and reaching $37.50 for the most senior.[93] Most boys who completed the courses appear to have headed into business, about twice the number of those who went on to college, chiefly to Columbia.[94]

The social origins of the students changed, at least insofar as we can tell from admission records (Classical Department for scholarship students only, but they were a significant sample) that identify parents' occupations.[95] No longer catering primarily to the poor, the school admitted most students from middle-class families. Sampling approximately twenty names at random at ten-year intervals from 1838 (when records begin), the differences in parents' occupations and circumstances by the end of the century are instructive.

> Admitted 1838–1840: sexton, widow, clergyman, iron founder, porter in bank, shipbuilder gardener, merchant, cabinet maker, weigh master.
> Admitted 1847–1849: paper hanger, physician, widow, coach maker, painter, rector, merchant, clergyman.
> Admitted 1859–1858: clerk, clergyman, sub-editor, agent.

Admitted 1867–1869: clerk, widow, clergyman, physician.

Admitted 1877–1879: silversmith, missionary, hatter, coachman, music, bookseller, widow, clergyman, hardware, insurance, lawyer, clerk (sewing machine).

Admitted 1888–1889: dealer in tailor trimmings, lawyer, clergyman, central magazine office, bookkeeper, organist (Trinity Church New York City), manager Autograph Register Company, insurance agent, physician, post office clerk.

Admitted 1897–1898: clerk, rector, organist, lawyer, secretary, merchant, cashier, decorator, veteran, florist, teacher, publisher, manager, bookkeeper, police sergeant, agent, gardener, coal dealer, engineer, real estate, dentist, fireman, architect.

We have personal records from this period of but one boy, George Leslie Stevenson, born in the city in 1863, and who entered Trinity's classical department fifteen years later.[96] Though the son of a lawyer, Stevenson too was a scholarship boy. He walked to school from 60th and Ninth Avenue, carrying his lunch. He went on to Columbia in 1882, graduated, and had a career in banking and with the federal government. There are two report cards from March 1879 and May 1880, plus the grade registers of his monthly performance that went into them and many others. He seemed an average student, and on the sickly side if abundant absences are any indication.

Two exercise books in religion over the space of three years survive. They might have been plucked from among the many others that do not survive from a century and more before that. Here was the old world of the orthodox Anglican catechism, drilled relentlessly into the young. Question: "What is the meaning of the word 'church?'" "What are the four marks of the church?" Answer: "One, holy, catholic and apostolic." "What is the meaning of 'holy?'" It was as pious at the end of schooling as at the beginning, though the subject matter grew heavier. Stevenson had a clear hand and a good memory, reciting at one commencement exercise the entire seventh chapter of Matthew's Gospel—in Greek.[97]

Beyond such classroom fragments and the sketches of surviving school plans, which changed little for half a century, we have hardly any elaboration of anything that might be called educational philosophy at Trinity before the end of the century. In the 1890s, a new rector and the final disposition of Baker Farm would introduce a new, if not yet fully modern, era at the school.

AN EPISCOPAL EDUCATION

During the three decades after the Civil War, the population of the city continued to soar as the expanding, industrializing economy generated new opportunities. The citizenry climbed past two million and was increasingly diverse as new waves of immigration brought in many thousands of Italians, Greeks, Poles, Romanians, and Bohemians, as well as a significant influx of Russian Jews. Many thousands of freed African-Americans also moved north to escape rural poverty in the South. Initially these immigrants settled in neighborhoods in lower Manhattan, on the Upper East Side, and in East Harlem, across the East River in Brooklyn, Queens, and the Bronx, and across the Hudson in New Jersey. As had occurred in the initial waves of non-English immigration before the Civil War, the arrival of newcomers profoundly affected the city's political and cultural life and stimulated fresh thinking and controversy about the purpose and utility of education and the organization and operation of schools. Trinity School, like most other religious schools in the city, did not participate in these debates or lend much sympathy to many of the reforms.

In the late 1880s and early 1890s Trinity was at last nearing a position to restate its distinctive claims with renewed vigor. Of course, the school had waited a long time to gain the benefit of owning Baker Farm, as the secretary to the board complained in 1886. It was "still accommodated in a hired house, no. 1517 Broadway [Longacre Square] where it lives and works in hope of it expansion into proportions large enough to meet the wants of the Churches in this city as to good Christian education. For this purpose it longs for the improvement of its unproductive property, in order to the increase of its free scholarships and of the number of its teachers, as well as the provision of a permanent site and building suitable for its operations."[100]

The convergence of several factors helped break the impasse. First, in 1887, the trustees gave up on an Upper East Side location, perhaps because of bitter experiences, but more likely because the neighborhood directly across Central Park seemed more congenial.[101] The Upper West Side was being carefully groomed into a middle- and upper-class enclave, with a rich and expanding array of cultural and religious institutions present or nearby. Several of these were especially attractive to an Episcopal school whose trustees numbered some of the city's most prominent Episcopalians. At the same time Trinity was exploring the neighborhood, the Episcopal Diocese of New York was finalizing plans to construct the world's largest cathedral on Amsterdam at 110th Street. Columbia was abandoning its landlocked midtown location for a new campus just north of the cathedral. Trinity Church was building a still another chapel of ease, St. Agnes Chapel, in the vicinity, on West 91st Street. Plans were afoot to build an Episcopal school for girls on West End Avenue. The neighborhood was well planned and co-ordinated, with rows of sturdy, attractive middle-class townhouses adorn-ing the side streets and elegant apartment complexes and a few mansions on Central Park West. Ample open space existed in Riverside Park, Morning-side Park, and especially Central Park. The neighborhood was also well served by public transportation, including the recently completed extension of Broadway, as well as the Ninth Avenue "El."[102]

Two years later, the state legislature amended the statute governing landed endowments of "religious, educational, literary, scientific, benevo-lent or charitable" corporations. The amendment raised the income such corporations could earn on property to $100,000 per year, calculated on the basis of 5 percent of $2 million, the new upper limit on landed endow-ment.[103] As noted already, the old limit of $15,000 in landed income per year fixed in the 1806 act of incorporation had constrained Trinity's options and thwarted the 1840s attempt to change its legal name. The new statute meant that the school no longer had to be circumspect about realizing greater in-come from Baker Farm. Over the next several years, the property was sold off, piecemeal, netting a total of $1.375 million.

Perhaps in anticipation of these events, the trustees had taken an option on ten lots on West 91st Street adjacent to the site on which St. Agnes Chapel was being built. They also commissioned plans for a new, four-story school building of solid stone, enough to double capacity. The intention was not only to raise the number of scholarships, from 72 to 100 to 125 by 1895 but also accommodate many more paying students.[104]

While these plans were taking shape, the school was obliged once again to relocate temporarily. In 1889, William Astor informed the trustees that he had alternative plans for the Longacre Square property. Despite the efforts of the Astors to preserve the square as an affluent residential neighborhood, the pressures of development inexorably overtook them. Though it would not be rechristened as Times Square for another decade and a half, the site was already becoming the center of entertainment, nightlife, and trendy fashion it has remained ever since—an awkward place of residence for a church-affiliated school in any event.

The new location wasn't much better. Trinity moved north and east to Madison Avenue and 59th Street (627 Madison). The second floor featured a huge, airy room with additional rooms and a tempting capacity for as many as 500 pupils. However, the ground-floor tenant, the National Panorama Company, was a purveyor of precinematic audiovisual entertainments. For the short time the school resided upstairs, customers downstairs could witness energetic reenactment of the Civil War face-off between the *Monitor* and the *Merrimac*. It was not evidently a suitable situation, historical content or not. There were also complaints about "the great noise of the corner when the windows were necessarily kept open."[105] Within a year the school flitted on once more, back down to 45th Street just west of Sixth Avenue (108 West 45th), to a brownstone handy to the El. It would remain there until the move in 1894 to its permanent new home.

The trustees were eager that the new move and the growth of the school occur under new leadership. Rector Holden was in his early sixties and there were palpable indications that it was time for a change. Enrollment was down, especially among pay students, and there were apparently concerns about the quality of teaching at the school. After Holden resigned in December 1889, the entire faculty of five was terminated at the end of the academic year, and his replacement was given a free hand to hire new teachers.[106]

Forty-five-year-old Rev. August Ulmann was named acting headmaster in May 1890 while the trustees searched for a permanent replacement. They wrote to schoolmen in England, including the headmasters of Harrow and Rugby and the warden of Keble College, for advice, but they were favorably impressed by Ulmann himself. After just a few months, they claimed, "his energy of Administration had already transformed the body [of the school] and elevated its character with the promise of making it, in time, the best school in the City." He was appointed rector in February 1891.[107]

Ulmann had been born and educated in Germany, where he started out his career as a *gymnasium* teacher. In the 1870s he emigrated to America, finding work as a teacher at St. Paul's (Episcopal) School in New Hampshire, before entering General Theological Seminary in New York, class of 1884. Upon ordination, he took up parish duties as rector of Christ Church in Yonkers. From there he came to Trinity in 1890.[108]

As the trustees hoped, Ulmann proved a vigorous and able leader, though he made some curious decisions. His appointments to the faculty were well received and included Reginald P. B. Johnson, an Oxford-trained classicist, and Trinity School alumnus Edward A. Northall '75, who held a B.A. and an M.A. from Columbia. Another new hire was Franz Dohs, who arrived to teach gymnastics and calisthenics, a new subject for the school and a reflection of the rector's belief in training not only the student's mind and spirit but also his body. In his second year, Ulmann added John Norman as music instructor.

Meanwhile, a host of student activities and societies took form—the first of which we have record. The Missionary Society raised money to send to Africa or Asia or Native American reservations. The Library Association took charge of managing and adding to the school's collection of books. The association also sponsored the first surviving student publications. *The Trinity War Cry*, an episodic newspaper appeared in 1890. During the next several years it morphed through several names—*The Trinity Illustrated Weekly, Ephemerida*—before settling on *Acta Diurna*. Along the way, the paper came to include a regular column by the rector. Ulmann did not neglect the arts, starting himself a glee club and encouraging the activities of the Literary Society and the Drama Society.[109]

The Athletic Association fielded football, baseball, and track teams that competed interscholastically with independent schools like Collegiate, Drisler, Wilson, Kellogg, and New Rochelle Academy. Some "home" events took place on the grounds of the Union Athletic Club or at Bryant Park in Midtown, or in Central Park, or at the Berkeley Oval in Morris Heights, a short hop by train from Grand Central Station. The Trinity School Chess and Checkers Club appealed to more contemplative competitors.

All this activity gave the school a distinctively new and modern feel and contributed to rising enrollments. In Ulmann's first year, Trinity taught 116 boys, up from seventy-five five years earlier. At the same time, the number of paying students jumped from three to sixteen, an upward trend that Ulmann and the trustees were eager to see continue. The rector estimated that enrollments would at least double with the opening of the new building on West 91st Street.[110] Tuition ranged from $100 to $250 depending on the track, with the highest amount for the final year of college preparation.

The burst of activity and new optimism at Trinity in the early 1890s, however, masked Ulmann's deeply conservative views of education. He strongly supported the traditional structure and curriculum of the school, which he emphasized by introducing Latinized terminology to describe them. Not content to accept the usual English names for the successive years at school—

"final year," "12th grade", "senior year," etc.—he rechristened what today would be, in descending order, grades 12 through 8 as Prima, Secunda, Tertia, Quarta, and Quinta (Sexta and Septima came later). Teachers became "Ordinarii," with the Oxford-credentialed Reginald Johnson as Ordinarius Primus, teaching students in their final year; Trinity and Columbia grad Edward Northall as Ordinarius Secundus, teaching students in the penultimate year and so on.

Ulmann reluctantly admitted a few changes to the curriculum to accommodate the expanding entrance requirements of Columbia and other colleges then emerging as regional and national institutions. In 1864, Columbia's new president, Frederick A. P. Barnard, had embarked on a twenty-five-year tenure that would transform the institution from a small traditional college into a large, diverse university with innovative degree programs in law, medicine, mining and engineering, architecture, teaching, and political science. For undergraduates, Columbia, like Harvard and a few other pioneers, offered advanced training in science and mathematics and an elective curriculum that enabled more subjects to be taught and allowed advanced students to specialize.[111]

At Trinity School, these trends demanded a response. By 1890, a bare but increasing majority of students planned to go on to college and needed enhanced preparation, particularly if they hoped to attend the Columbia School of Mines. For the latter, Trinity added courses in chemistry and physics, though initially it was science by the book, as the school possessed no laboratories before the move to West 91st Street.[112] Ulmann was not inclined to tinker further with Trinity's curriculum, however. "It was far better," he asserted, "to teach a few subjects thoroughly than many subjects superficially." He also took a dim view of "the college elective system," which he believed the means of "killing all education and filling the professions with incompetent men."[113]

Although Trinity was sending an increasing number of boys on to college, Ulmann doggedly portrayed the church school as an end in itself, certainly not a college preparatory school. Trinity, he argued, was a self-contained and self-sustaining community of intellectual and moral purpose. Now, not next, mattered most: "The church school is not an institution where boys are simply crammed for college or a scientific school, as the geese of Strassburg [sic] are crammed for the knife of the manufacturers of paté de foie gras.

Such a cramming process may produce the desired result . . . but the effect upon the mind is generally unsatisfactory, often disastrous."[114]

It is worth dwelling a while longer on Ulmann's philosophy of education because it exemplifies a traditional approach to schooling that, at Trinity at least, persisted not only through most of the nineteenth century but also into the twentieth. Ulmann's thinking also illustrates how an articulate Episcopal clergyman participated in the major intellectual controversy of the day, the debate between science and religion in the decades following publication of Charles Darwin's *The Origin of Species* in 1859.[115]

As noted, Ulmann believed in schooling body, spirit, and mind: There were games and exercises for the body and chapel for the spirit; everything else was for the mind. He thought about the mind as distinct sets of faculties and explained how a church school endeavored to cultivate them all equally and produce in boys an "all-sided growth and unfolding."

By *perceptive* faculties, Ulmann meant the five senses, two of which, hearing and sight, belonged to the proper realm of the church school, which rejected "the material theory of some scientists" that life was the consequence of natural forces. "We hold to the ancient account of the creation of man that the Lord God formed man of the dust of the ground and breathed into his nostrils the breath of life and man became a living soul." There were pedagogical implications of this ancient story. The body was by nature dead. The soul gave it life. The body contained the organs. The soul supplied the faculties animating them. Students needed to be convinced of their duty to develop whatever faculties they had—choices mattered more than ability—and they had to find the right channels to do so: "the eye and the ear must be enabled to grasp with ease and precision anything which is presented in the ordinary walks of life, whether it be a sum of arithmetic, a fact or a date, an anecdote or a speech." In math more important than solving intricate problems was the ability to do work rapidly and correctly; the best training was not with a book, which could be examined at leisure, but at the blackboard under pressure, where with problems dictated orally both the eye and ear learned to hear and see correctly and quickly.

Math trained in just one direction. Languages were the more perfect tool for sharpening the perceptive faculties: "the reading from the book, the rapid survey of an exercise on the board, the constant oral intercourse of pupil and teacher, enable the pupil to read and hear precisely, grasp exactly a sentence and passage and fully understand its meaning." The five languages taught at Trinity—English, Latin, Greek, German, and French—qualified: "An eye which is able to read correctly and rapidly the literature of five languages, more or less, of course—boys are not men—and an ear which can quickly and precisely take hold of anything said in five languages, is able to do anything and everything in this line which may be required by ordinary life."

Retentive faculties meant memory. Writing about it, Ulmann sounds a little like a critic of web surfing today. "The inordinate craze of newspaper reading with which our generation is so horribly afflicted" . . . the "glancing over of a vast amount of stuff which we cannot and do not care to remember" besieged memory. Then as now, information seemed everywhere, knowledge nowhere. A church school countered this danger by teaching discrimination: how to avoid the pernicious influence of careless reading and how to use carefully chosen literature, not newspapers or magazines, to train memory. He disliked notebooks and commended instead memorization, as a boy progressed, of constantly larger portions of prose and poetry, of course in all five languages.[116]

If today the tendency is to separate religion from pedagogy, then it was to integrate them. It was in Ulmann's thinking about the role of *reasoning* in education that the essential churchiness of Trinity in that era surfaced fully. We sense that his views even then were embattled, outside if not yet inside the walls, but he liked a fight and thought this above all was something worth fighting for. If indeed there was a trouble brewing with the larger world on this point, then a church school like Trinity ought not shrink from the test. Rather, it ought to stake out its territory precisely and let itself be known for its moral distinctiveness, not its worldly sameness.

A good Victorian, Ulmann was not speaking so much of education in church doctrine (though he certainly believed in that too), but the application of "right reason" arising from faith to overcome the daily temptations of selfishness and materialism.[117] The age, he believed, was full of them. Just read enough newspapers: "Everyone for himself; get all you can, keep all you can; a dollar never tells how it was gotten; men want to be humbugged; a stolen dollar buys as much as a dollar earned." Reason trained thus in the school of the world was a poor tutor as to what was right or wrong, wise or foolish, what was the best way to use ones's faculties and discern right opportunities. A church school understood reason differently, as a gift of God, and it could be read in other sorts of maxims: "Love thy neighbor as thyself;

love thy enemy; not slothful in business; lie not to one another; be not over-come of evil, but overcome evil with good."

Those other perceptive and retentive faculties, sense and memory, gathered up bits of the world and stored them safely in the mind, where it was reason's task to examine, weigh, classify, compare, draw conclusions, and decide then what action to take. Reason was like "the master workman in a factory, who lays out the work, assigns to each workman his share and tells him how it ought to be done." Now this sounded and sounds like education, *sub specie aeternitatis* however. For the true master was never far off stage. Education as training was a practical business where naturally "we go to our fellow men who, as we suppose, have their reason trained and developed in the proper and best manner and endeavor to learn from them. They help us to the best of their ability." Yet it doesn't always work out, "for when we present the result to the Master, we find frequently that we are all wrong. The Master is God."

This grates on modern sensibilities. Few headmasters, even headmasters of Episcopal schools, talk that way anymore. That Trinity's did then, however, is noteworthy, as the school pivoted into the twentieth century. At Trinity, remember, boys learned no science until the 1890s, and Ulmann's philosophy tried gamely to tackle the tensions science brought with it and that, since Darwin especially, had riven the church. Some churchmen battened down the hatches; some sought accommodation; some both. Ulmann made it sound simpler than it was, but at least he looked it square in the eye. Some things we can fathom and reason out with our intellectual powers; others we can't and must accept on authority and receive by faith. He thought this applied as much to the sciences as to religion. Didn't it demand, he wondered, as strong a faith "to believe in the doctrine of atoms and the molecular theory, as in the fact of the Trinity and the doctrine of the Incarnation?" Nobody had ever seen an atom or a molecule. Their existence could only "be proved by reasoning, and is usually accepted by faith on authority." Ordinary people, with no astronomy and insufficient math had no way of knowing that the sun was 95 (his number) million miles from Earth, but accepted it on faith in the science that told them it was so. Or again, "by faith they receive the doctrine of the law of gravitation. They cannot see how, but they believe that the planets are kept in their orbits by the nice adjustment of centrifugal and centripetal forces." To a degree, this even anticipated C. S. Lewis on the endlessly knotty relations between science and religion. Both men enjoyed flipping around the tables: "If the scientist can really *prove* so little, and asks us to accept so much in the realm of nature by faith, can he call us unreasonable, if we ask the same faith of him in the sphere of spiritual things?"[118]

Obviously, Ulmann's rock-ribbed orthodox conclusions would give way to other orthodoxies. Rational inquiry plus piety, reason kept humble by faith: These were notions that did not travel particularly well into modern times. Because they did not, Trinity then sounds inescapably remote even though, as then it was, just moved to the building still familiar to us. It was also apart from the world around it, then.

PUBLIC REFORM

The reform movement born in New York City in the 1880s in answer to the corruptions of Tammany Hall and the social problems associated with mass immigration, poverty, and slums loaded onto the schools heavy expectations both to transform individuals and to rescue society. Reformers, patricians and experts alike, saw the public schools as tools for social engineering on a grand scale and with benevolent purpose. Education took on new goals and was addressed by new theorists. Followers of the Swiss Johann Pestalozzi and the German Johann Herbart attacked traditional methods of memorization and pointed to the importance of psychology and ethics. German Friedrich Froebel started the kindergarten movement, which came to America in the 1850s. Psychologists William James and G. Stanley Hall turned old tables upside down, arguing that education must fit the child, not the child the curriculum. Curriculum had consequences. Schools needed to be made more like life. Any of this required better teachers, and under the leadership of Nicholas Murray Butler, a philosophy professor at Columbia College and head of the Industrial Education Association, a college for teacher training was established in 1887 and chartered five years later as Teachers College (a year after that part of Columbia). Butler became the overall leading light for school reform and head of the Public Education Society of New York, which relentlessly hammered away to increase the number of schools, update their curriculum, and replace local administration with a centralized professional system.[119]

Upon the reformers' total triumph in this third great "school war"—legislation centralizing the system was passed in 1896—followed the period of unprecedented innovation in what the schools did and how they did it, described by education historians Lawrence Cremin and Diane Ravitch.[120] Policy changes put philosophy into action, and demography reinforced it as child labor and compulsory attendance laws achieved for the first time in New York nearly universal public education. So large and fine a net caught up every sort and condition of child, especially as reform took hold at the same time that the new immigration from southern and eastern Europe brought a vast ethnically diverse population into the city's mix. Many had no English and no preparation (and no inclination some would say) for a traditional academic curriculum. What was at first called the "new education" and came to be called "progressive education" (and was coincident with the New Immigration) abandoned the traditional understanding that the schools' basic purpose was to teach everybody the three R's, and that those unfortunates who couldn't or wouldn't learn them were simply out of luck: Nothing else was on offer. Curriculum diversified following the social work/settlement house impulse: There would be manual, vocational, and industrial programs, programs for cripples and slow learners, for the deaf and the blind. Evening trade and elementary schools taught those who still worked days. Summer school was invented.

In the 1890s the plates shifted. Traditionally understood as the place where students mastered subject matter, the school under the progressives' hand would focus instead on meeting students' needs, however diverse those might be. In New York, it was a remarkably radical shift, praised at the time and excoriated later.[121] A close friend of Nicholas Murray Butler, fellow progressive William Henry Maxwell became first city superintendent of schools for Greater New York in 1898. Ravitch describes him as a man pulled two ways, "an autocrat with egalitarian goals," a paternalist smitten with democratic idealism.[122] Though he never questioned the duty to impose equal opportunity on all, he believed as deeply in the fundamentally ameliorative mission of the schools: "The best corrective of the evils generated by the accumulation of wealth is not anti-trust laws or other repressive legislation, but a system of schools which provides a training for all that is equal to the best which money can buy."[123] Education would overcome all life's obstacles. It was a daunting, widespread, and long-lasting claim.

It defined the future path of the public schools (whatever their charity origins), from which Trinity increasingly diverged, in part because it held fast to certain continuities. At the end of the nineteenth century, as at the beginning, Trinity taught content (including Episcopalian doctrine) to those who cared to learn it. Nobody was forced to come; nobody was forced to stay. That content changed some, but not hugely. Of course, it was believed that mastery of such content had positive worldly consequences: that somehow it would give students a better purchase on life, whether as an apprentice early on or as a student at Columbia later. To the extent that it took in poor children and potentially improved their prospects, it did address, narrowly, the issue of poverty, but poverty understood as an individual misfortune, not as a social problem. Christian charity commanded ministering to the poor who grew ever numerous, not amelioration of poverty abstractly through education.

August Ulmann, a democrat with elitist goals, did not talk at all like his contemporary William Maxwell, and this not just because Ulmann talked a lot about God. His claims for "the church school" were deep, not broad. It produced good college and business men, good Christian citizens (for his money the best kind), and, simply, good Christians. Ulmann was a priest after all, and a priest who worked for other priests (and some lawyers). Christ had come into the world to save it from sin's folly. If it was to be saved from poverty as well, well, that was how it would have to be saved still: one soul at a time.[124] Nowhere can we detect at Trinity the slightest creep toward environmentalism, the newer faith that surroundings trumped heredity, bad luck, improvidence, or other misfortune.

Trinity posed an interesting alternative model. Even as they began to do science at Trinity, to play at organized sports, do school publications and plays, even, that is, as the place grew to look more like a modern school that offered students in addition to academics lots of "activities,"[125] nothing fundamental changed in purpose and not much in procedure. It taught mental discipline and useful knowledge for a chosen few. It selected its students, still before the days of admissions tests, probing informally at any rate for desire and ability ("fit," admissions officers would say today). Trinity excluded. Public schools included. Trinity subsidized most of its selection. Public schools subsidized all of their students. However, Trinity subsidized by grace of endowment and did so case by case and conditionally; a privilege granted could be taken away. Public schools subsidized universally by fiat from taxes and the public treasury and did so unconditionally; a right once conceded was forever. Finally, Trinity controlled absolutely. Public schools controlled imperfectly at best.

Control such as Trinity enjoyed betokened independence and engendered isolation. Trinity appears to have been aloof from the second and third great school wars that had reshaped New York's public school system so profoundly by the century's end, turning that system into the dispenser of universal education for a polyglot population and an instrument of progressive social policy. Trinity lived elsewhere. Religious homogeneity—and thus ethnic homogeneity, too, Italian or Polish Episcopalians being rarities—was built in. In the public school realm, diversity was equally built in, a consequence of the universal-and-free principle applied to education in an ethnically mixed city. Homogeneity or diversity, elitist selectivity or democratic inclusiveness? What was necessity, what was virtue?

TRINITY'S PLACE

In 1893, when Trinity announced its intention to occupy new quarters on West 91st Street, an account in *The New York Times* recognized the school's hybrid nature in a brief characterization of its evolution from "a charity public school" in its early years to "now . . . partly a pay and partly a charity school."[126] Continuity was important in Trinity's progress through the nineteenth century. The school still educated most of its students for free, though it dispensed its charity not to the poor generally but to boys only, primarily from families of modest or middle-class means, and still sought to provide a substantial number with practical education, though more and more went on to college and professional careers. For all of its students Trinity aimed to teach Episcopal doctrine and discipline, though at the end of the century this was discipline not only of mind and spirit but also of body.

While minuscule in the larger scheme of vast, industrialized, and multiethnic New York City in the 1890s, Trinity offered a clear alternative to the secular public schools, as well as to most other religious schools. Even as they began to learn science, to play at organized sports, mount school publications and plays, even, that is, as the place grew to look more like a modern school that offered students in addition to academics lots of activities, nothing fundamental changed in purpose and not much in procedure at Trinity. After all, it was still a church school, still abiding by the charter of 1806. As best can be told, there were no foreign-born from the New Immigration among Trinity's student body; its tiny faculty remained solidly white, Anglo-Saxon (or just Saxon, in Ulmann's case), and Protestant—WASP, in the common acronym. Trinity was an Episcopal school, exclusively and contentedly so, and an unlikely destination for students who were not Episcopalians.

Following the reforms of 1890s and for the next half-century at least, the New York public schools were widely deemed to work well for all classes, colors, and faiths. Only two things made Trinity different: its traditional body-of-knowledge approach to schooling, overlain, and not lightly, with Episcopal Christianity. Trinity's close community self-selected itself on the basis of these two factors or, put another way, these were the factors that differentiated Trinity in the education marketplace.

The other line of the story describes how, within the confines of its world, Trinity grew first comfortable and then uneasy with the long legacy of self-selection and exclusive Episcopal religiosity. It was one thing to be steadfast, another to be static. In February 1895, when the school moved into its new building, once more directly in the shadow of Trinity Parish, these were surface ripples only on a calm well of assurance. New quarters—especially hefty stone ones, especially ones paid for in full in cash, especially ones nestled in a fashionable middle-class neighborhood adjoining an immense, newly built Episcopal chapel of ease—felt good.[127] The rhetoric at the dedication wasn't much different from the "speechifying" at its 150th anniversary back in 1859, and if long institutional histories move in arcs, then the moving into that place near century's end marked a zenith. There would soon be more students, more teachers, more activities—and more change. If you want to make God laugh, it is said, then tell him your plans. Ulmann, who liked to change the names of things but not the things themselves, must have told Him quite a lot, for in just a few years he found himself ushered involuntarily out Trinity's imposing new front door. Into his place walked a gentle caretaker to preside over a long, warm afternoon.

FIVE *Episcopal Twilight*

or years and years from the 1890s forward, a visual rendering of the four-story building at West 91st Street proudly faced off opposite the title page of Trinity's annual published description of itself, the *Trinity School Yearbook*. At first, these were full frontal, later slightly from-an-angle black and white photographs. Later still they became handsome etchings. For a then already venerable, two-century-old school but one that until the 1890s had been a migratory animal with no roof to call its own, the steadfastness of this visual imagery was likely no accident. Trinity equaled this one place at last, and this was a place that was built to last. The building looked solid, and it was. The authors were explicit about it. "The construction is of the most generous and substantial character, and insurance brokers have declared that they can suggest nothing to make the building more fire-proof than it is."[1]

That boast, repeated yearly for as long as the pictures appeared, which was into the 1940s, reflected confidence that Trinity at last had a good safe building where parents could send their sons and feel secure about it. They were right. The old building itself never yet caught fire. History, however, is filled with boasts that return to bite, as this one did in November 2005 when fire ravaged a small corner of a modern wing built long after the handsome 1890s edifice. It was a double bite, for the corner that burned happened to be the corner that housed the school's historical archives. Fire is the nightmare of every school and of course, better papers than people: No one was hurt in this blaze, and the school's current operation was not disrupted. Only history took the blow: "A School's Storied Past Is Charred But Endures" was how *The New York Times* headline writer put it several weeks afterward.[2] Most archives are but fragments, and so this one was too. After the fire, though, the fragments of Trinity's past became even less continuous, and for the period of time covered in this chapter, which is the last period largely beyond the reach of living memory today, the vacant spaces are particularly grievous. What follows therefore is a representation with more than history's usual holes. We know enough of the general patterns at least to fit the era plausibly into the story of a then already old school that in the early twentieth century seemed to have hit its prime, a place with a clear purpose, a fine home, a fresh leader.

Old themes continued to play in what appeared a serene new context. Small size and private means, churchy atmosphere, and high academic standards conspired to cement Trinity's status as an elite institution. While the school's physical migration appeared to have ended at last, not so the challenge of fitting itself into its physical and social surroundings. The New York neighborhood where it had chosen to situate itself did not stand still, even as Trinity contentedly seemed to. Between the beginning of this era and the end, the early 1900s to the late 1930s, there broke surface another tension, at first faint, between the claims of the charity tradition and the glimmerings of competitive meritocracy and the relative costs of each. At the beginning of this era, money, like location, felt easy. By the end of it, both felt hard.

In those days, a number of boys came to Trinity at the start of high school from the choir schools of St. Thomas Church on Fifth Avenue and the Cathedral of St. John the Divine just up the street on Amsterdam. There, if a boy's voice broke before he finished eighth grade, he went into the limbo of "acolyte land." If not, he sang on, gloriously, a few final months. The treble voice achieves unmatched purity and tonal richness just when it is about to change. The man's voice that gradually replaces it can become rich too, though never again so pure. Trinity then was something like that. It too had no choice but to grow up, in time. During the first decades of the last century, it gently approached that turning.

STEADY ON

A fatherly figure and more the churchman than the schoolman was how Clarence Bruner-Smith recalled the Reverend Doctor Lawrence Thomas Cole who came to Trinity as rector in 1903. Always dressed in clericals, Cole was the last of his type in two senses. He was the last Trinity headmaster to be an ordained clergyman and the last headmaster to be called not "headmaster" but "rector." Cole headed the school but did not quite lead it, at least not to the degree that all of his successors would be called upon to do. His immediate predecessor, August Ulmann, had tried perhaps too hard to lead and with bad result. Ulmann was a reformer with German ideas that had not gone down well, and he was one of a very few Trinity headmasters of record to be invited to go before he would have liked. Another priest with a scholarly bent but a different sort of character, Cole was hired to restore a steady course for Trinity in its then spacious and up-to-date new quarters on the Upper West Side. He did just that. This is probably the period of Trinity's past that best synchronizes with the character of a single headmaster. Not that Cole was a particularly strong leader, but he was a lucky one with a temperament suited to manage well enough through relatively settled times. For all his odd teutonisms, Ulmann had readied Trinity for an ordered progress across what appeared solid ground ahead, and that was what Cole dedicated his career to delivering. Doing so, he and the teachers and the boys of Trinity formed and experienced a school that, it must have seemed at the time, had in every sense arrived: a place that was everything their predecessors through a long fitful history had hoped it might become.

Cole was thirty-four in 1903 and well credentialed, with undergraduate and graduate degrees from the University of Michigan (1892, 1896), a divinity degree from General Theological Seminary (1896) in New York, and a Ph.D. from Columbia (1898).[4] He had done his time in parish and diocesan work in the provinces (Crawfordsville and Michigan City, Indiana) and was warden of St. Stephen's College (later Bard) before coming to the metropolis as rector of Trinity, with the charge to calm things down. He was good at it.

In the wake of the Ulmann disturbance, the board, itself then heavily clerical, must have kept some sort of an eye on his successor. Record of their interaction is sparse, but from their collective profile we might infer that they and Cole saw things much alike. Throughout Cole's time, clergymen trustees always outnumbered laymen. Some were well known and cut large figures in New York and national church circles: William Jones Seabury, long-time professor at General Theological Seminary, born in 1837, the son of Samuel Seabury and author of a manual for choristers and lectures on the apostolic succession; W. M. Grosvenor and Milo Gates, both deans of the Cathedral of St. John the Divine; Wilfred Robbins and Hughell Fosbroke, both deans of General Theological Seminary; David H. Greer, Bishop of New York; William T. Manning, another Bishop of New York and previously rector of Trinity Church; Ernest Stires, long-time rector of St. Thomas Church Fifth Avenue and Bishop of Long Island; William Bellinger, after William Manning long-time vicar of St. Agnes Chapel; H. Percy Silver, chaplain at West Point during World War I; Henry Lubick, Canon of Washington National Cathedral. Others but not all tended to be lawyers: John Van Vechten Olcott, who was board president in the 1930s, had been a New York congressman, a company director, and member of the New York City

Civil Service Commission; Charles F. Hoffman, who served in the 1910s, was in real estate (Hoffman Brothers) and also a trustee of St. John the Divine and Columbia; Lawson Purdy was president of New York's Department of Taxes and Assessments and president of the National Conference on City Planning in the 1920s; C. Aubry Nicklas, treasurer in the 1930s, was an accountant with experience in construction and engineering; John Erskine was a distinguished author, Columbia faculty member, and for many years a vestryman of Trinity Church. Most identified themselves as Republicans, with memberships at places like the University, Century, and Harvard clubs and the Downtown Association.[5]

Cole must have related to them easily and with their broad mandate settled the school into just the right groove to make them and everybody else happy. He was an easygoing administrator and father figure around the boys. He presided at chapel, taught the required courses in "sacred studies," liked to welcome "his boys" to school in the morning and shake hands as they left.

By benign default, the faculty ran the school then. This suited both rookies and veterans, teachers who came to Trinity young and stayed on until retirement. Sidney Small, who taught chemistry, physics, and biology for forty years, had himself been a Trinity boy, class of 1895, and then went on to Columbia. Ralph de Golier had come in 1920 and taught French until 1946, not neglecting, quite famously it was said, the sex education opportunities of French literature. He also coached the boys in chess and was observed to play three boards simultaneously—blindfolded. Dwight Holbrook taught classical Greek into his eighties, the sort of man who out of the blue would burst in on a younger colleague grading papers, with a bluff: "Remember, Mr. Bruner-Smith, they are not all inglorious Miltons!" Victor Bonsall, class of 1897 and then Columbia, first taught English and then Latin for forty-two years, and affected a personal antiquity to match his subject. Asked by a colleague if he had read the then hottest of popular novels, *Gone With the Wind*, Bonsall, a copy of Horace under his arm, replied that he hadn't, and wouldn't, read anything written since the fifth century A.D. Walter Keyes had become a master in 1896, was principal of the lower school for forty years, and kept a summer camp in Maine where many Trinity boys went as campers and worked as counselors. John Langford succeeded Keyes in the lower school ("he admitted boys to the lower grades testing them while they sat on his knee"[6]) and had taught English to Trinity boys since 1911, includ-

ing Humphrey Bogart and Truman Capote, bits of whose seventh-grade poetry and prose he saved, but these are now alas lost. Josephine Bartram
taught first grade for many years from 1919 and was married to Bertram
Bartram, manual training instructor. Elsie Bonsall, wife of Victor, taught
third grade also from 1919, and Edith Allen for many years took the fifth.
"Miss" Eliza Gascoigne had been at Trinity since 1898, and until she retired
no one at school knew she was married. Not all were the perfect match, but
most had special strengths enough. John Murphy taught history from 1920
until fired in 1939, an avowed socialist who never came to class without a
copy of *The Daily Worker* and who lived with his artist wife in the Chelsea
Hotel. Arthur Walter, who retired in 1936 a year before Cole, had taught
math for twenty-five years and was another Episcopal priest. Walter remembered how, when he had first come to Trinity, shellfish could still be found
in the Hudson at the foot of 91st Street.[7]

SCHOOL SPACE

Teaching and learning at Cole's Trinity, from the turn of the nineteenth
century to the end of the 1930s, from Roosevelt to Roosevelt, could be said
to have been contained in the West 91st Street building, with the cross
carved into the sandstone, as no mere building ever would contain it again.
It is, in part, the same building where headmasters, teachers, and boys (and
now girls) together form and experience their own Trinity in 2009. It is also
remote and faraway territory, so uniform and simple appear its outlines, its
rules, its mandate, the claims placed upon it.

As best as the record reveals, there was between the clarity of the claims
and the school's actual performance remarkable congruence. The Charles
Haight-designed building (it would never again be referred to as a mere
"schoolhouse" as its peripatetic predecessors were known in earlier centuries) was a source of identity and institutional self-esteem, and it etched
out in brick and mortar, tile and wood, rounded archways, peaked dormers
and tall windows, the four-square structure of the school life carried on
within it. The building, as completed in 1893, remained largely unaltered in
exterior appearance and interior arrangements until the 1950s. It had but
one primary entrance, at 139 West 91st Street, though "portal" is a better
word. Across the slightly inset-from-the-sidewalk south front extended five
archways, two casement windows flanking each side of the slightly wider
front door. The door was six steps up from grade, and one reached it

through a five-foot iron fence. There was a highly visible keystone at the apex of the arch over the doorway, which also marked the space between the words "Trinity" and "School" that were engraved in the lintel just above it.

The structure measured 125 feet wide by 100 feet deep, contained four floors plus basement, and was designed to (but never did until much later) accommodate up to 500 students or, as they were still called early in the century, "scholars." The interior layout, which was reproduced for the yearbook from the architectural drawings, was a study in symmetry and the appointments in modesty. The corridors were large, wide and open, an effect made possible by the fact that the classroom portion of the building was not much longer than it was high. The one hallway on each floor onto which opened four classrooms front and four back was less of a hall than a lobby, almost as wide as the classrooms themselves. Walls were white brick, floors gray terrazzo: hard bright surfaces everywhere. The classrooms were relatively small, designed for no more than twenty-five boys, and each contained its own cloak room, which was entered from inside the classroom, a feature intended to eliminate the crowding and hubbub that went with lockers in the hall.

Bottom to top, the building worked thus. The ground floor accommodated two primary classes and a trustees' room also used as reception and that connected with the appendage on the southwest corner of the building that was the rector's study and, above it, his apartment. On the southeast corner there was a library, and along the back and running the full width of the building a sky-lit pew-lined assembly or commons room large enough to seat the entire school, which it did, daily, for chapel. Stairwells east and west led up to eight more classrooms on the second floor, and eight more on the third. Above that, the footprint filled in differently. Three floors above the library, a dining room occupied the southeast corner and was backed by a storeroom, scullery, and kitchen where hot lunches were prepared. Adjacent, on the back, a sitting room, bedroom, and bath were designated for a live-in janitor. A chemistry laboratory occupied space next to the dining room, "perfectly fireproof," too. The rest of the top floor, front to back, went to a 3,500-square-foot gymnasium with locker room and showers on the front corner in the space that would have been the attic of the rectory. It was a big space with twenty-one-foot ceiling, fitted out with up-to-date fitness apparatus, and was in constant use. Primary and grammar school boys used it for half an hour every day for calisthenics and gymnastics under direction of the school's gym instructor. High school boys did full-hour afternoon sessions twice a week. Though there was still no schoolyard or playing fields, "the excellent effect of regular daily [if indoor] exercise upon the muscular development of the scholars has been clearly shown": jumping jacks and parallel bars on the fourth floor filled in. Throughout the building there were drinking fountains with filtered water cooled in coils of pipe packed in ice. There was a coal-fired central heating system and forced air ventilation. Lavatories were located by the stairwells, one per floor, "large, light, well-ventilated."

SCHOOL WORK

From outside, it looked something like a fortress. Inside, it was meant during school hours of nine to two or three, depending on the class, to be like a home. The rector ruled it sternly but benevolently, like the good "father" he was. By the time Cole was named to the post in July 1903, Trinity had been settled into the new building for ten years. Cole in the thirty-four years he would hold the job did nothing much to unsettle its functional arrangements, and if possible went about making it an ever more comfortable home. Like Ulmann, Cole was an ordained priest in the Episcopal Church and came with heavy academic credentials. Unlike Ulmann, he was solidly anglophile in his prejudices and a pacificator in temperament. That at least seems plausible in wake of the little we know of the discontent that had bubbled up in 1902 and led to Ulmann's premature departure, when he was still just fifty-eight.

Sometime between the 1901 and 1902 school years things took a tumble, or got out of hand as an earlier historian characterized it.[8] Ulmann related the "magnificent" opening of school in 1901: "this is the best opening of school we have ever had." A year later, he was a man alarmed. Parents were reporting that the teaching was bad and some removed their sons. "If a boy wants to work he can, but if a boy has no inclination for study he is let alone and consequently does nothing." There were also troubling reports coming back to him of faculty who used "rough means and uncouth language" with their students. If the problem was poor performance because of poor teaching and supervision, then the problem clearly was Ulmann's as headmaster (chief teacher) and he was right to worry. He addressed the matter directly with the faculty in meetings that fall and even called in Columbia professor George Odell to talk to the masters about best methods for teaching English. Parents of senior boys also complained that their sons were poorly prepared to get into Harvard and Yale, though Ulmann defended himself that every boy presented for college admission had entered, though some admissions had been conditional. The discontent, however, may have been systemic and related to Ulmann's policy of having teachers, particularly in the high school, teach all subjects and not specialize in the fields they knew best. At least we know that this was the one key policy that changed quickly under Cole.[9]

We know that Ulmann had put fancy Latin names on things and let his own German gymnasium experience influence his thinking about Trinity. Cole's antenna probably picked up the urgency of at least the appearance of change, and the easiest change was cosmetic. So, he jiggered the names of those things yet again. Organizationally, the school remained divided into the same three parts as it had before him, though with new labels. Ulmann's "English Department" became Cole's "Primary School." The "Intermediate Department" became the "Grammar School." The "Academic Department" became the "High School." The old English Department had sorted six-year-olds to nine-year-olds into English IV to English I, the youngest class getting the highest (roman) numeral. Ulmann applied his Latin nomenclature to his Intermediate and Academic departments and likewise designated seniority with inverse numbering. With eight years separating ten- and seventeen-year olds, Octava had designated ten-year-olds, Septima eleven-year-olds, and so forth up (or down) all the way to the Primas, the oldest boys at seventeen and eighteen. Cole simplified. As boys grew older, they progressed through just plain "grades," starting with first through fourth in the Primary School, fifth through eighth in the Grammar School. In the High School, it was unpretentiously "First Year" through Fourth.[10]

It did not take Cole long, however, to get down to substance. He deployed the talents of the faculty in the High School differently, with masters assigned to teach the subject or group of subjects where they were most proficient, not just grade-level work across the board. And he addressed anxiety about academic performance throughout the school by tightening up and formalizing the grade-to-grade promotion standards for advancement. To move up, students henceforth had to have a general average of 60 percent for the year and could not fall below 50 percent in any one subject. This apparently led to some quick winnowing. In his first year, of the 303 boys enrolled, close to a third were gone by the end of the spring term. This was dramatic. Apparently the axe fell for both disciplinary problems and poor academic performance, and must have had the effect of concentrating the minds of everyone who remained. The numbers that remained, the quantity of boys who came and went over the years, told the story of a school in a relatively steady state. In Cole's first year, Trinity enrolled 310 boys. In 1912, there were 285; in 1919, 297; in 1926, 317; in 1931, 300; in 1936, his last Depression-stressed year, 230.[11]

Excluding the rector, faculty numbered 21 in 1903, 19 in 1913, 18 in 1923, and 17 in 1934. They apportioned out among the three parts of the school with the same steadiness. In 1903, eight masters taught the high school; six took the grammar school, and four (all women) taught the youngest students of the primary department. Three teachers "floated," handling gymnastics, drawing, and elocution for everybody. The rector taught religion. The numbers were just the same into the 1930s, and never in the years in between varied more than a teacher or two, here or there.[12]

We have many of their names and can calculate their tenures, many of which were long and coterminous with and even reached beyond Cole's administration. Remaining records confirm Bruner's memory. Still serving in the high school when Cole himself finally retired in 1937 were Victor Bonsall, principal and English master who had come in 1902. Sidney Small taught high school science and came in 1901. Arthur G. Walter taught mathematics and came in 1912. Dwight Holbrook taught Greek and Latin and came in 1918. John Murphy taught history and came in 1919. In the Grammar School, seventh-grade teacher John Langford came in 1911. Arthur Roeder took the sixth since 1913. In the Primary School, principal and second-grade teacher Eliza Gascoigne took top seniority, having started out during the Spanish–American War. Edith Allen, for the fifth grade, came in 1902. Both Elsie Bonsall with the third grade and Josephine Bartram with the first arrived in 1919. Women exclusively (Mrs.'s and Misses) taught in the Primary School, men in the upper grades. They appear to have been a well-qualified lot, schooled at good colleges, several with advanced degrees. Columbia predominated, joined by Hamilton, Harvard, Rutgers, Yale, and New York University. Cole of course started out at Michigan. Walter Wildman came from Trinity in Connecticut, Bertram Bartram from Rochester, John Norris from Ohio State, and John Langford and Francis McCarthy from New York state normal schools at Oneonta and Pottsdam.[13]

What these faculty taught Trinity boys both flowed from the past and, gently, innovated around the margins. Continuity was especially remarkable in the younger grades, and the following progressions in curricula remained largely unchanged from Cole's first years to his last. Primary schoolers learned seven or eight subjects, depending on how they were described in different years. Arithmetic moved from simple combinations of numbers in first grade to number work to 100 in second, to addition, subtraction, multiplication tables and fractions in third, to long division, factoring, Roman notation, "practical problems," and "United States money" in fourth. Reading and spelling intertwined, first- to fourth-grade children learned from Readers and to spell simple words found there first, then more complex ones. Language (the label changed to "English" in the 1910s) started with "simple stories," moved to "reproduction exercises" and stories and short descriptions from pictures. By fourth grade there were punctuation and capitalization, dictation and writing from memory. Penmanship started with manuscript and in third grade went to cursive. Drawing fell under the same heading. The natural sciences first got attention in time devoted to what was called, straightforwardly, "Nature Study." Students learned about the germination and dissemination of seeds, and studied particular trees, flowers, insects, and animals, specifically animals and birds of the United States. Geography began in fourth grade (then in the 1910s pushed back to third): "general knowledge of the world and its peoples" at first, and later detail got added with a look at continents and oceans, hemispheres, the effects of heat and cold on plant and animal life, and the nature and use of maps. Illustrations were made with the globe and (in a strange echo of the Bell system) the sand table. History also first appeared in the fourth grade, with the teacher reading stories from U.S. history. This left only religious instruction, which meant Christian/Episcopal doctrine: the Lord's Prayer and the Apostle's Creed and simple Bible stories, the Ten Commandments, the Prayer Book catechism, and the seasons of the church year.

In the grammar school, fifth graders in arithmetic took on decimal fractions, greatest common divisors, and least common multiples. Rapid oral drill was the favored teaching technique. Then came more decimals, and work with weights and measures. Seventh graders learned about the metric system, compound numbers, and percentages. In English (Language in the Primary School), the grammar school continued drilling parts of speech and simple compositions in the fifth, more grammar and parsing in the sixth, complex and compound sentence analysis in the seventh, idioms and "peculiar constructions" in the eighth. Reading and spelling were folded into English in the 1910s.

Geography grew gradually more sophisticated over the middle years, branching out from the United States to the rest of North and South America, then Europe and Asia. By eighth grade, students were introduced to commerce and industry, means of transportation and communication, trade routes, and map drawing. History commenced from fourth grade, first with American subjects, then moved on to the history of England and Europe in sixth grade. Seventh grade brought boys back to the United States and introduced elementary civics. In eighth grade it was the "general history of the world." In science, Nature Study at first carried on from fourth to fifth, then was followed in sixth with "elementary lessons" in physiology, skipped across seventh, and resumed eventually in eighth with zoology, described as the life history of the lower animals, including "sex development." By the 1930s, this had become "various projects." Penmanship carried on (increasing exercises "for form and speed") across these years, while drawing and manual training appear in 1909 and occupied boys with construction from drawings, including by eighth grade simple furniture. Early in the century Cole appears to have pushed back on the timing of Latin and modern languages, which Ulmann had introduced in fifth grade, instead beginning them in eighth and seventh grades, respectively, and he soon pushed Latin into the high school. First grammar school lessons in modern languages had been in German, but gave way after World War I to first lessons in French. Trinity's attention to the basics of spiritual and physical education appeared even more steadfast, with daily gymnasium for all boys and a steady march through the Prayer Book catechism, Cranmer's collects, and lessons in church history.

There was only one notable structural shift, which came in the renamed "high school" during Cole's tenure. Columbia's standards for admission and after 1900 the uniform requirements worked out by the College Entrance Examination Board or College Board governed Trinity's high school curriculum.[14] In 1897, the newly renamed Columbia College established its own new curriculum, in style midway between Harvard's unlimited elective approach and Johns Hopkins's more rigid approach. Chemistry, engineering, and architecture were pulled out of the old School of Mines, and undergraduates studied a mixture of required and elective work in modern and ancient languages, history, mathematics, philosophy, political economy, and a natural science including laboratory experience.[15] At Trinity in what would appear to have been the same spirit, Cole simplified at least on the surface. Through the 1910s, the high school divided its offerings in each of grades nine through twelve into classical and scientific courses of study. The names "classical" and "scientific" now conjure sharp two-cultures divergence, but the differences then were subtle.

First-year high schoolers, for instance, in the classical course took English (Carpenter's *Rhetoric and English Composition*, Defoe's *Robinson Crusoe*, Scott's *Kenilworth*, Dickens's *Tale of Two Cities*, with weekly themes and exercises), Latin (grammar and easy prose composition, translation of *Fabulae Faciles*), German (conversation and Bacon's *Grammar*) or French (conversation and Chardenal's *Complete French Course*), mathematics (arithmetic first half of the year, elementary algebra the second), history (Woodburn and Moran's *American History and Government*), general science (recitations from Clark's *General Science* and supplementary technical periodical reading), and of course religious instruction and gym. In the first year scientific course a boy took both German and French but no Latin, studied English but not American history (Montgomery's *History of England*), and did freehand drawing. Sophomore classical boys started in with Greek (White's *First Greek Book* and *Anabasis*, Book I) and did ancient history. Scientific boys stuck with German and French, went a bit faster in math, and studied American history. Juniors in the classical course did Latin and Greek plus French or German and more ancient history. Scientific ones again did German and French, finished up American history, but added physics (Gorton's *High School Physics* with lab work). English courses were identical for both groups (themes based on the *Aeneid*, *As You Like It* and *King John*, Thackery's *Pendinnis*, Tennyson's *Princess*, Southey's *Life of Nelson*, Macaulay's *Essays on Madame D'Arblay and Frederick the Great*). In senior year, the classic course was an echo, a step further along. English included Egerton Smithy's *Essay Writing, Rhetoric and Prosody*, *Hamlet*, Palgrave's *Golden Treasury*, Emerson's *Essay on Manners*, and Macaulay's *Speech on Copyright*. Latin advanced to Virgil and Ovid and "voluntary sight-reading twice a week." Greek covered the *Iliad* books 1 through 3, book 4 or the Gospel of St. Mark, plus sight reading "for boys who need it for college entrance." In German they read Heine's *Die Harzreise* and Schiller's *Wilhelm Tell*, in French *La Tulipe Noire*. Boys in the science course learned the same English, German, and French, but took advanced algebra and solid geometry, and followed physics with chemistry (Brownlee's *First Principles of Chemistry* with laboratory work). For all seniors gym was voluntary.[16]

By the late 1910s, in the first two years of the high school, the classical/ scientific distinction had blurred, although sophomores had a choice between Greek or medieval and modern history. The last two years still divided, with classical boys getting to choose between Greek or physics their junior year, scientific boys still taking both French and German but no Latin or Greek, plus chemistry in their senior year. Starting with the 1922–23 school year the split was gone entirely, though there were choices for sophomores between Greek and mediaeval or modern history. Juniors could choose between Latin III or German I, and among Greek II, French III, and physics. Seniors selected between Latin IV or German II, and between Greek III and chemistry. The word "elective" first appeared in the year 1929–30 and was used in connection with the same options just described for juniors and seniors. There was little else to elect, and the fact that all these courses, classical or scientific, were taught by the same small faculty further mitigated the old divisions.

The record lacks any boys' or teachers' notes from these years, so we can no longer directly correlate substance with style. An earlier history mentions notes made by Victor Bonsall about Robert Southey's *Life of Nelson* that it illustrated "daring tempered by foresight" and "considerateness, integrity and persevering energy," presumably themes Bonsall drove home to his students.[17] In that spirit, the catalogue (presumably vetted if not written by Cole) told parents and prospective students what they could expect. That these words changed so little through his years suggests anyway consistent delivery of a reasonably satisfactory product. It suggests a straightforward teaching and administrative regimen. In Cole's early years, Trinity advertised itself as purveyor of the essentials of "a good English education." This meant concentration on the fundamental principles of a relatively few central subjects and the bodies of knowledge they represented.

Cole belonged to a lingering late Victorian generation more known for its self-control than its self-expression. He once used a curious figure, however, to describe what he thought should be going on inside those austere classrooms. "The school ought to be, among other things," he wrote in 1904 addressing students, "a kind of 'mind-press' to bring out of you all of what you have in you, and to help you put to practical use the knowledge you acquire in your classes." He went into the etymology of the verb "to express," the Latin *exprimo*, which means to press out, as in "oil from the olive, the juice from grape—that is getting out of these the good that is in them." Good schooling was a matter of both getting knowledge and getting knowledge out. "There are many very learned men who fail to take their part in the battle of life because they cannot express to others the great thoughts they have within themselves. Their minds are like sponges that are saturated or filled with water so that thy can absorb no more, and very often what they need in order that they may be of use to the world, is *to be squeezed* so that they may give out the useful knowledge they have in them."[18]

Cole's belief that schooling should enlarge a student's work and "kindle latent talents"[19] was nonetheless a long way from the notion of progressive education theorists that education was primarily about meeting the student's individual needs. Cole played safe with his pedagogy, putting the main emphasis on repeated drill, frequent and extended reviews of defined bodies of knowledge. It could not all be done in school hours. Homework, minimal in the early years, steadily increased with a boy's age and capacity, its on-time completion seen as evidence of his initiative and responsibility. Trinity was a day school, not a boarding school, however, and Cole and his masters necessarily shared power with parents. He did not hesitate to instruct them, much as he did their sons. On the matter of homework, he wrote that Trinity assignments could not be expected to be properly carried out unless a boy was quietly at home each and every school night: no "outside engagements" during the week, he told parents. They were also to be careful with any help they gave their sons. If a boy was up-to-date in attendance in class, no help, Cole said, should be necessary. Any boy who made an "honest effort" ought to be able to handle his own homework because the school took as a contract with parents the obligation to see that every child covered in detail every portion of the subjects assigned to his class. In return, the school expected from every student "hard work and cheerful compliance" with all the school's requirements. Without "industriousness" no boy, however smart, could hope to succeed at Trinity.

Between Cole's preachiness with parents and the one academic subject he himself was directly responsible for, religion, there was direct connection. Trinity was a church-sponsored school that taught a largely secular curriculum, "ordinary subjects," as Cole called them. It had a chapel (or a commons room that doubled as one), used it every day, and placed some emphasis on moral as well as intellectual and physical development. Sound academics were the obvious requirement of the contract with parents, but not the only one. Trinity also aimed at the "broader culture and discipline of the whole man," something that clergyman Cole believed was attainable only in an atmosphere "of good breeding, moral idealism, and religion." Thus Cole instructed his students in his faith, which meant the Christian faith with a clear Episcopalian flavor. Tone trumped doctrine, however. It was the influence of the daily Morning Prayer services and "general atmosphere of the school," he thought, that would most surely develop a boy's religious nature. Not every student was from an Episcopalian family, but every student went to chapel, learned the Christian pieties, and soaked up the language of the Prayer Book. A devout life, not mastery of his denomination's theology, was what Cole hoped to impart Trinity boys. No doubt of all the subjects taught there, it had also the hardest outcome to measure.

SCHOOL DAYS

Schooling happened at Cole's Trinity on schedule. Everyone started at nine o'clock sharp, Cole greeting boys at the 91st Street portal at the start of every day. Primary boys were dismissed for the day at 1:00 P.M., grammar and high school boys stayed longer, to 2:30, except on Fridays when all classes ended at 1:00.[20] However, it was central to the plan of the school that a boy complete the work assigned for his class for the day before he was dismissed, and when this did not happen masters had authority to detain the laggards and did so. "No outside engagements will be allowed to interfere with this arrangement." Trinity may have been a day school and of course took no responsibility for students outside the school day, but it did admonish parents that the school day in fact reached into the remains of the day at home. The school served hot lunch in the dining room on the southeast corner of the third floor, younger boys eating first, from 12:15 to 1:00, high schoolers from 1:00 to 1:45. "Simple food at moderate prices" was the official description. At least one real boy remembered it differently: "The food was awful, just terrible."[21] Boys living close by (the lucky ones?) were allowed to go home for lunch, with parents' permission. Cole kept office hours every day from 9:15 to 10:00 and from 12:15 to 1:00 and by appointment, and during the summer months he was available every day from nine to noon.

Boys growing up crave order and structure, and Trinity's nearly changeless routines and curriculum provided order and structure above all. A school is worlds within worlds, however, and the record of Trinity life that

from "The Four Stages of a Trinity Boy,"
Acta Diurna, June 1914

BOY STAGE ONE:
In the first place,
A Trinity boy of the Primary Grade,
To be quite correct, and properly made,
Should wear a blue cap, with a yellow "TS",
And be toted to school by his dear Governess,
When he marches to gym he should stand straight upright,
And hammer the floor with all of his might.
His lessons quite perfect he'll daily present,
And his teacher will give him one hundred percent.

ran parallel to the classroom world of Latin, math, and geography reveals richness beyond the catalog claims about relentless academic discipline and moral seriousness. School for boys is work to be gotten through en route to whatever might come next. It is also time to be well spent at that time, regardless of what might come next. This other-world of school peeks out in the remains of student publications and a few reminiscences that reach back to those years. *Acta Diurna* (daily proceedings)—the very name of the more or less monthly student newspaper from 1892 when it was founded by Sidney Aylmer-Small into the early 1930s, along with *Trinity Times*, which gradually took its place as the school newspaper from the mid-1920s—bespoke a place a-bustle with boys' life and not all of it mediated by adults. For every issue the boys wrote fiction and short essays, perhaps passed on, perhaps not, by English masters. "The Maid of Warsaw" (a "European romance") and "The Powder Boat" (a Civil War adventure set around Vicksburg) from 1909, "It Never Rains, But It Pours" (the rivalry of two boys for one girl that began with a risqué account of a telephone conversation where Elliot asks Alice out to the "Pink Lady" in Brooklyn), "The Organ" (apparently not by a musician: "Is it a freight train crossing a wooden bridge, or the cry of a sea-

sick peacock?") from 1911, "The Declaration of Independence" (a meditation on its importance in light of the Great War) from 1918, "The Devil Dog"
(an imagined story of the Western Front filled with "cheering American
boys destined to fill the gap that France's exhausted armies could not fill")
from 1919 and illustrated with an alluring Gibson-Girl-ish silhouette cap-
tioned "What a fool spring weather makes of a man!" Opposite the title page
of that issue appeared the honor roll of the fourteen Trinity alums who died
in the war: "*Dulce et decorum est pro patria mori.*" The same year, a luckier
alum reminisced about his trip to Europe on a cattle boat the last summer
before the war, and in 1925, a seventh grader wrote about a little "Christmas
romance" set in a wartime hospital, "A Fool There Was."[22]

Anniversary and graduation issues recorded valedictory and salutatory
addresses, praised athletic prowess, recorded notes about alumni, and printed
exchanges from other schools' publications. In his three-paragraph short
address, valedictorian C. A. Manning of the class of 1909 spoke about "in-
dissoluble bonds" between graduates and their soon-to-be-old school and
the privilege of graduating on the school's two hundredth anniversary. Spe-

BOY STAGE TWO:

O the Grammar School boy is the pride of your life;
Though he scarcely can whittle, he carries a knife.
His is useful in sundry and various ways:
He subscribes to the Acta, attends all the plays;
He sings in the choir, plays the drum and the fife;
And takes lessons in German, to bother the life
Of Herr Keil, the Professor.
His arithmetic lessons are never done well,
But no one can beat him in giving the yell;
Though his baseball and football are not over strong,
In spite of these facts, he wears his hair long.
For confidence, freshness, simplicity, joy,
There's nothing surpasses a grammar school boy.

cial thanks went to "the reverend rector, who has set for us to follow such an excellent example of Christian life," to trustees who "furnished the means," to faculty "who have so faithfully instructed us during the last four years." In 1911, valedictorian Winchester Donald Brunig talked of "more than the ordinary educational advantages" and praised Cole for his "knowledge of boys' characters" and his "strong sense of justice." Whether it was convention or a rule, such speeches all were short and all pretty much rang the same changes—reverent cadences representative of a whole era. They teased, too. In 1918, the senior class summarized its "statistics." Favorite pastimes in-cluded chewing gum, singing hymns, keeping still, and doing nothing. Under the list "He thinks he will be": aviator, musician, doctor, lawyer, busi-nessman, and soldier. Under "He will be": comedian, kicked-out, bench-warmer, bar-tender, broke. Under "dreams of," some boys pined for Prince-ton, more just for girls.[23]

Photographs of those classes complemented the portrait of the school building that began each year's catalogue. Taken on the school's front steps and reproduced across the vertical height of a page, they were studies in for-mality from the senior class on down, more straight faces than smiles. Every-one in the high school wore not a blazer and grays but a suit, and eighteen-year-olds in suits (rendered of course in black and white, as all probably in fact were) look older than eighteen-year-olds in something else: serious young men. Cole always posed with his graduates and always in his collar. A few freshman and some seventh and eighth graders could still be observed in knickers and knee socks, but everyone wore a tie, among them a few bows. Primary schoolers posed with Cole and their four female teachers, spread across the same front steps, a bit more disheveled, short pants abounding and even a sailor suit or three. Athletic teams posed in the gym, baseball players in white uniforms with the gothic Trinity "T" on their left sleeve. There were sometimes shots of the other interscholastic competitors in basketball, track, tennis, and the rifle team. (In the 1920s and 1930s, boys carried their rifles to school, on the subway.)[24] Grammar school boys played too, intramurally or "inter-class" as it was then said, baseball and basketball. During World War I, the fifth through eighth graders mounted a fife and drum corps that played, it was noted, to make the world "safe for democracy."[25] And there was a choir that sang at morning chapel: "Good singing at the morning service has much to do in stimulating and preparing us for the routine of the day."[26]

Athletics spoke, literally, to muscular Christianity and ideals of manli-

BOY STAGE THREE:
By your kind permission,
The High School boys are not boys at all;
They are men, every one of them, great and small;
And if you'll believe me, I'll tell you a joke;
When they get to corner, all of them smoke.
Each man has a chance to enter a 'Frat,'
And if he's elected, he's thankful for that;
But if he's rejected he goes off alone
And starts a fraternity all of his own.
The High School runs the Acta, and once a year for fame,
It gives a really, worthy play to perpetuate its name.
The High School men have dignity, school spirit, brains and poise;
Although they dress in modest taste, their neckties make a noise.
The High School men can tango; they dance quite up to date,
And when they do the "Turkey trot" they never "Hesitate."
And when the High School boys are made, they hold a fund of
  knowledge;
Some go to business, some to work but all get into college.

---

ness that Cole, like Ulmann before him, espoused. Everyone suited up and played at least in the gym, many on teams. An annual field day was held in late May in Van Cortland Park (also the home to Trinity baseball) and brought the whole school and alums together for sporting, competitive fun at the end of the school year. Classes of competitors were sorted out by a boy's weight, not his age, in hope of giving everyone a decent chance of success, and spectacle mattered as much as winning: In 1909, "Parents, sisters, sweethearts came up in crowds to see the big huskies and the little huskies perform." For newly designed medals that were "exceptionally heavy, the contestants strove like Greeks to win."[27]

It was a boys' school after all, and sports might be expected to have played a large role in "educating the whole boy." But so apparently did dramatics, the only other extracurricular activity in these years accorded something of the same attention as athletics. It is impossible to weigh exactly, but each year the Dramatics Society of the high school mounted a major production that in such a small school as Trinity would have had disproportionate impact. The plays were produced in the spring, at first at the Century Lyceum and the Berkeley Lyceum before moving in 1917 to the Plaza Hotel. Looking back, they all sound much the same, three-act comedies and "farces" with titles like "The Strange Adventures of Miss Brown" (1914), "The Time of His Life" (1917), "Hurry, Hurry, Hurry" (1921). The cast of players for "A Full House" from 1923 by Fred Jackson could stand for many in the genre and evokes a time of silly fun: "Parks, an English servant; Susie from Sioux City, a maid; Otilly Howell, a bride; Mrs. Winnecker from Yonkers, the aunt; Vera Vernon, a show girl; Dougherty, a police sergeant; and Mrs. Fleming, who owns the apartment." There was usually a accompanying musical program, that year by the "Canary Cottage Orchestra" with a program that included "Toot, Toot, Tootsie," "The Sheik of Alabam," and "Carolina in the Morning." Though the shows couldn't have lasted much past 11:00, the program noted the Grill at the Plaza stayed open till 1:00 A.M., for alums presumably.[28]

We have the plot summary from one of these zany efforts, "The Arrival of Kitty" (1919), a mix-up madcap where, as usual, the boys played the boys and the girls. It began with a summer hotel bellboy, Ting, taking charge in the absence of the manager. Enter William Winkler and his company of guests, Aunt Jane, Suzette her maid, and Jane who is Winkler's niece, who complain about the prices and quickly mix things up. Bobbie Baxter arrives and is in love with Jane, but when Winkler orders him away, Ting and Bobbie (old college friends) concoct a scheme where Bobbie stays, disguised as Kitty Benders who is expected by Winkler. He also expects the arrival of Benjamin More, whom Winkler wishes to marry Jane. More arrives, but before Winkler sees him he falls in love with Bobbie, who is dressed as Kitty. When the real Kitty appears, the confusion compounds, and when Winkler dismisses one Kitty from stage right, the other one enters stage left. Happy scene, curtain falls, loud applause.[29]

Cole was full of applause that first post-war year, 1919, for more serious reasons, too. He was a cheerful man who when asked how the war had affected the growing generation of schoolboys saw only the bright side. The war might have killed fourteen old boys and one master, but it also killed off the old American provincialism. Post-war boys were showing a fresh atti-

BOY STAGE FOUR:
Lastly,
The alumni are most funny men,
Who drop in on us now and then.
They always wear a restful smile,
As though they would the time beguile.
No matter how, in years gone by,
With taunting lip and wicked eye
They made the Master worry,
When they come back Alumni
They grasp the Master by the hand.
With words of joy and visage bald
They tell him how they loved him.
One said, "You don't remember me!
I used to sit in that back chair
And raise the deuce, I didn't care
About the precious moments then.
I wish I were back here again."
The Master smiled, for well he knew
The alumnus and the pupil too.
It takes twelve years and lots of fuss
To make a gorgeous Alumnus;
But when he's done and all complete,
He's proud to stand upon his feet
And give to Trinity the praise,
And drink her health through endless days.

—OLD BOY

tude to geography, once just an assortment of pink and brown bits on the map. "Today the schoolboy knows the natures of various peoples, understands many of their differences in language, race and customs, is familiar with their flags, the uniforms of their soldiers, the costumes of their civilians, and definitely visualizes their cities, villages and landscape." Geography had become an adjunct to history and broadened it: "In the past, we Americans have been content to paddle our own canoes . . . our viewpoint colored by provincialism and prejudice." Now boys were seeing the similarities (at least among the allies) in "Anglo-Saxon, French, Italian and other peoples" and that "we of the civilized nations must all stand or fall together, that we stand for the same general things." This was bound "to create on his growing and plastic mind a spirit of internationalism of the highest sort." The popularity of French was on the rise, and German he thought would return as the pendulum swung the other way, if only for reasons of sound self-interest: "In the great trade and industrial war sure to come between the English speaking and the Germanic peoples it will be essential for our professional and business men to understand the language of their competitors." The war had drawn attention to all sorts of technical gadgetry that naturally appealed to boys: electricity, wireless, aeronautics. Too young for the real things, Trinity boys made models in manual training class that Cole found fascinating. He watched one boy's test flight on the athletic field: "The propelling power was the result of an ingenious twisting of rubber bands, and the little plane a perfect duplicate of the real thing. It flew about 100 yards in each direction. Such work is a splendid mental developer for any boy, and is undeniably one of the great benefits of the scientific side of the war."[30]

Whether Trinity boys were really becoming a bunch of little Wilsonians, who knows? Cole certainly exaggerated. He was a man with a boyish streak. One detects little difference in what his boys said about themselves and their tone in saying it, between the "Trinity Boy" portrait from 1914 and Trinity through the 1920s. Politics, big events, the larger public world seemed remote. School sports, school spirit, school plays that were the furthest thing from serious drama, suggest a school that treated students forthrightly as the boys they were, and where the work was hard and the play was fun.

SCHOOL BOYS

On that template, Trinity produced, each year for all the years of Cole's tenure, a graduating class that never numbered much above thirty, and from which most boys went on to college. A few entered the military or "business" (generally a euphemism of boys whose financial circumstances kept them out of college, at least right away), though all, it is implied, got college acceptances.[31] In 1910, the listing of graduates still broke out into "Classical,"

"Scientific," and "Latin Scientific" groupings, though the destinations suggested little real difference. That year classical boys went to Amherst (John Carpenter), Yale (George Killian), Dartmouth (Allan McDougal), and the Naval Academy (William Popham and Battin Shelley). Scientific ones went to Yale (Hepburn Chamberlain), Princeton (Sandford Pegram), and West Point (Lambert Neff). Latin Scientific ones went to Amherst (Cecil Hall), Wesleyan (James Van Fleet), and Yale Medical College (Sidney Cornelius). The list from 1911 was typical of the college spread generally in these years: Trinity, New York University, Columbia, Lehigh, Yale, Harvard, Princeton. Five of twenty that year went directly into "business." Boys from the class of 1914 headed in addition to Dartmouth, Cornell, and Stevens Institute. In 1918, two boys enlisted in the Army's Aviation Corps, and one chose Worcester Polytechnic. In 1919, two went to MIT. Trinity's thirty-three graduates in 1931, beyond the usual northeastern and Ivy League suspects, could be found at Michigan (Cole's alma mater), Kenyon, Duke (two), and the University of the South at Sewanee.[32]

The roster of their names—references in school publications are to surnames, not Christian ones, which was how masters called the boys in those days—has about it a homogeneity comparable to what might have been found on the rolls of many an Episcopal parish of that era and indeed later ones. Trinity under Cole was an explicitly Episcopal place that attracted, mostly likely, a solid cadre of co-religionist families wishing that general atmosphere for their sons, though exactly in what proportion to non-Episcopalians is uncertain. The names, which of course could as likely have been the names of Presbyterians or Methodists or even Lutherans, we would today call WASP-ish northern European names: Chamberlain and Taylor, Smith and Bromley, Van Brooks and Symonds, McCullough and Muir. Before World War I, there were a number of boys of German or other clearly non-Anglo ethnicity: Donald Brünig, Arnaud Lachmund, Roderic Olzendam (all class of 1911). W. Dunkel and J. S. Hermann graduated in 1918.[33] Louis Kuehn, Trinity's sole Jew as best can be told, graduated in 1934.

We know little of the formal admissions process that took them all in; indeed, there probably wasn't much of one that extended beyond the rector's office where Cole looked candidates over, weighing traits he thought would make for their success at Trinity. The result was a like-sounding and of course like-colored pool. Some of them had come to Trinity early in their young lives. For the few years that records survive, in the 1910s, only one however, the Teutonic-sounding Donald Brünig, appears to have gone the full distance at Trinity, arriving in 1898 and graduating in 1911. In that class of twenty, seven boys had come up through the grammar school. Of 1914's class of sixteen, eight had. Of 1918's twenty, there were twelve. Of 1919's fifteen, there were only three.[34] This suggests that Trinity, though officially and proudly one school, did in fact divide into three parts, and that the three parts, or at least the two that divided around grade eight, were distinct entities with less than continuous student populations among them. Schools now, and presumably then, like well-performing students and families who come to stay. They reduce enrollment uncertainties and thus the cost and anxiety of finding replacements. Some Trinity boys, after eighth grade, obviously went off to boarding schools and so thinned the in-house high school pool. It would appear that a slight majority of the school's high schoolers were finding their way to Trinity from other places, doing as well there as Trinity "natives" and moving on successfully after that to the same sorts of colleges and careers.

Where precisely they had come from and how their origins might have changed over this long period is obscure. For the first reliable surviving record of their addresses (though not of their previous schools, though those likely as not correlate with public or parochial schools in those neighborhoods), we must reach forward to the very end of the Cole era, the school year 1937–38. The school then enrolled 260 boys, primary to high school, and the great majority not surprisingly were city boys. In the primary and grammar schools, students' home addresses divided more or less evenly between East Side and West (seventy-five East and sixty-five West), and those on the West Side were often but not always in the close vicinity of the West 91st Street school. Plus there were three suburbanites and six from boroughs other than Manhattan. In the high school, the numbers shifted in favor of the neighborhood. Thirty-three high schoolers came from across town, while sixty-one were from families on the West Side. Fourteen high schoolers then came from the suburbs and eleven from other boroughs.[35]

Relative proximity, of markets and customers, has determined the success or failure of many a business and other institutions too. While the numbers available for this period at Trinity are hardly conclusive, we do know that the neighborhood where Trinity proudly, and for years contently, found itself when Cole replaced Ulmann in 1903 was not the same neighborhood thirty years later. As it changed, there were bound to be associated anxieties in location-sensitive institutions situated there. It is not clear what level of anxiety visited Trinity, or that neighborhood change itself necessarily foretold dire consequences for the school.

LOCATION, LOCATION

When Trinity did finally land itself on West 91st Street in the 1890s, in a purpose-built building that it owned, not rented, it was with every plausible promise that the Upper West Side was becoming and would remain the place to be. The school had made that judgment not alone. The Ninth Avenue elevated railway had brought efficient public transportation west of the park by the 1880s and by the 1890s reached all the way to the Polo Grounds at 155th Street. Along side streets in the seventies, eighties, and nineties, residential real estate developers built rows of pleasant town houses, while on Riverside Drive the wealthy built more pretentiously in emulation of Fifth Avenue. The spread of apartment houses followed construction of The Dakota in 1884, as multiple-family dwellings shed, selectively at least, the old stigma of the tenement and took on solid middle-class respectability.

Advertisements in *Acta Diurna* afford a stroll around that mixed residential and commercial neighborhood and even hint of its ethnic mix. In 1906, Dover Farm Dairy still did business at 645 Amsterdam. Next door at 644, H. Neumann's Hardware also repaired furnaces, roofs, and dumbwaiters. Westminster Meat and Poultry Market traded at number 700. In 1909 "Alfred G. Davis—First class Fish and Oyster Market, Blue Points, Cape Cods, Crab and Terrapin Constantly on Hand" could be found at 587 Columbus Avenue. The boys could "After School Go Around the Corner to Pape's for Candy and Ice Cream, 646 Columbus Avenue between 91st and 92nd." J. M. Johannsen, "The Model Grocers," could be found at 686 Columbus. In 1914, "The Harvard" at 2371 Broadway shined shoes (5 cents) and cleaned hats. In 1918, Gross & Eschenberg, Grocers, did business at 611 Amsterdam near 90th. Between 92nd and 93rd on Columbus, Edward Haubner, "Fashionable Hair-Cutter," kept men and boys neat and trim. Frederick V. Sittig gave piano lessons at 153 West 80th, as did Marion Sheppard at 341 West 86th. By 1931, "Independent Radio Company" at Broadway and 88th offered Victor, Brunswick, and Columbia records and could "Make a Permanent Record of Your Voice, 50 cents and up." For the well-heeled, there was always Steinway Hall on West 57th where grands started at $1,375, with 10 percent down.

Regular presence through the years of others who weren't in the neighborhood suggest tastes and perhaps incomes. Brooks Brothers, then at Broadway and 22nd, pushed "Polo Ulsters, English Blazers and Mackintoshes." Rogers, Peet & Co. competed from three stores along Broadway with "Good Evening Clothes, Day Clothes, Hats, Shoes and Furnishings for Men and Boys." The Washington Shop, which was nearby at Broadway and 96th, purveyed "school colors in a tie, $1." At 214–220 East 23rd Street, James Potts & Co. sold prayer books, hymnals, and Bibles. Commonwealth Cigar Company in the Whitehall Building offered "A Quality Cigar for 5 cents." Then there were the New England summer camps: Camp Dudley, "Oldest YMCA, est'd. 1885," and Norway Pines on Casco Bay: "Healthy locale, approved sanitation, careful supervision."[36] The boys themselves sold the ads and learned something about how advertising worked in print publications. We do not know what ads cost, but Trinity boys believed that they had a list (themselves, parents, a few alums perhaps that could not have numbered a thousand) that posh advertisers should want to reach. Audience quality mattered. "An atmosphere of culture and refinement surrounds *Acta Diurna* families," their house ad to advertisers ran in 1918. "Twenty percent of them own their own motor cars, while 15 percent live in private houses. People of this character are worth advertising. By advertising in *Acta Diurna* you concentrate on a few hundred prosperous refined homes."[37]

"Refinement" was not just commercial, of course. Civic institutions had moved westward too and fed off the same sort of market—the American Museum of Natural History opened its first building in 1877, the Metropolitan Opera House in 1883, Carnegie Hall in 1891—adding cultural polish. Columbia University moved to its Morningside Heights location in 1897. Collegiate School moved to West End Avenue in 1891, soon followed by Trinity on 91st between Columbus and Amsterdam avenues. Mainline churches flourished there, too. Shearith Israel moved to Central Park West and 70th in 1897, and most conspicuously Bishop Henry Codman Potter of the Episcopal Diocese of New York announced plans in the late 1880s for what was planned to be the largest cathedral church in the world, the Cathedral of St. John the Divine at 110th Street and Amsterdam Avenue. Less conspicuous, but a part of the same general thrust of institution building, had been the decision in 1887 of Trinity Church to construct a chapel of ease on the Upper West Side to minister to the new neighborhood's prosperous and growing middle-class population. Named "St. Agnes," it would be massive, ornate, and, so it seemed at the time, built for the ages.[38]

The sad story of that great edifice and why it lasted hardly fifty years has been well told elsewhere, but it bears tangentially on its remote relative, Trinity School, as follows. Both institutions, chapel and school, were creatures of Trinity Church. The school of course had long been an independent corporation. The chapel was the church's direct offspring and ward. But the decision to place the chapel where it did when it did, which was also when and where Trinity School relocated itself, would end up holding several ironies. St. Agnes at first lived up to all the appearances of its physical grandeur, as a vibrant Episcopal home to the neighborhood and mission of Trinity Church on the booming Upper West Side. Its programs grew and flourished under talented leadership, particularly that of William T. Manning, vicar from 1903 to 1908 (then rector of Trinity Church and later Bishop of New York), and W. W. Bellinger, vicar from 1908 until the chapel's demise in 1943. In addition to a full roster of divine services, the place hosted a bevy of organizations—Woman's Auxiliary, Daughters of the King, Hospital and Flower Mission Committee, charitable Employment and Distribution Committee, Cadet Corps, Boy's Club, kindergarten—that served a diverse population and not just town-house dwelling Episcopalians. At its height early in the century, the vicar had five clerical assistants, an organist and choirmaster, and upward of 2,500 communicants. In 1903, a kindergarten was expanded into a free day school through the fifth grade, which in all likelihood attracted parents in search of Episcopal parochial education for their children but who could not afford or chose not to pay the fees of adjacent Trinity (for boys) or, after 1898, its sister school for girls, St. Agatha nearby (described later). The St. Agnes school, extended to grade seven in the 1910s and to grade eight in 1920, enrolled girls and boys together and, subsidized directly by Trinity Church, remained a free school until retrenchment began in 1918. It continued to operate until the end of St. Agnes itself, charging modest fees: $40 per annum for kindergarten to $100 for eighth grade. Trinity's Cole and Emma G. Sebring, headmistress of St. Agatha, apparently referred students to it,[39] which suggested to St. Agnes's historian close cooperation between "parallel institutions in the neighborhood."[40]

Parallel but different. From the 1920s on, St. Agnes, though maintaining the appearance of good health, began to slide. Though not formally a parish but a congregation within a parish, it depended on the parochial principle of drawing congregants from the local environs. A church that could not do that, and that could not depend on other subsidy, was doomed. Both sources of support faltered for St. Agnes at about the same time, and the result (per-haps hastened by the action of Cole's successor as head of Trinity School; see next chapter) was inevitable. Gradually its numbers, though large, began to decline, and in 1930 a survey commissioned by Trinity Church of St. Agnes's (and Trinity's) neighborhood showed why. That type of population—white, middle-class, and as it used to be said "Anglo-Saxon"—"to which the Epis-copal Church made an appeal was steadily diminishing."[41] The neighbor-hood was changing.

It was not just a local, parochial problem for Trinity Church, as it sought to "streamline" its activities, a term, though in keeping with stylistic inno-vations of the inter-war years, that was really euphemism for retrenchment that the Depression demanded.[42] Rather, the change that transformed the Upper West Side of the 1930s from that of the 1890s flowed from the rever-sal, starting in New York in the 1910s but evident in London and Paris ear-lier, of what had seemed an endless pattern of urban growth itself. The nine-teenth-century migration of Trinity School up Manhattan Island, as New York changed from Anglo-Dutch seaport to modern metropolis, like the building of chapels of ease by Trinity Church to serve new growing popula-tions, was driven by this dynamic evident then most recently in the late-nineteenth-century development of the West Side. The dynamic was not permanent, however, or at least its curve was not smooth. New York would grow again. But not for a time, and it was in that in-between time that St. Agnes Chapel (and St. Agatha School) fell through the cracks, and Trinity School had to learn to make some adjustments too.

Driven by suburbanization, the urge to spread and move out, the popu-lation of New York fell from just over 2.3 million in 1910 to just over 1.6 mil-lion in 1940, some 29 percent.[43] Some areas, however, like the Upper West Side escaped the general quantitative decline only to experience qualitative dislocation that was equally disorienting. Some moved out. Others moved in. Those who moved out were the white middle-class residents who lived in the stylish townhouses and new apartment buildings and who had made the area look such a promising field for Trinity Church, Trinity School, Protestants, and the educated and well-to-do generally, late in the previous century. Those who moved in, and who more than made up for the out-migrants in numbers, were both internal and external immigrants: black Southerners, Hispanics, and particularly Puerto Ricans, who in 1917 became American citizens, and, in the 1930s, European refugees from fascist Europe. Others migrated just within New York itself. As immigrants took hold, assimilated, and experienced prosperity, making the leap in one generation from Lower East Side to Upper West Side was not unknown. New York in general shrank; the Upper West Side grew more dense. But it grew more dense with newer New Yorkers, who were less well off than their Anglo predecessors for whom much of the area's housing stock had been custom designed and built. Owners made adjustments in order to match old housing supply with the new demand presented by a lower income market. Old townhouses (actually not that old at all) got divided up into rooming houses and even fell back into the dreaded category of tenement. What had once been large luxury apartments became more numerous and more crowded smaller ones. Jews, Catholics, Baptists, free-thinkers, the unchurched, but not Episcopalians filled up the old neighborhood where St. Agnes, and right next door Trinity School, still loomed physically so large.

Trinity Church decided early in the 1940s that as part of its ongoing streamlining, St. Agnes chapel had reached the end of its useful life, at least as an appurtenance of Trinity Church, and must be disposed of, though not necessarily demolished. By then few residents in the changed neighborhood, notes St. Agnes's historian, had much connection any longer with the place and few, at that time anyway, mourned its physical disappearance.[44] That fate, which was in large part the responsibility of Cole's successor, gets ahead of the story here. The demographic, neighborhood, and economic changes that led to the chapel's meteoric rise and thudding fall is context for Trinity School's own passage through the same years.

MONEY

Trinity Church would eventually off-load St. Agnes Chapel because, as the neighborhood changed, the market for the chapel's services declined but the expense of maintaining it did not. Trinity School would off-load at just the same time an appurtenance of its own for something of the same reasons. This was St. Agatha's School for Girls, which the New York Protestant Episcopal School Corporation, the independent entity that since 1806 constituted Trinity School and whose charter authorized maintenance of one or more schools in promotion of its aims, had established in 1898. There had been no girls at Trinity since 1838, and while the exact reasons for reaching out to that market sixty years later are not clear, it could probably partly be explained by the general opening up of educational opportunities for women in the second half of the nineteenth century and the founding of women's colleges like Vassar, Smith, and Barnard. Its stated aim was to provide girls with the fundamentals of a liberal education "in the hope that with their growth in power to understand and to learn they will develop a strong sense of responsibility and will take their places in the world as well-rounded members of society."[45] The new school opened at 257 West 93rd Street, then moved in 1903 to quarters in two adjoining brownstones at the corner of 87th and West End Avenue. At first it enrolled only grades one to eight but soon added a kindergarten and four-year high school. In 1908 it took up residence in a new purpose-built structure at that same West End address, one that for brick-and-limestone, Jacobean-styled stateliness and functionality rivaled Trinity's own quarters. In addition to classrooms, there was a roof-top play area and open-air gymnasium, a large indoor gym with showers and dressing rooms, a lunchroom, labs for science, and studios for art. More opulent than Trinity's, the baronial lobby featured a large fireplace, beamed ceiling, and heavy woodwork.

Through the 1920s St. Agatha's enrolled, for fees comparable to Trinity's, between 260 and 275 girls and educated them in a traditional academic curriculum that differed little from Trinity's, plus, as at Trinity, sound religious training. The high school offered both a general course and a college preparatory course, and there were a few gender-specific offerings then thought useful and appealing to girls, like sewing and weaving, ceramics and basketry. Methods were traditional: "untested theories of education are not made the basis of experimentation," though the school also claimed to adapt methods "to the individual student according to her special needs."[46] To 1910, some 20 percent of graduates went on to graduate from college; between 1910 and 1920, 40 percent; between 1920 and 1930, 64 percent. Most went to Smith, followed by Barnard, Vassar, Columbia, Bryn Mawr, Wellesley, and Radcliffe. St. Agatha girls acted in plays and played sports, and everyone was expected to conform to a formal dress code that for seventh and eighth graders and high schoolers forbade sleeves above the elbow. In gym, dark navy bloomers and white middy blouse with black tie were the drill. It was a middle-class Episcopalian place, before whose starchy headmistress for thirty-two of the school's forty-three-year lifespan, Smith graduate Emma G. Sebring, girls were known to curtsy.[47]

The financial health of Trinity during Cole's years is a composite of the two schools, which, though separate operating entities with regard to students, faculty, and facilities, rested on the same financial footing. Half a dozen checkpoints across the period illustrate the general relationship of income to expenses. The schools' income derived from paid tuition, rents from real estate, dividends, and interest. Of endowment income, dividend and interest income constituted the towering share during this period.[48] Expenses are somewhat less precise. Surviving reports made to the vestry of Trinity Church include a line item for "expense of school," which is not in fact that or at least not all of it, but rather the number of students enrolled multiplied by the fees charged them, however paid.[49]

In 1903, the "expense," that is, the fees due, of running the two schools amounted to $59,782 (Trinity $37,190, St. Agatha $22,592). Salaries constituted the lion's share of this number; that year they exceeded it at $60,502. That year the corporation had income of $168,494, which when one large extraordinary item tagged "St. Agatha's property fund" was subtracted left a surplus of $11,377. In 1912, income was $135,880, expenses $91,400 (Trinity $44,500, St. Agatha $47,000), surplus $37,700. In 1919, income was $163,500, expenses $115,600 (Trinity $56,600, St. Agatha $59,000), surplus $30,900. In 1926, income was $219,000, expenses $210,600 (salaries constituted $136,000, compared to $72,000 in 1919), surplus $8,400. In 1931, income was $231,000, expenses $227,000, surplus $5,600. In 1936, income was $152,000, expense $186,000, deficit $34,000.

For the same years, enrollment levels at Trinity wobbled but never wildly. In 1903 there were 310 boys, 285 in 1912, 297 in 1919, 310 in 1926, 300 in 1931, 230 (the low point) in 1936. (Tuition rates rose with grade level, in 1903 from $60 for a first grader to $225 for a high school senior, in 1936 from $250 for a beginner to $400 for a boy in high school.) At St. Agatha's, the curve rose, and fell, more steeply: There were 84 girls in 1903, 220 in 1912, 250 in 1919, 270 in 1926, 260 in 1931, and 210 in 1936.[50]

The connection point, and the variable on which the financial health of the school collided with Trinity's ancient warrant as a charity school, was the proportion of students who attended and whose parents paid for the privilege, and those whom the school paid, in effect, in order to get them to attend. Over the same time series, with the exception of one anomalous instance, in 1903 when the were just 8 free boys and 224 paying ones (full benefice or partial pay status is not uniformly broken out), full paying students were always in the majority, until 1936 when the balance shifted to 126 benefice boys to just 104 paying ones. In between, there were 168 pay to 117 on some level of benefice in 1912, 180 to 115 in 1919, 188 to 122 in 1926, and 170 to 130 in 1931. At St. Agatha's, the weighting indicates a generally higher ratio of tuition payers to benefice holders: 83 to 27 in 1903, 196 to 57 in 1919, and 202 to 62 in 1931. At Trinity, it may be less remarkable that paying students were indeed in the majority than the fact that boys on some level of subsidy constituted such a consistently strong minority. The cost of their subsidy was substantial, and the conditions for receiving it were never particularly well spelled out. "A number of benefices and free scholarships and partial remissions of tuition fees are granted each year," the Year Book repeated year after year, "to pupils who demonstrate that they need and deserve such concessions." Cole appears to have judged candidates subjectively pretty much as they came along, in his role as dispenser of Trinity's grace and favor.[51] It was an expensive habit.

Trinity's and St. Agatha's financial records at least were frank about it, as if it was a clearly accepted part of the business. Though "poor boys" (and girls, counting in St. Agatha) were no longer spoken of, worthy ones certainly were. In every year's report, "free education" was the line item that enumerated that sum needed from endowment to pay the fees of those who couldn't pay or who Cole (and Emma Sebring) decided shouldn't have to. The corporation's endowment (mortgages and bonds, but no equities) plus real estate rental income for this period ranged in value from $1 million to $3 million, and even the draw upon it required by an unrelenting high level of benefices for long did not exceed the income available from it.[52] In 1912, "outlay for free education" at both schools came to some $43,000 on an endowment of $1.6 million that yielded some $88,000. In 1919, subsidies called for $50,000 on endowment of $1.8 million yielding $98,000. In 1926, subsidies called for $111,000 on endowment of $2.3 million yielding $120,000. In 1931, $118,000 for subsidies came from income of $124,000 on endowment worth $2.5 million. Then in 1932, financial values, if not educational ones, changed, as the country and the city tumbled down into the Depression. Between April and June of that year, the corporation slid $26,000 into deficit as endowment income fell. Worse was to come. In the fiscal year ending in June 1933 the red ink ran to $44,000. Three more years followed with deficits over $30,000, and in 1937 moderated to $11,000.[53] When three relatively smaller deficit years from 1927 to 1929 are added in, this came to some $207,000 to be charged against principle.

This was dire but not devastating. In 1936 (June 30), the corporation's endowment in securities, which in 1932 had been valued at $2.4 million, had slipped to just slightly more than $1 million, its total assets slightly over $3 million. There was wrestling with both the expense and the income side. Salaries were reduced and maintenance deferred. Tuition was raised, collection tightened up, and benefices and remissions reduced (which also caused enrollment to slump).[54] When operations returned, modestly, to the black in 1938, it was due almost entirely to increased income on real estate held for investment. Readjustment of investments and the exchange of various properties in connection with the acquisition of 5 Riverside Drive and 450 West End Avenue resulted in reinstating much of the loss in income that had been suffered through the necessity of foreclosing a large number of mortgages and the consequent taking over of unprofitable and less desirable real estate. Income from tuition proved more stubborn. While Trinty's nudged upward, St. Agatha's went down.

Return to a small operating surplus was welcome relief but fragile, and though gains had been made in the right direction, treasurer C. Aubrey Nicklas delicately put it thus: "Our financial condition, while it has improved considerably, is by no means healthy." Moreover, a technical cloud loomed over the acquisition of 5 Riverside Drive and 450 West End in that other real estate was used in connection with those purchases, and the cost of the exchanged property was used as the basis for determining the book value of the new property. This resulted in the new properties being carried on the corporation's books for about $1 million more than they were actually worth. On other real estate, received as a result of foreclosure of mortgages and where liquidation was probable, further capital shrinkage could be foreseen. Added up, on the basis of the asset value on the corporation's balance sheets by the late 1930s, there was an erosion of the estate of some $1.25 million, "with no prospect in view of the recoupment of any part thereof."[55]

That of course must have been the frightening part: that a financial condition once deemed merely to have been "by no means healthy" might degenerate into one that was fatally unhealthy. Income in the short term could be enhanced just so much, and the two biggest expense items directly within the corporation's control were not, through Cole's time, controlled very much at all. These were the cost of subsidizing tuition and the cost of operations that could be construed as extramural, meaning the parallel operation of St. Agatha's, which, though it had its own tuition stream, shared the same sparse endowment resources as Trinity. The decision finally to address those costs belonged not to Cole but his successor, who would also conspire to buy St. Agnes Chapel from Trinity Church and promptly raze it to the ground for playing fields. St. Agnes, St. Agatha, and the charity tradition at Trinity would collapse in on one another at about the same time and for related reasons reflected in the corporation's generally weakening finances.

ALTERNATIVES

Those finances, however modestly buffered by endowment, related ultimately to the market for the educational services that the school offered. Absence of admissions records makes precision impossible on this point. All anecdotal evidence, however, points to a student body of middle-class boys (and at St. Agatha's, girls), who were mostly Protestant, and likely predominantly Episcopalian.[56] Names suggest few Italians, Hispanics, perhaps a Jew or two. Pictures reveal no people who were not white. In the large polyglot backdrop of New York City, Trinity and St. Agatha's were miniscule and elite, even more so, relatively, than the denomination that sponsored them. Among churched New Yorkers, Episcopalians represented a small minority, and only a small portion of those chose to send their children to Trinity and its sister. Demand for what these schools offered would appear to have been modest in this period. Though we do not know how many boys and girls might have been turned away, the persistent policy of tuition subvention would suggest that Cole's belief in Trinity's charity mission dovetailed with a need to attract students and fill places. Trinity and St. Agatha's after all were places that offered traditional academic schooling in an overtly Christian setting and, for many, made it available at a discount off the list price. It is possible to picture therefore a nonvirtuous circle in which relatively weak demand met a supply that, while not high-priced relative to the private competition,[57] was not free either and thus was at a competitive disadvantage with the public alternative.

New York's city public schools from the turn of the century through World War II offered a robust array of alternatives for all sorts and conditions of students. This was less by design than happenstance, as progressive and traditional ideas about schooling, how it should be administered and controlled, vied for influence and institutional power. The public system, while some criticized it as overcentralized, gradually took in and digested much of the essence of progressive theories about education and saw itself as a leading agent of social amelioration and progress. From limited old-time notions much shared by Trinity, that the school was a place that fundamentally dispensed literacy and numeracy—reading, writing, and arithmetic—progressive thought envisioned the school more expansively and extended the reach of its responsibility to areas once reserved to home, church, and community. This occurred at the same time that new immigration and compulsory attendance laws brought into the system children once bound for trade or the streets and that threatened to overwhelm it. Between 1900 and World War I, New York's schools register doubled to 800,000 students, many still requiring cultural assimilation and many, so it was thought, largely unsuited for traditional academic education.[58]

Thus began a duel that would last the century and more between competing ideals of education: progressives' penchant for "meeting the needs" of diverse students by broadening curricular offerings, and traditionalists who stuck by mastery of subject matter for all comers. The city experimented seriously with the Gary System (inspired by John Dewey and created for U.S. Steel's model company town in northern Indiana and an example, in pure culture, of progressive education ideas in action) as a solution to overcrowding and insufficient practical education. Opponents countered, likening the appearance of vocational tracking of children who tested poorly and whose needs thus looked less academic, to the old Lancasterian system and the specter of public schools fit only for those not bound very far up life's ladder.[59]

Ultimately, politics moderated reform ideology, and the city just built schools. In the 1920s, New York City spent $300 million to create places for 475,000 more students.[60] Progressive ideas, which earlier had focused on improving society through the agency of the school, shifted to liberating individual potential of school students and were, in the words of education historian Diane Ravitch, "bowdlerized beyond recognition." Social workers and psychologists descended on classroom teachers and principals to figure out which students needed what and who might be maladjusted and who was not. Meantime, the school bureaucracy standardized "even individualization" with practices and regulations that may have assured fair treatment for all but also rendered the whole enormous system mechanistic and impersonal.[61]

Demography reinforced the perception that the public system, however imperfect, was in fact a success for most New Yorkers. In the Depression, enrollment dropped (from 1.4 million to 827,000 between the mid-1930s and mid-1940s), federal assistance boosted personel and facilities, over-crowding eased, and the city's elite public high schools turned out high academic achievers. This was a period of lull between great waves of immigration, and it was deceptive. It was the same time when Trinity and St. Agatha, which displayed little if any infiltration of progressive ideas and were immune to public political battles over how best to educate the great mass of young New Yorkers, experienced their own falling enrollments and financial hard times. The connection here is indirect, but it is possible to surmise that if the public schools had not settled out as well as they did and performed at a level to satisfy most constituents, then there might have been flight to the private alternative thirty years before this occurred. That would have left the private schools overwhelmed too and, with their tiny capacity, would have rendered them necessarily even more elite than they became.

Between the end of the nineteenth century and the end of Cole's time at Trinity, the corporation dispensed on an average $72,000 per year in "free education," for the period some $2.5 million.[62] Had it not done so and had those funds been on account in the late 1930s, then its condition would have been far different when Cole at last retired. On the other hand, it is worth wondering whether if the corporation had not thus subsidized a substantial minority of its student body, might it not have foregone a substantial slice of that enrollment and slipped below that critical mass needed to conduct such a school of such a quality? (It is possible to argue that St. Agatha fell below that level anyway, but would it have fallen even faster without the lure of "free education"?) Whichever outcome, it is not hard to imagine Cole responding with a gentle "So what?" Surely God would provide for Trinity. He always had.

Cole was not oblivious and did his best. But he felt the bind. "I have tried to keep the total [benefices and remission of fees] down as well as I could and have made very few grants to new entrants," he wrote in 1936, "but of course the material increase in tuition rates makes the [dollar] total much larger than it would have been two years ago for the same number."[63] The problem was not the performance but the principle. At Trinity, Cole was the last apologist for the charity tradition in the Episcopal context, and as best we know was not particularly conflicted about the matter. Indeed, he believed that it was Trinity's moral responsibility *not* primarily to measure success by the sum of its accounts, or by the luster of its college placements (the very term belonged to the future), but by the quality of the life each of his boys lived each day at school, for the time long or short he had them there. Of course Trinity prepared boys for college, where most of them went; it was a "prep" school through and through. But Trinity was also a place inside Cole's head: a place unto itself whose worth related only indirectly to measurable outcomes. A Trinity education may have yielded no "degree," yet if all the Ivies had vanished just as any class of Trinity seniors from this era was set to graduate, they could still claim—and Cole would certainly have claimed for them—to be educated young men.

To this day, Cole's portrait hangs in the anteroom to the headmaster's office in the original 1893 building. He is dressed, how else, in clericals, and one imagines him cradling a prayer book. Matthew Dann, who had come to Trinity to teach math and French the same year that teacher/memoirist Bruner-Smith came to teach English, 1927, and who followed Cole into the rector's-turned-headmaster's office ten years later, wore for his portrait a business suit and cradled a ledger.

SIX *Managing for the Middle*

ometime in the mid to late 1930s, something changed. A younger rector soon to be called by the more secular title of "headmaster," layman Matthew Edward Dann, replaced an older long-serving incumbent, priest Lawrence T. Cole. Though it had been a long while since Trinity had had a nonordained head, this had happened before. Personnel changed routinely, but not the school necessarily, at least not much.

With this changeover however, from Cole to Dann, commenced one of the most significant transitions in the school's long history, certainly the biggest since the nineteenth-century shift from charity to private Episcopal school. It marked a divide the far side of which Trinity still travels toward an ever modernizing, secularizing institution. What inkling the school's leaders at the time had of this shift remains a question; key documentation is missing. We may suppose that the near view trumped the far, as they struggled with the day-to-day, year-to-year business of administering the institution. But those actions added up and in time left behind them something new.

Cole had headed Trinity in settled circumstances that did not really call upon him (at least not until near the end of his time) to lead it. All his successors, starting with Dann, would be expected to lead it and increasingly to manage it. Managing entails deploying scarce resources to achieve certain desired ends. For Cole, both the ends and the resources were more or less givens. For all his successors, the ends would from time to time be subject to occasional reinterpretation, and the resources would never again be taken for granted.

Historically, Trinity had never much felt at pains to explain itself. This was still decades before schools had departments of external communications, but the very notion of doing so was remote. If the place could be said to have had a "style," reticence described it: the Rev. Dr. Cole and his happy Episcopalian boys. This changed slowly, but we can spot the beginning.

NEW LOOK

Available testimony indicates that Trinity during Cole's era was nothing if not a warm and friendly sort of school, once a boy was ensconced on the inside. Beginning with Dann, it remained friendly but the attitude changed toward finding more boys. In part, this flowed from the financial hard times of the 1930s. Enrollment was wobbly, the 91st Street building was showing signs of wear, and once-grand visions beyond it (St. Agatha's) were wearing out too. In part, it was Dann himself. Though he had started out at Trinity in 1927 teaching French and then math, Dann was no academic. He had an M.A. in economics from Columbia (1927) and had worked as an economist at Chase National Bank. As he moved through assistant to headmaster positions (at Trinity, St. Agatha, and Trinity-Pawling), he made administration his specialty and left the classroom largely to others. His comfort and competence with the business side of schooling were evident in his appointment to the board of trustees in 1943, the first active headmaster to serve alongside the corporation's other legal governors.[1] This sensibility was evident from the outset.

Presumably Dann's work, the new 1938–39 edition of Trinity's Yearbook,[2] the school's public face to the world, came out in a larger trim size and sporting if not quite a new look then some notably fresh features. This was not just cosmetic. Dann's first catalogue opened with the same stately engraving of the West 91st Street building familiar for years, but no longer was the picture alone allowed or expected to convey the whole message. Beneath, someone had crafted new words. "Trinity School was old when the United States of America was born. For more than two generations before the Colonies declared their independence, the school had been training the boys of New York and its environs . . ." The appeal to history and not religion as identity, and a distinguishing identity at that, might have seemed an obvious one at so ancient a place as Trinity, but it suggests a key transition. It had not been put quite that way publicly, that is, for external public consumption, before. Whatever the value of history as heritage, the credential of longevity alone was not enough to do the job then at hand. That was making Trinity grow, and that took selling.

So the prospective Trinity parent and student were directed to look not back but ahead: "For leadership in all walks of life, and since 1709 Trinity has continued an unbroken record in this field in which she was a pioneer."[3]

That claim, that this is what Trinity was all about, was untrue literally. Eighteenth-century Trinity boys (and girls) had been trained up very modestly indeed and to lead nothing at all but just to get on. By later in the nineteenth century, many graduates of the upper school began to go to college and to elite ones at that, but then to advertise the idea of schooling for leadership was not the done thing. Starting in the late 1930s, however, Trinity adopted a more forward strategy. "Marketing" is an anachronism for that time, but from the way Trinity then began to describe itself, the need to capture and hold a market via claims of both altruism and utility is evident. This was because Dann had a different sensibility and training than his predecessors. Thus in the catalogue, the "what-the-place-is-about" verbiage (or statement of purpose) got moved to the top where it couldn't be missed. There were two parts to this—the aims of the school and the way it was organized to meet them—akin to a loose sort of strategy with a fairly rigid reinforcing structure.[4]

Trinity, it was said, aimed to send boys into the larger world with the "desire and capacity for leadership, and a strong sense of responsibility to society." To do so, it employed assets both ancient and modern. The school was obviously very old and implicitly had survived for good reasons: age impresses. That it was also claimed forthrightly to be "modern" appealed to the spirit of the times. In the 1930s modernism in art and architecture was an intellectual fashion, the word itself a rebuke to the fustiness of Victorianism. At its extreme in education, progressive, child-centered approaches to schooling made headway as disciples of John Dewey and Francis Parker experimented with a new generation of children. This was not Trinity, then or later: "Untested theories of education are not made the basis of experimentation." There was "openness," however, to "better methods" for preparing boys for college and "for leadership in American life." No two boys were alike, not exactly, and the differences required that the school "adapt it methods to the individual student according to his special needs." In some other setting or in another era, those might have been fighting words, code for a creeping child-centeredness and subversion of skills-mastery/body-of-knowledge pedagogy. With thundering modesty, however, the next sentence explained that at Trinity, openness to better methods just meant that "all classes are small."

The way organizations describe themselves seldom overlays exactly the way they actually behave. It would be decades, picking just two examples, before Trinity in striving to meet its markets would spice the curriculum with any significant electives and abandon coat-and-tie for everyday dress. But surface language is the place to look for first suggestions of change deeper down, and the words started to change with Dann.

There was new emphasis on facilities, the buildings and equipment that the prospective student could see. This took moxie, considering that Trinity's physical plant was by then showing signs of advancing middle age and deferred maintenance. Dann talked a good game even if he couldn't yet quite play one. To hygiene-conscious parents, he touted the West 91st Street brownstone as a place suffused with light and sunshine, with excellent heating and ventilation assuring "fresh air of regulated temperature at all times," with newly installed modern shower rooms and new lavatories with "the finest equipment: the best in sanitary facilities."

Cleanliness, godliness, and busy-ness: Aside from academics, the place sounded like a beehive or a Boy Scout troop. There was studio work in pottery, art, and sculpture at seats (pity southpaws) "so placed as to allow an abundance of light to fall on the desk from the left side of each boy." The gym may have been cramped but it was high up, "light and well-ventilated." The school's ample hallways were used afternoons for ping-pong and fencing. Outdoor athletics (in basketball and baseball Trinity competed in the Eastern Private Schools League) made use of playgrounds in Central Park, and for the older boys the school leased tennis courts. The rifle range, "carefully worked out to avoid danger" and with a ventilating system that changed the air every five minutes, occupied the basement. The Trinity Rifle Club boasted membership in the National Rifle Association, and the boys received "splendid instruction in the proper handling of guns" under the supervision of a master qualified as an expert marksman. The rifle team also competed interscholastically.

A student council represented all things lofty: "it provides the leadership and unified responsibility necessary to the maintenance of good student morale." Membership brought "honor, responsibility and privilege." For the brainy, there was a chess club that played every afternoon, for the artistic a glee club and orchestra ("boys share the pleasure derived from group singing" and "find music a delightful hobby"), a dramatics club ("to give members practical experience in the interpretation and production of outstanding plays," viz., in the Lower School "Six Who Pass While the Lentils Boil," in the Upper School "The Milky Way"), dancing classes (once a week in the evening for high schoolers, and in the afternoon for the little boys). The student paper, *The Trinity Times*, published every other week. Social events "of interest to parents and students alike" allegedly abounded: the Lower School Parents' Dinner, the Fathers and Sons Dinner, trips to concerts, musicals, and exhibits around the city, and of course each year's Closing Exercises where older boys graduated and prizes for everyone (twenty-five of them in 1938) got handed out.

Fresh and appealing photographs of school life illustrated all this, and what now looks charming was then intended to invite more applications. Upper School boys posed on the basketball court in what would have been shiny blue and gold striped shorts and black high-tops, concentrating on a (successful, the ball just about to dunk) free throw. Two unmasked fencers smartly crossed their rapiers. Middle schoolers in neckties, knickers, and knee socks made toy sailboats and biplanes in manual arts class. Third graders wove baskets and made pottery. Two first graders in shorts and short sleeves played at blocks.

Not everything was thought to promote the school equally well. "Religion in the School" got five lines, sandwiched between "Home Study" ("parents should be most discriminating in the kind of assistance they give their boys at home . . .") and "Transportation," which explained how the buses ran. This may have been because religion—that is, the Christian religion pretty much as set forth in the Book of Common Prayer—was such an assumed presence at Trinity that nothing much else needed to be said. Indeed, history got the credit, or the blame, for its presence. "Because of its origin and history, Trinity School lays emphasis on the moral and religious, as well as on the intellectual and physical development of its boys." That boiled down, formally, to opening chapel each morning and one period per week of instruction in church history and Christian doctrine, and informally to keeping the "high moral tone" befitting gentlemen in the making. No witness from those years remembers anything much more profound than that: Behavior trumped doctrine.[5] Or, the downplaying of religion might have been because Dann, though a faithful churchman himself, determined to put down Trinity's enrollment net as ecumenically as possible. Either way, anyone who happened to be less than fervent in the faith, and anxious about being stigmatized or proselytized, needn't have worried.[6]

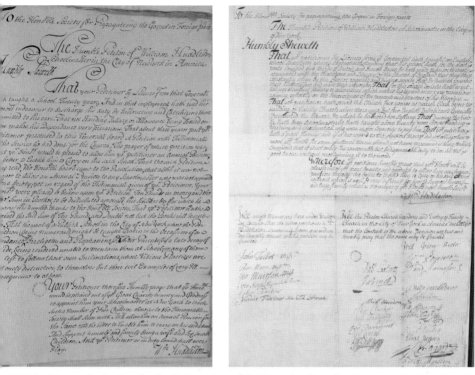

Petition to the Society for the Propagation of the Gospel, asking for the appointment of William Huddleston as schoolmaster to teach poor children in New York, 1709. (Trinity School Archives)

Fire destroyed the Charity School of 1750, reported in the *New York Weekly Journal,* February 27, 1750. (Trinity School Archives)

A bowl by silversmith Adrian Bancker commemorates the fire that destroyed Trinity's "new" school, halfway through the eighteenth century. (The Metropolitan Museum of Art, Anonymous Loan. L.1968.74 Photograph ©2008 The Mtropolitan Museum of Art)

March 5, 1750.   THE   NUMB. 372

NEW-YORK GAZETTE
REVIVED IN THE
WEEKLY POST-BOY.

With the Freshest Advices, Foreign and Domestick.

'Tis a miserable Thing to be injured by One, 'tis in vain to complain of.
       L. Veritam.

IN a well regulated Community, publick as well as private Vices, are discountenanced and punished; but when they are pass'd over, either thro' Fear of offending the Perpetrators of them, or to curry Favour with Men in Power, it then ceases to be a well regulated Community; and the Members that constitute such a Body, deserve to be treated with the utmost Contempt: When Magistrates are elective, the People think themselves safe from being oppressed; but when those chosen, neglect their Duty, and don't punish Offenders because of their great Estates, or Alliances, those Magistrates may then be justly termed Oppressors of the People.

It is a very melancholly Reflection, to think how different Punishments are inflicted for the same Crime; and that for no other Reason, but because the Quality of the Offender, and not the Heinousness of the Offence, is what the Magistrate considers. If a poor Fellow not worth a Groat, gets Drunk, rambles about Town, and meeting with a Man's Daughter, should offer any Violence to her; upon a Complaint made, he is immediately taken up, and put in the Stocks till he is sober; if then, he can't get Security for his good Behaviour, he is whipt, and sent out of Town: The Magistrate is extolled for his Justice in the Case, and we all say, If such Crimes are not punished, how can a Man's Daughter be safe in walking the Streets. On the other Hand; If a rich Man happens to be guilty of the same Offence, occasioned by drinking too much, upon Complaint being made, the Magistrate advises the Party complaining, to make it up; adding, that if the Gentleman had not been drunk, he would not have offered any Violence to your Daughter; and I am sure, says the Magistrate, I will answer for him, he shall ask your Pardon. Thus the Magistrate becomes an Advocate for the Gentleman, instead of a Judge; the Consequence of which is, that the Gentleman goes on in the same Course of Wickedness; full well knowing, that the Magistrate dare not punish him; and he founds his Argument upon this Reason, the Magistrate is elective; if he dares punish me, for abusing my Neighbour, he shall not be chosen the next Year, and I will make all the Interest in my Power against him. Had the poor Man that was whipped for the same Crime, presumed to have taken some more Liberty in his Cups, such as breaking open Doors, breaking Windows, and attacking People in their Houses, (which ought to be their Castles) the poor Man, without Dispute, would have been committed to Goal, without Bail or Mainprize, in order to undergo such Punishment, as the Law would inflict for such Offences; and if the Man had been so unhappy, as to have exercised his Fury upon the Habitation of a Man of Interest and Power, much Question, whether any Thing could have saved his Life, but a Pardon. Now, why the rich Man should be acquitted, and the poor Man put to Death, for the same Crime, I leave to the Learned in the Law to determine: I confess, I can't reconcile it to the Notions I have of Right and Justice. I believe your Divines will tell you, That no Wealth, tho' ever so considerable, will acquit a Criminal before a Tribunal, whose Justice is immutable.

Self-Love is so prevailing a Passion, that we are really blind to our own Imperfections; yet Men are seldom so abandoned as to injure their Neighbours; either by Word, or Deed, till they have deprived themselves of the little Reason God hath given them; and then, not only their Tongues, but their Hands are let loose, to wound and abuse all those that are so unhappy as to differ from them in Sentiments. Walter Moyle, Esq; in a Charge he gave to a Grand Jury, says, "Drunkenness for this last Age, seems to be "the prevailing Vice of the English, and has justly rendered us the "Scorn and Reproach of all our Neighbours, who pretend to more "Civility and Politeness of Manners: This Vice is its own Nature "carries so much Brutality with it, is so notoriously contrary to "the Laws of God and Man, is so scandalous to the Profession of "Christianity, and so unworthy of a rational Creature, that the

" bare naming it, is exposing it to the Abhorrence of all good " Men, and it needs no Aggravations to make it blacker."

I have no Intention, by any Thing I have said, to prevent People from taking a chearful Glass; so far from it, I think it one of the grand Cements of civil Society: It is an old Observation, and I believe a true One, That where good Sense is fashionable, and a genteel Behaviour in Esteem, Gluttony and Drunkenness can be no reigning Vices.

Perhaps I shall be told, that the Doctrine I advance is of dangerous Consequence, that it is putting a poor Man upon the Level with a Rich, and such Things ought to be avoided; To which I say, the poor Man hath as much Right to Justice, as the Rich; that he is as useful to the Community, in his Station, as the wealthy Man, and ought to have his Liberty and Property equally protected; and all Governments where that is not done, their Duration must be short. I shall conclude, that in this World nothing is permanent, that which does not grow better, will grow worse.

Mr. Parker, Your inserting the following Lines on the Loss of the Charity-School, which was destroyed by Fire, on Friday the 23d of February last, will oblige several of your Readers, particularly Your humble Servant,   W.

COME, see this Edifice in Ruin lye,
Which lately charmed each Spectator's Eye;
See, and lament the well proportion'd Frame,
Consum'd by a relentless cruel Flame.
On the bold Structure when it first was rais'd,
Each kind Contributer with Pleasure gaz'd;
They gaz'd, and wish'd it might remain in Peace
To Ages: and, the Christian Flock increase,
Mourn, Mourn, ye Orphans, its untimely Fate,
See, and lament the Shortness of it's Date;
Founded for you, in Charity design'd
To improve your Parts, and cultivate your Mind.
But let our just Concern, for that give Way
To grateful Thoughts, which we are bound to pay;
God's House remains, let that our Thanks excite,
With Gratitude this Miracle recite.
The Flame fierce flying touch'd the hallow'd Spire,
The Flames attack'd it, and the Winds conspire
To set the Church, the House of God, on Fire.
But now, God's interposing Power we spy,
To save his Temple he himself draws nigh;
Nought but a Power Divine, in such a Case,
Could give the Means employ'd the least Success,
They too deserve our Thanks and great Regard,
Who gloriously such mighty Dangers dar'd.
On, may they live to serve and bless the Lord,
And with his faithful Church his Love record.
Let us go with Joy into his House of Prayer,
And sing with one Consent his Praises there.

Extract of a Letter from Capt. Badger, of the Brig Sarah, belonging to this Port, dated Madeira, January 18, 1749.

" Ten Days after my Departure from New-York, and in the
" Lat. 35, 20. Long. 56 and 52, I met with a Ship in Distress,
" full of Water, and sinking; I immediately got out my Boat,
" and brought the People, Twenty-Five in Number, on board my
" Vessel: This Ship was from Boston bound to Barbados, and
" belonging to London, commanded by Andrew Dewar. The
" Number of Men on board, obliged me to the Allowance of a
" Pint of Water and an Half, a Man for twenty four Hours; upon my Arrival
" here the British Consul took the People under his Care.

City of,   Pursuant to an Order of Common
New-York,   Council, dated the 23d of February, 1749.
NOTICE is hereby given to all Persons who are indebted to the Corporation, to come and discharge what they respectively owe in Arrear, without any further Delay, to Isaac DeBrer, Esq; &c.

Contemporary poem, marking the fire that destroyed Trinity's "new" schoolhouse in 1750. (Trinity School Archives)

Trinity accounts in the eighteenth century were simple, but meticulous. This sample from school ledgers for 1761. (Trinity School Archives)

Trinity has stood as an independent corporation under the laws of the State of New York since 1806, with provisions periodically revised. This version is from 1841. (Trinity Church Archives)

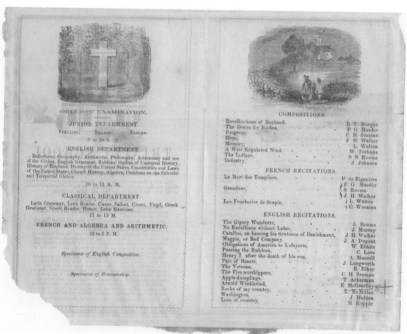

Semi-annual program of examinations, 1856. Exams lasted all day and emphasized oral presentation. (Trinity School Archives)

2.

Receipts:—

<table>
<tr><td></td><td></td><td>$. ¢s</td></tr>
<tr><td>1857. May 1.</td><td>Amount of Balance in Bank.</td><td>4050,97</td></tr>
<tr><td></td><td>Interest collected,</td><td>950.</td></tr>
<tr><td></td><td>Ground Rents.</td><td>2235.</td></tr>
<tr><td></td><td>Rents,</td><td>4300.</td></tr>
<tr><td></td><td>Bond and Mortgage paid off.</td><td>3200.</td></tr>
<tr><td></td><td>J. N. Wells, nett am. Rents "Baker Farm".</td><td>1208, 32</td></tr>
<tr><td></td><td></td><td>15,944, 29.</td></tr>
</table>

Payments:—

<table>
<tr><td>Salaries,</td><td>3,369, 09</td></tr>
<tr><td>Beneficiaries,</td><td>1942, 50</td></tr>
<tr><td>Taxes and Insurance,</td><td>482, 28</td></tr>
<tr><td>Repairs and Supplies,</td><td>811, 63</td></tr>
<tr><td>Books & Stationary,</td><td>939, 82</td></tr>
<tr><td>Rev Dr Morris, 3 quarters Stipend,</td><td>1200.</td></tr>
<tr><td>Annuity; Taxes & Expenses "Baker Farm",</td><td>2535, 90.</td></tr>
<tr><td>Rent to 1st February,</td><td>372, 42.</td></tr>
<tr><td></td><td>11653, 64</td></tr>
<tr><td>Balance on hand :</td><td>$ 4290, 65°</td></tr>
</table>

The Annual Income of the Corporation (Exclusive of the Baker Farm)
may be estimated at , as at present rented and invested , as
follows: viz:—.

Financial record, 1857. (Trinity School Archives)

Trinity School.

FOUNDED 1709.

Report of *McGeachy* for the
Month ending *June 3d* 185*9*.

SUBJECTS.	Number of Lessons in the Month	MARKS.	Number of absences from Lessons.		
RELIGIOUS INSTR.	7	52		Total Marks for Lessons,	1101
LATIN,	20	157		Credit for Punctuality,	200
GREEK,	20	191		Credit for Behaviour,	200
MATHEMATICS,	20	141			1501
ENG. GRAMMAR,				Deduct	
SPELLING,				(a) For Days Absence,	
COMPOSITION,	14	94		(b) Demerit for Lateness,	
DECLAMATION,				(c) Demerit for Behaviour,	
READING,	9	65		Nett Total,	1501
WRITING,	12	119		N. B.—10 is the greatest credit for each Lesson.	
GEOGRAPHY,	11	102			
HISTORY,	8	63		*The Parent or Guardian is requested to return this paper with his signature affixed, as soon as possible after inspection.*	
FRENCH,	12	117			
GERMAN,				This Report is considered *Good*	
SPANISH,				CHARLES D. MORRIS, Rector.	
	133	1101			

M L McGeachy

The Rector wishes to impress upon Parents the importance of a careful scrutiny of these Reports. An abstract of them is periodically laid before the Trustees, and their attention is specially called to the regularity or irregularity of each boy's attendance. It is the fixed resolution of the Board not to suffer any boy to continue to share in the bounty of the School, who does not, by his conduct, diligence and punctuality, show that he and his parents appreciate and are anxious to retain the advantages of his position.

The June 3, 1859, report card of Charles Edward Alleyne McGeachey.
(Trinity School Archives)

Trinity scholars in 1881. (Trinity School Archives)

Longacre Square in 1891. Trinity occupied 648 Seventh Avenue (or 1521 Broadway),
the building with three awnings, behind the lamppost, at the far right, from 1873
until 1888. The crossroads of Seventh Avenue and Broadway was renamed Times
Square in 1905. (Photography Collection, Miriam and Ira D. Wallach Division of
Art, Prints and Photographs, The New York Public Library, Astor, Lenox,
and Tilden Foundations)

View of Madison Avenue at 59th Street showing number 627, Trinity's home for the 1889–1890 school year. (Milstein Division of United States History, Local History and Genealogy, The New York Public Library, Astor, Lenox, Tilden Foundations)

Students in 1893 in front of 108 West 45th Street, Trinity's last stop before moving to the Upper West Side. (Trinity School Archives)

The Trinity football team in 1893, the heyday of "muscular Christianity," an idea that all-boys, Episcopal Trinity took seriously. (Trinity School Archives)

Charles Coolidge Haight (1841–1917), architect who designed Trinity's building at 139 West 91st Street. (Courtesy of Peter L. Donhauser)

The exterior of Trinity's new building as it appeared ca. 1908–1916
in a photo in Lawrence Cole's scrapbook. (Trinity School Archives)

Imposing entrance bespoke serious intention. The Great Hall of Trinity's 139 Building, which once led to the chapel, and today leads to the lower school library and (now as then) the head's office, met all the requirements. (Trinity School Archives)

August Ulmann, Trinity's rector 1890–1903, was the first to preside on West 91st Street. Ever in academic garb, he looked as old as his charges looked young. (Trinity School Archives)

Lunch is served in the first dining room on the third floor of the 139 building. Ulmann, it seems, never missed a photo opportunity. (Trinity School Archives)

The Class of 1896 with Rector Ulmann (*seated center*). (Trinity School Archives)

German-born Ulmann attempted curricular reform and placed new emphasis on physical fitness. Here, Trinity's first gym, atop 139 West 91st Street. (Trinity School Archives)

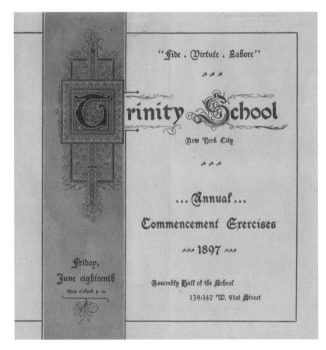

"Fide . Virtute . Labore"

Trinity School

(New York City)

... Annual ...

Commencement Exercises

1897

Friday,
June eighteenth
three o'clock p. m.

Assembly Hall of the School
139-147 W. 91st Street

Twenty-two boys graduated from Trinity School on June 18, 1897. (Trinity School Archives)

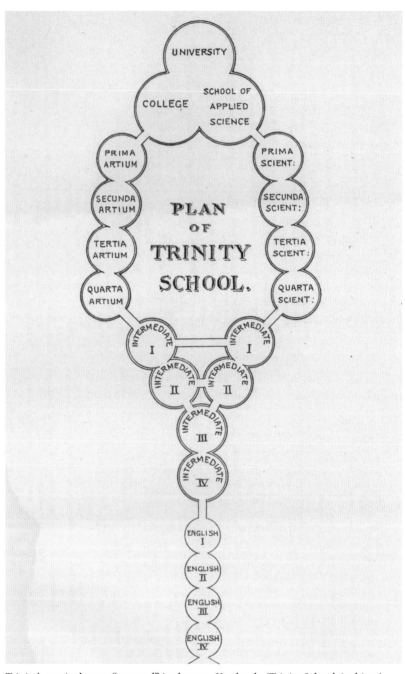

Trinity's curriculum as "mapped" in the 1900 Yearbook. (Trinity School Archives)

St. Agnes Chapel, a "chapel-of-ease" of Trinity Parish, on Columbus Avenue at West 92nd Street, was completed in 1892 in order to meet the needs of the Upper West Side's growing middle-class population. Viewed here from the Columbus Avenue "El." (Museum of the City of New York, The Wurts Collection)

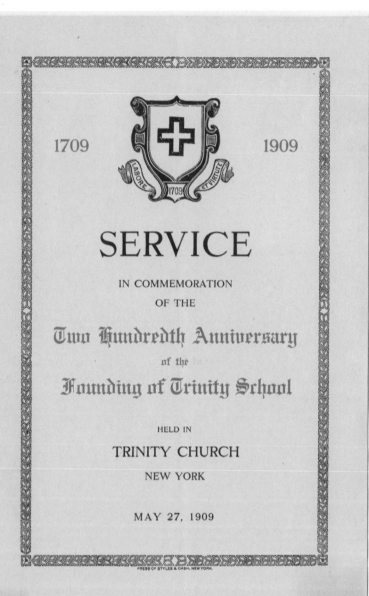

1709　　1909

SERVICE

IN COMMEMORATION
OF THE

Two Hundredth Anniversary

of the

Founding of Trinity School

HELD IN

TRINITY CHURCH

NEW YORK

MAY 27, 1909

Trinity School celebrated its 200th Anniversary on May 27, 1909,
with a formal service at Trinity Church . . . (Trinity School Archives)

Program

FIELD DAY

FOR THE BOYS OF

Trinity School

On the occasion of the

200th Anniversary
of the School

————

COLUMBIA OVAL

————

Friday, May 28th, 1909

... and a field day at the Columbia Oval. (Trinity School Archives)

In the 1910s, when Trinity dramatics called for females, males had to suffice.
Here student Frederic Prescott Hammond poses in costume for a 1916 production.
(Trinity School Archives)

For decades, the school day began in the chapel of the 139 building with formal liturgy from the Book of Common Prayer. On Fridays, the boys knelt for the Litany. (Trinity School Archives)

Varying degrees of attention during chapel. (Trinity School Archives)

Chemistry class, ca. 1920. (Trinity School Archives)

Trinity's baseball team, ca. 1920, posed at Columbia University
where games were often played. (Trinity School Archives)

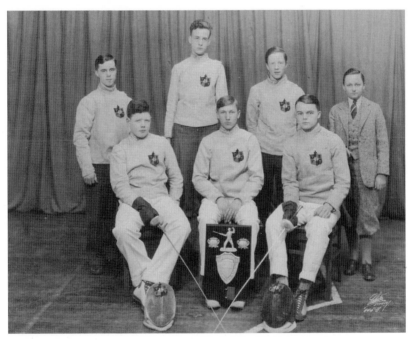

The fencing team in the 1920s. Longtime master Clarence Bruner-Smith
thought fencing, especially, built character. (Trinity School Archives)

Then as now, chess attracted intellectuals: Trinity's team in 1933.
(Trinity School Archives)

The fatherly Lawrence T. Cole was rector of Trinity from 1903 to 1937 and its last leader in Holy Orders. He was not known to appear but in clericals. (Trinity School Archives)

Cole, white hair beneath the American flag, was Trinity's longest-serving head and the last to be called "rector." Trinity paid tribute to him at a retirement dinner at the Astor Hotel on June 3, 1937. (Trinity School Archives)

Matthew Dann followed Cole as rector in 1937, though the title soon changed to "headmaster." Trained in finance, Dann managed Trinity through hard times and when the pool of potential students was still small. (Trinity School Archives)

St. Agatha's School for Girls on West End Avenue at 87th Street opened in 1898 as Trinity's "sister" school under the aegis of the New York Protestant Episcopal School Corporation, Trinity's formal, corporate name. Declining enrollment and dismal finances forced its closure in 1941. (Trinity School Archives)

St. Agatha's at first enrolled only grades one through eight; eventually a kindergarten and an upper school were added. (Trinity School Archives)

The 1938 board of Agatharian, the St. Agatha's School yearbook. (Trinity School Archives)

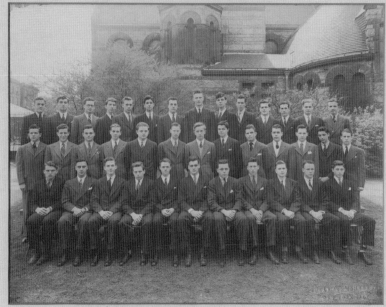

· Class of 1941 ·

Green · Gandy · Barbey · Conn · Stone · Lewis · Livingston · Seekamp · Stevenson
Leek · Elmendorf · Gibbons · Gordon · Boatrite
Evans · Meerbott · Groebli · Johnson · Raisbeck · Goodnough · Nicholaus · Scott · Lange
Prewitt · Fraser · Georgopulo · Williams
Finch · Storie · Lindemann · Krause · Street · Makel · Burns · Davis · Wildman
Heath · Roemer

Boys too soon to become men: wartime awaited the class of 1941.
(Trinity School Archives)

The rifle club marked out another era at the all-boys Trinity.
(Trinity School Archives)

In the 1950s, Trinity's littlest boys wore ties and everyone shared the 139 building. (Trinity School Archives)

Through the 1960s, Trinity's dress code was uniform and uncompromising. The return of girls in 1971 complicated things. (Trinity School Archives)

The "Annual Terror," pictured here in 1958, referred to final exams administered, and carefully monitored, in the gym. (Trinity School Archives)

West Side Urban Renewal Proposal, Plan B, 1958, which called for combining brownstone and tenement rehabilitation with new housing in Trinity's neighborhood. (Trinity School Archives)

THE TRINITY TIMES

Vol. 36   WEDNESDAY, DECEMBER 20, 1967   No. 5

This picture, taken from the east side of Columbus Avenue, shows the gaping hole where some day soon Trinity Towers will rise. Gone will be dear old Schuyler's Market. But in its place will stand a tribute to Trinity and all that it represents.

Vacation Begins At 12 P.M. Today

This year, the school again will hold the traditional Christmas Carol services preceding the holiday recess. Following the precedent set last year, there will be a separate service for the Lower School in the afternoon to enable working parents to attend.

The Lower School service will begin with a processional, "Once in Royal David's City." Then "Personent Hodie" and "O Come, O Come Emanuel," the well-known Early Plainsong hymn will be sung.

The service then will continue with the traditional hymns, carols and lessons, ending in a blessing and Adeste Fideles" in Latin.

The Upper and Middle School service is comprised of much the same music with the addition, however, of several more sophisticated pieces, including "An Earthly Tree, A Heavenly Fruit," by William Byrd, an excellent example of word-painting and Madrigal, sung by the Middle School Glee Club. For this service the lessons are read by both faculty and student readers and both the **Magnificat** and the **Nunc Dimittis** are sung. The solos in the hymn, **We Three Kings**, sung by Woody

Fannie Hurst Is January Speaker

Fannie Hurst, once called "the Sob Sister of American fiction," is coming to Trinity to speak at an assembly on Jan. 15th. Born Oct. 18, 1889, Miss Hurst spent her childhood in St. Louis, and graduated from Washington University (St. Louis) with a B.A. in 1909.

At the age of fourteen, she first had a verse masque printed in "The Saturday Evening Post." During her university years, her work began to appear in "Reedy's Mirror." In 1910 she traveled to Columbia to do work in the English department and "went into training for fiction" in slums, sweat shops, department stores and eventually in Europe.

She was encouraged by Robert Davis, a promoter, and turned out her first book of short stories, **Just Around the Corner,** in 1914.

Fannie Hurst works six hours a day with what has been noted as "immense vitality." Her main interests in reading are science, history, and exploration. Her favorite work is **Lummox,** published in 1923.

Pier Paolo Pasolini's "The Gospel According to St. Matthew" will be seen here on Jan. 20th. Called "...probably the finest religious film," it is extremely realistic yet emotional.

'Times' Evaluates Student Council

By Dirk Roberts

With one trimester of the year completed, it becomes possible to make valuable judgments on the actions and achievements of our Student Council. The **Times** believe that this year's Council has already exhibited a definite capacity for achievement which makes it necessary to discuss the new Student Council critically.

One issue to discuss is the supposed new spirit of the Council. Is "your Student Council on fire," or not? There is evidence for either a negative or a positive answer.

Several weeks ago, President Meeker asked each member of the Council to submit to him individual reports stating how the writer felt the Council was progressing and bringing up any suggestions for action. This affords an excellent opportunity for the President to listen to individual opinions and new ideas. However, only two members, both members of the Junior class, bothered to submit reports. This is one of several incidents which reveal that there is really no new spirit in the Council.

On the other hand, there is also (**Continued on Page 4, Col. 3**)

"George M." Chosen As Theatre Benefit

Mrs. Withers Hardee, Theater Benefit Chairman, recently announced that Trinity has succeeded in obtaining a new musical "George M." as its Spring Theater Benefit Evening. The Evening will be held on Wednesday, April 17, 1968.

Ordinarily, the spring fair and the spring benefit alternate from year to year; however, because of space limitations, Trinity decided to replace the fair this year with a theater benefit. The purpose of the benefit is to raise money for the new building. Workers have already begun tearing down all apartment buildings on the site and hopefully, the new building will be finished sometime in 1969.

The show, which will open at the Palace Theater in April, contains many well-known songs by George M. Cohen. The musical will star Joel Grey, who has recently played in "Cabaret," and the book was written by Michael Stewart of the smash hit "Hello Dolly."

There will be a reception following the performance. Ticket prices are to be announced soon by Mrs. Hardee.

THE TRINITY IMAGE

Compiled by the TIMES Staff

Two weeks ago the **Trinity Times** took a formal student poll at the Spence, Hewitt, and Lenox Schools and an informal one at a fourth school to get an evaluation of Trinity students by members of grades 9-12 of the girl world. The **Times** wishes to thank all the headmistresses of the girls' schools involved, as well as Mrs. Kalman, Lisa Lyons, Missy Lindsey, Mrs. Joe Naith, and Wendy Flink, without whose help this paper would not have been able to publish this poll.

Though this poll may be indicative of nothing, the **Times** does hope that you will enjoy reading this and looking at yourselves through the eyes of New York girls.

The poll is divided into three parts: two paragraphs, an evaluation, and a series of ratings. The first of the two paragraphs challenged the

Answers:

"He is attractive, nicely dressed, witty, and has a terrific smile . . . He tries hard but doesn't always succeed. But you gotta say they're good kids . . . Blond hair, wild, all over girls . . . Either 4'6" or 6'4" . . . Long blond hair, cute, but very conceited . . . He wears white socks . . . Trinity boys are all typical, that's their problem. They are conformists, but they're not so bad.

"He is fairly attractive, a little loud, but in a cute, funny way. When alone with a girl he is a perfect date — but when with other Trinity boys he becomes unattentive . . . He wears white socks . . . A typical Trinity boy is considerate, polite and good looking. He should have a wonderful personality and be able to mingle with girls easily . . . Laurent de Montmollin.

The *Trinity Times*, December 20, 1967, glimpsed the empty space soon to be filled by the Hawley Wing and Trinity House. (Trinity School Archives)

THE TRINITY TIMES

Vol. 36   THURSDAY, MARCH 14, 1968   No. 8

Trinity Expands Summer School; Adds Grades 2-6

This summer from June 24 until August 12, Mr. Pasanen will head a greatly enlarged summer school program. While the program included grades seven through twelve in 1967, this year it is being expanded to accommodate grades two through twelve. In the Upper School, the classes offered will be basically the same as last year.

The courses in the mathematics department will be algebra I, algebra II, geometry, and algebra preview (a forerunner to algebra I). Also, the same foreign languages will be available: French I-III, Spanish I and II, and Latin I and II. Grammar and composition, as well as literature and composition, are holdovers from last summer. Film and verbal communication is a new course. Of the new courses offered last year, history of philosophy, American history, advanced physics, history of Russia since 1900, driver education, and typing, all remain. Of these courses, all can be taken for credit except algebra preview.

As usual, summer school will be coeducational. Last summer, from grades seven to twelve, one hundred boys and girls attended school. Naturally, this year with the addition of five extra grades, there will be a greatly enlarged student body.

A student may take one or two
(Continued on Page 2, col. 3)

Mano '59 Has 1st Novel Published

Recently, D. Keith Mano, a Trinity alumnus, Class of '59, finished a book which was published by Houghton Mifflin Company. The title of Mr. Mano's novel is **Bishop's Progress**, and it deals with an important moral topic of today: the scientific standpoint of medical progress vs. the ethical code and foundation of Christian Church.

Representing the latter side is Whitney Belnap, Episcopal Bishop of Queens, a brave, likeable, compassionate man who is in the hospital with serious heart trouble. His antagonist, Dr. Snow, often portrayed as the "Temptor", is pushing the Bishop by horrible means towards breaking down and choosing the easy wrong. That is, in his serious condition, the Bishop must decide whether he will confirm his faith in God and entrust his soul to God, or turn his faith to scientific processes, thereby prolonging his physical life. After Trinity, Mr. Mano, graduated **summa cum laude** from Columbia University and also did some acting off-Broadway and with the National Shakespeare company.

New York Times Host to 'Times'

By Dirk Roberts

Last Friday, the junior and senior staff members of the **Trinity Times** visited the New York **Times**, The N.Y. **Times**, founded in 1851, has steadily expanded and become the most respected and informative newspaper in the world. The center of operations for this worldwide organization is a skyscraper off Times Square. The Trinity **Times** staff members were given a tour of the facilities in this building.

The students first visited the studios of WQXR, the radio station of the **Times**. The station has the largest record and tape library in the world. The students watched two announcers conclude a music program and saw the beginning of the hourly newscast. The office is a complex set of studios centered around the engineer's booth.

The students next visited the museum operated by the **Times**. The museum is on the tenth floor and is open to the public. It contains exhibits tracing the history of printing and the progress of the paper through the past century.

Following this, the staff traced the path of an imaginary article from its assignment to a reporter to its actual appearance in the **Times**. This tour included visits to the Newsroom, the Composing Room, and the Press Room.

The Newsroom is the center of operations for the 450-man reporting staff based in New York. The room is filled with long lines of grey desks. Here, a reporter receives his assignment for the day early in the morning. Then, when he has covered his assigment, the reporter returns to the Newsroom and writes his article. The room also contains teletype machines from fifteen news services including the Associated Press, Reuters, Tass, and the United Press International. These agencies constantly relay news to the
(Continued on Page 4, col. 2)

Randy Charles, grade two, looks at the construction through the new fence surrounding the site. Blasting has just begun to clear the bedrock.

Freshmen Benefit From Orientation

This year, the fifty-seven members of the Freshman class have had a series of orientation sessions. In the first few weeks of the academic year, the freshmen attended lectures on the set-up of the school and on basic school policy. Following these talks, the freshmen took a study skills course taught by Mr. Garten.

During the current trimester, the third-formers have been introduced to a tri-weekly sex education course. In addition to putting forth the technical aspects of human reproduction, this course, taught by Messrs. Paskin,
(Continued on Page 2, col. 3)

Council Proposes Two New Projects

The second trimester was certainly not as productive as the first for the Student Council. In the first trimester, the council proposed and passed the Senior Project, the first student-initiated action ever passed by the faculty and administration; began publishing the **Student Council Review**; and sponsored a dance for the students. This trimester the council has unfortunately not been able to produce as many material gains for the students.

This trimester the Council has instead undertaken several very ambi-
(Continued on Page 4, col. 4)

Catenaccio and Garren Elected To Cum Laude

In its first two meetings this year, the Trinity Chapter of the Cum Laude Society approved drastic changes in what had been previously a very clear-cut but limited program. In addition, the members voted two seniors into the Society — Robert Catenaccio and Brent Garren. It should be noted that admission at this time marks these two as the highest-ranking seniors. The balance of the candidates will be installed either during the final trimester or in a ceremony in conjunction with prize day in June.

The Society, which was established in 1906, was instituted into the Trinity framework in 1934. Traditionally, the Headmaster of the school serves as president of the local chapter, and other persons of the faculty who merit the honor are admitted to the chapter.

It was the feeling of the Trinity Chapter that it had been remiss in not electing eligible faculty members and honorary members. In order to correct this negligence, the present members are considering proposed faculty members and persons not directly involved with the school for honorary membership.

Another privilege which the chapter has been loth to exercise is that of accepting up to one-tenth of the junior class as "continuity" pro-
(Continued on Page 4, col. 2)

Forty-Five Attend 'Tiger at the Gates'

Students have continued to show great interest in Trinity's theater parties, organized by Mr. Mayer.

Three weeks ago forty-five boys, the largest number this year, went to see Tiger at the Gates by the French writer Giraudoux. About four or five days later a group of boys went to see **Rosencrants and Guildenstern are Dead**.

Tiger at the Gates got mixed reviews, some highly praising it, and others, such as Clive Barnes', of The New York Times, not so enthusiastic. Mr. Barnes said that the play seemed outdated to him, which was not at all the impression that Mr. Mayer and many of the boys had expected.

Rosencrants and Guildenstern, on the other hand, received very high acclaim from almost all the critics. The theater parties were organized to fit in with school as much as possible. For example, Rosencrants and Guildenstern coincided exactly with the end of the twelfth grade's study of Hamlet. The play focuses on two minor characters from Hamlet who
(Continued on Page 2, col. 3)

On March 14, 1968, even the smallest boys got a look as construction began. (Trinity School Archives)

Construction of the Hawley
Wing and Trinity House,
underway 1968. (Trinity
School Archives)

A cartoon in the *Trinity Times*, November 27, 1968,
caricatured social transformations taking place in the
late 1960s. (Trinity School Archives)

Richard Garten served as headmaster (1964–1975) through times of unprecedented change at Trinity and oversaw construction of the Hawley Wing and Trinity House. (Trinity School Archives)

Robin Lester became headmaster in 1975 (1975–1986) and presided over Trinity's successful transformation into a competitive coeducational independent school. (Trinity School Archives)

Christopher Berrisford (headmaster 1987–1991) sought to shore up Trinity's finances and professionalize its administration. (Trinity School Archives)

A bell, which had made its home in the steeple of St. Agnes Chapel until the Chapel's demolition in 1944 is raised to the bell tower atop Trinity's new building at 115 West 91st in 1997. (Photo by Kevin Ramsey, Trinity School Archives)

The steel frame of the roof of 115 West 91st Street opened in 1998, which provides a purpose-built home to Trinity's middle school and includes two gymnasiums and expanded physical fitness facilities. (Photo by Kevin Ramsey, Trinity School Archives)

Trinity's "Mr. Chips" and its longest-serving faculty member (1927–1971), pictured here in the Great Hall in the late 1940s. (Trinity School Archives)

Henry C. Moses came to Trinity as head from Harvard in 1991. Under his leadership, Trinity defined afresh for itself the role of the sacred in a secular society and advanced diversity to the center of the school's mission. (Photo by Kevin Ramsey, Trinity School Archives)

Today, the women's and girls' roles in Trinity productions are played by women and girls. Here a scene from the middle school's production of *Bye, Bye, Birdie*. (Photo by Kevin Ramsey, Trinity School Archives)

Chapel continues to play a central role in school life. Weekly services for all divisions, and seasonal celebrations like the middle school Celebration of Light are part of the fabric of Trinity School. (Photo by Kevin Ramsey, Trinity School Archives)

Trinity athletics in the twenty-first century
(Photos by Kevin Ramsey, Trinity School Archives)

"The conversation between student and teacher is the heart of our school . . . "
(Photo by Kevin Ramsey, Trinity School Archives)

Trinity's youngest in the pool, where every lower schooler is taught to swim.
(Photo by Kevin Ramsey, Trinity School Archives)

PIVOT POINT

Dann meant all this to signal a new tack, if still on course toward an old destination. He appears to have enjoyed wide mandate. An inch-thick letter book survives that documents the changing of the guard and the congratulations Dann received on the new job. It reveals a striking range of acquaintance from parish priests to Wall Street lawyers, from high-toned headmasters to local vendors hustling business.[7] Bill Weissinger, class of 1933, wrote: "I hate to see Dr. Cole go, as he and Trinity School somehow seem to be almost one being in my fond memories of my days there. However, if said memory does not fail me, Trinity is getting a mighty good man to fill Dr. Cole's shoes" (March 26, 1937). From "Fred" at NW Ayers & Son Advertising headquarters in Philadelphia, and who apparently knew Dann on the links: "I look forward to hearing your 'cuss' words again next summer" (March 29, 1937). A parent (Theodore O. Wedel) quoted Kipling: "Bless and praise we famous men—Men of little showing! / For their work continueth, / And their work continueth, / Broad and deep continueth, / Great beyond their knowing" (March 31, 1937). From the top of the hierarchy, Bishop William T. Manning sent a telegram (March 23, 1937). From the bottom, Lower School boys wrote sweet notes in pencil on lined paper, each one carefully marked in the upper left hand corner, "answered." From Broward Craig: "Dear Mr. Dann: I am very glad that you are going to be rector of the school since Dr. Cole is retiring. I hope that you are rector as long as Dr. Cole has been." Signing "Your little friend," Lewis Charles Popham III wrote: "Dear Mr. Dann, I am so glad that you will be Headmaster of Trinity School, but I am sorry that Dr. Cole will leave us. I hope you will have a nice Easter."[8]

Cole was sixty-eight when he officially resigned on July 1, 1937, after thirty-four years as rector. Scant record remains of the precise dynamics of his departure, though there is indication of some impatience with his leadership. It is clear that Dann intended to do things differently, but not exactly how. He became Trinity's leader in stages, between his appointment as assistant headmaster[9] in June 1935 and elevation to the top job two years later. Having come to Trinity in 1927, he was not even one of the more senior faculty. That he must have been on the track to succession early can be inferred from events during that interim. He appears to have had close allies in board members John Erskine, English professor at Columbia, and the Rev. Frederic S. Fleming, rector of Trinity Church. Fleming thought Dann's revamped yearbook a breath of fresh air. "You have done a capital job," he wrote, "especially as I recognize some of the barriers you have had to hurdle. It is definitely a step in the right direction, and I hope a good omen for the future."[10] It is possible that "barriers" referred to reluctance on Cole's part to promote the school, to matters of his old-fashioned style, or of course to money. Dann and Erskine appeared to have worked together closely to move things ahead or at least prepare the ground for when a new regime would be set in place. That this was a complete secret from Cole seems far-fetched, but neither is there any paper trail leading back to him.[11]

"Thank you very much for your letter," Dann wrote from his summer address in at Camp Marienfeld in New Hampshire to Erskine in late July 1935, "telling me that the Trustees elected me Assistant Headmaster of Trinity School."[12] Six weeks earlier, Erskine had thanked Dann for his "proposals for Trinity"—evidently Dann was invited to propose something new by trustees looking for something different—and said he was eager to talk in person. In the meantime, Erskine would only say that the trustees had voted a 25 percent rise in tuition and that all benefice boys would be expected to pay at least $100, no small steps: "These limits had to be fixed in order to secure even a fighting chance of weathering next season."[13]

Record of board deliberations are lost as are Dann's proposals, but Erskine (a professional writer) wrote between as well as on the lines. Obviously, much had been said already. Dann appears to have wanted a different title but couldn't get it. Erskine and the board evidently had their new man but were being careful. "I am afraid the title will be Assistant Headmaster for the present. That version seems to the Board for many reasons advisable, and it will make little, if any, difference to your influence." It would appear that Cole was being eased out, and it is possible that he resisted or at least was prickly about it. Erskine anyway wanted no scenes. In his note formally telling Dann he had the number-two job, the sense of frustration relieved is unmistakable: "I hope this means for you and for the rest of us the beginning of a very happy and successful work at the School." It would take some tact however. "You will have the problem of improving School conditions without seeming to reflect on Dr. Cole and without giving offense to him. Since you and he are the gentlemen that you are, I foresee no difficulty."[14] Erskine signed off, though, saying call any time.

The episode is worth recounting for what it suggests about Trinity at its first big pivot point in thirty-three years. This change was different from the change from Ulmann to Cole. It was not a personnel problem but an institutional one, and simple fixes wouldn't work. Some tenseness was natural, but the new man's more radical plans definitely needed to wait for a clean changing of the guard. The new yearbook put forth a more appealing face to prospective customers, driven by Dann's anxiety about enrollment and that the school might fail. In private he even anticipated that the whole show might need to move on.

Again, we have it from Erskine's side: "I am much interested in the idea of securing a foothold on the east side for elementary classes—both for Trinity and St. Agatha. If we could establish such a foothold, we might then go on to the idea you and I discussed, of moving the upper schools to the country." So might have ended the career of 139 West 91st Street. Muriel Bowden, headmistress of St. Agatha, was a strong promoter of an East Side option. Erskine, who worked at Columbia and lived on Claremont Avenue (though later on Park Avenue), first was cool to the idea. But, he wrote, "I am becoming a convert."[15] Dann was likely in favor, and they all talked it back and forth through 1936 when Cole was still nominally in charge. Another board member, the Rev. Henry Darlington, had a plan of his own, which he floated at least with Fleming and Dann, to merge Trinity and the day school of the Church of the Heavenly Rest at 90th and Fifth Avenue.[16] There is cryptic mention of "negotiations" with Montclair Academy in Montclair, New Jersey, being called off in November 1936. The board apparently dithered until, we surmise, wartime put any such big moves on hold. In September 1939, there was talk of acquiring "the most attractive plant" of the Hackley School (a nonsectarian boys boarding school in Tarrytown, founded by Unitarians in 1899), and active negotiations with the Pawling School in Dutchess County (see later discussion).[17] There things simmered.

The willingness even to look at changes so radical as moving east or moving out or some combination of the two bespoke the level of anxiety surrounding the transition from Cole to Dann. It was the late 1930s and times were hard, as they had been in the late 1830s, which had occasioned another re-think of what the then charity school was all about and how best it might move forward. (The answer then: Drop girls, slim down, emphasize Episcopalian identity, focus on "preparatory" education for a few boys.) Dann appears to have appreciated the urgency as well as the delicacy of the new situation even before he was formally fully in charge. Somebody, obviously, needed to do something soon. Through all the thrashing about for the right path ahead emerged more modest, probably lower risk alternatives than

Dann might have wished, but at least they were, literally, close at hand. These involved the two neighboring Episcopal institutions named for saints Agnes and Agatha. And by then, Dann would have the title he needed to carry out the plans.

Cole's formal letter of resignation was accepted by the board in January 1937, when Dann was elevated to rector effective the end of that school year.[18] At that meeting, Erskine wanted to get on with it and asked Dann for a memorandum distilling his plans for the future. The memo is lost, but it was Erskine's stated understanding that it would "fall in with the general plan that we have discussed—of country day schools with branches in the city for the younger scholars."[19]

Dann no doubt complied with the paperwork and then got moving. At the end of January, he sent Erskine two reports, "The Present Situation" and "The Future Development of Trinity School." The first looked ahead just to the next school year; the second outlined "the possible courses which seem open to us."[20] Neither document survives, but the themes might be guessed from the changes in the catalogue and subsequent events. Trinity could not stand still as, Dann thought, it pretty much had done under Cole. It would embrace a survival-through-growth strategy that depended for success on making the school more attractive to more boys with parents who were willing to pay. More attractive, to Dann, most immediately meant more space, perhaps in the country but if not there then space closer by where the boys could not just work but play.

MONEY

To say that Dann as he stepped into his own viewed Trinity as a business as well as a school would be to draw the distinction too sharply, but he did see Trinity the school as a place with certain business aspects. He saw himself as its administrator, even its executive, as much as its "head" master or teacher. (In this strict sense, the old term "rector" might therefore have been more apt than the "headmaster" that replaced it, except for its clerical association, for Dann was laity.) At least, his were the actions of someone alert to the concept of supply and demand as they related to the dispensing of educational services, and to the fact that the demand for Trinity's services must not be taken for granted. It is very clear that Trinity's ancient warrant as a charity school, which Cole held sacred, held little charm for Dann. Everyone needed to pay, at least something. Dann attended to both the revenue and the expense sides of the ledger. Slowly, he raised tuition. Scrupulously, he monitored what got spent. He probably had as much respect for school "spirit" and tradition as any of his predecessors, but he was no sentimentalist. A month into his first year in charge, 1937–38, he reported to Erskine that there was "a fine spirit, and I am much encouraged." But this was because, he went on to say, "we have a splendid enrollment in our lower school, and I believe our income will show an increase over last year."[21] Nothing pleases a chief executive like an improving set of books. Trinity's would be a year-by-year slog however. In 1940, he reported to board member and treasurer C. Aubrey Nicklas that tuition receipts looked to come in $5,500 over the previous year, but that operating budgets remained squeaky tight. (With no padding, small, unforeseen if inevitable bothers became big problems. That winter the sidewalk along 91st Street was condemned and, indoors, the dumbwaiter collapsed, exceeding the repair budget by $445.[22]) At the close of the 1942–43 school year, he told new treasurer William G. Brady, Jr., that Trinity collected "every penny" of tuition. "This must be close to a record in the private school field."[23]

Of course, every penny of tuition was not and never would be enough. Two trends, however, are significant of Dann's new discipline. Sampling, starting in 1940, Trinity enrolled 308 students, 32 on full scholarship, 98 with partial subvention, and 178 who paid in full. Two years later, with a total enrollment virtually the same (305), free students fell to 24 and partial paying ones rose slightly to 103, for a net gain of 3 for the full-pay to less-than-full-pay ratio. In 1944, with enrollment up to 333, fully free students were down to 17, partial paying ones down to 93, and full payers up to 223. In 1952, with 321 enrolled, there were 17 full-scholarship boys, 42 who got some help, and 262 who paid full fare. In 1955, with enrollment of 325, things slipped back slightly with 17, 62, and 246, respectively. In 1959, of an increased enrollment of 420, 325 paid full tuition, 29 went free, and 66 fell in between. Nudging up the income by holding down the subsidy yielded mixed results. The other trend was a general improvement in operating results or school expenses relative to fees collected ("net school income before depreciation"). In 1940 it was negative $19,402, in 1943 negative $18,033, in 1944 negative $7,819, in 1952 positive $3,880, in 1955 positive $5,502, in 1959 negative $1,775.

The school's other income, from which operating shortfalls were met, came from a modest endowment, at mid-century valued at approximately $700,000 divided between a small bond and equity portfolio, twenty-four mortgages, net rental income on real estate, and income on the school's only substantial bequest at that time, the Alan Hawley estate, of which Trinity was residuary trustee.[24] Endowment income oscillated but generally slid: $64,442 in 1940, $39,831 in 1943, $48,904 in 1944, $31,979 in 1952, $31,974 in 1955, and $30,498 in 1959. The conclusion would be that it was necessary to run harder to stay in place. Expenses also rose steadily, particularly salaries: $58,589 in 1940 to $70,202 in 1944, $103,358 in 1952, $121,011 in 1955, and $186,097 in 1959. General expenses rose over the same period, $16,853 to $62,426.[25] It was not until the late 1950s that the school operated reliably in the black. What also mattered was how it was spread. In their own ways, St Agnes Chapel and then the Pawling School added. St. Agatha School subtracted.

CREATIVE DESTRUCTION

In the sad story of St. Agnes Chapel, Dann's strategy for Trinity of prosperity through growth and finding new markets met fortuitous opportunity. Two market imperatives dovetailed, robbing the neighborhood of a fine old church but renewing the lease on life of one at least fine old school. The problems of St. Agnes Chapel related directly to neighborhood change.[26] Erected in 1892 when the Upper West Side boomed as a fashionable destination for the middle classes and was promising ground for the missionary work of the mother parish of Trinity Church, already by the 1920s St. Agnes had become for the church a "problem chapel." By the 1930s, the problem of St. Agnes, which was immense[27] and immensely expensive to operate, had become acute. By the mid-1940s, both chapel and problem were erased into history.

It wasn't lack of people, but rather people of the right sort. Population of the Upper West Side in fact became more dense in the 1920s and 1930s, but with newcomers, many of them Roman Catholics and Jews. Episcopalians, relatively, dwindled, and other parishes already in the neighborhood (St. Stephen's, Christ Church, St. Ignatius, St. Matthew's, and St. Timothy, plus the looming Cathedral of St. John the Divine) more than met local Episcopalian demand. The urban mission work of churches then tended to be denomination specific, with each branch of the faith looking after its own. With fewer and fewer Episcopalians to look after, as reflected in declining membership and financial support, St. Agnes, though hardly forty years old and built of stone and steel to last the ages, became a premature white elephant. Or so a "streamlining" (its term) Trinity Parish judged it. The demand for the church's services had changed—literally, the demand had moved—and the parish needed to divest underutilized real estate and redeploy its assets.

In the distress of Trinity Church, Trinity School found opportunity, if certain conditions could be met. Thus the second market imperative: that of Trinity School to make itself more attractive to more paying students by boasting better facilities, or else probably fail. It did not need another chapel. It did need space to grow, especially for physical education and athletics, and St. Agnes sat atop adjacent prime space, its parish house filling the lot directly east of Trinity's own brownstone schoolhouse on West 91st Street. Dann had visions of more classrooms and beyond that, on the 200-by-300-foot parcel that was occupied by the chapel itself and the rectory, of playing fields all Trinity's own. In its desire, the school was not at first without competition. In 1942, the Greek Orthodox Church proposed purchasing St. Agnes and putting it to use, as it stood, for its own faithful, this even though Greeks were not much more abundant in the immediate neighborhood than Episcopalians were. Dann and the Trinity Board then moved quickly.

To rector of Trinity Church Frederic Fleming (ex officio on the board of Trinity School), the school proposed a rent-with-option-to-buy arrangement whereby they would assume all the costs of St. Agnes's operation, assuming no restriction on future use. The school offered $50,000. (In 1892, the buildings alone had cost close to $600,000.) It took the Trinity vestry over the summer of 1942 to approve the deal. It was left to Bishop Manning and the standing committee of the diocese of New York to bestow the final imprimatur, which came in November. Eighty-year-old William W. Bellinger, the last vicar of St. Agnes and also on the school's board, though "deeply grieved," went along reluctantly.[28]

Trinity School took over on July 1, 1943, and to Dann not a moment too soon. Fleming deftly handled the public relations: "With rapid development of the City of New York, Trinity Parish has endeavored throughout her history to keep abreast of the movements of population, and to throw her strength into one neighborhood after another as occasion demanded." For Trinity School (whose own nineteenth-century migrations up Manhattan he might have been describing), which "had its origins in Trinity Church itself," this meant opportunity "to provide more adequately for its rapidly growing enrollment and activities." Here Fleming clearly had the cart before the horse: Enrollment only inched up and it was the activities that were intended to get it there. As to any continuing obligation to meet "the spiritual needs of St. Agnes' people" and the possible continuing use of the chapel as a place of worship, Fleming fudged and made no public reference to Dann's desire, which he surely knew about, for the land, not the building, which is what motivated the deal from the school's side to begin with.[29] Yet the deal was historic in one modest sense, as one reporter noted: "The 247-year-old grantor and the 235-year-old grantee are believed to be the most ancient who are parties to any deed in New York County."[30] Not everyone was happy with the decision and how it was handled. From left-of-center, Dann confidant Erskine slammed his establishment vestry colleagues: "They thought the building of a chapel on the West Side had proved a business error. They wanted to take the loss and balance the books."[31]

That was hard, and the other interpretation of the meaning of the episode—that the long-term benefit of Trinity School should be seen as fair compensation for loss of the obsolete chapel, however lovely—is as persuasive. Dann in any case proceeded unsentimentally and without apology.[32] Until the wrecking ball struck, that is, for the 1943–44 school year, Trinity used the great chapel once a week for its war memorial services (though not for its daily ones), but even while the school still technically only leased the property from Trinity Parish, demolition plans for the chapel building were being made. Manning, who himself had served as vicar of St. Agnes, 1903–1908, sadly gave his approval to Fleming, who presumably gave permission to Dann. Once the deed was in hand, it was school business alone. The school tried to sell everything of the contents of any conceivable use or value, from the high altar to the organs, the bells, the stained glass, right down to prayer books and hymnals. It appears to have been a fire sale, however, and much just disappeared in demolition. The building itself was destroyed without much adieu between June and October 1944. Few structural elements survived either. Mosaic floors were crumbled to fill the foundation hole.

Where the chapel had stood, Trinity boys played ball starting the spring of 1945, Dan boasting about the boost it gave school athletics. The two other buildings that had been part of St. Agnes met different fates, but in line with the same strategy. The vicarage, which stood at 115 West 91st Street, became a dormitory for the small number of boarders that Trinity began to take in during World War II and continued with until the Pawling connection (see later discussion) reassigned them to the country and Trinity returned to all-day status. With the end of boarding, the old vicarage, which was called "The Residence," was turned to faculty housing until 1955, when it too came down to make way for the school's second gymnasium. The third structure, the parish house just to the west at 121 West 91st, survived where it stood by process of incorporation with the old 1894 school building and would later be designated a historic landmark, a status that did not exist when destruction originally had threatened. It would become a historic landmark only as shell, however, as most of its interior spaces metamorphosed again and again to different uses. But out on the street, the number "121" in stone relief still marks the spot.

CITY GIRLS

St. Agnes Chapel fell, literally, before the urgency of Trinity's need for space to spruce itself up and attract more boys. Trinity's second experiment with girls, if not coeducation, which had begun with the opening of St. Agatha Day School for Girls in 1898, fell, figuratively, before the corporation's marginal finances in the 1930s.[33] If Trinity could not do all things well, then it would discriminate and do what it had done the longest, which was to prepare boys for college. The view that if one sex or the other should be so prepared then it should be males stirred little of the opprobrium it would later. Trinity's decision to off-load its money-losing sister operation in 1941 came with routine expressions of regret and sincere ones of relief. Though St. Agatha girls looked back fondly on the schooling they received there right up to the end, St. Agatha had been sliding for a decade. Muriel Bowden, who succeeded founding headmistress Emma G. Sebring in 1930, inherited a hard job in hard times. Faculty salaries dipped below other area schools, and good teachers were hard to find and keep. Enrollment had peaked at 275 before the 1929 Crash and then slid, to 233 in 1932, to 175 in the final year. The school building, completed in 1908 and every bit the rival of Trinity's, was too big, and not even the appearance of boys, who were admitted to the first four grades toward the end, filled it.[34]

That was one of Matt Dann's ideas, however, and probably was never intended to fix St. Agatha. From the mid-1930s when Dann first started to work into the leadership position, his mandate was to fix Trinity. After the long drift of Cole's "the Lord will provide" laissez-faire headship, Dann needed to act quickly, and St. Agatha was an urgent problem needing to be addressed or else. With no endowment of its own and with enrollment falling to little more than half capacity, a shaky faculty situation, and pensions to fund, St. Agatha reported a deficit of $30,000 in 1937. Dann and the Trinity/St. Agatha board went after expenses and revenues. Salaries and pensions got cut, and an attempt was made to broaden St. Agatha's curriculum beyond college prep by adding an eight-month secretarial course. The idea was to recruit girls who had finished their junior year of high school elsewhere and who might be attracted to the St. Agatha experience by a practical curriculum of shorthand, typing, business practices, speech, and bookkeeping. They hoped to avoid the appearance of a two-class school: Everybody dressed the same—"in the high school sleeves above the elbow are not permitted"—and participated in the same extracurricular activities. But few new girls came. In 1940, headmistress Bowden resigned amicably and without hint of blame, and Dann moved in as terminal caretaker for what turned out to be St. Agatha's last year in business. He made the most of it. There was much brave talk about combined school spirit, and activities between Trinity boys and St. Agatha girls ratcheted up: joint plays, choral concerts, dancing classes for the younger boys and girls, just plain dances for the older ones. Littlest boys were even enrolled in the primary grades.

It amounted to but a brief respite before the inevitable end. In February 1941 and after a decade of rising deficits, Trinity School announced the closing of St. Agatha. Board president Erskine carried the grim message to a meeting at the school of students, parents, and staff. Some were gracious and understanding, others angry and suspicious. The alumnae association offered a nice letter for the record, thanking Emma Sebring, Muriel Bowden—and Matthew Dann—for all their efforts down the years and expressing the hope "that at some time in the future St. Agatha may be reestablished."[35] It never was, and families with daughters as well as sons would wait another thirty years before the Corporation of the Protestant Episcopal School of New York would open doors to both sexes. The St. Agatha school building by comparison had much life left in it. Trinity promptly sold it for $155,000 to the local Roman Catholic Archdiocese, which recycled it first as the Cathedral Preparatory Seminary and then as the St. Agnes Boys' High School. So St. Agatha was reincarnated as St. Agnes, both once sacrificed for Trinity.

COUNTRY BOYS

Announcement of the decision to shut down St. Agatha came almost exactly one year after Trinity had backed away from another potentially en-
tangling alliance with another failing school, but this one for boys. The
world of Trinity on West 91st Street and St. Agatha on West 87th was about
as urban a world as could be, and by the 1930s one that appeared to many to
have reached, and passed, its peak. The same demographic change (new and
different ethnic neighbors and relatively fewer and fewer middle class Episcopalians) that had emptied the vastness of St. Agnes Chapel and led Trinity Church to abandon it was no doubt also observed with uneasiness by
Dann and the Trinity School board, who harbored their own ideas about
moving or merging or at least guarding their flanks if the neighborhood
slipped too far. Trinity board records from this period are sparse, but we do
know that as early as 1935, that is, even before he was fully ensconced at
headmaster, Dann plotted with John Erskine and St. Agatha headmistress
Muriel Bowden about possibly calling it a day on the Upper West Side, picking up stakes and starting out fresh somewhere else. Specifically, the
thought had been to move the younger boys and girls and high school girls
to an East Side location and the high school boys to the country. The East
Side possibility never got beyond the talking stage, but the country prospect
actually happened, at least in part.

Beginning early in 1939, Trinity entered quiet negotiations to merge with
or to take over (which was not exactly clear) an Episcopal school even more
ailing than itself.[36] The Pawling School in Pawling (Dutchess County), New
York, sixty-five miles north of Manhattan, had been founded by Frederick
Luther Gamage in 1907, earlier the head of St. Paul's School in Garden City
on Long Island and before that teacher of Dann's father at Delaware Academy in Delhi, New York. Pawling was a mere babe by Trinity standards, but
one with what looked like a relatively short life expectancy. Never high up
in the boarding school ranks and eking out a meager existence, Pawling
School suffered from the unhealthy combination of slight endowment and
declining Depression-era enrollment and was slipping fast. From the hole it
was in, Trinity must have looked a comparative pillar. Dann later remarked
that the idea first surfaced in 1937, at lunch with an old acquaintance, travel
writer/broadcaster Lowell Thomas, who expressed Pawling's need for some
sort of partnership.[37] The terms of the proposed agreement certainly sounded
advantageous to Pawling, if only to ensure survival and some continuity, but

should also be interpreted as a measure of Trinity's only slightly better disguised anxiety about its own future and its eagerness to find fresh quarters (160 country acres) if not as an alternative at least as an option. Under the deal, Pawling was to retain its identity though probably with a hyphenated name, the aging founder got to keep his house, and he and several others would get pensions. Pawling would get six seats (a minority) on a new combined board. Dann was to become "supervisory director" over both schools (a new headmaster being appointed for Trinity) and would have full authority over both the heads.[38] Trinity also would have been obligated to pay off Pawling's debts, guarantee its bonds, and make improvements in the physical plant—"and make Pawling a beneficiary of its large endowment fund."[39]

Trinity of course did not have a large endowment fund, by any objective measure (its then most recent benefaction of consequence, the Alan R. Hawley Trust of 1938, was yet to be unlocked and monetized), though it was better off than Pawling. As the months passed, however, Trinity apparently cooled. As if an echo of the Phony War that at that moment held all Europe in suspense, Wesley Oler wrote to fellow Pawling trustee John Burnham that "we have no final word yet on the Trinity business and it has dragged out into a war of nerves here that has all of us somewhat on edge."[40] By early February 1940, the deal had died. Though in their last ditch and probably foreseeing what this would mean for their school, the Pawling negotiators recorded no bitterness toward their Trinity counterparts but rather charged up the failure to the times. "Had times been normal all of these things would have been accomplished," "but with Europe torn by what might easily become a world conflagration, and our own country so filled with economic, social and political uncertainties, the Trinity Board feels it would not be wise to spread itself in any way at this time."[41] Who knows whether it was really the war or just cautious trustees who took their fiduciary responsibilities seriously and understood the principle that the merger of two weak organizations does not make one strong one? Whatever the reason, their reluctance spelled for Pawling the end of the line. In 1942, the school closed (though the corporation did not dissolve), its campus soon leased by the U.S. Army for a cryptography unit and later a rehabilitation center for Army Air Corps fliers.

The idea, however, was not dead but dormant. Soon after the war, Dann, smitten as ever with country visions, resurrected the Pawling project and this time pulled it off. When the army vacated and returned the campus to

the Pawling trustees in 1946, they decided not to try to start again independently but to consent to takeover by Trinity for the price of the mortgage. As
noted, during the war, Trinity had operated a small boarding department of
its own as a convenience to the sons of fathers going into the service and
housed it in the old St. Agnes vicarage.[42] But with no desire to become a
boarding school permanently, at least not in the city, Trinity needed a place
to put the boarders it had and so saw Pawling's availability opportunistically.
That an associated boarding option fairly nearby might also be attractive to
Trinity middle schoolers whose families desired their sons to board for high
school was probably the immediate strategic rationale, with the insurance
of Pawling's green acres against the possible abandonment of the city altogether the long-term one.

In any case, Dann moved quickly to bring Pawling back to life, even en-
listing schoolboy labor. On Thursdays, he loaded Trinity boys into his
Chevy and put their teenage energies to work tearing down some unattractive accretions added to the campus during the army's occupation. He
wanted something new at Pawling, and he got it. He oversaw a $150,000 ren-
ovation before the school reopened for classes in the fall of 1947 as, reported
the press, "an annex of Trinity School." While such language offended some
Pawling alums, the break with the past was deliberate.[43]

This was accurate, partly. First, Trinity added its venerable name to its
new ward. "Trinity-Pawling," Dann claimed, was the inspiration of his
friend Frank Boyden, headmaster of Deerfield Academy and high up the
prep school pole, who thought the best way to jump-start enrollment at the
revived school was to make it look like part of Trinity and hope that some
of Trinity's academic reputation would rub off. Though impossible to measure, it may well have helped.[44] There were some sixty boys at the restart,
which would grow to some 300 over the next twenty years.[45] Trinity also
gave Dann, or half of him. From 1947 to 1955, Dann served as dual headmaster of both Trinity and Trinity-Pawling. A bachelor[46] with his whole life to
give to his job and, in stark contrast to his predecessor Cole, a crusty worka-
holic, Dann seemed to love the challenge. The miles he put on his battered
"woody" station wagon to-ing and fro-ing between town and country could
not be counted, and as Trinity-Pawling resuscitated and post-war Trinity
too prospered, he thought himself the luckiest of men.[47] The schools shared
one board (Trinity's), but not faculty. No one commuted but Dann. Glover
Johnson,[48] Trinity class of 1919, paralleled Dann's dual role, serving for years

as president of the board. Another Trinity alum (class of 1900), trustee from the 1930s and Dann's close friend, Robert Carleton, who lived in nearby Garrison, New York, became one of Trinity-Pawling's, but not Trinity's, greatest benefactors.[49]

Yet Trinity/Trinity-Pawling remained an odd sort of mating. The two schools shared leadership and many intangibles but lived apart. Both were traditional-not-a-hint-of-anything-progressive, all-boys, blazers-and-ties sort of places.[50] Both had and used chapels according to the old Episcopalian rite. Where they overlapped, in grades eight through twelve, their curricula were similar and similarly unadorned. Both practiced combined classroom/playing-field pedagogy aimed to turn young adolescents into educated gentlemen fit for proper colleges. Sports teams from the two schools competed with one another, vigorously. But of the two motives for the union from Trinity's perspective, neither was confirmed by later events. Trinity-Pawling did not serve as an in-house catchment for Trinity eighth-graders thinking about boarding school,[51] and Trinity's leaders themselves never again thought seriously about quitting town for country and so had bought an unnecessary piece of insurance. The relationship was nice but not necessary, at least not necessary for Trinity. Thus eventually it ended (in 1977, after much hemming and hawing)—nicely enough.[52] Of course, the relationship had been absolutely necessary for Trinity-Pawling, which almost certainly would never have come back to life on its own. Though Trinity acted out of its own institutional anxieties, experience proved those anxieties moot. That left in the end, out of the whole thirty-year episode, only a gift: of survival from one independent school to another.

The linkage did, however, prompt the next leadership change at Trinity, when Dann's double burden became too heavy, in his own and the trustees' judgment.[53] Dann favorite Hugh C. Riddleberger was an alum (class of 1934) who had returned to teach math and coach tennis and football at Trinity in 1938 for $1,000 a year. After the war, he returned to the Trinity faculty, and then with the start of the new combined enterprise Dann invited him to the country as assistant headmaster at Trinity-Pawling in 1947. When Dann finally had to choose between the two schools and chose Trinity-Pawling, the decision in 1955 for Riddleberger to become his successor at Trinity was a relatively easy one.

The Trinity-Pawling story, like the St. Agatha story before it, raises an interesting clinical question about the value of horizontal expansion and of growth by acquisition in education. In the business world, it is common at the outset of an acquisition or merger that the value of the acquirer measured by its share price typically falls, at least for a time, while the value of the target rises. If the merger is wisely begotten and skillfully executed, the value of the new entity can indeed rise as bosses on both sides fervently hope. Mergers are also fraught with the perils of misbegotten aims and poor execution and can destroy value as easily as they create it. In the world of schools, no such hard measure as share price defines value, and judgments are ever subjective. However, Trinity's experience with its sister and brother institutions should probably be judged as net value drains. St. Agatha had seemed a pervasively good idea at the time (the turn of the nineteenth century), rather as St. Agnes had seemed at the same time to the vestry of Trinity Church. But both enjoyed brief flowerings, and St. Agatha took ten costly years to shut down. Trinity-Pawling cannot help but have drained Trinity too, and the entire venture is now imaginable only in the context of the relative organizational simplicity of both schools in that era, and of their still largely settled philosophical assumptions. By temperament a one-man manager and no delegator, Matt Dann into the 1960s still functioned as his own development director, alumni coordinator, college placement officer, and omnipresent cheerleader with "his" boys, as well as being chief executive officer and trustee of the corporation. Moreover, he managed his schools largely by benign fiat, and nobody ever much questioned his style. He produced results in keeping with his intentions. He probably saved Trinity, in part by terminating St. Agatha, in part by acquiring the property of St. Agnes on extremely favorable terms. Certainly, he saved Trinity-Pawling. His success should also be judged relative to his starting point. As his longtime close friend Clarence Bruner-Smith, who was becoming the school's academic leader during Dann's administration, remarked after Dann was dead, "What Matt Dann had done was simply incredible, but it was in many ways because the school was at a very low ebb."[54] If Dann had followed the business career he started out to and had become chief executive of a profit-seeking enterprise, he would have been one who kept a sharp eye on the stock price. He also would have had a reputation as a turnaround artist.

TEMPLATE

If Dann was single-minded about putting Trinity on a sound financial track and keeping it there, the "it" that was the focus of his labors made the job easier. At least in the routine of its operation it caused him few additional headaches. Boys themselves changed as they moved up the ranks, but Trinity as an institution in these years was in relatively steady state, its days and seasons if not quite unchanging then largely unreflected upon. This apparent stability is best viewed in the context of external changes whose path eventually, but not yet, would cross with Trinity. Viewed from the highest altitude, the mid-twentieth-century world beyond Trinity changed too, moving through depression and wartime to a (surprisingly) prosperous postwar. From a lower level, the world of New York City experienced its own changes, with the chief one that impinged on Trinity being the change in its immediate neighborhood, once so fashionable but become shabby.[55] At the level of the market for primary and secondary schooling in New York City, Trinity existed against the backdrop of the general success of New York's vast public school system in educating most young New Yorkers, the richest and brightest often as not included among them. This fact left the demand for private alternatives cool and calm.[56] From a later perspective, Trinity amidst the swirl of the city begins to look like an island. Then, it did not, particularly. E. B. White could have had it mind, writing in "Here Is New York" (1949): "New York blends the gift of privacy with the excitement of participation; and better than most dense communities it succeeds in insulating the individual [or institution] (if he wants it, and almost everybody wants or needs it) against all enormous and violent and wonderful events that are taking place every minute."[57] Serious questioning of why this institution was here (or there), of what it was for and how it should go about its business, still lay largely ahead. The template seemed satisfactory and self-evident. The daily job was fitting things to it.

From the printed record to remembered testimony, the evidence confirms that the school's interior academic life—its substance, style, tone, and texture—looked at the end of the 1950s remarkably like it had looked in the 1930s and early 1940s. Sameness should not be mistaken for dullness, however, or lack of choice for lack of challenge. We do not have his testimony, but Lawrence Cole himself, whose view reached back through the entire first half of Trinity's twentieth-century experience and who died in 1956, would have had to look hard to find much (beyond a few new faculty names) unfamiliar or anything profoundly amiss.

Trinity continued to organize itself on a twelve-year plan (the phrase "country day school plan" crept in after the merger with Pawling), divided into a Lower School covering the first eight years and beginning with grade one, and an Upper School or high school that took boys to the point of entrance into college or, as was still said into the 1950s, "into business."[58] The idea was that this meant a continuous track and a "complete curriculum," which was most profited from when a boy went the whole distance. Some did; many didn't.

The school year began the third week in September and followed a time-honored round. There was a mix of sacred and secular holidays—three days off for Thanksgiving, two weeks for Christmas, Lincoln's and Washington's birthdays separately in February, ten days for Spring Break in late March and early April, Good Friday and Memorial Day. Graduation fell on one of the first few days of June. The school operated five days a week, with Saturdays only for makeup work or detention duty. Everyone started with chapel at nine, presided over by a chaplain in lieu of Lawrence Cole who had done the job himself. The littlest boys, grades one and two, had lunch at noon and were dismissed at 12:30. Third through eighth graders (or "second formers," in the English usage as then used interchangeably with the American "grades," through grade twelve or sixth form) worked on until 2:30 and then went to supervised outdoor athletics until 4:00 or 5:00. There were football and soccer in the fall, basketball, boxing, wrestling, skating, and gymnastics in the winter, baseball in the spring. Lower school boys got to school and got home on dedicated school buses, one route for the East Side of the Park, a second for the West. Upper schoolers too began at nine and along with seventh and eighth grades went until 2:30, thence until 5:00 for various athletic and extracurricular activities. Everyone was required to attend physical fitness classes, and to elect other activities that might be athletic (football soccer, baseball, basketball, tennis, wrestling, and track) or might not (rifle, chess, ping-pong, dramatics, glee club, band, art, shop).[59]

Academics at all levels meant straightforward body-of knowledge fundamentals, as it had for decades. The first four grades laid the foundation in reading, writing, and arithmetic. Grades one and two shared an identical list of arithmetic, reading and dramatics, spelling, conversational French, manuscript writing (penmanship), music, art, and religion ("sacred studies"). Grade three added English, social studies, cursive handwriting, and science, while physical education replaced less formal games and recreation. The upper four grades of the Lower School followed the standard curriculum of the New York State Secondary Education Board. By grades five and six, boys got a taste of industrial arts (shop/woodworking). Seventh graders (first formers) learned Latin as well as French, and second formers began algebra. The Upper School curriculum was designed to meet college and scientific schools entrance requirements that stipulated sixteen units to receive a diploma. These included four years of English, two of algebra, one of plane geometry, two years minimum of a foreign language, two years of science, and one of American history. Every boy had to carry at least four courses all of the time.[60]

The life of the mind had the edge, in time anyway, over body and spirit. With the exceptions of religion, civics, and physical education, all classes met four or five class periods per week. Third formers marched through English 1, algebra 1, Latin 1, general science, community civics, sacred studies, and physical education. Fourth formers took up English 2, Latin 2, world history, biology, and French or Spanish. Fifth formers went on to English 3, Algebra 2, modern (European) history, French or Spanish, and Latin 3 or physics. In their sixth-form year, Trinity boys finished out with American history, trigonometry and solid geometry, chemistry or a fourth year of Latin, economics (starting in the 1940s), or mechanical drawing (starting in the 1950s).

Report cards went home each quarter, with written faculty comments at the midyear and end of school. Formal examinations occurred twice a year, at midpoint and end, with final grades worked out based on exam results plus daily work. Starting in 1941 (and through 1954), the school began participating in the standardized testing program of the New York-based Educational Records Bureau. This included a battery of tests (Kuhlmann–Anderson Intelligence Test for grades one through six, the Haggerty Reading Test for grades three and four, the Sangren-Wood Reading Test for grades four and five, the Traxler Silent Reading Test for grade six, the Junior Scholastic Aptitude Test for grades seven through nine, the American Council Psychological Examination and Iowa Silent Reading Test for high schoolers), on which Trinity boys generally performed above public school level and at or above the median for independent school pupils at their respective levels, "showing relatively high academic aptitude and reading achievement." The median IQ of a Trinity boy was 121.5 in 1943, 125.4 in 1946 (the two years for which summaries exist), though there could be a wide range of individual results. One Trinity first grader in 1943 scored an IQ of 76, one sixth grader 158.[61]

It is impossible to recapture the application process much beyond cata-logue descriptions, which suggest a level of informality probably inherited from the Cole era and that persisted long after him.[62] Entrance examina-tions and placement tests clearly were not standard in this era, with empha-sis appearing to fall on previous scholastic record, indication of a boy's "good character and general promise," and of course the all-important inter-view with the headmaster.[63] This might account for such occasional wide spreads in intelligence scores, though the school's general high ranking in the college placement scales spoke well enough for whatever subjective judgment it was that let some boys into Trinity and kept others out.

For promotion and then graduation, the bar does not appear to have been onerously high. In the Lower School, the passing mark was D, and boys who did not manage even that and failed in a subject were required to make up the deficiency within "some reasonable time" or drop back to a lower grade. The passing grade for each high school subject in which a boy had to accumulate units for graduation was 60. However, the admissions process linking elite prep schools and elite colleges was more subjective then too, and based on its graduate placement Trinity had reason to be pleased with things as they were: From the classes of 1947 and 1948 Trinity graduates trooped off to Amherst, Columbia, Cornell, Duke, Harvard, Kenyon, MIT, Princeton, Swarthmore, Trinity, Virginia, Williams, Wes-leyan, and Yale. Many did so, moreover, on the basis of "certification" alone. A number of top colleges then admitted freshmen essentially on the good word of their prep schools without benefit of entrance examinations. Trin-ity, due to its "high academic standing" in the those circles, participated in certifying those sixth formers who showed "definite academic promise" and who in the majority of their courses had achieved minimum lofty grades, not of 60 but 70. It took a standardized test neither to get in, nor to get out.[64]

FACULTY MATTERS

The quality of the academics that shaped test scores and determined col-lege placements was faculty business. No record of faculty/headmaster meetings survives, but Dann day-to-day at least must have deferred at least to his two academic right arms: Bruner-Smith and John Langford,[65] princi-pals respectively of the upper and lower schools. The job of transforming boys of "good character and academic promise" into "college men" belonged to them and other real teachers.

Trinity's in the 1940s and 1950s was a small crew: twenty-two in 1939, twenty-one in 1945, twenty-six in 1949, twenty-eight in 1954, and thirty-six in 1959. An earlier history suggests that Dann may have done some house-cleaning that strengthened the roster.[66] We are left now with names, year-book photographs, and fragmentary personnel files that indicate at least the tone, if not the details, of how he related to faculty. On taking over in 1937, he put everyone of them on a year's probation, and stated that his decisions would be based on performance and loyalty, to him. "In retaining the staff which I have taken over from Doctor Cole, for one year, I am giving each master the opportunity to demonstrate his loyalty to me, his ability, and his readiness to cooperate with the exacting demands of the new regime," he wrote (this to his friend Bruner-Smith, but the same to everyone). "During the year I shall evaluate the organization and will retain those masters whose efficiency, loyalty, personality and cooperation measure to the stan-dard which I shall require."[67]

The vocabulary was fairly direct: "new regime," "efficiency," "coopera-tion," "loyalty." It would appear to have been a shot across the bow of low-performance teachers, though it is frustrating not to know specifically who they were or how Dann measured faculty performance. There are occa-sional hints at the locus of dissatisfaction. To Bertram Bartram, who taught manual arts and math in the Lower School, Dann in a letter otherwise iden-tical to that sent to Bruner-Smith in 1937 pointed out "the weakness in the Lower School faculty, of having no master qualified to assist in the after-noon athletic program. I hope this weakness can be corrected, or I shall have to make changes which will bring to the department men who com-bine teaching and athletic ability."[68] Certainly Bruner-Smith was no low performer and possibly was excluded informally from the stern tone of the letter.[69] Dann probably hoped to have a salutary effect short of dismissals, on which the record is largely but not entirely silent. In 1939 Dann dismissed long-time "physical director" William H. Simpson, Jr., who in consideration of his long association with the school was paid a full year's salary. Also in 1939, he let go part-time chaplain the Rev. George Hall when Trinity Church rector and school board member Frederic Fleming offered to share one of his staff for less cost.[70] Wartime soon strained most labor pools, including male schoolteachers, which made for a sellers' market and made employers grateful for what men they had. Thenceforth, however, everyone at Trinity got a contract, one year at a time. Everyone served at the pleasure of the headmaster with provision for resignation/termination on thirty days' no-tice. Starting in 1942, each contract also contained a war clause: "If the school should close as a result of the bombing of New York your contract terminates as of the day of closing. In the event of an evacuation your con-tract terminates as of the day of evacuation."[71]

Employment records for the years before Dann do not survive. Whether or not yearly contracting was also then the rule, the important change wrought by Dann was closer scrutiny of how faculty actually performed year to year. He made it clear to faculty that he was a headmaster who paid attention, and that what he paid attention to most was feedback from par-ents. Of course, he had come into Trinity's top job facing strained budgets, weak enrollments, sagging physical plant, and, apparently, some faculty flabbiness. In 1937, this was an immediate anxiety, but it reflected an endur-ing conviction. Every contract letter for years opened with the same verbiage that wrapped up in good words a dire warning. In addition to a master's ob-vious classroom responsibilities, "there should be a cheerful readiness on the part of a master, to accept special duties in connection with the carrying for-ward of the work of the school." Teaching at Trinity was not for nine-to-fivers. Expect to arrive early and stay past closing. Expect to attend every chapel. Expect to attend conferences and keep up with one's field. "The wel-fare and happiness of the boys must be a primary consideration. Frankly, the boys make our jobs possible, and the masters should be ready to make per-sonal sacrifices in their interests."[72]

It was the part after the "frankly" that probably was meant to have the two-by-four-on-the-forehead effect. Unhappy students meant unhappy parents, and parents paid or didn't. Trinity was a choice for people who had other schooling options for their sons, most importantly a then still-esteemed public system. Teachers constituted every school's front and middle and back line, and to Dann the test of a good one was not complicated: "A successful teacher must have a genuine friendliness for the boys and should enjoy their companionship."[73]

The flavor of his correspondence with faculty through the years de-scribes the patience with detail of a good administrator running a fairly small shop, trying to attract, motivate and retain talent. In March 1941, Thomas K. Brown III, a young New York University Ph.D. who taught Spanish, French, and German, petitioned for more money because he had just gotten married, because the cost of living was going up (he enclosed a clip from *TIME* that prices were up 45 percent over pre-war levels), because he had high replacement value ("It's unlikely that you could find another teacher who could handle three languages with any sort of competence and the salary for two would far exceed mine"), and because he had a 4F draft classification and thus would be around and would be in demand. He said the figure he "had in mind" was $3,000. Dann offered him $1,800. Brown took it (in four days and asked the headmaster to be on the watch for any tutoring jobs).[74] In April 1945, Dann hired Judson C. Loomis as director of music for the 1945–46 school year for $2,500, to teach the boys of the Lower School and to restart an Upper School band program, only to have Loomis resign in June because of money and the wartime housing shortage. Loomis had gotten a too-good-to-turn-down offer from a boarding school that came with "a whole house, light, heat, laundry . . ." He wrote Dann that he had spent two months looking for an apartment in New York and the best he could do was "the waiting list of the Van Tassel Apartments in Tarrytown." Of course Dann released him from his contract but was miffed. He had just helped place "two other good men in music in other schools" and would have used one of them at Trinity had he known. Now it was midsummer, when shorthanded headmasters had to scramble. "So far as the housing situation is concerned," he closed, "I could have given you some help had you called upon me."[75] In 1947, Dann was somewhat more successful with Trinity alumnus Charles D. Walker hired as director of music, and together they plotted over their mutual keenness for a new chapel organ, even presenting to the board a $9,000 proposal including a complete stop list from Boston builder Aeolian Skinner.[76] Alas, Walker too stayed just two years. (The organ took a bit more time.)

Others, it seemed, had stayed forever. When alumnus of the class of 1895 Sidney Aylmer Small, science master since 1901 and senior master in the Upper School, retired in 1941 because of ill health, it was Dann who wrote the special memorial and resolution to the board, laying it on thick and likely enjoying himself: "His devotion to his Alma Mater . . . his loyalty to us . . . the high quality of teaching it was his gift to dispense . . . the beauty of his character and its superlative ideals." Chips lived.[77] Highs do not stand without the lows, however, which could be very low, as with the (blessedly rare) headmaster's nightmare that occurred in 1947 when a master was forced to resign because of "a sex problem" with a Lower Schooler.[78]

TWO BOYS' LIVES

The yearbook listed faculty deferentially in order of seniority, and most of the turnover was "natural," from retirements and not terminations. It was a stable fraternity/sorority of respectable provenance. Columbia predominated (Dann had his B.A. and M.A. from there), with Trinity, Harvard, Yale, New York University, Williams, Hamilton, and Rochester reliably represented plus occasional outliers from Virginia, Sewanee, and Oxford.[79] All in the Upper School were white men ever in suits (Dann, always pictured with them, usually in pinstripe), and in the Lower School white men and women in high-collared dresses. The students they taught looked anyway likewise monochromatic, to the eye at least, with names identifiably Anglo/Irish/ northern European: Brown, Craig, Evans, Hadley, Hastings, Parker, and Smith.[80]

In the 1940s and 1950s and counting neither St. Agatha nor Trinity-Pawling, Trinity grew respectably, enrolling between 241 (1940) and 420 (1959) students, all boys, with Upper School graduating classes numbering steadily in the thirties. It did so while reaching out to no discernibly new constituencies. Directories indicate a fluctuating but steady mix of boys from both East and West sides with a few from outer boroughs and the suburbs. The nicely scrubbed faces that stare out from the pages of class yearbooks are almost uniformly white (this in a city that was far less so but yet unroiled by civil rights), and came from families of which a steadily increasing majority paid full fees for their sons' schooling. Trinity was a Christian/ Episcopal prep school for a tiny number of boys from New York's middle class.

"Middle-class-ness" in America has always had as much to do with the sense of one's prospects as with the level of one's income, more a matter of self-selection and self-identification than of family ties, ethnicity, or religion. In the New York City of the 1940s, still a patchwork of small provincial neighborhoods, and when $20,000 was a handsome wage, Trinity could afford its modesty. Two old schoolboys report on how that felt. One's name is relatively prominent in the records of the school: his father on the staff as school doctor, he himself a boy who went the full Trinity distance and later did distinguished service as a trustee. The other's name is less known, but as a boy with brothers who went to Trinity after him and as a Trinity short-termer, he is more typical.[81]

Broward Craig entered the first grade in 1934 and graduated from the twelfth in 1946. His grandfather was a New York City policeman, his father a solo-practicing pediatrician who made house calls for $5 a round. The family lived on East 96th Street and their son rode the cross-town bus to Trinity, when he didn't ride with his father who also served as Trinity's doctor. In those days, Craig remembered, "you were known by the company you kept," and if there were friends in your neighborhood who went to Trinity, that was where you wanted to go too. The Craig family were Episcopalians, the kind who didn't much go to church but recognized Trinity as "very much a church school." Craig the father worked six days minimum and slept on Sunday afternoons; Craig the son made weekend calls with him, waiting outside in the car. He recalled taking French in the third grade, time spent in the old St. Agnes Annex, tastes of early football, and awe felt for head coach Duffy Dougherty, who went from Trinity to the big time at Michigan State. Moving up, he learned more about Dann, a tightly wound spring of enthusiasm who though no athlete himself also coached junior varsity (JV) basketball, and for a time taught, too, math in the Upper School. Dann "ran the show." When, as head of the Student Council in the mid-forties, Craig found it hard to get excited about wartime paper drives, Dann commanded, "Get excited!" He did. Though it exaggerates and is not exactly confirmed in the record, Craig's description of Dann's relations with the faculty—"he went through teachers the way Sherman went through Georgia"—captured a certain truth about a man whose personality and style were "very definite." The school was "his life. He was there all the time. Bruner-Smith was his best friend." Craig remembered teachers going off to war, two fraternities ("for the achievers" and not socially exclusive), graduation in the chapel with faculty in regalia. Boys stood up in class to answer questions and wrote a good deal at the board. There was no honor code, but classes were small, masters watchful, and "it never came up." In an era still favoring self-control over self-expression, boys behaved or at least knew how to watch out. The worst transgression? "Smoking and you were out—even down at the corner."[82]

John Beebe was six years younger and started out his school days at the Oberlin School on the East Side, where his family lived in rented apartments, first on 82nd and then on 79th streets. His father was an insurance broker, his mother (like Craig's) stayed home, the family part of "a relatively subdued society." As he grew toward middle school, the family wanted an

Episcopal school but without any hints of snobbery. Trinity had that reputation. Beebe had just turned eight in 1941 when his parents brought him for the admission interview with Dann: "an imposing man with a big presence and very sure of himself." Beebe passed muster, but "did not know a soul." He too rode the cross-town bus, and later was allowed to walk across Central Park. Two brothers, three and nine years younger, would follow him to Trinity (and follow him out). He recalled wooden desks with flip-up tops; Miss Hand, his math teacher, who made multiplication fun by making a ball game out of it; Lower School principal John Langford, "a real gent, who had exquisite penmanship even at the blackboard"; football (right guard) in seventh grade on the dirt lot where St. Agnes used to be, and wrestling in eighth grade. He was a catcher in baseball, and learned basketball "very methodically" in the old gym that was just "too tight for showy lay-ups and slam dunks." He was a good athlete and a middling student. Through middle school, Beebe found Latin a challenge, but also found that it was "easy to pad your grade by being a polite, attentive student." Most students "were OK academically, some extremely good." He remembered one Jewish boy, and religion as an "accepted part of school life." He had no awareness that either family money or social standing mattered much among the boys, and parents, his anyway, kept respectful distance, showing up as expected once or twice a year for parent–teacher nights. He did not know Craig but did remember his doctor father. Wartime impinged little on Beebe's Trinity—"we had a very narrow exposure to the world"—except for "lots of Spanish rice and filler in the lunch room." Beebe would have been perfectly happy staying on at Trinity: "I was regimented there, every day the same nice routine." But that had never been the plan. His father had gone to The Hill School in Pennsylvania and so, without comment or complaint, would he, leaving Trinity after the ninth grade in the spring of 1947. No thought was given to Trinity-Pawling, which would start up that same autumn desperate for students. Hill was the Beebe school. It too was old (relatively, founded 1851), it had a proper chapel, fine faculty, football, and was of course all boys. Hill and thence Princeton would claim a larger part of Beebe's latter-day school loyalty than farther off Trinity, but Trinity had done its job and prepared him well.[83]

AT THE MARGIN

Dann's strategy for prosperity through growth appeared to work, or at least it worked in general. There was one significant disjuncture between aims and performance. For a school that proudly offered a "full twelve-year program" for boys from the time they were near-toddlers to the time they were near-men, not many students went the full course. Only a third to a quarter, often less, of graduating seniors between 1944 and 1960 had been at Trinity for more than eleven years. Large majorities clocked less than three.[84] This meant two things. The Lower School did not feed the Upper School as the catalogue said it ideally might have done, with most Lower Schoolers continuing their education elsewhere (boarding school, public high school, families moving away). The Upper School meanwhile succeeded by attracting a majority of its boys from families up to then outside the Trinity fold but shopping around and who eventually landed on West 91st Street. Once they did, there is scant indication that any were not well pleased.

Dann worked hard to fix the school's weaknesses in order win students. This meant winning them at any and all points of entry. "Twelve years" sounded nice and no doubt then conferred the optimum (just as it would many years later, when the principal entry point into Trinity was its intensely competitive *kindergarten*) of steadfast nurture in education. That not more parents availed themselves of that opportunity for their sons must be explained by the available alternatives, chiefly one suspects public schools widely deemed to work well or well enough, and lack of anxiety that if their sons did not get into and carry through at Trinity they would not get into the Ivies or suffer some other crippling disadvantage in life's next steps. Dann and his faculty did not want or need large numbers; they needed to fill the desks they had. Their even-then aging school building clearly limited size of enrollment, but it was probably the market that limited it too. If it was as hard as the numbers would indicate it was to retain boys for the long haul, however advantageous "twelve years" was claimed to be, then Trinity's evolution in these years is better understood as chipping away at the margins of schooling. Dann after all had worked in the business world before he got into education and probably understood that the margin is where profit is earned and business success determined. As a sum of examples shows, this was neither dramatic nor glamorous, but it built for permanence bit by bit.

In 1944, when St. Agnes Chapel so unceremoniously disappeared, it was just one more bit. Mundanely, the site yielded a football field, and in winter a skating rink. In springtime, tennis, baseball, and track teams took advantage of a place to practice right at school, with the result that participation and performance in athletics at Trinity soon improved. It was all dirt and cinders and nothing fancy, but it did the job. Sports and winning teams attracted boys, and in space-starved Manhattan the school's transformation of an underused house of worship into hard-used playing fields was a strategic coup at the time, however cavalier it would look to preservationists later. It was endless blocking and tackling. At the same time they worked hard to provide for playing fields, Dann and treasurer William Gage Brady, Jr. (class of 1904) converted the school building's heating system from coal to oil, renovated the library, and moved the shop to more spacious quarters. In 1946, Trinity inaugurated its first faculty advisor system, which assigned to each boy a teacher to counsel him on problems inside and outside of school. The acquisition of Pawling added another arrow to Trinity's competitive quiver. The same year, plans moved forward to remodel the chapel and plans were drawn up, pending financing, for construction of a new gym to replace the one originally on the top floor of the 91st Street building. Though the new gym was delayed, a contract was signed for a new chapel organ, one of Dann's pet causes. The chapel renovation was finished in 1949, with the help of Trinity Parish and friends of the school, and was furnished out as a dual-use chapel–auditorium. Obstructive concrete columns came down, once-drab walls got dignified wood paneling, indirect lighting supplanted old-time globes, and new heating and air conditioning were installed. The new space was dedicated in March 1949 with a performance of Benjamin Britten's "Saint Nicholas" cantata by Trinity boys helped out by young ladies from Spence.

Space renovation served the cause of improved educational services that were additive. In 1950, the school rebuilt and re-equipped the physics laboratory, more or less untouched since the 1920s, in anticipation of refitting labs for biology and chemistry as well. In the Lower School, the shop was reconditioned and a manual arts instructor added to the faculty. Arrival of the new organ finished off the chapel renovation. The next school year, the lower main hall got a facelift with couches and armchairs better to welcome visitors, and the new chemistry lab reached completion. Alumni meanwhile stepped forward with the beginnings of a fund dedicated to constant improvement of the physical plant, with an eye specifically on the long-sought new gym. In 1952, two new committees took shape, first for the time in embracing both faculty and students, for the purpose of planning assemblies and expanding the library. The school band got the boost of a new director, and intramural athletics joined the more competitive interscholastic program to help build Trinity boys' bodies along with their minds and spirits.

To make them all feel part of the team, Dann upped the dress-code ante. Coats and ties had been the rule for all except the smallest Trinity boys since time immemorial, but starting in 1953 all students would sport regulation Trinity blazers, smart crest, Latin motto, and all, on the breast pocket. This was uncontroversial, partly because it was then more rule than exception in the prep school world of which Trinity saw itself a part. It was not just a matter of joining the crowd or of sartorial taste (Dann's own ran to natty double-breasted pinstripes), but of efficiency and equality. Dann thought dress uniformity, not just similarity, simplified things and was "conducive to a more democratic way of life."[85] Not that Trinity was a democracy, but among its "aims" was to ready boys to live in one. Competition and rivalry in clothes, even in an all-boys setting, distracted from the true business of schooling. Blazers banished it.[86] Students did get the occasional small tastes of self-rule, however. The Student Council that year got a broadened brief that included responsibility for Trinity's work program previously under supervision of a master, and the advisor system got renewed emphasis, affording students the opportunity to see and discuss their grades with a master before grades and comments went home to parents. The alumni society continued to raise money toward the new gym and meantime resurfaced the tennis courts.

Through the early 1950s, Dann kept two faces about him: the strenuous embodiment of optimism and school spirit that the boys reported, and the fretful one he kept to himself and his fellow governors. He saw independent schooling as a service business that juggled three big variables: enrollment, which represented demand; faculty, which represented the intellectual capital that supplied it; and physical plant, which was necessary both to keep out the rain and be attractive enough to help lure families to Trinity. Enrollment, it is now clear, was reasonably resilient, which did not mean that its steadiness and modest growth could be taken for granted then, and Dann presumed nothing. Gently, numbers and tuition nudged upward.[87]

Faculty salaries, though, were ever a problem. In 1952 Dann reported that despite small increases made each year, the scale at Trinity had fallen behind competing schools, ranging as it did from $4,450 (Upper School Senior Master Bruner-Smith), $4,300 (Lower School Senior Master John E. Langford), and $4,000 (Physical Director Dudley Maxim) at the top end, to

$1,200 (Alexander Maigi, instrumental music) at the bottom.[88] (Dann that year was paid $6,000, his secretary $3,600.) The demand for increased salaries was a constant drumbeat. "Good help is difficult to secure, regardless of the level or the job [and] there is little we can do about it since the market is a competitive one." Though confident the school was operating with a lean faculty roster and with the lowest possible overhead, Dann thought that "it is in this area of [faculty] costs that the real school problem exists." Talent cost.[89] Dann's successor, Hugh Riddleberger, felt no different and harped on it from the very start: "The present salaries seem quite unrealistic and we cannot hope to encourage an able and stable faculty unless we are competitive."[90] A year and a half later he complained of "weak points [on the faculty] which will be eliminated only if we can offer tangible inducements to better men. There are areas of real mediocrity which will do Trinity harm in the future, but it is impossible to replace them with stronger men unless we can offer some worthwhile benefits." Trinity's average salary by then (1957) had risen, to $4,200, but that was still only the starting salary for New York City area public school teachers. It was the early days of what would become an enduring refrain: how to live in New York on what Trinity paid? With the norm of double-income families still far in the future, Riddleberger worried particularly that Trinity could not hold married men. "We have 13 who are married out of 31. This is far out of balance."[91]

BOYS' VOICES

What administrators did—how they attracted and managed and stretched the resources to do it—tells a story from the top down. Most of the individuals ever to pass through Trinity were students, largely oblivious to matters of strategy and finance. We have some of what they left behind from those times. Together they etch a picture of Trinity at mid-twentieth century that looks simple, innocent even, when compared with a later Trinity where the student newspaper could headline an article on the school's condom policy.[92] Buttoned up or down as the case may have been, repressed, certainly controlled—pick any 1950s cliché, and Trinity reflected it: blazers, white boys alone, plain-Jane curriculum with few electives, a rifle range in the basement, a Coke machine dispensing fizzy water in green glass bottles for a dime.

"Hackley Conquers Blue and Gold in Final Period 13–6"; "Sports Program is Planned for Year"; "Council Elections Held in Assembly of Upper

School"; "New Secretary and Master Join Staff"; "Charles Essig '37 Killed in Service." Headlines from page 1 of the school paper, *The Trinity Times,* for October 27, 1943, sound timeless, for those times: the round of school doings, generally heavy on sports and some dramatics, In the paper, the Upper School always came first, then a page for the Lower School, and then, on the editorial page, the boys on the paper staff having fun playing at journalism.[93] From the perspective of later years when engagement with communities beyond the school would be encouraged and even expected, the insularity of this record is striking. World War II was something of an exception. The notice of the death of Charles Essig in a plane crash in the Aleutian Islands, the third Trinity boy killed in the war up to then, was an example of the double consciousness that the war evoked: The notice appeared sandwiched between a photograph of the varsity football team beat that week by Hackley, and a boxed notice for "Trinity vs. Riverdale at Riverdale, Election Day, 2:30."[94] The voice of little boys may have captured this spirit best. On the Lower School page for November 1943, Tom White, a fifth grader, wrote a poem about "Winter": "I like to have a snowball fight / Until it gets quite late at night, / I like Christmas with all its joys / I like Santa when he brings toys." Two columns over, sixth grader Tony Russell wrote one about America's then enemy, "The Japs": "The Japs are a yellow race—they snoop around in every place; / But when an American comes around, / There are no Japs to be found—For the Japs are a yellow race."[95] Classmate John S. Gleason admonished everyone to save paper: "If you are a smoker you use paper in several ways. Cigars and cigarettes have paper coverings. Milk bottles have paper tops and milk containers are part paper. In these critical times our government wants us to save, save, SAVE!"[96] Another sixth grader, Chisolm McAvoy, wrote a short report on the experience of his Uncle John landing in Sicily—"the Italians used wooden bullets . . . if Patton wasn't there we would never have held the beach"—who later mustered out with an honorable medical discharge and, the nephew reported, with a new attitude on life: "He said he was sick of war and wanted to earn a decent living for his family."[97]

The war was of course closer for high schoolers, with a large proportion of graduating seniors entering the army or navy. Dann initiated a duty, honor, country military supplement to the paper in 1943, with a growing honor roll and short reports on Trinity men in service. A special prayer was offered each week in chapel for old boys in uniform. Come home soon, and safe: "We are proud of you and we await the day when peace returns to our land so we can welcome you back to Trinity."[98] In the first half of the 1940s, some 300 Trinity alums served in the armed forces, along with ten faculty. Eight alums—Charles H. Essig 1937, Jack Watson 1929, Halsted L. Hopping 1919, Colin Campbell 1937, Edward Nelson 1937, Ellery Huntington III 1942, Clarence MacLean 1934, Eldred Kerry 1937—died in uniform.[99] Through the war years, "Buy Bonds and Stamps" ads interspersed with the time-honored ones from Brooks Brothers, Rogers Peet, and Reid's Ice Cream. As the post-war period approached, fifth- and sixth-form Trinity boys partici-pated in a forum for schools in the New York metropolitan area organized by the Foreign Policy Association (FPA) on "the economic, political and so-cial difficulties which are bound to confront all nations at the conclusion of the present conflict." Trinity was assigned South Africa for its particular field of study, which, a mature-sounding *Trinity Times* editorialist wrote, "may seem remote to most Americans, yet it has a race problem very simi-lar to that of our own South." Whether or not he was reading directly from the FPA literature, he sounded ahead of his times: "Until the bulk of the American people realize how highly interdependent the world of today is, they cannot grasp the absolute necessity of post-war cooperation with other nations."

Maybe, but Trinity boys still were boys who read in the adjacent "Chalk Dust" column about lower things: "By the way, have you ever considered the interesting subject of the crap-shooting movement in America? I knew a crapshooter once. A great guy. Positively brilliant. Killed in a razor fight last year. Too bad. Well, the game was originated in Africa, we believe. Brought over on a slave ship by a fellow named . . ."[100] All of this, along with sweet notices for school dances in a gym decorated with blue and gold crepe paper streamers, passed the mindful eye of the faculty sponsor, English master Bruner-Smith. Mothers ran the Trinity Exchange: "Clothing, books, sports equipment, lots of Trinity caps, rainwear. We have blue suits for cash. Will each boy please bring in a tie? Come in and use your credit."[101]

Into the 1950s the tone persisted of an earnest ordered interior world in-sulated from but not deaf to the outside. Get involved. Boost school spirit. Support the teams. Go to the dances. Occasionally lend a hand outside school even, as at the Yorkville Youth Center where Trinity boys helped out with needy children.[102] Behave in chapel. Be informed. When the Korean War broke out in 1950, a *Trinity Times* editorial admonished boys to be ready "physically and scholastically" for national service: "It's Up to You."

Trinity boys needed to "work to perfect all our abilities so that they may be a benefit to us, and we to our country, for there will be a great demand for able leaders in the future."[103] Cooperation is important. "The Draft and You" counseled boys that eighteen-year-olds were not being drafted "yet," and "to continue with your plans and hope for the best." Best, if possible, to enter the armed forces with the maturity gained in college. Facts changed every day but "the most important thing for us to do now is to keep our marks high, and our goals in front of us."[104] Mature as this sounds, the real adult presence was never far off, particularly Dann's, and one senses a lid tightly screwed on. "Disciplined Education," the headline of a 1953 editorial, echoed his philosophy of Trinity: "Freedom of the individual comes from discipline, rather than discipline from freedom of the individual." The student editorialist continued that Trinity was "as liberal in our policies as discretion allows . . . but we stop at the uncontrolled and uncontrollable bedlam which all too often results from the undisciplined, so called progressive, education."[105]

Not all Trinity boys, however, were disciplined all the time, and after-school social life Dann sometimes thought was out of hand and an issue that touched on school–home relations. Distressing upper school absenteeism on Monday mornings, he primly told Trinity mothers at tea in December 1953, was likely because too many boys stayed out too late at night and "indulge in too active a social life." This was most likely because boys did not have enough responsibility at home. "There is a tendency," he contended, "for parents to do things which are often against their better judgment." The mothers apparently agreed, adding dark worries about "un-chaperoned parties and party crashing."[106] No doubt more to a headmaster's liking was the wholesome relaxation afforded by the refurbished school snack bar, with its vending machines for Coke, fruit juice, and crackers (all set carefully out of sight for a more attractive appearance), cozy knotty pine paneling, tables and chairs with smart red leather cushions, walls hung with college banners and "catching murals." It was open all day but mainly an after-school spot for "the T. S. Gentlemen to congregate."[107] Some enterprising gentlemen were not beyond temptation, however, and it wasn't long before someone pilfered eight cases of Coke empties from the snack bar: "We pity any boys who have stolen bottles for the paltry two cents each brings. But this large-scale disappearance is due mainly to an equally large-scale lack of consideration; those bottles should not now be missing, and the Times should not now have to be reminding students of their responsibilities."[108] *Et in Arcadia ego.*

Seniors traditionally produced the yearbook, and the class of 1954 produced one shot through with Shakespeare. They then learned the Bard from masters like Bruner-Smith and Stanley Willis, and it was schoolboy stuff. But Shakespeare is filled with boys and with stories of what it means to become a man. That is probably how it was taught at Trinity, as much with moral as literary purpose. The bottom-up truth that it conveys now is about how schoolboys then had fun with high language. "Teach me, dear creature, how to think and speak" from *Comedy of Errors* introduced the section on the faculty. "I am a gentleman of blood and breeding," from *Lear*, introduced the sixth-form boys. Senior John Knowles Buckner, who was salutatorian, Cum Laude Society, varsity soccer, basketball, and baseball, and "close to being the elusive all-around boy," was tagged with "Tis an office of great worth, and you an officer fit for the place" from *Two Gentlemen of Verona*. Lawrence Evans, who was bound for Princeton after the full twelve years at Trinity, mostly loved messing around with boats: "I desire no more delight than to be under sail and gone" from *Merchant of Venice*. Charles Danzoll was a Virginian who impressed even stickler Bruner-Smith with the power of his vocabulary: "Well said: that was laid on with a trowel" from *As You Like It*. "My salad days, when I was green in judgment" from *Antony and Cleopatra* introduced third, fourth, and fifth formers; "And one man in his time plays many parts" from *As You Like It* brought on extracurricular activities. "Where to you with bats and clubs" from *Coriolanus* introduced sports. "Then the whining schoolboy with his satchel and shining morning face, creeping like a snail unwillingly to school" from the Seven Ages of Man in *As You Like It* finished up the little boys of the Lower School.[109]

About Trinity boys' borrowings from the Bard there was nothing unique. They might well have borrowed the idea, perhaps even the very quotes, from other schools' yearbooks. Adolescents striving for profundity still so indulge and still bring grins to grown-ups. This is because of the peculiar mix of seriousness and fun, the heavy and the light that may be unique to that age group: young people (still only boys/men in the case of 1950s Trinity) just on the threshold of stepping out from home and school and into college, work, the military, but not quite over the threshold either. Few of those boys would have said Trinity under businessman Dann had not been hard. Fewer, if any, would not have confessed it had also been fun.

OLD BOYS

All schools that last have alums, and, ancient as it was by American standards, Trinity by mid-century had thousands. Its claim over them, however, was historically slight, if not in terms of sentiment, which to the limited extent documented was rich, then certainly in terms of institutional utility. Starting in the 1890s, alumni organizations had sputtered, and there is no record of deliberate, administration-directed activity intended to organize alumni for continuing involvement with and support of the institution until Dann's administration. In 1938, the first full year of Dann's tenure, appeared the first issue of *The Trinity Alumni News*, a descendent of earlier on-and-off attempts of alums to communicate regularly with one another around school subjects. This was not the same thing as the school communicating with alums around the subject of supporting alma mater with more than expressions of warm feeling. Even though sustained formalized alumni giving was still a thing of the future, some alums did express their feeling of obligation to give something back and pressed others to join them. "Whether we had scholarships or not, we must be aware that the education we received there was of far greater worth than the relatively small amount of dollars and cents that we actually paid," wrote alum and board member T. G. Cortelyou. "It is to Trinity's thorough preparation that most of us owe whatever measure of success we may have attained, and it was there that the foundation upon which our later studies were set, was first formed." For a first modest fund drive to furnish the rehabilitated school library, little bits, not just big checks, were welcome. Just about everyone could, and should, manage to part with fifty cents maybe even a dollar or two: "So let's keep Trinity on top—we have no Eton or Harrow in this country and it strikes us that Trinity with its genuine traditions is the closest approximation that we can offer—so forego the next Scotch and soda or two and send in our check."[110]

For a school that looked about as monochromatic indeed as Eton or Harrow, Trinity alums had at least diverse tastes. For high rollers, there was "The Trinity Club," organized by younger alums on property, owned by Yale University, known as Yale Farms in Greenwich, Connecticut. The building was formerly owned by the Greenwich Polo Club and surrounded by forty acres, where gentlemanly sport was the thing: softball, touch football, badminton, horseshoes, and skiing and sleighing in winter. For those wishing something less strenuous and more modest there were beer parties: "the first one, held early in February [1938, we do not know where], was a big success, if what we can learn from mousing around among the boys who were there is true. It was a grand party, and the price was only fifty cents for all the beer you could drink. Our next one will be held after Lent is over."[111]

As in play so in work: Alumni notes began to appear regularly in the Trinity Times in the 1950s and recorded boys-turned-men with wide-ranging careers in and beyond New York.[112] From the class of 1938, Ralph Calaceto was an adjustment manager for Ohrbach's in Newark. Martin Albert ran a photography equipment business in Richmond. Charles Scully supervised a rehab program for the Veterans Administration in Washington, D.C. From 1941, Herman Livingston managed a radio station in Grand Forks, North Dakota. Classmate John Fraser was married at St. Thomas Church Fifth Avenue with a reception aboard the *Kungsholm*. From 1942, Eric Neff was at Oxford. From 1943, Lawrence Luhrs worked as a petroleum consultant in Saskatchewan. From 1946, future trustee Broward Craig was an army lawyer stationed in Charlottesville. From 1947, Fritz Kenny was finishing up Johns Hopkins medical school; Tracy Scudder and George Selly were pursuing their medical educations at Columbia. Leonel Mitchell and Douglas Pimm were ordained deacons in the Episcopal Church. Will Ackerman worked for Dictaphone in Bridgeport. Alfred Boote was in the navy in Alameda, California. Former Marine Miguel del Rio (an early-appearing Hispanic name) worked with a Texas oil company and was posted to the Gold Coast of then British West Africa. John T. Henderson lived in the West Village in Manhattan, a script writer for Mutual radio and TV. From 1950, alums were just getting out of college: Richard Amill from Brown, Herbert Fanning from Swarthmore, Walter Millis III from Amherst, Charles Sheldon from Williams, Peter Trent from Princeton, William Kohl from Kansas State. For this generation of alums, family vied with career, and correspondents reported lots of weddings fresh out of college and babies that came along quickly.

MID-CENTURY

Neither the Pawling connection, nor the blazers, nor the boys-alone, nor the easy middle-class-ness of it all would last. The then still relatively straightforward, nonelective curriculum was bound to change. Still, it is possible to see in this vanished Trinity the rudiments of institutional maturity. It had taken the school 250 years to get to this solid-seeming spot.

When that anniversary observance began in September 1958, President Dwight Eisenhower was nearly halfway through his second term in office, and events did not let him coast to the end. The previous July, American Marines had landed in Beirut to forestall a Nasserite coup. In September 1959, Soviet Premier Nikita Khrushchev visited the United States, including a stop in New York and a stay at Camp David, during which plans were laid for a summit meeting the next summer to address the status of Berlin and other Cold War issues. Then on May 1, 1960, the Russians shot down Gary Powers's U-2 spy plane, flummoxed Eisenhower, and collapsed the Vienna summit. Not to mention a vice-president/heir apparent he didn't much care for, Ike was an old man with a lot on his mind. Yet there survives in the Trinity archives a note on White House letterhead from March 1959 addressed to Trinity headmaster Hugh Riddleberger and signed in Eisenhower's unmistakable sweeping hand: "As Trinity celebrates its 250th Anniversary, I am delighted to send greeting to its students, faculty, alumni, and friends."[113]

We do not know how this got arranged or who arranged it, though a fair guess is then New York governor and fellow Republican Nelson A. Rockefeller, who sent a letter, too, and with whom some Trinity trustees and alums likely had ties. Rockefeller's writers were less disciplined than Ike's. Nineteen fifty-nine in New York State had been dubbed the "Year of History," commemorating Henry Hudson's exploration up his namesake river and Samuel de Champlain's foray to his namesake lake. Trinity's 250th meshed nicely with "history," and the governor's note homed in on the school's chosen anniversary theme, "A Time for Rededication." "There never could be a more fitting period for this theme than the day in which we live, a day teeming with new challenges and new problems. It is encouraging to everybody to know that Trinity School is so rededicated. May it stand as a beacon of culture and spiritual rededication for generations to come."[114] Eisenhower's writers kept it simpler: "I understand this historic institution was founded in 1709 to provide training 'in piety and useful learning' . . . and I add my congratulations, best wishes," etc.[115]

Presidents routinely sign thousands of such communications, and who knows if Ike even read what he put his name to. But the old-timey words—"piety and useful learning"—sounded credible coming from the small-town boy who went to West Point, became famous in wartime, and then became president. Until he became surprise president of Columbia University in 1950, Eisenhower had probably never gotten close to a private school, and his speech/letter writers too worked with canned words. The ones they thought best represented their boss in this instance also best represented Trinity at that moment in its long history. A fancier fellow in every respect than Eisenhower, Rockefeller had nattered on about New York and rededication (to what, exactly, was a little vague). Ike spoke plainly of piety and utility. Not that he knew anything about the school firsthand, but Trinity through the 1950s remained a remarkably plain, pious place. The old president's stately signature underscored it.

Both letters were solicited for and presented publicly at the biggest do of the anniversary year, a dinner on the Starlight Roof of the Waldorf-Astoria on April 27, 1959, "ten dollars per cover, black tie preferred."[116] The formal portrait of the event survives: massive Trinity School banner above a head table that seated twenty-two, and a room packed close with sixty-seven (at least) tables for ten: faculty, parents, and boys (it would appear from middle school on up). Heavy hotel plate, little tassled lamp shades on table candelabra, black lace and pearls, ashtrays and cigarettes. There appears to have been no wine, just water carafes and Coke bottles: The boys were present.

As Ike was told, Trinity at 250 still was a pious place, and church services bookended the year. On September 28, 1958, a special choral evensong at Trinity Church set things rolling: "The Order of Service is in the Book of Common Prayer, pages 21–34." In addition to identifying the service music (Thomas Morley's four-square *Magnificat* and *Nunc dimittis*) and sturdy hymns ("Glorious things of thee are spoken," "Christ is made the sure foundation," "St. Patrick's Breastplate," "God of our fathers"), a service leaflet printed a brief history of the school, a list of headmasters and anniversary sponsors (who included Ralph Bunche, Thomas E. Dewey, Grayson Kirk, John Olin, Red Barber, and Herbert Hoover, none of them alums, but a fascinating group nonetheless), and the school prayer: one great rolling period of "ripe wisdom," "true knowledge," "gallant living."[117] On Trinity Sunday, May 24, 1959, another festival evensong (Stanford in C), this one at the Cathedral of St. John the Divine, rounded things out. Headmaster Riddleberger read the first lesson, Upper School principal Bruner-Smith the second, trustee Glover Johnson '19 gave the greeting, the Right Rev. Horace Donegan, C.B.E. and Bishop of New York, the sermon. Everyone finished with "O God our help in ages past."

Fun filled the in-between. In March an "extraordinary attraction" marked the anniversary in the form of an all-faculty play, Morland Cary's "Love Rides the Rails." Boys clapped for favorite teachers and staff in silly roles, some of them in drag. Riddleberger and Bruner-Smith played railroad workers and patrons of the Paradise Café. Others played a nightingale named Lolita and a buxom dance-hall hostess. French teacher Paul Bolduc arranged the songs, and the Mothers' Organization saw to "genuine costumes of the period" (the 1890s). The school also got its story into the press beyond just the Trinity community, with stories in the *New York Times* ("250th Year at Trinity School is Marked by Bishop Boynton at Church Service," September 29, 1958) and long-since vanished journals: the *Herald-Tribune* ("Courses Growing at Trinity School," September 28, 1959), the *World-Telegram* ("250 Yrs. Can't Alter Trinity School's Ideals"), the *Journal American* ("Note 250th Year of Trinity School"). The trustees did what trustees increasingly would be expected to do. They established a 250th anniversary fund with the objective of raising $750,000, for faculty salaries, student scholarships, new science laboratories, new endowment for science and chaplain's chairs, and physical plant modernization including improved playing fields: "Independent, or so-called private, schools give leaders to the nation in numbers out of all proportion to the number of students they train, [and] must have an assured future if the nation is not to lose an inestimable source of strength."[118]

The education-for-leadership theme raised there, in terms of money, Dann had raised in the 1930s, framing it as one of Trinity's attractions and another reason to send one's son there. It is impossible to measure. All graduates by this time went on to college and then on to professional lives. In the school year ended just before the anniversary, 90 percent of Trinity graduates did not just get into college but got into the college of their first choice.[119] But did that make them leaders? It did in the sense that then still under 40 percent of American high school graduates, private and public together, carried on their schooling past the secondary level. College men (and increasingly women) led by definition, if only because there were still so many others so much less well schooled than they.

At its 250th, Trinity sounded confident and comfortable with itself because so much could still be so safely assumed. Undoubted purpose aligned with a simple plan and, more or less, with resources and the market. The commemorative booklet produced for the anniversary looks and feels not much different from the school yearbooks from the late 1930s: sepia-and-white production values, filled with happy pictures of masters and boys. The camera caught three of them, unnamed, in one particular image fantastic for its innocence and today hard to imagine meeting "appropriateness" standards in any school publication anywhere: a trio of flat-topped, crew-cut, shall we say fourteen-year-olds cutting up in the gym's fancy new tile-and-chrome gang showers, naked nearly to the level of embarrassment. The shot looks "natural" (of course it is cropped), the caption—"Cleanliness (after Godliness, of course) comes a little easier in the new showers"—artifice.

As with the showers, so with the neighborhood, soon set, it seemed, to get its own squeaky-clean new look. "Did you know," wrote a breathless Riddleberger to alums in 1959, "that the twenty square block area around Trinity School is to be rehabilitated? The plans are approved, the money is in hand and the work shall begin shortly. The miserable block to the south of us will be razed and new apartments and a park will take the place of the old-law tenements. What could be more encouraging?"[120] There followed renderings of the two tower block apartment houses that would face Trinity along 91st Street and a plot plan of the whole project from 87th to 97th between Amsterdam and Central Park West. "Urban renewal" in 1959 still looked, like Trinity boys in the shower, fresh and innocent.

Not for long: Everybody grew up. The tensions and alarms of the 1960s and 1970s would press the need to grow up more quickly and, more deliberately yet, to guide the school's evolution.

SEVEN *Dividing Line(s)*

oday, Trinity's oldest trustees who are alums were students in the late 1960s and 1970s. Recalling the embarrassing performance of the basketball team when he played on it in those years, one of them confesses with just a hint of nostalgic chagrin, "Well, y'know that was because we were all, well, a lot of the time, half-stoned." The great lightening up, breaking loose, reconsidering, questioning of authority that beset the country then carried Trinity partway with it. There was an attempt to unionize the faculty; boys' hair got long; girls' skirts got short. Vietnam, civil rights, and the culture of protest showed up on West 91st Street as unruly seniors, evidently intent on expressing themselves, trashed the student lounge. Trinity then was not always a happy place, and by the daily look of it, about as far as could be from the muscular Christianity, kneeling-at-chapel-serenity of Bunny Cole's or Matt Dann's day.

Under leadership perhaps sometimes too stiff, sometimes too friendly, and with boards slowly taking larger corporate responsibility for money and mission, Trinity grew and changed faster than before, sometimes lurching a bit along the way. Three stimuli merit attention here. First was the matter of the neighborhood on the Upper West Side where the school found itself, but which was no longer anything like the place it had been when the decision was made to build the big brownstone schoolhouse there back in the 1890s. What had once been fashionable was fashionable no longer. As Trinity evolved, putting the last vestige of "charity" long behind it and having positioned itself as a leading college preparatory school, the gap between school and its setting yawned wide. In the context of the times, aloofness was not a policy option, and tensions demanded an institutional response. There were neighbors to placate, redevelopment earnestly and opportunistically to embrace, lawsuits to damp down. Building of the Hawley Wing/Trinity House committed Trinity to the neighborhood when it might well have picked up and, in keeping with a long habit, moved yet again. It also committed Trinity to becoming a larger and more elaborate school. This related to a second stimulus toward greater diversity within the school. Diversity was in part a function of larger enrollment capacity and the need to fill it. It was also a consequence of the withering of single-sex (or at least all-boys) education generally and the social pressures of the times in favor of coeducation, and of the civil rights movement and pressures for some degree of racial integration. A third driver of change was fresh internal leadership that embraced Trinity's strategic repositioning away from a genteel Episcopal school with limited market appeal to an elite independent school where places were highly desired.

A CHANGING ENVIRONMENT

Trinity or, officially, Trinity Episcopal Schools Corporation was a private entity funded without state subsidy and free to choose and price its services and to discriminate among its customers. Its neighborhood until the 1960s was the product of private market forces, too. Over time, the quality of the neighborhood's building stock had varied directly with the income levels of its residents. As those rose and then fell, what had once been fashionable environs became unsightly ones. Long brownstone blocks so handsome at the turn of the nineteenth century, and some of them destined to be handsome again at the turn of the twentieth, in between became slums. If bad environments make bad people or at least make life harder on good ones, then the West Side, starting not that long after Trinity moved there, had a problem on its hands. It was a problem of economic and social dimensions. It prompted a public response and thrust Trinity into a swirl of forces portending risks and opportunities.

The news of impending West Side redevelopment that Hugh Riddleberger breathlessly announced at Trinity's 250th anniversary in 1959 was but one corner in a vast canvas of mid-century urban improvement. Robert Moses, its chief conjuror, changed the map and the look of New York City more than any one individual before or since. Progressive visionary, ruthless power broker, misjudged master builder, and subject of one of the twentieth century's great biographies, *The Power Broker* by Robert Caro, Moses provokes conversation and controversy still. The subtitle of Caro's book—"Robert Moses and the Fall of New York"—declared the long-fashionable viewpoint, though as perspective lengthened—revisionism visited even the subject of Robert Moses and more sympathetic interpretations emerged.[1] From the 1930s to the 1970s, Moses reimagined both how New York ought to look and how New Yorkers ought to live in it, and he turned many of those visions into buildings, bridges, expressways, playgrounds, and pools.

In the process, much was gained that New York still takes great pride in. Much too was lost that New York forever regrets. Trinity School does not appear in the index of Caro's biography, published in 1974 and in print ever after, nor does Moses's name appear prominently in the archives of Trinity School. But it was Moses's plans for the urban renewal specifically of New York City's Upper West Side that drew one dividing line across Trinity's modern history, propelling its own physical growth and renewal and reforming its relationships with those around it.

Moses, who as a young man lived at 95th Street and West End Avenue and endlessly walked the city, was no stranger to the West Side. In the 1930s as Fiorello LaGuardia's Parks Commissioner, he put into action some of his first great schemes there: the Henry Hudson Parkway built on landfill, and 132 acres of new playgrounds and ball parks in Riverside Park.[2] It was the Federal Housing Act of 1948, however (which Moses helped draft), that catapulted into policy his agenda for massive slum clearance and residential reconstruction. This took time, but the subsequent course of "urban renewal" on the Upper West Side eventually intersected with Trinity's smaller story.

Since the mid-eighteenth century when it moved from the shadow of Trinity Church to Varick Street, Trinity recognized at least the challenge of changing neighborhoods and the need for some response. Under Matt Dann, in modern times, its takeover from Trinity Church and thence demolition of the obsolete St. Agnes Chapel was such a response, though an opportunistic one without much public dimension, at least none that Trinity (school or church) then acknowledged. If not quite "urban renewal" as the phrase would come to be understood, Dann's demolition partook of the hell-for-leather Moses spirit.[3] Old structures that no longer served their first purpose ought to make way for others that met current needs, even if, as in this case, the need was for no structure at all but only a cinder-strewn playground.[4] Thence and through the 1950s, even as it struggled to make itself more attractive to more middle-class families, Trinity watched the deepening decline around it: squalid neighborhood versus genteel school for boys from nice families. This was difficult. And it was not a difficulty that the school alone, acting privately, could do very much about, short of, once again, picking up and moving on probably out of Manhattan. It is speculation to guess how much longer Trinity might have stayed the course on West 91st Street had urban renewal not come along when it did, but probably not as long as it has.

On New York's West Side, no doubt the most famous monument to Moses's way of thinking about cities is Lincoln Center, imagined and realized between 1959 and 1966 out of the San Juan Hill area around the old Lincoln Square and the slum setting for Leonard Bernstein's *West Side Story*.[5] By this time in his long career, Moses had opposition, and he did here. Opponents protested the planned demolition loudly and in vain, with Moses trumpeting that the only solution to "urban blight" was surgical clearance.[6] Also by this time, Moses had come to see arts and culture as a catalyst for urban revival, and the cluster of institutions (the Metropolitan Opera House, the New York State Theater, the Julliard School) that the world would come to revere as Lincoln Center proved to be just that. Ground was broken for the project on May 14, 1959, which was in the midst of Trinity's own 250th anniversary year, when two months earlier President Eisenhower had signed the congratulatory note to Trinity referencing its long history of pious learning. At the Lincoln Center ceremony, Ike put in an actual appearance, looking on benignly as master builder Moses rang all the changes on what would be this, his most glittering project yet. These included his famous remark likening urban renewal to getting breakfast: "You can't renew cities without displacing people any more than you can make an omelet without breaking eggs."[7] He emphasized not just the what, but the how of what was about to happen. The Lincoln Square renewal project, he boasted, was to be made possible by model public and private cooperation, with commitment of federal and city funds, the enticement of "private risk capital," and the generosity of numerous philanthropic individuals and corporations. The presence of "our chief executive," Moses thought, crowned the whole endeavor.[8]

No other renewal project ever sparkled quite so grandly as Lincoln Center, though the same spirit—whereby "urban rot" (a favored Moses phrase) would give way to urban renewal as the great city stemmed flight of the middle classes to the suburbs and revived itself as a place to live and play as well work—animated others. The West Side Urban Renewal Area located just a few blocks to the north and that so excited Hugh Riddleberger on the occasion of Trinity's 250th brought the full meaning of Moses's thinking into Trinity's own back (and front) yard. And it enabled Trinity to piggyback its private institutional needs on the public cause of neighborhood renewal, drawing, in part, on public resources.

Planning for the West Side Urban Renewal Area began in the mid-1950s, and it produced something more nuanced than the slash-and-burn approach for which Moses would be widely pilloried. By this time, his methods had stirred sometimes furious opposition, led most famously by economist and urbanologist Jane Jacobs, who fought successfully to save a vast swath of Greenwich Village from a highway. The plan for the Upper West Side, however, as put forth under City Planning Commissioner James Felt, proposed rehabilitation and spot clearances, not wholesale bulldozing and massive tower blocks. Several layers of public agencies—the Housing and Home Finance Agency of the United States, the New York City Board of Estimate, the Housing and Redevelopment Board, the New York City Planning Commission—would oversee West Side urban renewal. It is important to understand what was being attempted and what it was hoped to avoid.

The West Side project bespoke a progressive impulse to restore, to renew, if necessary to rebuild, a neighborhood fallen on bad times. The target area, a twenty-block area between 87th and 97th streets and Central Park West and Amsterdam Avenue (which put Trinity at the western boundary and midway north to south), was the product of adverse history. From the 1880s, when the area had been a highly desirable one and brownstones were built to accommodate the well-to-do or at least aspiring haute bourgeoisie and when a stable working-class population inhabited blocks in the shadow of the then steam-driven Columbus Avenue El, through the 1910s and 1920s when modern elevator apartments crowned Central Park West, the area bloomed. With the Depression, however, housing construction slumped and then ceased altogether, while population continued to grow. As landlords reworked old real estate assets to meet increased relative demand, rents rose and overcrowding ensued. The setback that began in the thirties turned into a long period of stagnation. By the mid-1950s, surveys showed that 10,000 New Yorkers were living in apartments fit for half that number. Wear and tear rose along with rents and hard use, and buildings deteriorated. Old tenements and brownstones got subdivided into single-room accommodations that often housed not individuals but whole families. Those who were able, or became able, moved out as soon as they could afford to, and neighborhood instability increased. Of the 18,000 families who lived there in 1956, only 5,300 had lived there five years before. Crime and unsavoriness reared up. "Blight and decay," in the phrase of the time, set in. In the best Jacob Riis/Dorothea Lange tradition, a single photograph in a publication promoting the renewal plan crystallized the cause: two West Side youngsters, one white, one perhaps Puerto Rican, peering out from behind the bars of a squalid basement room somewhere on West 94th Street.[9]

What actually occurred was envisioned as a model exercise in neighborhood rescue. "For the whole city, the project is a huge demonstration that it is not necessary to blast a neighborhood off the map and start afresh to build a good one." Rather, the planners explained, it was preferable "to save the old while building the new; to maintain diversity in people and housing while making the area more livable."[10] Dating from a time when historic preservation had barely got started, this sounded enlightened and in general turned out to be. The plan rested on a combination of three techniques of renewal. Where present structures were beyond economically sound rehabilitation, some demolition would be required. But others, most of the old brownstones, in fact, would be rehabilitated or conserved. Rehabilitated brownstones, some requiring only minor repairs, others more extensive remodeling including new plumbing, heating, kitchens, and baths, would yield 3,100 new housing units. Another 3,600 units were already of high-enough standard to require conservation only. The best buildings, of course, bordered Central Park, but far from all of them.

A land use plan assigned every property in the project to its designated category. "Redevelopment" meant demolition and replacement: Substandard housing would come down, replaced with 7,800 new apartments in a range of rents but with emphasis on low and middle incomes. Three hundred and fifty rehabilitated brownstones would transform overcrowded single rooms into standard apartments. A new public school, playgrounds, more open space, and better traffic flow accompanied the improvements in housing, and the neighborhood would continue to be ethnically and economically integrated. Some disruption of course was to be expected. Slightly more than half the 11,000–plus families in the project area would be able to stay on where they lived; just less than half would need to be relocated either into new housing in the area or in other neighborhoods. To the unlucky ones, the city made a promise. "THE PLAN AFFIRMS THE LEGAL RESPONSIBILITY OF NEW YORK CITY TO RELOCATE THESE FAMILIES TO DECENT HOUSING WITHIN THEIR MEANS"[11] (capitalization original).

The plan also promised that churches, private schools, community organizations, and other neighborhood institutions would be retained. The block where Trinity had found itself since 1894, when the neighborhood was in its heyday, between 91st and 92nd and Columbus and Amsterdam, was to continue in a mixture of uses. The existing Trinity facing south along 91st, the property immediately behind it facing north along 92nd, and the southeast corner at 92nd and Amsterdam and occupied by Central Baptist Church (founded in 1846, "The Friendliest Church in New York City") were designated "public and semi public" and would be conserved as they stood. So would the southwest corner, which was residential. Brownstones to Trinity's immediate west along 91st and along 92nd were also to remain "residential" but were marked for rehabilitation. The area to Trinity's immediate east, fronting along Columbus between 91st and 92nd, was marked for new, tax-abated, residential development, as was the plot just to the south across 91st. The far greater portion of that block across the street from Trinity was planned for residential development, too, but of the public housing variety.[12] This was by far the largest of the just three public housing areas planned for the whole project.

However sensitive to preservation and rehabilitation it may be have been, the West Side Urban Renewal Project was also large, in the best Robert Moses mode. It required large financing. Public funds through Title I of the Federal Housing Act were catalysts for the project, but most (83 percent) of the estimated cost of $151 million was to come from the private sector.[13] Private investors who participated in the rehabilitation phases of the plan were assured "technical assistance and other advantages," while the Limited-profit Housing Companies Law of 1955 ("Mitchell–Lama" after sponsors, New York State Senator McNeill Mitchell and Assemblyman Alfred Lama) promised to subsidize construction of a portion of the 4,200 housing units defined as "middle-income," which meant those renting for under $20 per room per month.[14] It was there that opportunity opened for Trinity.

SITE 24

Trinity in the mid-1960s was under the leadership of a new headmaster and an aging board. In 1962, Hugh Riddleberger had resigned, with goodwill all around but suddenly, for an affluent suburban opportunity at University School in Grosse Point, Michigan. Riddleberger had become headmaster of Trinity in 1956 by easy default, when the trustees (sending him first on a round the world cruise) decided that Matt Dann was overstretched in running both Trinity and Pawling and on his return gave him Pawling. They gave his assistant Riddleberger, without further search, Trinity. When Riddleberger left, Upper School head and English master since 1927 Clarence

Bruner-Smith was pressed into additional service as interim headmaster for 1963–64. He did so as duty but not happily and with no desire to continue.[15] The board made calls. Richard Garten, like Riddleberger and just a few years younger, was an old (scholarship) boy, Trinity class of 1939. He was the son of an Episcopal priest and a native New Yorker with an M.A. in history from Columbia. Garten was forty-three in 1964, an Episcopalian, married with three sons, and experienced in the business: He had taught at Riverdale and since 1960 had been in charge of his own school, the Park School in Indianapolis. He recalled surprise when Trinity rang but answered without much hesitation. New York was home and so was Trinity. It was also a step up. He moved east the summer of 1964 and went to work that fall.[16] Riddleberger had lived in Rye and commuted to work. Garten would live in town. In addition to salary and clubs, he received rent-free residence in a seven-room co-op apartment owned by Trinity but nowhere near it, overlooking Central Park at 98th Street and Fifth Avenue.

Garten seemed a comfortable fit with Trinity as it then was. He came with no particular mandate, to a school internally at ease with itself but set amid a local world that wasn't. This inconsistency had not been enough to give Garten pause, at the beginning anyway, about the attractiveness of the Trinity position. In turned out to occupy much of his headmastership. The neighborhood problem was getting hard to ignore, and the solution of sorts that soon presented itself, while persuasive, would not be simple. Trinity's uneasiness at the decline of its West Side environs had to do with more than just distaste for unsightly tenements across the street and the awkward fact of a nice school situated in a slum. The location of the school affected its reputation and its market, and Trinity increasingly felt the need to bolster the former in order to secure the latter. Enrollment nudged upward in the late 1950s and early 1960, but limited space constrained thoughts about serious growth. Conversely, limited size constrained the quality, or at least the variety, of offerings that might make Trinity more attractive to more families and so spur growth could it be accommodated. As baby-boomers came of school age, Trinity had begun to pick at the problem of growth and improved facilities with construction of its first new gym since the original version atop the 1894 building, in the late 1950s, and Garten arrived at a school that enrolled some 442 boys, a historic high. But no one was comfortable: The old building and the annex groaned. The financing mechanism for the new gym had been illustrative, however: a $300,000 ten-year first mortgage from the New York Bank for Savings, for which the case was made that the increased operating income derived from additional tuition fees would provide adequate funds to amortize the mortgage. This in fact proved to be the case.[17]

The West Side Urban Renewal Project presented a unique opportunity to accelerate growth of the school but on even more favorable financial terms, providing a way could be found to slip Trinity, as a private nonprofit corporation and a religious though not parochial school, into it. This required creativity and connections. Trinity trustee and parent Eliot Lumbard, partner at Townsend & Lewis and an advisor to Governor Nelson Rockefeller, offered both. In the 1960s, Lumbard became chief legal architect for what would become the dual-purpose building project known as the Hawley Wing/Trinity House. Dwarfing the old 1894 building, the project focused on the immediately contiguous tract of land between the existing Trinity and Columbus Avenue, and 91st and 92nd streets, designated in the West Side plan as "Site 24." To participate in the scheme, Trinity had to conform to relevant government programs. If it did not, the opportunity would pass "into the hands of private housing speculators."[18] In June 1964, the New York City Housing and Redevelopment Board, agent for all government programs regarding the West Side Urban Renewal Area, formally designated Trinity as the prospective "sponsor" of future development on Site 24. This meant that Trinity exclusively stood to benefit from all available government programs for development there.

New housing was the objective of the West Side plan. Larger school facilities were the objective of Trinity, but the Housing and Redevelopment board quickly ruled that Trinity could not have sponsorship of Site 24 for school purposes alone. It welcomed, however, a plan that combined housing and school facilities. Throughout 1963, Lumbard and a team of architects (Brown & Guenther), attorneys (Demov & Morris), and general contractors (Thompson-Starrett) worked without compensation to evolve a plan they believed would satisfy requirements for maximum government aid to the overall project and also meet Trinity's space needs.

To the architects Garten enumerated them in dismal detail. Current deficits were severe. To seat the whole student body in chapel required "usage of 105 folding chairs." The library could accommodate no more books and not enough students. There was no adequate study hall facility. Classrooms were insufficient for each class to have its own homeroom and each teacher a home base. The snack bar and student lounge, underground and lacking natural light and ventilation, "border[ed] on violating city codes." Administrative office space was diminutive. Insufficient lunchroom seating meant costly extended serving time from 11:15 to nearly 2:00P.M. Even at present enrollment, there was no space for a language laboratory, or a proper infirmary, or an audiovisual room, or a manual training shop, or a place of musical instruction. Athletic facilities, once a source of pride, were so no longer. Locker rooms were inefficiently planned and used. The playing field, "treasure that it is," was too tight for interscholastic competition in football or soccer. The two tennis courts doubled as a faculty parking lot. There was no swimming pool, and no place for fencing, wrestling, or handball. The very young boys had no playground at all. And not the least of all, the school as it then stood could offer no faculty housing, which meant "that married and familied [sic] men are difficult to attract."[19]

The Lumbard team members addressed the school's space shortfall and the government requirements for use of Site 24 with an ingenious plan for a hybrid building. They proposed a new two-story school building to cover the entirety of Site 24 and to be integrated with the school's existing facilities along 91st. The new construction would provide a purpose-built facility for the upper school (which was anticipated then to expand to 300 students, for a total school population of some 700), together with classrooms, laboratories, faculty offices, lounges, and 800–seat combined chapel/theater/auditorium, a swimming pool, showers, and lockers. On a portion of the flat roof above, there would be a large open play area, enough for two tennis courts, volley ball, primary school playground equipment, and an outdoor hockey rink for the winter months. Gymnasium space would be doubled by raising the roof of the current gym on new outside columns, making possible an entirely new second floor. A cantilevered walkway eight feet high would start in the new building, be attached to the present, and connect with the old buildings in the main lobby. The existing chapel would be converted into library space, the dining room expanded. With the high school moved to new quarters, the top floors of the 1894 building would be freed up for occupancy by the lower grades, which, with growth, would need more space of their own.

Thus the school. Its realization, however, depended on the public component of the plan, which, in New York City style, meant building up. Rising on columns out of the new school building would be a separate housing

building of 25 stories containing 200 apartments, to be owned by a corporation separate from the school but whose stock would wholly controlled by
Trinity. As Site 24 sponsor, the school would sell the air rights over the
school to the new corporation.[20] Rents would be in the middle-income
range as required by Mitchell–Lama, and housing units would not begin
until five floors off the ground. This was necessary to assure that the flat-
roof play area of the school qualified as the necessary "community facility"
for use of apartment tenants as a park-type area when not required by the
school (during summer vacations, most of most weekends, all evenings).
The school could not be had without the housing, a requirement turned to
the school's advantage through its general control over tenancy and the
reservation to Trinity faculty of a number of units at below-market rents.
There would also be an underground garage for 140 to 150 cars.

The whole project was estimated to cost some $6 million, $2 million for
the school (plus $250,000 for furnishings), $4 million for the housing,
which included $200,000 in land costs, which was about half of real value.
Just as the building was essentially one structure meeting two different
needs, so the financing had to be broken in two and then added up.
Mitchell–Lama funds would be available for 90 percent of the land purchase
and would provide a $3.6 million construction mortgage for the housing
portion. It was figured that Trinity would need to advance only $200,000
equity capital to the housing corporation to build the building, and under
the law would receive a 12 percent return on that investment ($24,000). The
housing subsequently would qualify for real estate tax abatement of 50 percent as stipulated in the West Side Urban Renewal Plan for Site 24.

The awkward part was that construction of private school buildings could
not be financed under any present public program. Lumbard forecast that
half of the construction mortgage for the school portion could be obtained
in the private market, and that Trinity would need some $1 million for school
construction. The land occupied by the school building would be tax ex-
empt. The advantage of the joint building concept, however, was that certain
of the school costs could be quite legitimately allocated to the construction
of the housing portion (such as certain major supporting columns), with the
cost of such items coming under the 90 percent Mitchell–Lama-backed
housing mortgage even though the (private) school directly benefited.

More or less, this was what Trinity House and the Hawley Wing physically became and more or less how they were paid for. Early in 1965, Trinity

formally voted to proceed as official sponsor of Site 24 development and the two-pronged building program, and it began to clear its decks for the extended action that was to entail.[21] Howard Craig, parent and long-time school physician and trustee, was enlisted to chair the small oversight committee that would manage the process. "I am aware of how these matters work, having gone through a recent installation at the New Rochelle Hospital, of which I have spoken before," wrote Johnson, sounding like a man with some sense of what they were getting into. "If you think the present delays are annoying, you should just prepare yourself for negotiations with the staff of the Housing and Redevelopment Board and all the clerical clearances that are required. In the words of the late Mayor LaGuardia, patience and fortitude are essential ingredients."[22]

It is interesting that more than a year later, the daunting size and complexity of the project appear still to have given some pause. The question was raised not about the imperative of expansion as such, but about the wisdom/necessity of undertaking it in connection with Site 24. Why not "go it alone" and just build a new Trinity on the then-existing playing field site? The reasons against were not inconsequential. One was money: Additional sums would have to be obtained through fund raising or mortgaging or both, if the Site 24 plan was followed. Site 24 also promised management headaches—"plain bother"—involving as it did, and as Johnson foresaw, "various government agencies." The playing field alternative would be "easier and less involved." Then there was the specter of a coming "inflationary swirl," and "the larger the building project, the larger the risks."[23]

The pros, however, carried the day, and to the limited extent that the school's leadership could foresee possible positive consequences of Site 24, they made good guesses. There was flexibility: more options for development of future contingencies within its immediate neighborhood. If Trinity did not develop Site 24, a "private speculator" would. Such development might well be inimical to Trinity's interests "from aesthetic to tenant reasons." Faculty and staff stood clearly to benefit from a Trinity-controlled apartment house and low rents, to say nothing of the athletic and recreational facilities that came with the plan. The total of such space would be greater under the Site 24 plan than what could be accomplished by roof-top use of new buildings atop the present playing field alone, and "adequate athletic facilities are one of the disturbing weaknesses of Trinity at the present time—especially for older boys, and particularly for those instances where families are making comparisons with schools in the country." Even on the matter of money, the additional sums for Site 24 development "are not so much greater as to carry the decision by themselves."[24]

Trinity took the risk and moved ahead. That the school portion of the project was called the "Hawley Wing" indicated the remaining part of the financial equation. The Hawley Trust, a restricted bequest that dated from the 1930s (see chapter 6), was carried on Trinity's balance sheet at $1.00, since by the original terms of the bequest the trust fund was not distributable to Trinity School for fifty years (not before February 16, 1988). By the mid-1960s, however, the Hawley Trust consisted of securities with market value of close to $2 million and easily represented Trinity's single most sizeable financial asset, if it could be released and monetized.[25] The fund's value far exceeded the needs of its original purpose, which was the granting of ten modest cash prizes to graduating seniors, and a grander use now beckoned. It seemed to be the key to the opportunity that West Side Urban Renewal represented, and to paying for Trinity's share of the public/private apartment-plus-school building that would enable Trinity's growth and guarantee its continuing presence on the West Side of Manhattan, indeed in Manhattan altogether.

Board president Glover Johnson's law firm, White & Case, proceeded "to explore the matter of invading the Hawley Trust." In due course, the Trinity corporation applied to the Surrogate of the County of New York and the state attorney general to break the Hawley will and get access to the capital before its time, planning to apply $1,250,000 of it to building the eponymous school building. Trinity argued that, had he known, Hawley surely would have approved, despite the will's troublesome restriction on investments in real estate.[26] The state proved agreeable and did not argue, deciding that using the funds for the renewal program on the school site "was in accordance with the intention of the testator." Trinity's part of the financing package had two additional components. One was an additional mortgage. The record was good here with the New York Bank of Savings, to whom Trinity had argued successfully in the course of modest physical expansion in the 1950s that larger enrollment did not increase operating expenses in proportion to the gross income realized from additional tuitions. This time, it was proposed that, as had been the case with its earlier $300,000 mortgage, it was feasible to amortize a mortgage upward of $1 million through the increase of the student body by upward of 300. In addition, it was pointed out that more students (or their parents) would mean more annual giving now and more alumni giving, eventually. Moreover, even with $1,250,000 of Hawley money to be spent on brick-and-mortar construction, Trinity would still have at hand marketable securities in excess of the principal amount of its new note. They were opportunistic but prudently so.[27]

It was also determined that an internal fund-raising campaign would be necessary to complete the financial package. Early in 1966, the school launched "The Trinity Fund" with the aim of raising upward of $4 million. Three million was designated for immediate building requirements of the new school structure (not the apartment tower), and $1,250,000 to restore the money being diverted from endowment (the Hawley Fund), or, as it was put with a forward-looking spin, "as endowment for Trinity School's long range investment in people."[28] These were large numbers, in the context both of the times and of the history of the school's own less than robust fund-raising. That the goal, however, was achieved suggests a level of professionalization in matters of external affairs then new to Trinity. High stakes—as one piece in the puzzle of West Side renewal, the project was extremely visible and put Trinity in the public eye as it had never been before, and it was costly and rested upon a hopeful "build it and they will come" assumption—meant serious time requirements from busy trustees. Outside fund-raising counsel was retained at the beginning, both to probe giving capacity of the school's parents, alumni, and friends, and to assist with a campaign. This entailed interviewing of trustees and much sifting of names and categorizing of prospects against targeted giving levels. There was one primary target, however, at first thought essential to the entire effort. This was Trinity School's mother institution and "historical patron," Trinity Church.

The approach of school to parish suggested a certain presumption about the value of tradition. The school leaders aimed high, asking for a challenge gift of $500,000. To get it, they pulled at all the stops. At one level, it was the approach of one member of the Episcopal family beseeching another member, in language that then still made everyone comfortable. The school had its "origin in the parish." From this "felicitous association of parish and school" had risen the school's "unbroken tradition of Christian education for worthy boys" as "intelligent and religious beings." Trinity was now at work educating its thirteenth generation of them. School promised church that the half million would go to construct the new chapel (to be called "The Rectors' Chapel" to commemorate two and a half centuries of school rectors, though they hadn't been called such since Cole): the "inspirational heart" of the school and "the single place of worship for every teacher and boy." They were deliberate with the vocabulary, and the operative word was still "worship," not "gathering," or "assembly," or "reflection." Without the church, the school shamelessly claimed, "parents and other friends who are sensitive to the historical relationship will be discouraged and the amount of funds to be secured from fund-raising activity will be very substantially reduced, endangering the scope and quality of the entire project."[29]

That, potentially, seemed a compelling argument if not a load of guilt. The parish partly agreed, donating half the asked-for amount in the form of a matching grant. Though somewhat disappointing, it was not small change either.[30] The appeal however was couched not in terms of tradition alone. This particular Episcopal school, like the larger Episcopal church to which it still claimed allegiance, approached a period of internal change more wrenching and more imminent than it knew. At those great broadening-out, secularizing currents the language of Trinity's fundraising appeal hinted. It spoke not of just thirteen generations of pious Trinity boys, but of "the wish to help meet the education needs of the City, as well as the opportunities in a neighborhood renascent through urban renewal." Indeed, the school's chapel itself was no longer to be quite that, or at least not that alone, but in addition "the springboard and center for the program of social work in the Community to which the boys are committed."[31] The "chapel" was to be a theater for both school and community programs in drama and music. By its "ingenious subdivisibility into three self-contained chambers," it became lecture and study halls through the school day: practical and trinitarian, ancient and modern.

The broader fund-raising thrust of the "Trinity Fund" was communicated in professionally produced campaign materials that emphasized the modern prospects with a less sharp salute to the past.[32] This began with the title of the main booklet, "A Commitment to Superior Education in an Urban Environment," and headmaster Garten's summary of what it was all about. Trinity needed to be a greater force in the community. It needed to enlarge itself in order to provide the variety and quality of academic and athletic and civic activities that the families of "pace-setting boys" expected. Trinity's nineteenth-century physical plant was incompatible with "the needs of a generation destined to live in the twenty-first century." The unfolding West Side Urban Renewal Program was not to be ignored. It mandated that the time to get Trinity moving was now.[33]

The timing of all this was determined by politics and policies external to

Trinity. From the highest altitude, it belonged to the Robert Moses vision for renewing New York City's physical structure in accord with a for-then progressive urbanist template. The external push coincided, however, with matters internal to Trinity, which as a private corporation bore sole responsibility for its own future. The cliché of course simplifies, that institutions either change and grow or wither and die. At this point, however, it was no imagined anxiety within that Trinity needed to grow in order to prosper.

INTIMATION OF DIVERSITY

One prescient line from the Trinity Fund booklet even spoke of the importance of sustaining a student population not just strong in talent but "rich in diversity." As that word would later come to be understood at Trinity and in education generally, the photographs with which Trinity promoted itself to potential givers in 1968 bore no hint and might have been plucked straight from school publications of the 1940s and 1950s. The boys all are white ones and still wear crested coats and ties, about the only distinguishing concession to fashion being the white socks of that era.[34]

Photographs are historical. Renderings can be aspirational. Trinity, as it then prepared to grow and through what would become the thirty-plus years from then to now when it continued endlessly to punch out, build up, and fill in the physical plant on West 91st Street, also began to reimagine itself in other ways. The second half of the Trinity Fund booklet presented an image of a bright new Trinity with "modern" fluorescent-lit spaces and filled with angular contemporary furnishings, and that wasn't that far off from the way the Hawley Wing actually turned out, though in the promotional renderings the ceilings looked deceptively high. It too was filled, at first, with boys in blazers and who, after a certain style of commercial-art illustration from that time, go faceless. They are generics, almost. For the artist tinted a number of those faceless faces to look different, with complexions other than white. These near-stick figures, for they were just likenesses and not yet real boys, bore the group label then thought polite but that a later generation would find uncomfortable: "Negroes." When the subject first arises in the written record, demurely in the 1950s, polite Trinity people merely said "colored." Wrote Hugh Riddleberger to trustee Howard Craig in 1957: "I talked to you earlier about the matter of colored candidates . . . I have an excellent candidate by the name of Charles A. Johnston, who will be ready for Form One in September. We tested him in the latter part of January and the results were extremely high. The boy is an attractive youngster and he comes from an obviously refined and cultured family. His father is a teacher of the physically handicapped at an institution in Brooklyn. The father has applied for scholarship assistance and I am both able and willing to give it to him provided the Board feels they wish to accept this youngster. I leave the problem in your lap and I hope I can get a positive answer in the not too distant future. I don't see how we can continue to side-step this issue without getting ourselves into considerable difficulty."[35]

Whatever the labels, discussion of racial integration and thence cultural diversity at Trinity, as at many schools, steadily increased in volume in years to come, and by the late 1960s Trinity would count some twenty African American students.[36] At Trinity at that moment, the issue still was spoken of largely within the context of growth, improvement, and change generally, as that was spurred on by the Hawley Wing/Trinity House project. If, all of a sudden, it became possible to build (as it did) and to fill (which wasn't yet quite as certain) a much larger Trinity, then should that new physical space shelter simply a larger version of its immediate past predecessor? Or should it become the setting for something else in addition? The answer did not come all at once, but the coincidence of so large a building project and the social turmoil that so unsettled the late 1960s and 1970s portended a different sort of Trinity as well as bigger one. The answer would have racial, religious, and gender components. Slowly, Trinity would become less white and less Christian (see chapter 8). More suddenly, it would become less male.

GARTEN AND GOVERNANCE

As the tower and school went up, starting in the spring of 1968, and as board members worried and worked to make sure all the sums came out right, some of Trinity's littlest boys (grade 2C) recorded the event in words and childish drawings from their own vantage. "Trinity Tower's Things," from Robb Roehl: "It has a swimming pool and a tennis court and a gym and a play ground and a field and a lunch room and chapel. I hope it will be finished by the time I get to third grade." From Daniel J. Woo: "Trinity Towers looks like this. Trinity Towers is 22 stories high. It has a swimming pool and is very modern. It has new laboratories and a new library and a beautiful modern chapel." From Robert Oberuetter: "I think Trinity Towers is going to be a good building. I think it will look like the Empire State Building when you get inside it." And from "Michael B.": "Trinity Towers is tall, very tall!!! It is 30 stories, that high! Trinity School has 4 stories. The building has 3,000,000 windows."[37]

Well not quite: "Windowless New Wing Will Have Pool and Air-Conditioning" was how high schoolers in charge of the school newspaper more soberly headlined the coming of Trinity House, though the sense of excitement was much the same.[38] But perspective does matter. From low down things look big, and around the construction site the contractors cut diamond-shaped viewing portals at levels low enough even for little Trinity fellows to get a glimpse.

From farther away, things look a part of their landscapes, and the new Trinity came to look a part of its. The building that little boys once marveled at would come to seem less marvelous, but it still stands and fills its purpose: Trinity House looking like one high-rise among many, though with lots of balconies, the Hawley Wing another flat-topped concrete box of modernism in large-building architecture, though with a nice-for-the-time brick veneer. Garten and the Rev. Dr. John V. Butler, rector of Trinity Church, troweled in the cornerstone at a formal ceremony on April 15, 1969, and deposited memorabilia: a school yearbook and a copy of the *Trinity Times*, school catalogues and brochures, a description of the curriculum, a tape recording of a chapel service, even an earlier history of the school.[39] And there were nonwritten artifacts then still proudly emblematic of Trinity: a blazer patch and buttons, an athletic letter, and a school tie. Wondered one dreamy boy writer at the time: "Who will want to know about us in the twenty-first century?"[40]

After many delays, the Hawley Wing finally opened for educational business halfway through the 1969–70 school year—a year that would mark the midpoint of Garten's tenure as headmaster. Three hundred and thirty boys (thirty below capacity), grades seven through twelve, moved in, a huge relief to the overcrowding in the old 139 building, but into facilities that were "*still* not ready—the chapel, the pool, locker rooms, AstroTurf field, teacher offices and seminar rooms are unfinished," moaned Garten. Boys and parents reacted positively despite the lack of paint and flooring and other amenities. "People still look *ahead to* rather than *at what* we have. It will be something; it is already, in spatial terms, an unparalleled asset"[41] (emphasis original).

The blazer patch and school tie then deemed representative were to vanish soon enough, and with them something else that proved more worrying. The professed purpose of the Trinity House/Hawley Wing undertaking was to take advantage of the opportunity, presented by West Side renewal, to keep Trinity competitive through expanded enrollment and enlarged improved facilities, particularly in the Upper School. This was where dropouts from the full twelve-year course were heaviest and where brick-and-mortar seemed to matter most. Athletics mattered in high school, and Trinity's were below standard. While city Trinity could never have the playing fields of a country day or boarding school, the new plan addressed the athletic-space shortfall seriously. Good teachers of course mattered even more, and Trinity already had a fine reputation in this department. But good teachers, however idealistic, liked good facilities and a nice place to work, too. The two factors, quality facilities and quality faculty, were inextricably linked.

So was the quality of the students, still boys alone. The issue then did not focus as sharply on the determinant of academic aptitude as it later would. Eliot Lumbard, the lawyer/trustee/parent who played the leading role in the building project, saw Trinity as it had been for a century at least, as a middle-class sort of place, and foresaw no change flowing from this as a consequence of the new building. "Trinity is *not* a rich boys' school," he explained to outside fundraising counsel. "It does not try to cater to high society. Its target—solid middle class with sights on scholastic achievements as preparation for good college" (emphasis original).[42] Certainly no thought was expressed that by offering fancier facilities Trinity would attract or, heaven forefend, seek out fancier, better heeled clientele.

Lumbard's assessment was probably still right in essence, but not completely in fact. In the course of the Trinity Fund Campaign, lists were compiled of the best giving prospects. These included, of course, alums who had gone on to business or professional success, but they also identify a small but not tiny cadre of Trinity parents and past parents whose job titles, affiliations, and addresses would suggest other than middle-income status. Thirty-six current and past parents (of students the oldest of whom would have graduated in 1955) were listed as top prospects, including Charles G. Bludhorn, Chairman of Gulf and Western Industries; Victor Kiam of Sarong Consumer Products; Sidney Kahn of Lehman Brothers; Maurice Clairmont, chairman of Lee National Corporation investment bankers; Eliot Janeway, economist and president of Janeway Publishing and Ventures; Richard Brown of Metro–Goldwyn–Mayer; Maxwell Geffen, chairman of Blue List Publishing and director of Standard and Poor's; Charles

Wolf, a hotel and real estate developer; Leonard Lauder of Estée-Lauder; James Cassidy, vice-president at Hill and Knowlton; and L. Jay Tenenbaum, partner at Goldman Sachs. Names in media and entertainment stand out: Edwin S. Friendly, Jr., a vice-president at NBC; actress Arlene Dahl, wife of wine importer Alexis Lichine; actor Fernando Lamas; Mary Tyler Moore, wife of Grant A. Tinker of NBC; *Herald Tribune* writer Judith Crist; "Today" show host Hugh Downs; author and etiquette consultant Amy Vanderbilt; and Kitty Carlisle Hart of CBS's "To Tell the Truth," widow of playwright Moss Hart and doyenne-to-be of New York City arts and culture.[43]

To the extent that Trinity then could be said to have been generally middle class, however, it was by the measure of mainstream mid-century American sensibilities also solidly inclusive. It could be seen as exclusive only in that it turned away girls (and single-sex, particularly all-boys, education then was only on the verge of its great decline in the 1960s and 1970s) and boys who weren't white, though this it hoped to change. "The school desires to become integrated," Lumbard continued, in apology for its not being so yet. "The school recently made a concerted effort to recruit Negro boys—but couldn't find them—based on the school's admission standards. A few however are attending."[44]

As it planned for, built, and began to use its new building, Trinity at that point appeared to Garten as a work in progress and open to change, at some pace yet to be determined. That the Hawley Wing would transform Trinity at a leap into a larger, more elaborate institution seemed to him obvious and desirable. Garten himself was a transitional figure, arguably the last headmaster with any natural feel, perhaps even preference, for the old-time style of Trinity at mid-century: the Trinity that Cole even earlier passively oversaw and that Dann and Riddleberger accepted and then more actively managed. Though temperamentally a poor fit with the 1960s, Garten was no reactionary either and could be described as conservative only by comparison with his younger successor, Robin Lester. While Garten might have liked to have run the school on the old top-down Dann model, he knew those times were slipping away. The Trinity House/Hawley Wing project was trustee-driven and trustee-managed at its core, and presaged a future where activist board members, bigger budgets, and higher standards for administrative performance would be the rule, while the internal educational life of the school would be more and more faculty-managed with periodic episodes even of student influence.

When Garten came in 1964, Trinity enrolled over 400 boys. Five years later, the plan was for 600, to grow to 700 as the new building came into full operation. By the 1974–75 school year, the last of Garten's tenure, kindergarten through grade twelve counted 760. To maintain small class size and close student–teacher relationships, the faculty increased, too, from forty-one to eighty-five in eleven years, an enviably low 1:9 ratio.[45] Garten thought this highly promising, even though it meant sacrificing the intimacy of the old smaller scale Trinity. Greater size compensated with, in his words, the opportunity for "diversity, appropriateness, and excellence." Some care with the words is important here. By "diversity," Garten did not mean diversity as a later generation would come to know it, as centered on matters of racial, ethnic, and gender identity of students and faculty. He meant, more simply, a broader curriculum: more choice, which in his view only enabled Trinity better to deliver on the age-old rhetoric about the boys being the point of it all. In the high school the year he arrived, 164 boys studied among some thirty courses. In 1970, 225 boys elected among forty-five offerings. Some of this represented authentic curricular broadening, that is, new subject material not taught before. Besides basic and advanced courses, juniors and seniors by the mid-1970s could choose from an array of for-credit electives: in English, Time and the Hero, Journalism, Creative Writing, Works of Carlos Castenada; in math, Introduction to Abstract Algebra, Number Theory, Computer Projects; in history, Twentieth Century American I and II, Twentieth Century European I and II, and Psychology; in science, Ecology, Biological Anthropology, History of Science; in Classics, Homer and the Historians, Classical Tragedy and Comedy, Pre-college Latin, Classical Lyrical Poetry; in religion, Ancient Israel, Philosophy of Religion, Jesus and Paul, Comparative Religions, Christian Theology, and Religious Themes in Literature. What was useful was not always academic: Typing was offered and encouraged, for no credit.[46] Some of it represented more of the same, that is, more than just one course or section in each discipline and grade level (i.e., in the old style: "Ninth Grade English"). Trinity now offered section levels matched to the capacity and preparation of the boys. This is what Garten meant by "appropriateness."

"Excellence," however, applied to everything that the school did and so has a more contemporary meaning. It did more and more, though this was as much building on past heritage as it was pure innovation. Given the lift associated with the new building, excitement about improved and expanded extracurricular life came naturally with enhanced athletics and club/interest groups. If winning mattered, Trinity's interscholastic sports performance between the end of World War II and the mid-1960s had been lackluster at best, with few championship teams and seasons. Winning did matter at least to morale, and by the late sixties Trinity coaches and athletes were turning in ever better performances. After two decades of lackluster showings, the football chalked up three winning seasons between 1965 and 1969; there was rising interest and success in soccer, and there were strong wrestlers and swimmers. Not all boys competed on teams, but everyone played at something and everyone enjoyed the improved opportunities that the school's new facilities offered. Garten thought Trinity still had a long way to go in tapping all the boys' interests and talents, but contributions of boys "with ideas and leadership" outside athletics seemed on an upswing. Senior class projects blossomed, and faculty loosened, lightly anyway, some of the old strictures. Seniors, starting in 1969, were granted the privilege of using any unscheduled school time as they themselves judged best. Opportunity to "fly alone" was how Garten gently described the trend.[47]

Garten, forbidding to some in person, had a nice touch with words at least on paper, at ease summoning in a single sentence Tom Paine, Patrick Henry, the Book of Common Prayer, and Janus at the Gate looking both retrospectively and ahead, all of which fit the times when he was in charge. He liked James Madison best, however, which was probably apt. As Trinity grew, and its interests grew more tangled, Madison's advice for running a republic resonated on West 91st Street. Trinity was "trying to reconcile competing factions: adults and first graders, a tempestuous community and a less-cloistered school, our heritage and our freedom, responsibility and the richness of our talent with the paucity of our dollars." This was alternately uplifting and depressing. Whichever, it was also increasingly a community-wide effort.[48]

FRACTIOUS TIMES

Apart from the adrenaline kick that attended planning, building, and adapting to a new building, there is about Trinity in the late 1960s and 1970s a feeling of anxiousness. It is the feeling of being pressed, of running to stay in place. Tuition levels seemed too low, and indeed were lower than comparable schools in New York. It had long been policy, even as Dann first began to raise it, nevertheless to keep the price of a Trinity education well below such competitors as Riverdale and Horace Mann, and somewhat under Collegiate School. The stated purpose was that Trinity should remain attractive to middle-class families—in the prevailing language, "families such as clergymen, teachers and professional people." That desire might be described as a legacy desire and one that was beginning to conflict with financial realities. Capital costs aside,[49] the necessity of teacher salary increases pressed relentlessly on every administration from Dann, who resented it, to Garten's successor Robin Lester, who lived by it.

By the late 1960s, there was distinct pressure to fudge the history if the future demanded it. Parents, as the purchasers of private schooling, needed to understand (this was 1968) that the bargain they were getting was too good to last. It was "a great privilege to have their sons educated at Trinity School and they should realize that what they are paying for this education is insufficient by today's standards."[50] Garten recommended raising the bill $200 for 1969–70, an order-of-magnitude increase that seems modest by later standards but on a percentage basis (30 percent for kindergarten, over 10 percent for high school) was not trifling.[51] Even with more money, though, new faculty members were hard to find and keep, as the Vietnam war roiled the education world and the market for teachers in particular. Selective Service teaching deferments were much sought after, even as local draft boards demanded stronger evidence of "irreplacability." Garten speculated, and surely not alone, that there were many young men then in teaching who would not have been but for the war and who were unlikely to stay past their twenty-sixth birthdays, which was the upper cut off for conscription. Turnover among junior teachers was always high anyway, and the unsettledness of those years probably accented it: "The 'losses' this year (1968–69) are high: four on leaves of absence, one is to marry, two to graduate school, one to take a Federal job, two are not offered contracts, and one is difficult about it and there are muted cries for 'tenure.'"[52]

Bristly young faculty bespoke the rebelliousness of the times and no doubt communicated some of it downward to students not that much younger than themselves. Of course, students in the late 1960s had their own ways of rebelling and needed little prompting, even at Trinity. "As you all know from the public media," Garten fretted to the board in the Fall of 1968, "we face a rising tide of student action against the establishment. High school children are widely copying the attitudes and actions of college students." Some students in the city had formed a High School Students' Union whose propaganda had appeared on Trinity bulletin boards, and some Trinity boys tried to form a chapter.[53] Probably no leader since then would dared have used the phrase "high school *children*" referring even to Trinity eighteen-year-olds, but Garten was a leader stuck with one foot in each of two worlds and knew it. He knew what world he preferred personally, but he hesitated institutionally, and so Trinity tripped ahead.

Some school administrations seemed to embrace the spirit of the times more easily. Horace Mann sent a letter to its parents justifying relaxation of dress codes that fundamentally blurred the distinction between faculty and students: "We have some teachers whose hair is over their ears (so do I) . . . and I do not think we have a right to ask of the boys what we do not ask of the man. We have beards among the faculty and moustaches; and if our boys—whom I believe to be perfectly normal adolescents—wish to try beards or moustaches, more power to them."[54]

Garten, who wore a conventional haircut and horn-rims, was more cautious at Trinity. The matter that lurked here was student participation in policymaking and the threat of division within the school community driven by ideology and politics. Again, elsewhere it seemed foregone: "I am asking the Community Council (note: it has more student than faculty votes) to review a number of long-standing policies established in the past by the faculty, and we as a faculty will abide by their judgment." This last clause, Garten said, was the key one since the Trinity student council passed similar resolutions calling on the school to relax its rules on appearance, specifically to modify the jacket-and-tie requirement, leaving trousers, shoes/boots, even the style of jacket—"athletic, Nehru, mod, traditional"—open to student–parent choice. Students awaited, presumptuously, "response from the administration."[55]

Garten and the board plainly did not like much of what they saw happening around them in New York and shuddered that it might happen to Trinity, too. They feared that the "malaise" of the colleges had spread down even into grade schools and that Trinity had its own "dissidence and dissidents, some of them finding good quarterbacks among teachers just off disturbed campuses." On top of responsibility for things once left to families, like sex, manners, and attitudes, and new ones like drugs (a problem first mentioned in the record in 1969[56]), there was a palpable generation gap within faculties, with a core of older teachers and a new corps of "contemporaneously oriented young fellows right off restive campuses" but "too few men in the middle years of service" who might help bind things together. One divisive issue was time off to "march," to protest. Young teachers demanded it, for themselves and for boys, and without penalty. Some families wanted it too. How to respond?[57]

In the spring of 1969, Garten reported forlornly that Trinity was the only high school left in Manhattan that was holding the line on attendance, appearance, attitude. At one girls' school, all the seniors left each day at noon. At another, students with two "study halls" and taxi money could "visit boys anywhere." At the "most traditional," all were in pants. At boys' schools, Trinity was nearly alone with blazers. Scarsdale high schools had effectively ended study hall, leaving students free to "learn" anywhere or "use their time as they see it in preparation for the freedom of college."[58] Strident calls from the young and some of the not-so-young for fuller voice and greater freedom multiplied, but what of responsibility? It was easy to lose, even at Trinity. As the Hawley Wing crawled to completion and tight budgets for furnishings dictated spartan interiors, Garten suggested to the boys that they set themselves the challenge to raise $6,500 for their own lounge: "Typical of the times, they are reluctant to do it—preferring instead to get it without working for it."[59]

How far to go to let students help determine the policies of the school such as compulsory chapel, smoking, study hall? How to respond to calls for changes in dress and decorum? How much to allow students to participate in student "movements" within the school? How far to explore coeducation, independently or by merger? The answers, to the first three at least, came piecemeal into the 1970s and 1980s, and what seemed at the time dire threats to the established order of education at Trinity proved in the long run not to be. Near the end of the tenure of Robin Lester (1985), Garten's successor as headmaster and a very different personality and leader, Trinity would appear to have weathered things better than Garten may have feared. Little if any responsibility for governance had trickled down, littlest of all to students. Chapel remained mandatory for all students and teachers, its thrust less sectarian than earlier but its purpose large as ever.[60] There was still afternoon and Saturday morning detention for (the list is nonexclusive) chewing gum, swearing, cutting class, or violating the dress code. There was suspension for rudeness, plagiarism, and smoking. There was expulsion for theft, possession of drugs or alcohol in school or use of them anywhere during the school day, and for serious breaches of integrity. The student council ("Senate") oversaw student activities, "organizing dances, etc." The dress code might have slipped from old-time "uniform ethos" but still was recognizable. For boys: jackets, long pants (not jeans), shoes and socks,[61] either a turtleneck or a shirt and tie. For girls, more complexly: either ankle-length tailored straight-legged slacks with blouse, collared or crew-neck sweater, collared shirt, or turtleneck *and* a tailored jacket or blazer, or knee-length skirt with a blouse . . . or a knee-length dress (not a sun dress or strapless dress). No one, boy or girl, was allowed to wear jeans, painter's pants, T-shirts, or sneakers. Everyone had to be "in code" from 8:30 in the morning until the end of school.[62]

GIRLS

On the fourth question, however—coeducation—the consequences would be profound, if hardly dire. The issue arose in the late 1960s and belonged squarely to the spirit of the times, when in the name of nondiscrimination and equal opportunity all-male bastions of higher education and then secondary education opened classrooms, even dorms, to women and girls. Trinity had had no girls since the 1830s, that is, since before the time when it began to refashion itself in the prep-school mode. That girls had been present for more of the school's history than they had been absent was to many a largely forgotten fact. Trinity by the 1960s had been all-boys since a time far beyond living memory, and its obscure coed history figured hardly at all in the return of girls in the 1970s. What did figure was the coming presence of the Hawley Wing and the mandate for growth.

The record is not sharp, however. The building of the Hawley Wing was in no small part an opportunistic response to West Side redevelopment, which enabled Trinity to double itself at a swoop on favorable financial terms. It would renew an old plant, help keep an old school up-to-date and competitive, and cement it securely to Manhattan. Formal discussion about whether an enlarged Trinity could or should include girls dates at least from 1968. At a board meeting otherwise dominated, as most then were, by construction progress and costs, Garten noted that he was "giving thought" to an alliance with a girl's school (unidentified) in the hope of coordinating extracurricular activities for both schools, and there was suggestion that Trinity create or acquire an East Side feeder school, perhaps even one with girls.[63]

Talk then sounded general and long term. Garten claimed still to think that in a city of eight million there would always be enough families of the sort who wanted single-sex schooling for their sons. One senses the thin edge of a wedge, however, in discussions with Spence, Nightingale-Bamford, and Collegiate for a coed interscholastic seminar, and a rumored approach to Spence for some reciprocity in attending classes.[64] Trinity boys themselves seemed of mixed views, no doubt like their parents and perhaps depending on whether they had Trinity-eligible sisters.

School jokesters sounded off predictably: "The education of women is the greatest waste of energy in the 20th century." . . . "There are two sanctuaries in New York City into which women should not intrude. One is the men's lavatory and the other is Trinity School; both should be preserved." More serious types judged it a matter of tradition and wondered if coeducation would damage or enhance Trinity's proud one. Practically, these adolescents anticipated the chief argument later taken up by advocates of single-sex schooling, especially for boys, when it began to come back into fashion in the 1990s: that good schools above all demand intellectual concentration, and girls are, well, distracting. Others countered that coeducation simply was the coming thing: Riverdale had long had a girls' school, and Fieldston was totally integrated. Moreover, since the top colleges were all doing it (Yale would admit women that fall of 1969), logic said the top prep schools should too. A particularly thoughtful school editorialist raised the history-based objection to all-boys as an obsolete remnant of Victorianism and saluted what would become a hackneyed criticism of all-boys schools like Trinity, which was that they the created an artificial environment for students, divorced from the "real world." Trinity's already "diversified study body contains boys of different faiths, races and backgrounds, which contribute greatly towards making an enriching experience for all." No doubt, but girls, too? Could anyone though "reasonably doubt that any boy's education is complete if it is conducted in the absence of girls?" It all depended, one supposes, on the interpretation of "complete." How could "any Trinity boy really understand girls—any more than an Episcopalian understands Jews, or a white understands blacks—if he does not live and learn with them at school? The answer to this question is not easily found."[65] Indeed, it still hasn't been.

The seriousness and relative maturity of the discussion spoke well for Trinity boys. Students have good antennae and are generally hard to fool about what the real issues are in a school, and coeducation clearly was "in the air." Garten continued to move in that direction, and a special committee of the board was established to examine it.[66] As changes go in large institutions, this one moved rapidly, certainly more rapidly than the planning and building of the Hawley Wing, which it trailed by about one year. In January 1971 the standing committee of the board, on recommendation of the school committee, passed the resolution authorizing the headmaster to accept girls as students in the last four years, or the high school program. For the record, chairman of the school committee Otto Kinzel affirmed that making Trinity coeducational was "overwhelmingly supported by the faculty, students and parents."[67] Board president Glover Johnson told *The New York Times* blandly that girls' abilities and assets would make the school "a happier place."[68] With the admissions office already busy with boys, Garten himself handled enquiries and applications from girls and set about seeing to the necessary space alterations, chiefly the conversion of the old kitchen in the old St. Agnes parish house into a locker room adequate for ninety girls. (The Hawley Wing already had girls' restrooms for summer day campers.) That fall, with the first female students on the premises, it all seemed a breath of fresh air, the girls in Garten's estimation "a hit in every way."[69] Asked by a female reporter whether the decision had been influenced by the women's liberation movement: "'We do not feel threatened by placard bearers,' said Mr. Garten, smiling thinly."[70]

Among the faculty, reactions varied from men to women, of whom there were then three teaching in the high school. History teacher J. Heyworth militantly declared that the coming of girls meant that "male chauvinist attitudes have to be reassessed and broken down" and called for "critical self-analysis on the part of the male population." The school psychiatrist fretted that the problem would be of boys faced with high-level competition from girls. Some teachers were cautious: "I don't see any problems, but I don't see well." Science teacher B. Baker thought the move would help boys "see girls as people, not as idealized sex objects" but worried about their potential "for exerting a distracting effect on the students." (Students seemed to think such distraction would be welcome.) History teacher Lyle Redelinghuys took the stand that girls make for "a more meaningful social reality" but added that the girls themselves stood to benefit from participating in "an already structured institution." Pretty much everyone agreed that one way or another the presence of girls would bring about "a more civilized school" while altering in yet unknown ways the nature of a Trinity education. Bruner-Smith, Upper School head and then senior master, was conservative. Much in favor of a more civilized Trinity, he thought it a pity that an element of choice had been lost, believing that there was still a demand for traditional all-boys schools in New York and that it was sad to see Trinity leave the field. He was also realist: "I'm not going to fight the flood. I've taught both boys and girls, and successfully."[71]

Largely, all the faculty did teach both boys and girls successfully, though integration took time and not everyone, mainly the girls, was pleased at its pace. Four years out, at near the end of Garten's tenure, the issue, though firmly settled in principle, could still be unsettling for those who lived it. The student paper did a survey on the status of things at the start of the 1974–75 school year and confirmed general satisfaction (among students, the great disgruntlement had been among seniors the year the change was announced but before it was implemented—perhaps born of jealousy?), with the most frequently mentioned problem being that by stimulating academic competition the presence of girls had made the school less relaxed. But as students dwindled who had experienced all-boys days, few any more bemoaned loss of the alleged old-time male solidarity.

That did not mean that girls' progress was easy. Implementation was remarkably laissez-faire. There is record of scant effort on the part of the administration, beyond fixing up lavatory and locker rooms, actively to manage the transition: admit them, and all will be well. This resulted in some rough edges. Female teachers were still few (the first had arrived in the Upper School only in 1970) and found the coming of female students to bring a more balanced perspective on the classroom experience. Female students of course varied by individual, and the record is skewed toward those who spoke up to complain, sometimes angrily.[72]

An easy target was the sports program for girls: Boys took precedence. After four years, there were 108 girls and one female gym teacher, and she not full-time. Girls in the first years were limited largely to volleyball in the fall, basketball in the winter, and track in the spring, but there was little effort to get a dance program or organize soccer, field hockey, tennis, swimming, fencing, or lacrosse teams for girls only. On the occasions that a girls' softball team was allowed on the turf (as the playing field atop the Trinity House garage came to be called, after its AstroTurf covering), "it was lucky to get a corner." Attitudes and behavior changed gradually. Soccer and lacrosse came first as noncompetitive intramural offerings. Tennis waited on the search for scarce courts, but history master John Hanly agreed to coach a girls' team that year (1974). At first, boy spectators at girls' events laughed or weren't there at all. In time, they became cheerleaders. Use of the school's one bus was always a problem: Not even the girls' varsity volleyball team got to use it if any of the boys' teams, even lowly ninth graders, were in need.[73]

The disjuncture between intention and performance was not to do just with athletics, if senior Caroline Franklin was to be believed, but was systemic across Trinity. After four years, no one doubted that girls were at Trinity to stay, but had Trinity "advanced to the point of totally accepting girls as students instead of co-eds"? It was an interesting distinction, and appeared beneath a headline that touted not "girls" at all, but "Women at Trinity." A survey suggested Trinity thus far had failed in its obligation to treat all students the same: "I made a big mistake in coming here. The opportunities for sports and activities for girls are just awful. Sometimes I just feel caged in." Another: "I love this school; but I love it for my teachers and my friends, not because I feel it loves me. I don't feel that I should have to fight and struggle for the things I need in my education." Or another: "It's understood that girls are a growing part of the community, and I feel the administration is waiting for us, but I also feel that they should present suggestions." Teachers, it was felt, did treat girls equally as scholars, though not universally: "When I get a 1 in class, I feel I should apologize for being smart. I feel the school still wants us to be dainty little girls who will be good mothers, not good scholars." The intelligent girl was respected if not accepted. And of course there was the dress code, from this time forth a puzzle for this school and many another. Two years into the change, girls banded together to petition, successfully, for the right to wear pants. It was, they said, not a matter of good grooming. Feminists or not, they had a point, given the way boys then were dressing. "Making a girl wear a skirt is like making her wear a badge that says 'I am female.' We are not here to show off our legs." Of course that could have been answered by longer skirts, but legs weren't the point. Equal treatment was, and here the girls got the better of the argument. "Wearing pants would not bring down our appearance. Girls tend to care if they are clean and attractive. The boys in this school wear ragged jeans, dirty old ties, and torn jackets. They wear the same pants every day for a week, yet girls who look presentable during the winter months [from the start, pants had been allowed in the cold season] are suddenly unsuitable in fall and spring!" One frustrated girl summed up, "Do they really know we're here?" Another responded that "they" would know only if girls asserted themselves more. Another countered that to assert yourself you have to feel secure.[74]

Classics teacher Frank Smith, something of a traditionalist, offered a little perspective. He thought that for the first couple of years too many of the new girls tried to imitate the appearance and manners of the boys because of a lack of confidence, even suppressing their femininity for a protective covering. "Has ever so much time been wasted by intelligent people in discussing the right to wear pants?" He even suggested a Dean of Girls, "a woman of personal charm with special understanding of the girls' situation." That never happened, but if girls were to make Trinity softer and somehow "more civilized" they could at least assume a more active social function: "Isn't it amazing, that there has not been a single dance a Trinity in these four years?"[75] Amazing indeed, whoever was responsible.

POWER SHIFT

Read literally and close up, it all sounds very earnest, which is an age-specific trait of bright teenagers. From farther back, the whiff of something sweet, boyish and girlish, hangs on, but as if against rising odds. Some of it seems just whining: School was supposed to be hard, wasn't it? The girls would figure it out, just as every boy had had to do before them. "I feel" was not a construction that would have gotten a boy with a complaint very far in Matt Dann's office. But these were not Matt Dann's times. It may indeed just be the voice of the whiners that we hear, the spoiled offspring of a permissive era.[76] The shortfall in athletics, for instance, was far more likely a problem of scarce resources than malicious neglect, as some students made it sound. It cannot be fully dismissed as such, however. The rumblings over the coed issue fit in a larger context of uneasiness that settled over Trinity in the early 1970s and that set the stage for another change in leadership and a profound change in tone.

Some of the angst may have been a consequence of the very pace of change. Even internally, there had been a great deal of it since the mid-1960s, when there was still talk of quitting Manhattan for the country. That ended once and for all with realization of Trinity House and the Hawley Wing, which ultimately scotched the awkward Pawling connection. Precipitously, the urban school doubled in size. Attention went there, and Pawling, ever a financial drag, had for Trinity no even residual justification.[77] Trinity changed qualitatively, too. Faculty grew, much of it young, some of it restive. Curriculum broadened, it was said, to satisfy demand for more choice and, after a mantra of that day, to become more relevant. A kindergarten got added at the bottom. Girls got added at the top and before long at the bottom, too. Retrospectively, much of this seems to have been conceived and managed in remarkably ad hoc fashion. One small committee oversaw the great building project. One or two lawyers (Eliot Lumbard and Glover Johnson) primarily nursemaided it. One committee looked at coeducation. No one in particular looked much at the neighbors. It was a lot to absorb and not surprising that some things should slip out of sync.

One of them was the headmaster. This was unfortunate and sad, for Richard Garten had managed Trinity responsibly through times the likes of which he could hardly have anticipated upon his arrival from Indianapolis in 1964. He talked and wrote about the changing world of schooling frequently, with feigned amusement about subjects he knew to be dead serious. In 1971: "Evolution, evolution, evolution—the sensible way for schools to meet the changing needs of students. Trinity will continue to alter details but not be blown by each wind. In the eight [*sic*] years since 1964 when the present Head came, the school world has been buffeted by pressures about fake alphabets and color alphabets; sex education; drug education, sensitivity training; independent education, affective education, and the open classroom—nearly a national craze a year. And we have neither ignored nor gone whole hog on any or all."[78]

For ten years he had met all this head-on, honestly, and with steadfastness, perhaps with a measure too much of steadfastness. At least, by the early 1970s, with the new building built and girls inside, discontent began to bubble up that he was ill-suited temperamentally to manage. He was devoted to young people, particularly Trinity's little boys, and fit, in many respects, an older schoolmaster model. In less extraordinary times, a man after such accomplishment as his might have rested a while on his laurels or looked forward to a comfortable coast toward retirement. But that was not Garten's fate.

Garten had a tendency, or the appearance of one, that clashed with two groups of Trinity constituents, faculty and students, and then finally alienated a third, the trustees. He was dismissive.[79] Examples were countless, and individually many seem silly. But they were cumulative, and a long-lived administrator knows how carefully everybody keeps count and how important it is to stay just ahead of it. In the spring of 1971, there was great brouhaha at Trinity about hair length, along with the wearing of denim, icon of social protest and individual self-expression. "Decision Pending On Hair Proposal; Trustees Consulted."[80] That headline in the school paper may bring a grin to fifty-something Republican alums with graying, thinning hair and who now look back on the episode nostalgically, but to teenagers at the time and to numerous of their faculty mentors it was serious business that went to the heart, it was claimed, of the character of life at Trinity, a life being judged by ever more nonacademic measures. The issue was a recent vote by the Student–Faculty Senate overwhelmingly in favor of new hair regulations. The students were restless. Their new proposal would have abolished any restriction on hair length, conceding only that it be kept neat. (Nothing was said about clean.) In addition, students were to be allowed beards and moustaches. The changes were to be put into effect the third trimester, for the student Town Meeting vote was taken in March. The Student–Faculty Senate had received the Town Meeting proposal enthusiastically, giving it a hefty majority: 16 in favor, 2 opposed, 3 abstaining. The proposal was then presented to the headmaster for his approval: Constitutionally, the headmaster and the trustees exercised ultimate power over all aspects of school life and were consultative only to a degree. Garten dithered and delayed. He might better have said "no" outright. He consulted both the Parents' Organization (who established its own committee) and the board, and meantime fell back on procedure. It was policy, he responded, to make no change in operational procedures during the course of a particular academic year, but this looked like a dodge: "This annuls one of the major student demands which was to begin the new regulations at the commencement of the third trimester." Senior Peter Sonnenthal, ardent partisan of long locks, thought it should be up to boys and their parents, not the school at all. But student "demands"? This was new. Karl Connell, another senior, sneered in the ultimate put-down of the day: "A slow withdrawal of restrictions from Trinity School is like Nixon's withdrawal of troops from Vietnam."[81] Garten could sneer too. Responding to a proposal in the Faculty–Student Senate to give students greater freedom to cut classes: "I question whether parents in college or secondary school who are straining to pay heavy tuition will entirely cheer that their children will have less time in association with their teachers."[82] "Children," as with "demands": the deadly difference of language.

Perhaps it never would be resolved, only endlessly mediated. Garten, not a great mediator, was the first who had to face it. Dress and hair were emblematic, and the interest lies less in the detail than their persistence and the quality of the discourse that swirled about such "school life" issues that once had seemed so settled. Three years later, in 1974, which was also Garten's last, Garten bent and allowed boys to wear jeans with their jackets, while girls were permitted boots and pants. Many students looked forward to the administration eliminating a dress code entirely. Give an inch, take a mile: "The only tradition that really counts is that of a high quality education which can be achieved if a student is wearing a jacket and tie or a T-shirt and sneakers." Garten responded that a dress code was tradition, that tradition set a tone, and that tone mattered in a school. Students said facilities, community spirit, and a good quality faculty were part of tone too.[83] So the words sailed past.

A reason that Garten appeared dismissive could be that he was afraid, of change and of how to manage it, or a certain type of change anyway, for no one could say he had not led the charge for growth and for girls. He had reason to be afraid, and he certainly was not alone. The articles abutting the "hair piece" in the *Trinity Times* evoked surrounding dark times and not exactly the quotidian school-day subjects that had appeared there in 1964: "NYU Counselors Explain Draft Laws"; "Squatters Seize 90th Street Building, Hold Other Sites"; "White-Third World Forum Organized."[84] "Spring Anti-War Plans" filled an entire page. Much of this was noise. There were still grown-ups on the board and on the faculty, and school carried on: "Waste Paper Drive Helped by Students," "Cheering Improves at Football Games," "Charlie Brown Set As Spring's Musical." Parent and film critic Judith Crist organized a Trinity film festival of comforting fare, including Walt Disney's "Treasure Island" and Terrence Rattigan's "The Winslow Boy." Racquel Welch was noted "among the amazing effects" in "Fantastic Voyage."[85]

No one could deny, however, a certain raggedness that not the nicest new quarters could hide. There was talk of division, fear, and distrust, and the chief fault line was the one between the administration and everyone else. School chaplain David Bird, a young priest of unmistakable "what would Jesus think and do" sympathies, brought God into it in a chapel talk in February 1974 that definitely stirred the pot. If Trinity was to call itself a Christian school, a religious school, even "a human school," how did it demonstrate its concern for values of love, compassion, understanding? Not very well, apparently. "God would not be sickened by our standards of dress or speech [likely a direct jab at the headmaster, who often was appalled], but by the atmosphere of the place, by the fear and discontent which lurk in every corner." If Trinity was to be true to its name and teach the love that binds Father, Son and Holy Spirit, it needed to get to work addressing a "fear among the students that was preventing any feeling of community from materializing." Other faculty members concurred: It was a hard but true message that needed to be sent.[86]

On the receiving end, it was surely not what Garten wanted to hear. Measuring the extent of "fear and discontent" is subjective territory. Memories from the time confirm it generally if not universally.[87] All close communities are in some degree hothouses, and schools among them grow their share of exotic faculty plants and radical student journalists. The Rev. Bird may have been one, and students, even protesting and demanding ones, are followers of such like-spirited teachers. Administrators have less luxury of expression. By the end of that school year, Garten had been at Trinity a decade, and he remained reticent even as the temperature rose in the ranks. There was, after all, a bright side. He had watched enrollment increase 75 percent, faculty 100 percent, the plant 200 percent, the budget 400 percent. The school was filled with new people and things. True, the old intimacy had been lost, and some of the style—"marble to cinder block"—but for educational quality, fiscal stability, and confidence in the future, he thought Trinity and himself on solid ground. "I hope," he wrote to the board as the 1973–74 year ended, "you share this with me."[88]

THE CHARMER

They did not, at least not enough. Garten announced his resignation the following October, to be effective at the end of the 1974–75 school year.[89] What if anything happened that summer is unclear, but it is likely that the discontent that reached the board was cumulative and had to do with nothing in particular and much in general. Age and style probably mattered as much as any substance. The theme can be inferred from how the school committee of the board, which quickly constituted itself as a search committee, went about looking for a successor. It was notable that at the very start they asked two members of the faculty and one student to join them. The teachers were classicist Frank Smith and historian Ross Coles, chosen by vote of the faculty, and the student Stephens Johnson, chosen by the student body. Two of the three women board members also served: Mrs. Richard I. Ulin, president of the Trinity Parents' Association, and Mildred J. Berendsen, longtime headmistress of The Chapin School.[90] Chairman Broward Craig, a Harvard-educated lawyer, Trinity class of 1946, was second-

generation Trinity, son of Howard R. Craig, since the 1930s school physician, then trustee and head of the Trinity Towers building committee and
on the committee that had selected Garten as headmaster.[91] He invited suggestions from the full board and announced that the committee would employ an outside consultant to help with the search (Carl Andrews, a former
headmaster of Collegiate School, who had become a headhunter).[92] They
got right at it and had major screening done by Christmas. To a query from
trustee Robert Parks, Rector of Trinity Church and a parent, about what
kind of man—there appears to have been no thought given to it not being a
man—they had in mind, Craig responded, someone of sound academic credentials, who was in young middle age (between 35 and 45), and "who was
able to develop a good rapport with students and faculty." Mrs. Ulin meanwhile polled parents (thirty-five responded by November, 5 percent), who
reported the "recurrent request" that the new man be able to "relate mean-
ingfully to students and faculty."

Therefore we suppose that Garten hadn't, or that he had ceased to. Perhaps he had changed in office as people often do, grown in some respects,
hardened in others in response to the outside insidiousness he saw infect-
ing Trinity. He later stated that the death of his close friend and board men-
tor Glover Johnson in October 1973 made him feel more alone and that his
and Trinity's paths were diverging.[93] No one ever said that he was not competent academically even administratively. Before him, Cole had stayed a bit
beyond the optimum age and needed to retire. Dann got himself over-
booked at Trinity and Trinity-Pawling and was told to stay in the country.
Riddleberger left young, for another, more congenially suburban, opportunity and under no cloud. Of Trinity's modern heads, Garten in his departure probably most resembles August Ulmann, Cole's predecessor in the
1890s who served for a relatively short time and whose forceful ideas or, we
might say, temperament, angered enough people to warrant an invitation
out before he was ready to go. Garten was no more ready to go than Ulmann, certainly not ready to retire. He was an alum, parent of two sons at
Trinity, a New Yorker, and leaving Trinity where he had made a huge mark
hurt.[94] Temperamental competence was the order of the day, however. To
lead it, Trinity wanted a wholly different personality. In the hackneyed
phrase of that era, Trinity wanted a people person.[95]

The committee foresaw the school operating in a continually changing
environment in the five to ten years ahead, academically, socially, culturally,

and were careful to solicit views close to the ground. The committee pre-screened more than 100 candidates (one internal candidate did not get past the preliminaries), winnowed twelve semifinalists to five who were asked to second interviews, and then to two, whom they brought to the full board. One was a priest, the Rev. Thomas Shaw, headmaster of Episcopal School, New Orleans. The other was Robin Lester, chairman of the history depart-ment just a few blocks away at Collegiate School. At forty-nine Shaw was senior, well known in headmasters' circles, "an extremely competent admin-istrator, experienced, mature, thoughtful, humane." Moreover, they saw someone who knew how to manage resources and accomplish "pragmatic results." Shaw was the proven quantity, and the two faculty representatives were highly impressed. Frank Smith liked that Shaw was ordained and had "the necessary spiritual qualities" and that he was particularly experienced with younger children (Episcopal New Orleans was a lower school, nursery through eight). A board member whose brother's children were being taught at Shaw's school described him as someone who was flexible and not wedded to the past, although with traditional values.[96]

Robin Lester, though, had the sparkle. He was just thirty-five and looked even younger, a native Midwesterner and well credentialed academically: education at the University of St. Andrews in Scotland, two degrees from the University of Chicago, one in the school of education, one a Ph.D. in his-tory. He had taught in urban and suburban public schools and at Columbia College in Chicago. He came to Collegiate and New York in 1972. From the very start of their comparison of the two finalists, the Trinity committee homed in on the soft qualities. Shaw had experience in running a school, but Lester had "creativity." Both men were highly intelligent, but they found Lester exceptionally "energetic and articulate, an ideal communicator." Shaw was ordained, but they liked Lester's academic distinction and the Chicago doctorate and didn't even mind that he was a Presbyterian and so potentially the first non-Anglican headmaster in the school's history. He was certainly also its most secular. In the committee's judgment, "he had the potential spark of greatness."[97]

These were worldly, prudent men and women, and their tilt toward Lester, the younger, less experienced man, surprises. But one must remem-ber the context for their deliberations. It was almost as if they were saying what they didn't want. They did not want any chance of another Garten. Garten couldn't keep up and had ceased to "get it," with students and faculty.

The committee had faith that Lester would. Craig and committee members Michel Fribourg, head of Continental Grain Corporation, and Eliot Lumbard, the politically well-tuned lawyer, were highest on Lester and may have carried the others with them. They recognized the fact that Lester had had no top administrative experience but thought Trinity could adequately support him while he got it. His academic credentials in social and educational history they thought would well dispose him to understanding the unique urban milieu in which Trinity then found itself, and, again, they all remarked about his ability to communicate. Everyone at Collegiate thought him a great teacher. But what else might he bring, and could he run a school?

Here, and it is their own figure and thus not flip to say, Trinity rolled the dice. "The choice between Dr. Lester and Rev. Shaw involved a decision between gambling for greatness or choosing someone with proven ability and competence." Shaw was apparently content, a success where he was, a man already in charge. Lester wanted to be and was overtly on the move: He made it known that he had a standing offer to become headmaster of the University of Chicago Lab School. So they jumped and decided to offer Lester the Trinity headmastership (and, if he didn't take it, to offer it to Shaw).[98] Lester accepted in April, at a salary of $25,000 plus housing, club memberships, and occasional use of a school car. In June, Garten received a respectful testimonial dinner at the Union Club and a silver tray with the trustees' signatures, in facsimile. "I will always prize my association with Trinity," he said in farewell, "and I will patiently wait for the verdict of time."[99]

Discounting trustees' official politeness, the verdict at that time from much of the rest of Trinity was harsh, the sense of relief at imminent regime change palpable. "This year marks the end of an era of sorts . . . characterized by an almost complete lack of contact and mutual understanding between the administration and the rest of the school community." With good schoolboy/girl hyperbole, which should also be discounted but probably less, student editorialists tarred the departing administration "an ominous punitive monster" with but one answer to complaints from disaffected students or faculty: "Because it's good for you." The school was factionalized to the point of "crumbling."[100] That was in June and the last days of Garten's term. In September, with Lester in the top job, the talk was all of "a new era," even a new office. Responding to complaints that the headmaster needed to be more accessible to Upper Schoolers, Lester fitted out an auxiliary office for himself in the Hawley Wing in space that had been a computer room—

"with no battery of secretaries or maze of passages, one will simply walk in"—and even allowed a student, Laura Chancellor, to choose the color scheme.[101] He invited faculty and parents into the old brownstone where few had ever been before. He would teach every day but not at first, as might have been his prerogative, senior or Advanced Placement (AP) courses, but ninth-grade ones.[102] He liked to joke around with students and was unself-conscious about being silly. A year into the job, the new headmaster appeared on the front page of the school paper, pipe in mouth, bound to a chair, two pretty female staffers behind him mouths taped shut, pistol-wielding student in Arab dress to the side: "Dr. Lester Kidnapped by ALA; Terrorists Hold Language Lab." The ALA stood for Adolescent Liberation Army (after Simbionese Liberation Army, the kidnappers of Patty Hearst in 1974) and explained its action as a "response to Dr. Lester's edict Tuesday in which the dress code was modified mandating that all students wear white sox and carry the King James Version of the Holy Bible with them at all times."[103]

They were nice opening touches, though Lester was no pushover either, over the summer treading into the dress code mire and unilaterally banning jeans for the school year to come.[104] But expectations about change were generally not disappointed. Partly, it was the way he said and did things; the board was right about his skills as a communicator. One could see that much from the pictures. The *Alumni News* reported the changeover with a photograph of Garten, stern and ramrod-straight in buttoned blazer and horn-rims, posed, plausibly, beside the cornerstone of the Hawley Wing, still with a touch of Latin and adorned with a cross: "Trinity School, Founded 1709, Anno Domini 1969." Lester smiles back from across the page, slouched in modish tattersall-checked sport coat before some sort of art poster, the only visible script in Chinese.[105] Lester and Garten worked amicably on transition matters that summer, and Lester officially took charge August 1. Garten left town for Florida. He also left, empty, the cooperative apartment that the school had provided him on Park Avenue. In another nice touch, the new headmaster, his wife Helen, and their two small children would live in the old brownstone apartment at the west end of the 139 building where Bunny Cole used to read the *Herald Tribune* mid-mornings —over the store, door open.[106]

Student and faculty testiness about arbitrariness and poor communication aside, Garten left Lester a school objectively far from the rocks. College admissions looked fine, a mix of ivies and less exalted but well-respected schools not much changed since the 1950s. At the other end, twenty-three boys were enrolled in the full-day kindergarten, with a half-day section probable. First grade suffered from a buyers' market and admissions were weak, with families appearing to hesitate (at least Garten thought) at the change in administration, the cost of transportation beyond fees, and fear of the bad neighborhood. It looked like a seller's market in the middle grades and high school. Garten thought "until American women decide to have larger families again" the bulge at the top and weak bottom would likely continue. The fall of Lester's first year, the school would enroll 791 with design capacity of 800. Money was tight as ever, "people are having trouble paying their bills," but the school was running in the black, if only just.[107]

LESTER AT TRINITY

Lester was a teacher at heart, and the fundamentals of teaching and learning at Trinity got his early and sustained attention. He is remembered as a faculties' headmaster, who managed teachers with flattery and seldom threats, though this style did not prevent some early weeding-out. By the start of his second year, he had asked five teachers to leave and offered two others only conditional contracts. But what he really thought was wanting at Trinity was not just good teachers but the right structures to enhance or at least not impede the challenge of education. He began carefully. In the Lower School in 1976, he added a fourth section to the first grade and gave new assistance for scheduling and organizational matters to principal Caroline Roberts. Thinking and planning, in which principals, department heads, and faculty all participated, evolved gradually toward a new middle school structure, centering on seventh and eighth grades where, he believed, Trinity needed to do a better job.[108]

In the Upper School, principal John Hanly got an assistant principal, chemistry teacher Kevin Bleakley. Lester saw Trinity heading in the direction of a division between academic and student affairs, which was not original to it but was important to sort out internally and very carefully with faculty and staff consultation. In general, he saw department heads handling curriculum and academic affairs, including evaluation of members of their departments. Equally important in the Upper School was redesign of the position of form master or class advisor, with self-initiated job descriptions and supplemental stipends. Form masters concerned themselves with all aspects of student life and "walk that fine line between disciplinarian and student ombudsman." The driver here was the need to prevent Trinity, which had become one of the largest private schools in Manhattan, from becoming an impersonal institution, part no doubt of the perceived "Garten problem." (Garten was certainly not oblivious, but Lester set about addressing it.) He wanted a big school that was "localized, personal and humane."[109]

He also supported early innovations in the Upper School curriculum: One was the requirement of a five-meeting-a-week writing workshop in addition to the regular ninth-grade daily English course, under the supervision of George Mayer and department head Donald Hull. Good writing takes years to develop and he didn't want to "oversell," but he did want to get started. Ninth graders would also be required to take one or two trimesters of a group of humanities subjects including music, art, drama, and ancient and medieval history. Modern European history for tenth graders was instituted as a prerequisite for the study of American history in eleventh grade. Physical education had grown lax in years immediately previous, with many Upper Schoolers "escaping" entirely, with faculty collusion—"pass" grades for courses not attended—and Lester determined to tighten up. Seeing how far things had slipped, he predicted to the faculty that "if we were going to have a student rebellion at Trinity, it would be over our attempts to meet our expectations and the New York State mandate regarding physical education." He placed responsibility for attendance and record-keeping with the principal, just as with any academic course, and at the same time searched for less unattractive gym uniforms. Resurfaced outdoor courts and a new gym floor helped, too. Lester's first year also saw the little-lamented suspension of interscholastic football at Trinity, and in its stead development of an intramural touch football program under the direction of Trinity's renowned coach Dudley Maxim. Fifty to seventy-five boys and girls of every proficiency played, afternoons on the AstroTurf field atop the Trinity House garage: a big improvement and far better use of resources, thought Lester, over the fifteen-boys-butting-heads model from the old, boys-alone past.

On girls, Lester thought Trinity had made a start, but just a start. It was one thing to have admitted girls to a boys' school, another to become genuinely coeducational. "The addition of girls to Trinity has been an exciting and proper development for the boys and faculty who were already here. We want to make it just as exciting and proper for the girls who joined Trinity." He worked straightway to initiate gymnastics, an activity highly popular in the best all-girl schools, and brought in three young women coaches and teachers (Cindy Greenwald, Leah Holland, and Pamela Pattison) also to serve as role models for Trinity girls.[110] The larger issue, however, was whether girls in the Upper School could truly be equals at Trinity if they had not had the opportunity, as boys had, to have been a part of it from the start. There is little hint of movement here under Garten, a strong believer in differential boy/girl development at early ages, but it was clearly in the air among faculty and parents and one of the issues that Lester picked up early and pressed forward. In April 1977, a faculty committee was appointed to study the matter and convey preliminary views to the board.[111] Lester along with key board members saw the extension of coeducation as a front-line faculty issue: Were the teaching staff opposed, the issue would die there.[112] The issue was probably less controversial than the admission of girls in the first place, however. School psychologist Lois Berman was assigned to survey the forest of literature of boy/girl learning issues, the sense of which was that while there were differences in what boys/girls find easier to learn, there were no differences in how they learn. Girls, for instance, had greater verbal ability; boys were better at math and in visual and spatial areas. But these differences did not appear until the late elementary years (age ten or eleven), and before that there were no consistent observable differences at all. Boys, it was thought, were more vulnerable to learning disabilities, but overall there was no difference in overall level of "intellectual functioning" between the sexes. It was all unthreatening news.[113] Outside consultants were commissioned to do the definitive work.

They made some useful discoveries about the mood and the market.[114] Internally, the mood was pervasively, if not quite universally, in favor. A survey indicated that three out of four faculty members supported girls throughout; indeed, some suspected that the issue had already been decided.[115] Lester assured all that it hadn't and wouldn't be made in favor, without faculty support. Parents generally were well disposed too—"coeducation is great, it's the natural approach, let's get on with it"—and fears about the safety of the neighborhood for their littlest ones seemed minor. Students, no surprise (one boy one girl from each high school grade were interviewed), approved heartily, and they too assured that transportation of little children to Trinity should not present a problem. Frankly: "The West Side is not nearly as scary as it was a couple of years ago." Students also argued that the ever-fraught transition to high school would be easier for both boys and girls if both girls and boys had advantage of the same Trinity middle school preparation.[116]

Externally, the market appeared to promise success. Administrators at similar schools[117] concurred that although competition for able students was always keen, Trinity should profit from the situation of the West Side in particular, which contained a "new breed" of families: "demanding, willing to sacrifice." Larger trends also supported optimism, with National Association of Independent Schools statistics promising rising day school enrollments. New York City was expected to experience modest annual enrollment growth, from 16,366 in 1968 to a projection of 17,737 in 1981. Independent schools pride themselves on being "families," a notion reinforced by the number of Trinity families, literally, that would like their daughters as well as their sons in the same school. Of Trinity's enrollment of 785, there were then at least 425 siblings who either were or shortly would be school age, 269 of them girls, and 191 of those attending private schools in New York City other than Trinity. This seemed to indicate a significant supply of female candidates already close within the Trinity fold. Geography was telling too. Of that 785, 353 or 45 percent lived on the West Side, 432 or 55 percent on the East Side; of the 135 girls already in the Upper School, 58 lived West, 77 East. In kindergarten through grade 4 the geographical split for little boys was almost identical, all of which indicated that Trinity should have no difficulty in attracting from a pool of candidates on the East Side unafraid of traveling to the West for school.

Not only had coeducation to be highly desired among all the school's stakeholders and the market for it confirmed to exist, it also had to be doable, on the ground. This looked promising as well. In terms of academic program, there was no reason to think that curriculum and instruction provided for boys would not be entirely suitable for girls. Trinity teachers, it was assumed, both men and a handful of women, were properly qualified to teach girls as well as boys. In terms of guidance and activities, it might be necessary to deploy faculty talent differently, to be sure, for instance, that in grades 5–8 there would be male counselors for boys and female ones for girls. Attention would need to be paid to evening out extracurricular opportunities.[118] Physical education posed the most obvious challenges, and here it was anticipated that more staff would be required (there were then five men and two women on the physical education staff). And of course, there would have to be additional girls' lavatories and locker rooms.[119]

Plumbing, however, was the only anticipated alteration to physical space, because the change to full coeducation was subject to the requirement that the overall size of the school would remain the same. With an already full enrollment in all grade levels and because boys would not be dropped to make way for girls, coeducation in the lower and middle schools would be a gradualist affair, with places first offered to girls at kindergarten and first grade levels, then moving upward year by year. At that rate, the school would be completely coeducational in 1988. "First" girls, those earliest in the process, might need special attention to compensate for their relatively small numbers, and the school would need to spell out clearly to prospective families the complete program for coeducation as it stretched into the future. Planning was one thing; execution was everything. "If the decision is made to go to coeducation," Mariana Leighton, principal of the Lower School put it, "it is imperative that we do a first class job with the first kindergarten girls, or surely enrollment problems will develop. Providing a happy and successful experience for those first girls can make or break co-education."[120]

It was, and they did. Trinity did decide to embrace coeducation school-wide, and its implementation on a "cascading" basis was well done. Lester thought, clearly, that the most useful thing to come out of the studies leading up to it was neither confirmation of a general internal consensus in favor nor the challenge of facilities changes, but the predictions about the market for such extension. Nor was it just prediction. In January 1979, there were already twenty sibling applicants for the ninth grade, sixteen of them girls. This suggested strong satisfaction of Trinity families with the education their children were currently receiving and the desire to have others of their children receive the same. Were girls to continue to be excluded from the lower grades, Trinity ultimately must frustrate this demand, thus dividing families, forfeiting high-quality enrollment and risking empty desks in its by then enlarged plant.[121]

Parent and student satisfaction with any school is largely a function of faculty performance, in turn a function of academic preparation/competence, attitude, and management. Across the two decades when Richard Garten and Robin Lester were headmasters, a period that encompassed the biggest building project since the 1890s and the readmission of girls at all levels for the first time since the 1830s, Trinity's teachers, some with gray hair and some with long hair, purveyed a broadening menu of courses but within the steadfast context of traditional education. Never did Trinity even flirt with unstructured progressive styles: new (or renewed) substance within old structures.

At Lester's replacement of Garten there was among Trinity's some seventy-five faculty members a nearly audible sigh of relief, in part relief from the appearance at least of Garten's administrative arbitrariness. "They, the faculty, could take votes, but they were subject to my approval or disapproval. There was 'democracy,' up to a point," as Garten later looked back on his tenure without regret. "I was not the most popular headmaster."[122] Lester probably was, and he liked it.[123] No more than Garten does he express regret at the way he ran the school.[124] Young, energetic, and something of a genial whirlwind, he correctly saw that the faculty needed improved tending. Money, he also recognized, always helped. He made improved faculty salaries an early, uncontroversial priority: He was a first-time headmaster, but he had always been a teacher and appreciated the profession's financial anxieties. Teachers to Dann had been a "you pay them what you have to" necessity; to Garten they were sometimes political adversaries. To Lester, they would be friends. He set out to regularize their lives and in particular not just to improve salaries but make them look fair. With help from board members Broward Craig and Michel Fribourg, and with the overwhelming vote of the teachers themselves, he worked toward a published salary scale in 1976. The scheme moved everyone onto a grid that correlated levels of years of teaching experience with levels of education. Illustrating from the four corners of the grid, a beginning teacher with one year of experience and a bachelor's degree would earn $9,000. A similarly green teacher but with a Ph.D. would earn $9,750. At the other end, long-timers with twenty-five-plus years in the classroom earned $16,400 with a bachelor's, $17,150 with a doctorate. There were intermediate grades for M.A.'s and A.B.D.'s, and nowhere, vertically or horizontally, did increments "step" by more than $200 or $300.[125] Supplementary stipends for heading a department, serving as form master, or some other administrative task were in addition. There would be no differentials between Lower and Upper schools, and some women faculty who had not before been paid close to equitably found themselves in for sudden raises. Lester liked teachers who were not beginners. Newly signed faculty in the late 1970s averaged six to eight years experience, a level he thought Trinity students deserved and that, from a management standpoint, helped reduce "surprises." As one standout case in point, he was able to hire in a competitive situation "an impressive young black teacher for our English department . . . a four-year veteran at St. Paul's."[126] In the same spirit of transparency and with the agreement of chairman Broward Craig, he showed faculty the budget.[127]

The other side of better pay and improved hiring was more formalized faculty evaluation. Among independent academically oriented individuals such as were attracted to prep-school teaching, particularly at the high school level, this could be awkward and it took some time. It evolved constantly but had an overall frame. Lester wanted a system that was simple and direct, with the key members being department heads in grades seven to twelve, and the principals in kindergarten through six. Each department/division developed its own standards for good teaching, to be coordinated by the headmaster into a "universal standard of excellence." Department heads met with each of their teachers, wrote down their commentaries, and discussed them with the teachers. Comments then went to the headmaster, who in turn met with each faculty member and discussed them again. A marginal evaluation could lead to a conditional contract letter for the year ahead (all contracts, as they had been since Dann's time, were for one year). A conditional letter stated explicitly the school's expectations of the teacher for the year ahead and threatened non-renewal beyond that if performance did not improve.[128] In 1978, a new faculty manual was published, detailing policies and procedures new since the last one six years earlier and explaining straightforwardly how things worked.[129]

Lester's new structure took effect at the beginning of the 1978–79 school year. It reflected his anxiety to mitigate the impersonalism of a big school such as Trinity had chosen to become: "A school of 800 students and 1500 parents served by a faculty and staff of 100 can obviously be a complex, austere institution."[130] Thenceforth there would be three Trinity's in one, not quite schools within a school but functionally discrete divisions focused on their own age groups of students. The school divided into a Lower School (kindergarten through grade 4), Lower Middle School (grades 5 and 6), Upper Middle School (grades 7 and 8), and the Upper School (grades 9 to 12). Three new principals joined ranks with John Hanly, already head of the Upper School. Mariana Leighton, who had served as head of the Lower School at the Allen–Stevenson School, led the Lower School. Joseph A. McCord, a fifth- and sixth-grade social studies teacher at Trinity since 1972 and author of the curriculum "Man: A Course of Study," took on the Lower

Middle. To head the Upper Middle, Lester first turned inside to Theodore Scull, who had come to Trinity from St. Bernard's School and taught history and English. When Scull left teaching to pursue a career in travel writing, Lester recruited Donald Graff, a classics and history teacher who also taught a course in filmmaking for middle schoolers, to become principal of the Upper Middle. Graff, who came from an Episcopal school in Hawaii, in Lester's estimation combined "outward gentleness with inner steel" and proved a happy antidote for "the kind of laissez-faire approach employed by some previous administrators in the seventh and eighth grades." Australian Kevin Bleakley, a chemistry teacher whose wife sang as a principal in the New York City Opera Company, joined Jesuit- and Oxford-trained Welshman John Hanly as assistant principal among Trinity's oldest boys and girls.[131]

Smaller, more manageable units were the aim, though a problem remained in that the number of units no longer matched the physical space. After the move to the Hawley Wing in 1971, it had been assumed that seventh and eighth graders could be mixed successfully there with Upper Schoolers, something veteran teacher Bruner-Smith dismissed as "predictably unworkable."[132] Hanly and Lester strongly concurred that a physically separate Middle School with its own autonomous teaching staff must be the goal. Until then, Upper Middle Schoolers would find themselves "in the upper school but not of it in maturity, aspirations and accomplishments."[133]

Managing some of those awkwardnesses and generally tending to issues of "student life," the teachers who also served as Trinity's form masters grew in Lester's estimation and were keys in developing the fuller sort of community he had in mind. That same year, Emily Park, a Pembroke graduate, handled the fifth grade, Jo Belknap, a former math teacher at Brearley, the sixth. History teacher Pam Pattison and science teacher Eric Kuhn shared the seventh, Upper Middle School football coach Charles Patterson and Katherine Pappas, an A.B.D. in English literature, the eighth. Admissions director Wells McMurray and Bill Sweeney, director of theater and a Trinity graduate himself, handled the ninth. John Romano, the math teacher whom John Hanly said more students asked for than any other in the Upper School, served the tenth. George Herland, who combined teaching chemistry and modern European history and was at work on a dissertation in intellectual history at New York University, served the juniors. English teacher Alice Horton and chemistry teacher/assistant principal Bleakley served the seniors, together "dispensing even-handed justice in the halls."[134]

Whether Lester could have gotten very far with any of this, or for that matter with anything at all involving the faculty and the day-to-day life of the school, without Hanly is doubtful, as he himself admitted. Hanly was British, trained in English and smitten as a young man with America. Trinity's Frank Smith, also British, had recommended Hanly to Garten, who hired him in 1967. He stayed nineteen years, taught English, became head of the Middle School, then the Upper School, then finally interim headmaster on Lester's departure.[135] Lester's measure of Hanly bespoke his own muddle about tradition and change. It is easy to depict Lester as a great loosener-up after Garten days, as command-and-control style made way for a collaborative one. He praised Hanly, however, for holding up the model of the old-fashioned schoolman: married to Trinity, friendly but at a distance, not authoritarian yet authoritative.[136] This contrasted with a younger cadre of faculty and some no longer so young but comfortable with the antiestablishment egalitarian spirit of the times and who encouraged palsy relationships with students, particularly in the high school. Lester observed that when young alums returned to visit the school, however, these were the teachers they had most quickly outgrown.[137] No one ever outgrew Hanly, or Bruner-Smith, or Paul Bolduc.

Bolduc came to Trinity in 1946, hired by Dann: "He wanted to teach students to speak French, not just grammar and vocabulary."[138] He did so with high art and was an accomplished pianist besides, and when he died of a massive coronary on the dance floor at the senior prom in 1978, just sixty-six, the school went into shock. There were two memorial services, one a formal affair with a committee chaired by trustee Michel Fribourg with remarks from two headmasters (Dann and Lester) and a eulogy from classics master Frank Smith, but one right away, the very next day, at the school, for the students. Lester made attendance compulsory for the high school so that, he said, "they sense the tradition and continuity of our school and in order for them to see how we honor our fallen colleagues."[139]

Teachers like Bolduc were memorable, sentimentally, to hundreds, even thousands of students over many years. They were important at that time as representatives of a type that seemed both old-fashioned and just what Trinity needed more of, looking ahead. Starting with the time of Robin Lester, the second of two areas of responsibility, once implicit, their parameters easily assumed, became more urgent and challenging. In the academic sphere, the school had and for long had had a relatively clear contract with students and their parents, with clear expectations and consequences. In the social sphere however, the ground was less clear and not always or even often happy. What to expect, demand, enforce in general student behavior and what to do to ensure that a Trinity schooling addressed "the larger lifetime interests of our students"? How to define "social" as well as academic excellence? Two years into his job at Trinity, Lester voiced these worries directly to the faculty, hoping, he said, to address long-term "the pervasive sense of unease and powerlessness many of you have noted."[140] Peel back the cajoling, "we're all in this together" team spirit that he cultivated with teachers, and there remained this troubling substance. The "old" schoolmen were old only in the sense, typically, of calendar age (Bruner-Smith, Trinity's classic of classics, was seventy-five in 1978) and in the fact that they were all still males who had become the teachers they were when teaching boys alone. They were anything but old-fashioned when it came to what and how they taught boys and (after 1971) girls. On this point Lester was dead certain, and it became a central theme in his analysis of what currently ailed teaching, and thus schools, far and wide.

Could it be, he mused, that the problem was with the colleges and universities and that secondary schools just mirrored them? Trinity, with its academically self-conscious faculty, "has had its share in this development." A recent Carnegie Foundation for the Advancement of Teaching report, "Missions for the College Curriculum," addressed the deficit among faculty members who were strong in their own fields but weak in their contribution to general education. Moreover, the colleges had abrogated pretty much completely any responsibility for students' personal lives. The schoolmen, with wide-ranging interests and commitment to "the whole student" in an out of the classroom, knew better. But the trend at the secondary level and in prep schools was toward teachers with fancier academic credentials (Bruner-Smith only ever had a bachelor's degree) but who took more reluctant interest in and commitment to the student's extracurricular school life. Of course it was not either/or, and the tumultuous social and cultural environment of the day made things harder and probably accelerated faculty retreat from responsibility in areas beyond the books. Student populations were not as monochromatic as once, and teachers further found themselves asked to handle "areas of student behavior with which we are little familiar and sometimes distinctly uncomfortable." Lester could certainly say that again. In the spring of 1976, his first year on the job, students conducted a poll of Trinity tenth to twelfth graders on a variety of nonacademic topics, and the school paper published in detail the steamy results. Who knows how accurate it was, but even discounted for adolescent posturing it suggests a mood.[141]

It all wanted some ballast. Lester envisioned youngish old schoolmen (and -women), teachers competent in their fields but without particular academic ambition and who recognized the danger of an overemphasis on academic performance coming at the cost of "the total student experience."[142] But who knew? "It is of course too early to see," Lester wrote in 1979, "whether the generation of teachers that came of age in the turbulent late sixties and early seventies will prove good schoolmen and schoolwomen. They *are* demonstrably attractive; they *are* bright; but, they are also self-centered— which almost seems to characterize the kids [not a Garten word] who came out of that period of our national history. I choose to believe that with proper shepherding, these young teachers may prove dedicated caretakers of the young and of our cultural heritage. We shall see what we shall see"[143] (emphasis original). "Total" is a dangerous modifier, but it fit. Lester had big thoughts that had a way of putting people on notice and often sent them soaring, but he did not attempt sharp definitions or lay out road maps. As they evolved at Trinity during and after his tenure, the best of such "schoolpersons" would acknowledge the need to relearn the balance afresh each year.

LESTER AND THE BOARD

If there was a yin/yang quality to some of this, it was because the school in the 1970s and 1980s was awash in a diversity of currents, internal and external. Faculty, student, curriculum, and "student life" matters, in the much larger school that Trinity had become, strained vision and performance from day to day. Managing it beyond the day-to-day was no easier, and it was there that the intersections between Trinity and the world outside became most hazardous.

Something of the same freshening spirit that accompanied the coming of Robin Lester visited the board that hired him. Trinity's board (officially the "Trinity Episcopal Schools Corporation") historically had been a quiet, fraternal affair, its business conducted privately in Wall Street offices and old clubs, and since the days of Cole, but especially Dann, deferential to the headmaster. It met formally three times a year, attending to routine finances, with a nod to school matters as reported by the headmaster.[144] Separate subcommittees were rare because the business of the school seemed so routine, something that began to change most noticeably with the Hawley Wing/Trinity House project. Thence, the issues of coeducation and raw relations with the neighborhood that flowed from West Side renewal and the role Trinity played demanded more and more of the school's official governors. It is a retrospective temptation to ask about the quiet old ways, "what was hidden?" Probably nothing. Rather, they bespoke a reticent style and more easily shared values and assumptions of that era: prudent Republican men and women in suits. Comparing the board's composition across twenty years reveals remarkable steadfastness. In 1955, the apogee of old-time, all-boys, headmaster (Dann)-in-charge Trinity, the board consisted of twenty men, including four clergymen, lawyers, and businessmen. Seven were alums. In 1975, at the start of Lester's era and with an enlarged, coed Trinity looking already a lot more like its future than its past, the board looked not that much different: twenty-one members, seventeen of them male, a dominant mix of lawyers, bankers, and businessmen.[145] It did, however, begin to see itself differently.

As if in anticipation of new challenges, the board in 1975 restructured. This was not radical, but it was suggestive. For decades there had been a number of life trustees, men (and women) once on, never off. In 1975, there were ten of them, including two women (Mildred Berendsen, headmistress of The Chapin School, Mrs. Robert Carleton, widow of a Trinity alum and great benefactor of Trinity-Pawling), and three ex officios (Paul Dudley Moore, Bishop of New York, Robert Parks, rector of Trinity Church, and William McGill, president of Columbia University). What exactly entitled one to "life" status was always a bit blurry, but basically it said something about large benefaction (Mrs. Carleton), historic relationship (the two priests and college president), or distinguished service (lawyer Eliot Lumbard was a lifer, as was Matt Dann, then headmaster of Trinity-Pawling, then still part of the "corporation"). Consensus was universal for change. The position of life trustees looked musty and suggested sinecure; it also potentially overloaded the board with people who, however competent or deserving, did not circulate.[146]

The board appointed a subcommittee chaired by Eliot Lumbard plus Richard N. Colhoun, Christopher Doyle, and Edwin Heard to draw up necessary revisions to the by-laws, which would also require approval by the

State Board of Regents in compliance with New York education law. They consulted the by-laws of other places, including Dalton, Collegiate, Chapin, and Nightingale schools, as well as Columbia and the University of Pennsylvania, and returned a reform package on which agreement was "substantially unanimous."[147] The underlying principle, Lumbard said, was to provide a more democratic board and to permit the continued growth of the corporation.[148] In substance, it abolished the category of life trustee, with the board henceforth to consist solely of term trustees serving three-year terms renewable for a second consecutive term. After a one-year hiatus, a trustee might serve yet again. There were two subcategories: the persons who held the offices of president of Columbia, Bishop of New York, and rector of Trinity Church, to whom invitation of membership for the length of their respective tenures would automatically be extended, and the presidents of the alumni and parents associations as ex officio trustees for the terms of their office. It was also stipulated that no headmaster of any school operated by the corporation would serve as trustee, ex officio or otherwise, though they might do so if elected after retirement or other separation. The matter of the board representing "broader constituencies" was discussed but apparently still premature. With a salute to the importance of "a well-rounded board," it was left that the nominating committee should look at the subject each year as it proposed candidates for trusteeships. Once the change was approved, the procedure was for all sitting trustees to resign on condition they would be re-elected as term trustees with terms to be decided by lot. Thereafter, in each year in which a third of the board would stand for re-election, those being re-elected or those being elected for the first time would serve full three-year terms.[149] As to number, there were to be no more than thirty and no less than fifteen trustees, and a retirement age of seventy was agreed necessary to ensure a young and vital board. Business would be conducted through the usual executive, operations, finance, nominating, and schools committees, with ad hoc groupings as necessary. Further, on motion of erstwhile life trustee Mildred Berendsen, it was unanimously approved that all references to "Headmaster" henceforth be changed to "Head of School."[150] Both schools of the corporation then had girls, and the prospect of a female head was not impossible.

Other prospects were more likely. Board and "head" interacted centrally on the business aspects of the school's life. These centered in turn on matters of demand for Trinity's services and what it cost to supply them.

Throughout this period and notwithstanding a moment of enrollment soft-
ness in the early grades as noted by Garten and confirmed by Lester in his
first years, Trinity easily ran at close to enrollment capacity, then around 800
students, kindergarten through twelfth grade; it gave preference to siblings,
endeavoring to be "a school for families."[151] What it took in, it nicely turned
out, dispatching seniors to a steady list of top colleges. Lester, as steadily,
pushed for and the board approved tuition increases, from the 1976 levels of
$1,730 for kindergarten, scaling to $2,740 for high school, to, in 1985, $6,215
and $7,200 respectively. He saw it as a problem from the start and not just of
his tenure but as consequence of a much longer legacy. It proved less of a
challenge to fill up Trinity's big new plant with a steady stream of boys and
girls than it did to service the debt and tuck-point the buildings, one of them
eighty years old. "Somehow we were proud of lowish tuition," one cha-
grinned trustee put it, "even though we had built the most expensive building complex in Manhattan."[152]

In 1977 the price charged for a Trinity education was $200 to $600 lower
than other major independent schools in New York City. As the School
Committee and trustee Berendsen had made clear the year before, this was
directly reflected in comparatively lower faculty salaries and levels of scholarship aid at Trinity. Despite recent raises and conversion to a scale, Lester
in 1979 worried that new faculty recruits, whether veterans or relative newcomers to teaching, were all single, "as our salaries are insufficient to support a family."[153] Moreover, the gap between operating expenses and tuition
income yawned ever wider. Lester thought that the only answer lay with
leaning harder on current consumers for current expenses, and that larger
amounts given by trustees and friends of the school could better be reserved
for building long-term endowment and for endless capital needs (a purpose-
built middle school looming the largest).[154] This turned out to be a profound insight, but not necessarily in the way he initially meant it. Tuitions
could never keep up, for costs would escalate too. What he might have suspected however, but could not have foreseen with certainty, was the phenomenon whereby consumers (here, of elite independent education in New
York City) come to perceive greater value in that which is higher priced. For
years, the fear had been twofold. High tuition would violate the spirit of
Trinity's history: Charity schooling may have been long dead but not the
notion that Trinity remained, at its core best, a school for "deserving" boys
(and lately, girls) from ordinary families. Second was the fear that high tu-

ition would in fact drive away the market of middle-class families, the school's bread and butter since the second half of the nineteenth century. This was a plausible enough fear as long as the "free" public school alternative was still an acceptable choice, as it was well through the first half of the twentieth century.

Make Trinity more expensive? Dann had done so, but on another order of magnitude and in a different context. In the 1930s, the school awoke to the folly of giving away its services, however modest their cost. More families paid more, but so thin was the apparent market that the fear of empty places overrode any thought of aggressive pricing. Dann competently tidied up and may indeed have saved the school at a critical juncture. It is key to remember, however, that the school was much smaller then, contentedly less ambitious, and less beset by troubling times. By the 1970s and 1980s, it was bigger, more complex, and with walls highly permeable to troubling times. In this fact lay both threat and opportunity.

The same commotions that roiled, albeit gently, through Trinity also roiled through New York and its public schools. Once admired as a model of primary and secondary urban education, that vast system educated the vast majority of young New Yorkers and would continue to do so long after it ceased to be a model in any positive sense. Its stumbling, however, freshened demand among the ever-small but growing minority of New York families with imagination, inclination, and means enough to entertain at least the thought of a private-school alternative. "Flight from the public schools" had become an evening news cliché by the 1970s, when New York City went bankrupt, and its beleaguered public schools fell in reputation along with its subways. It was usually spoken of in the same breath with phrases like "flight to the suburbs," or, more ominously, "white flight." Trinity too once had thought of fleeing the city but had taken another, tougher choice. Instead of green pastures, it invested hugely to renew and enlarge the physical plant in a marginal urban neighborhood whose comeback was then anything but assured. It was a sizeable bet and, as it turned out, a good one. This was so, long term, because of the reputation its investment purchased: as a Manhattan school of traditional ilk, coed, with a pool and gym and a playing field—and tough teachers who knew how to turn little children and clever adolescents into successful college applicants.

Make Trinity more expensive? Lester figured there was no other choice, as Trinity completed its metamorphosis from old-time Episcopal school to elite independent school. By the 1970s and 1980s, that choice or lack of it would have consequences disproportionate to whatever additional revenue it brought in, as demand for such high-quality educational service proved startlingly insensitive to price. These consequences were partly virtuous but not entirely. So ferocious became the appetite for a Trinity education that price no longer deterred demand but may even have enhanced it, if the measure was the line at the admissions office and the selectiveness in which the school subsequently luxuriated. Raising the price thus solved one problem, and solved it better than anyone might prudently then have guessed: Places were full and so was the pipeline. Even as it solved that problem, though, raising the price created another. Who got to come? Who might enjoy the privilege? If demand was intense and tuition revenue was important, then might not Trinity, whose unrelenting high standards defined it as an academically elite school, become Trinity whose high price defined it as a school primarily or even solely for the economic elite, and a New York City economic elite at that? The question, driven by economics, both resonated with an old one of what Trinity was for and hung over debates about diversity—of talents and types and the benefits and costs of securing it—that would fill the early 2000s and beyond.[155]

It all looked good—indeed, suspiciously so. How to coordinate academic with financial success? How to balance the income and expense sides while maintaining even expanding the purposes of the institution? By the mid-1980s, Trinity's fees were near the top among New York City's independent day schools. Its endowment, then some $2 million, ranked eighth after Ethical Culture, Brearley, Chapin, Collegiate, Dalton, Nightingale, and Spence.[156] This income stream supported an operation that, like its competitor schools, was extremely labor-intensive, with salaries and benefits accounting for between 60 and 70 percent of operating costs (at Trinity in 1984, it was 65 percent). The other major expense items at schools like Trinity were plant maintenance and scholarships or student financial aid, at Trinity that year 12 and 8 percent, respectively. Like most schools, Trinity depended heavily (90 percent) on tuition income to meet the payroll, pay the mortgage, fix the roof, and subsidize desirable students, with just 1 percent of operating income coming from endowment, and 3 percent from fundraising and contributions.[157]

Controlling expenses, in Lester's time, was exceedingly difficult. Trinity had the largest and most expensive physical plant in Manhattan. Until 1980, ten years after the building of the Hawley Wing and Trinity House, Trinity's budget showed no item for building renewals and replacements, with the result that maintenance got postponed and piled up. The first-generation AstroTurf atop the garage, which had given Trinity its own unique urban playing field, needed replacing by the early 1980s, and the hugger-mugger of old buildings (139, the St. Agnes "Annex," and the 1950s gym) it had accumulated demanded pointing, roofing, routine mechanical updates that could be frightfully expensive. If keeping out the rain was necessary but dreary, paying the staff, who could talk back and walk away, was necessary but electric. Faculty starting salaries by the mid-1980s ranked eighteenth among New York independent schools, and the entire salary scale fell in the second fifth of competitors. Counted as a percentage of budget, scholarships at Trinity then ran at 7.6 percent, which was behind Ethical Culture at 15.3, Collegiate at 9.8, Brearley at 9.4, Chapin at 9, Dalton at 8.7. Nightingale came in next at 7.3.

Stress abounded, centrally the stress between two facts. "I believe we are at the top or near the top in the quality of education we are providing," Lester wrote, adding, "I believe most observers of Manhattan independent schools would agree." He was right: There were waiting lists, families left competitor schools to come to Trinity, students and parents were energized with school life, college admissions never flagged. But it was as if Trinity had jumped to the head of a very competitive pack in an increasingly pressure-cooker atmosphere, yet was looking as if it might not be able to sustain its lead. Without addressing the second fact, of its comparatively weak showing in faculty salaries and scholarships (which purchased, in Lester's phrase, "student diversity"), a cushionless Trinity could certainly fade.[158] With every year still a race to the finish, this despite a two-pronged capital campaign initiated in 1979 to raise $3 million to deal with maintenance and remodeling issues and address faculty benefits and scholarships,[159] tension did not abate. There was precious little room for maneuver.

LESTER AND THE COMMUNITY

There might have been even less had not one other troubled area of the school's life at last come right. It is possible to view the enormous changes at Trinity between the mid-1960s and mid-1980s as both willed and imposed. Pushed first by Garten, then by Lester and most faculty and parents, Trinity reopened to girls and so doubled the size of its market at just the time implosion of the once mighty public school system set afire demand for top-quality independent education in New York City. Garten and the board chose this initial course for the high school. But the record is equally clear that had the faculty not relented about full extension of coeducation just a few years later, then it would have gone no further and left Trinity a hermaphrodite. That coeducation proceeded successfully as it did is hard to imagine however absent the Hawley Wing. That project too, of course, had come about by choice, to a degree, and calculated risk taking. But would it ever have come about outside the context of West Side Renewal and the promise, but just the promise, that a once fashionable but decayed part of town would be fashionable once again? Without the threat, and the opportunity, of Site 24, could Trinity have found a way to grow enough in order to stay on West 91st Street? It might, of course, have reacted differently than it did; it might have ignored the threat and failed to realize the opportunity altogether. It made a better choice, but it had to be prompted by a challenge from outside itself.

The consequences that flowed from that decision, to embrace renewal and creatively align a private interest with a forgone public policy, could not all have been foreseen. What might have been guessed at was that henceforth Trinity would find itself engaged with, sometimes embroiled with, its neighbors on new terms. For decades after moving to West 91st Street in the 1890s, Trinity had had no "neighborhood relations" in any formal sense at all. Trinity was what it was, which was pretty much the same year after year. The neighborhood was what it was, which changed a great deal over the years. The status quo of that relationship was not ultimately sustainable.

Everyone noticed, including students, who like students everywhere in the 1960s were beginning to look outward and ask grown-up sounding questions about the world around them. "Trinity, for many years a shining star in the midst of poverty and despair, is beginning to come to the realization that it can no longer stand peacefully on the side, aloof from the problems surrounding it," wrote one young journalist in a *Trinity Times* opinion survey in 1969, "while the neighborhood drowns in a sea of illiteracy and frustration." Opinions about the old school varied among the locals, reflecting the fractures of the neighborhood. One elderly white woman who thought Trinity students "the nicest kids in the world" and described young Puerto Ricans as "little monsters," in response to the question "should Trinity remain isolated" answered, "Yes: Trinity should mind its own damn business." A local white shopkeeper who knew the street described the same chasm differently: "The black youth envy and despise you; trying to educate these people is a lost cause; don't stick your neck out for them." A young Asian woman thought Trinity needed to do more: "As regards being a good neighbor, Trinity has failed." A Puerto Rican youth was more graphic: "They come in their nice blue jackets and clean white shirts and hide in their nice clean building." A black teenager said simply: "They close their eyes to what's around them when they're here, and they keep them shut till they get to Fifth Avenue."[160] Hurts and hazards cut both ways. Trinity students were easy game for muggers, and worries about street safety were real. "In order to lower the mugging rate," the school contracted private security services to monitor both entrances.[161]

Such was context. It was at the level of high policy that cracks became crevices and not long after the concrete was poured for what would become the Hawley Wing/Trinity House. No good deed goes unpunished for long, and so it was that in October 1971, freshly moved into new quarters that would have been unimaginable a decade before and having become, it thought, benevolent landlord of a modern high-rise apartment tower housing a prescribed proportion of low- and middle-income neighbors and some of its own faculty, Trinity found itself in court in an extended action as politically dubious as it was probably legally sound. The root external problem was the shifting political nature of West Side Urban Renewal, which dated from the early 1960s and was ever a work in progress. Trinity's creative involvement with Site 24 was one part of that puzzle and a critical one for itself and the city: It was defined in carefully lawyered contracts, in mortgages, and finally in immovable brick-and-mortar. Other parts of renewal moved less smoothly and witnessed greater finagle. The other part that mattered directly to Trinity was Site 30, the parcel of land directly across 91st Street from its nice new building.[162]

The city had been eager that Trinity as the oldest and largest area institution be involved in West Side renewal, and Trinity's decision to sponsor development of the contiguous Site 24 had been made with certain understandings. The one that proved critical and that triggered the legal imbroglio of the 1970s was how exactly the new and renewed housing envisioned for the area would be divvied up between middle- and lower-income people and the impact such division would have on the quality of the neighborhood environment. The city amended its plans numerous times during the 1960s as to what the balance should be, finally settling, so Trinity would claim, on a ratio of 70:30 (middle to lower), and that the total number of lower-income units would be 2,500. Trinity House, the housing half of Trinity's involvement in Site 24, was tenanted roughly on that basis. Site 30 was originally designated for the same mixture, but in 1969 the city planning commission reneged, claiming that the number of low-income units originally proposed was no longer sufficient to meet demand, and that Site 30 would be re-designated as a predominantly low-income project, a high-rise building accommodating 160 units for the poor. The decision was not exactly clinically pure, but shot through with local politics. Already, opposing community groups had polarized the issue along class and perhaps racial lines. The Strycker's Bay Neighborhood Council and the United Tenants Organization, vintage 1960s "grass-roots" neighborhood outfits, claimed to speak for the (largely nonwhite) poor and provided legal and organizational support for increases in the amount of low-income housing and in defending squatters who occupied, among others, the old buildings on Site 30, daring eviction. Prospective national, state, and local elections only raised the volume.[163] On the other side, the Committee of Neighbors to Insure a Normal Urban Environment, or CONTINUE, mobilized middle-class property owners, some of them investors drawn to the area's remarkable collection of 350 brownstone row houses, others residents of the stately inter-war vintage elevator buildings along Central Park West. It opposed concentration of low-income housing anywhere in the area, and its rhetoric could be colorful, railing at middle-class victimization at the hands of "maniac liberal politicians" and "professional povertycrats."[164]

In the lawsuit that Trinity filed in October 1971 to halt construction in face of the switching of Site 30 to low-income housing, these two ideological foes became the plaintiffs of record, a fact that might have signaled the bitterness of the encounter to come.[165] There followed for nine years a see-saw of argument, decision, appeal, and remand, in which Trinity lost and won, won and lost. This much of the legal narrative (which produced thousands of pages of testimony from scores of witnesses and hundreds of exhibits) bears recounting here. Led by outside counsel Eugene Morris (who had also shepherded the Hawley Wing/Trinity House construction project) and with Trinity Board member and attorney Eliot Lumbard never far into the wings, Trinity argued along three lines. First it claimed breach of contract in the city's decision to redesignate Site 30 and allow additional low-income tenants into the area. Moreover, the designated figure of 2,500 low-in-come units Trinity took to mean the "maximum not be exceeded." The city would argue back that flexibility had been part of the concept of the plan from inception.[166] Flowing from the numbers was the second argument, which had to do with "tipping," which described the white flight that oc-curred when too many nonwhite people move in and was a concept recog-nized in the courts.[167] Trinity contended that the proposed conversion of Site 30 added to the low-income projects already on West 91st Street would result in an over 80 percent low-income concentration and would mark the tipping point. Unless reversed, the area would revert to a pocket ghetto and segregated slum—opposite the intention of the entire West Side renewal plan and illegal besides. Trinity's argument on this point blurred the eco-nomic and racial focus, perhaps because of CONTINUE's racial diversity. Witness Roger Starr testified that "in the Area there are a fairly considerable number of non-white homeowners and if the neighborhood tips they will get out along with the white people getting out." What was feared, the plain-tiffs argued, was not black people, but poor black people who would "tip" the area to become all-black, period. This was important, since racial segre-gation was recognized as a federal constitutional violation. Economic seg-regation was not.[168] The third line of argument was that the plan violated the National Environmental Protection Act of 1969 and that the Depart-ment of Housing and Urban Development (HUD) had not undertaken a full environmental impact statement. Trinity argued that the lapse was more than procedural and failed to take account of the "social and psychological" consequences for the urban environment that would result from conversion of Site 30 to low-income housing. HUD indeed was ordered back to present alternative sites, and argued successfully that any switch would cripple the plan with two years' delay and impose negative environmental consequences of its own.

Trinity lost, in law, on all but the environmental issue, and there it was not, finally, sustained either.[169] It all took a long time, however, enough in fact to accomplish by delay what could not be achieved by injunction. By the time it was settled, the fashion for such old-style high-rise public housing projects had faded along with the funds to build them. What resulted and what stands today is a middle-income building with the entrance on the other side that does not even face Trinity.

The specter that Trinity then feared and that prompted legal action proved in time a phantom. Trinity won for losing. With economic resurgence in the 1980s and 1990s, the neighborhood indeed tipped, decisively, but in all the right ways. The middle class stayed; all sorts and conditions of men and women mingled more or less benignly; property values went up and up. In all ways external to Trinity, the tale of West Side Urban Renewal had a virtuous ending worthy even of Hugh Riddleberger's rosy visions far back in 1959 (see chapter 6).

In ways internal to Trinity, the episode illustrates not only the inadequacy in this instance of legal measures alone to accomplish a policy aim but the potential of extended legal action to lay open conflict and dissent. After Trinity's first volley was knocked down in U.S. District Court in 1974, special counsel Morris warned the board of dark consequences if the decision was let stand and, ever the good advocate, strongly urged carrying on through the courts. The board did and at first was vindicated, when a federal appeals court promptly reversed the district court and blocked the low-income project.[170] When the prospect of a lawsuit had arisen in 1971, the board pressed ahead boldly. When it looked to turn into a long and dirty slog, consensus frayed. The board's two clergymen, the Rt. Rev. Paul Moore, Jr., Bishop of New York, and Dr. Robert Parks, rector of Trinity Church, dissented. Moore and Parks took their dissent public. Whatever the merits of the legal argument, Parks said that in his view "the filing of an appeal can only further confirm the opinion of many people that Trinity School has no real concern for low-income people" and that "the alienation that results from it (the suit) may not be worth it." They appealed to all the way back to Trinity's charity origins, declaring continuation of the suit "counter to this tradition."[171] Moore in particular was a clergyman well toward the left end of the spectrum in a once conservative denomination ("the frozen chosen," as Episcopalians were sometimes called) rapidly realigning itself with liberal causes along the central theme of social justice. The lawsuit made him squirm, an embarrassment sullying an allegedly Episcopal institution but one that the church obviously could not control. They were right, about the appearance of things anyway: Trinity was easy to make look the villain. Morality seemed all on the side of the defendants, if one accepted that social justice was what vocal "low-income people" (once called simply "the poor"), or of their appointed spokesmen, said it was.[172] Moore did.

So did Robin Lester, the new headmaster. Lester was appalled at the lawsuit, which he thought small-minded and needlessly antagonistic.[173] But

Lester was not, at the beginning, quite yet in charge. The suit had started squarely on Garten's watch, and though not leading the charge, Garten wholly supported Lumbard and his partisans in initiating legal action and following through, whatever it might take. When Lester appeared in 1975 it was with the express intention that he would play the conciliator and improve relations with all Trinity's constituents, including the neighbors. The tide turned. He took the charge seriously and took it up enthusiastically, appreciating that Trinity had been going through a rough patch that was partly of its own making, partly not. The part that was, he would do his best to ameliorate. He forsook the fancy East Side apartment on Fifth Avenue overlooking Central Park where Garten had lived, and moved his family into the old brownstone on West 91st and thus became, literally, a neighbor too.[174] He understood acting and the importance of being seen. His very first week on the job, Lester opened Trinity's swimming pool to residents of nearby Goddard Riverside low-income apartments: "I was in the pool with black kids and so forth from all over the neighborhood."[175] Lester's own politics were leftist, and his friendliness with local area politicians and neighborhood activists adamant that Trinity relent in its suit was controversial but effective.[176] In 1978, Trinity did relent and dropped out of the litigation, leaving CONTINUE to carry on (all the way to the U. S. Supreme Court). Eliot Lumbard resigned from the board in protest,[177] but relief was pervasive among those weary of controversy and the diversion of energy and resources it caused.

It was not, after all, as if Trinity had not tried to be a good neighbor in other ways. Here, Lester could build on others' work before him. They did not at first call it "community service," but Trinity students had long stepped out quietly to lend a hand. Garten had pioneered the Broad Jump program established in the 1960s to offer academic enrichment to disadvantaged children, and Trinity had partnered with an enterprising Bronx public school teacher, Garry Simons, to found Prep for Prep, which reached out to bright public school children and their families with the specific aim of admitting the topmost performers in the program to top independent schools, and so also diversifying the admissions pools and advertising Trinity's commitment to minorities.[178] Prep for Prep was staffed mostly by public school teachers who wanted to see their best students challenged; participants did intensive academic work at Trinity in the summer and returned twice a week throughout the school year.[179] Garten related a lovely story, given that the time was the summer of 1968: "We picked up four Broad Jump boys for Trinity, three of them financed by a $7500 grant we received for each of two years to back Negro and Puerto Rican boys. One of our regular boys who was a tutor this summer was held up on the East [!] Side. When he had emptied his pockets, one of the 'robbers' saw his Trinity blazer and had it all given back. He said, 'It's an OK school. I went there this summer and this kid helped me.'"[180]

There had long been a summer day camp drawing children from outside the school-year community, and from the inception of the Hawley Wing/ Trinity House project the need to make some of its facilities available to neighborhood groups for sports and recreation was on the agenda even if the logistics were subject to evolution. In community relations, particularly where the community was diverse and packed tight, as it was on the West Side, perceptions mattered and called for sensitive management. In 1978, Lester appointed Lyle Redelinghuys, formerly head of the history department and an Episcopal deacon, to the special job of dealing with community affairs.[181] A hundred students and faculty then participated voluntarily in the school's student–faculty service group, working in a number of community activities. One destined for school lore was the Thanksgiving Day dinner served each year to the neighborhood elderly, in Trinity's spacious new cafeteria. In 1977, the effort landed Trinity a three-column front-page story in *The New York Times* the morning after, with two photographs of fresh-faced, name-tagged Trinity students helping out around the table and others wheeling a West Side senior across the street toward school. Some of the boys and girls doing the serving were little ones. Lester, no surprise, got quoted. "The younger they are, the better the old people like them. The kids have to endure endless hugs and squeezes and kisses, but they don't seem to mind." Eighty-two-year-old Rupert Smith, born in Tobago, didn't. Smith had spent years as a waiter at the Century Club and found being served a real treat: "I do hope to be back next year, with God's blessing, of course."[182] It was very sweet—and smart and a far cry from sour stories about lawsuits.

PART WAY

Lester may have liked to think of himself as a radical, but he was a careful one.

He was ever polite about and toward his predecessor, who had after all managed eleven years at Trinity with arguably more successes than failures.

Lester too would manage eleven years at Trinity. He thought that long enough: any longer, and the risk rose of identifying oneself with the school, and when that happened faculties grew wary and boards restive. Through the 1970s and 1980s, the school responded less and less anyway to the hand of any one leader. Lester represents probably the last moment, however, when one leader was sought who had answers to all the school's multiple and complex challenges. It was hard-nosed lawyer and political infighter Eliot Lumbard, no sentimentalist, who had said that hiring Lester would mean "gambling on greatness."[183]

Lester figured it a gamble, too, and knew his weaknesses (he was never, he admitted, comfortable with finances),[184] but he never doubted he could do the job. Many, faculty and students especially, agreed. He also thought himself lucky. For someone of his modest administrative credentials and youthfulness to have become head of one of the oldest schools in America, luck had to have had something to do with it. At the time of his hiring, trustee Mildred Berendsen, headmistress of Chapin, had remarked that in addition to other more objective qualifications, true affinity for the city was essential in the Trinity headmaster or "head," as was the official term.[185] Here, Lester shone. He was an outsider to New York, who came in the classic fashion to love the city. But he admired it less for its natives than for its newcomers, because of its history as a magnet for talent (like himself) from everywhere else.[186] In the end, neither Trinity nor New York held him. He left subsequent marks on schools far away, on the West Coast and in the Midwest, but he probably peaked at Trinity. Certainly that is where he was happiest.[187]

He came into a school fighting with itself and with the world outside, and he helped calm, restore, and inspire it. It is hard to imagine a rougher time. Perhaps it was the right time for a young man brimful with faith and energy and who did not yet know any better. Lester was a starter, and a very good starter, but he hardly finished the job. As a Presbyterian ("Let's hire the Calvinist," Robert Parks had joked to the search committee in 1975), Lester was a fatalistic—make the world into something God might once again be proud of—optimist. "We do not believe in educational utopias at Trinity," he wrote to prospective families toward the end his tenure. "We do believe that any structure or system is only as good as the people we place in the school to help your child grow and learn."[188] If physiognomy is any clue, the work that took took its toll. In 1975 he was thirty-five and looked twenty-five. In 1985, though dapper as ever, he was every bit his age and looked older.[189]

Lester trailed a warm glow of human closeness that can still be felt at Trinity, and he left a mixed management legacy for others to attend to. He too got a portrait, a nice enough painting by Dian Friedman. It hangs in the anteroom to the headmaster's office in the old 139 building, on a wall to itself opposite Cole and Dann, with Garten off to the side. Lester poses, at ease, awash in academic robes: the radical, approachable "Dr. Lester" looking out toward the street. Later in life, he claimed to have asked his one-time teacher at the University of Chicago, renowned historian and Librarian of Congress Daniel Boorstin, for advice on how, getting started in the schooling business, he should style himself: "What am I supposed to be called?" Bow-tied Boorstin flashed back: "Oh look, in education, 'Doctor.' Make sure you take advantage of that."[190] He did.

EIGHT *Elite Education*
in a Democratic Society

obin Lester correctly perceived Trinity's fundamental attractiveness in new terms, as an academically powerful, coeducational, kindergarten-through-twelfth grade independent school, in a market where demand far outstripped supply. He did not perceive all the consequences of that insight. Sustained growth created demands on governance and finance that had little precedent. Lester was not the only one at first to miss this, and he labored under the disadvantage of probably unfair expectations. Hired and blessed by board members who then crossed their fingers and hoped for "greatness," Lester was the last "here, you do it" headmaster.[1]

A year before he left, Lester told a story that had an eerie forward resonance. He had made it "traditional" for the kindergarten classes to visit him in his office each year (which accounted for the many stuffed animals that furnished it), where he read to them from books by his wife Helen (an accomplished children's author), invited them into his home, and entertained them with a playful slide down the banister. Through all the giggles, one serious little fellow reportedly asked, "Dr. Lester, how can you afford this place?" Lester replied, "I can't—it is loaned to us for a time."[2]

Lester was speaking high-mindedly, about how Trinity belonged to no one headmaster, to no one generation of teachers or students, but to "the centuries." (It was just then marking its 275th anniversary.)[3] The truth was that it was Trinity that probably could not have afforded Lester for much longer. The school publicly reported its financial condition only starting five years later, in 1990, and it reported an operating deficit that year of some $150,000 on an operating budget of $10.5 million. In fact it had run much deeper in the red for several years, and the trustees hoped and expected a new leader with weight and experience would set things right.

While Trinity by the middle 1980s appeared a happy enough ship, as an institution that dispensed increasingly sophisticated and expensive educational services and maintained a large and awkward physical plant, part of it nearly 100 years old, it was sailing close to a lee shore. The fate of Lester's successor illustrated this. The trustees thought the school could be run by a strong headmaster, stronger at least than Lester. They learned that the job was more complicated and demanding than in the past, requiring better management of a variety of constituencies, with a large budget and contentious administrative and policy issues ever in the balance. It was more than any single person could achieve and required reconfiguration of roles and responsibilities.

John Hanly's year as interim head, 1986–87, sustained the warm high spirits of Lester's time, and kept the ship, educationally at least, on an even keel. Hanly soon proved his administrative talents elsewhere, but at Trinity he was ever the teacher (of English, then head of the Upper School), and so he would be revered ever after. His one-year appointment echoed similar service done by Bruner-Smith two decades before, between Hugh Riddleberger and Richard Garten. Bruner-Smith had never had any other intention than getting back into the classroom as quickly as possible. With Hanly, the interim headship was an up-and-out maneuver: With a year in charge of Trinity, he would be ready for his own school and soon got it.[4] But Hanly like Lester, was a faculty man, too, and while charged with one awkward errand in the form of a tough personnel decision, he was a placeholder who gave the board time to find the next permanent head.

The choice was Christopher Berrisford. A transplanted Englishman fifty-eight years old in 1988 (Lester had been thirty-five in 1975), Berrisford held degrees from Harvard and Oxford and on paper must have looked the sure thing.[5] Most importantly, he had successfully led two other independent schools in the United States—St. Mark's School in Dallas (1963–69), and the Harvard Westlake School in Los Angeles (1969–1988). Both gave him high marks as an administrator and as a fund-raiser. "Besides," concluded British schoolman Hanly, "he's an Oxford man: what more could we ask?"[6]

BERRISFORD

When Berrisford arrived in 1987, it was with the typical good words: "Trinity is a community enriched by an unusual combination of talent and energy. It is an exciting place to be. One is constantly being delighted by a challenging question, an original thought, a friendly gesture and a disarming smile."[7] It did not take him long to get down to work however, and it could not have been easy.[8] There were issues of both style and substance. Berrisford had a formal, some said even imperious, manner that matched his distinguished good looks and Oxbridge pedigree and accent. He was not a man who made friends easily around the school, certainly not compared to the back-slapping, never-forgot-a-name Lester. Berrisford liked to communicate on paper, a memo writer to a community used to being talked to, or talked up. Certainly Berrisford made few friends on the faculty, which some said Lester had favored to the point of pampering. The new headmaster's manner, and his plans, invited a rocky start. That was what he got.

Berrisford was a thoughtful man and started his review of Trinity from high up, with philosophy. He was also a seasoned administrator who related philosophical matters to practical ones. Trinity's philosophy, he thought, was not clear. Partly this was the times: Schools everywhere were being put upon to do more than they had in the past, and the temptation was to add activities out of expedience but without philosophical conviction. While he admired the Trinity he inherited, he found it hard to explain in comparison to other independent schools in the city. "We need to define our position, both so that we can establish priorities in terms of time and money, and so that we can tell prospective parents what they should expect from us."[9] He set up Philosophy and Curriculum Review committees composed of senior faculty, which would consult with Planning and Academic committees of the board to hone objectives, and, with that in hand, would move on to review the school's schedule and curriculum and start discussions about what was taught, how it was taught, at what level and at what length.

He also thought a school as allegedly good as Trinity should not be afraid of measuring things. "Evaluation" was the fateful word, which to Berrisford meant setting goals, reviewing them regularly, and redefining them on the basis of previous experience and trying to improve. This was not radical theory. He liked the idea of being able to monitor progress. One of the biggest lapsed areas lay at the very heart of the school, with the faculty. When he arrived, there was no description of a normal teaching load or of additional expectations. He put to work a faculty evaluation, committee chaired by a senior teacher, Carol France of the Upper School English department, inviting self-evaluation and staunchly defended evaluation against all comers.[10]

Berrisford understood independent schools and Trinity, his latest one, unromantically as providers of specialized educational services for which was charged a price determined by costs and competition. The on-the-ground everyday provider of those services, within the school, was the faculty, and it was central, he believed, to the health of the institution that teachers teach efficiently. To some ears and probably most faculty ears, talk of efficiency in education sounded and still sounds oxymoronic, if not crass. To Berrisford it was just economic reality and intended neither to threaten nor offend, but he could not avoid collision.

It occurred at the intersection where faculty representative committee and trustees' operations committee met to discuss salaries and benefits. Faculty as ever was anxious about money and the daunting challenge of living in Manhattan on teachers' pay, and a change of guard in the headmaster's office occasioned a predictable push for more. Berrisford was not in principle unsympathetic, but the numbers told but one story. Trinity's student/teacher ratio, a crude measure of work load and one window on efficiency, was then 7.6:1 and far beyond the limits normally considered to be productive in private day schools.[11] Berrisford admitted that Trinity's rambling hugger-mugger physical plant imposed some unavoidable obstacles to running things efficiently but argued that an effort at least must be made to recast the school operationally in a form that would put tuition dollars into pay packets in line with competitive schools in New York. He did not believe, however, that this could be accomplished through fund raising (at least not at first) or by raising tuition. First, it was an internal matter of "setting some priorities and defining our expectations."[12]

He knew what he was up against, in general, in terms of conventional wisdom to do with the beauty of small classes, but the facts were otherwise. "If there were evidence that the small ratio of teachers to students produced measurable educational gain, then we would have some difficult choices in front of us," but, he argued, there was none. "There is nothing in any literature of which I am aware that argues this. In fact, the arguments go the other way and suggest that clear priorities, reasonable class size [i.e., not unreasonably small] and a focused program help students to obtain better results." There was no way to raise pay without increasing productivity. This had philosophical and budgetary ramifications. He asked the principals therefore to review the school's operations and daily practices in their divisions and to recommend where they could cut costs by 20 percent. At the same time, he sought to reassure Trinity that the changes he foresaw would not endanger the jobs of full-time classroom teachers or extracurricular programs. Nonetheless, just thinking about cost reductions was a start toward establishing priorities, and "it is an essential exercise for us to undertake at the moment."[13] He also thought Trinity's bookkeeping was outmoded and incoherent, and that long-time business manager John Ryan was not the man to fix the problem. Controls on expenditures were lax and a sensitive issue, and Berrisford insisted that charges be made against appropriate budget lines even if those lines overdrew.[14] Only then, he said, could the board have a clear picture of which operations cost more than anticipated. He instructed Ryan to reorder Trinity's accounts according to new standards set by the National Association of Independent Schools (NAIS), and in time he replaced Ryan with a new hire of his own, Joan Dannenberg.[15]

Into early 1988, the surface at least seemed reasonably calm. Berrisford tried hard to couch his changes as improvements to an already good thing, but he was steadfast that changes had to be made: curriculum review, regular evaluations, simplified decision making, general tightening up of administrative matters.[16] It was not just that he was a new man, but a new man who found himself in the unenviable position of taking on an institution in more dire circumstances than had perhaps been represented to him. With written record slight and remembrance reluctant on this point, it is foggy about just what Berrisford was told about Trinity's finances and about the collective character of its faculty. His roll-up-your-sleeves-and-get-right-down-to-it style suggested he was a quick learner, whatever he knew at the start, and that he was not unused to the fact that all institutions traverse peaks and from time to time valleys. Trinity in the late 1980s and early 1990s was beyond doubt in a valley.

Since at least 1983, Trinity's operating budgets were overspent, often by substantial sums: $750,000 in 1984–85 (Robin Lester's penultimate year), $203,000 in 1986–87, $623,000 in 1988–89, deficits that as a proportion of expenses ranged between 2 and 9 percent.[17] Everything cost more. There was debt to repay from the Hawley Wing, ever-escalating maintenance costs of an aging nineteenth-century plant, and of course the eternal lion's share of what it cost to run any school: faculty and staff wages and benefits, which increased approximately 100 percent during the 1980s. Against growth-driven escalation in expense, revenues refused to keep up. Borrowing from the school's modest endowment filled the gap, which, however, slowed growth of the endowment, upon which in turn depended the school's long-term prosperity if not its year-to-year survival.

It is with such financial context in mind that Berrisford's years at Trinity must be judged. The inheritor of a school bleeding red ink year after year, with well-entrenched forces who bristled at his presence almost from the start, and with a board less steadfast than he in confronting the symptoms of an ailing institution, Berrisford faced daunting challenges and long odds against success. It is a sad fact that his name remains identified with one of the least happy chapters in the school's history.

Berrisford's fall was a tale of colossal misperceptions, and a lesson in how the long arm of past experience would not let the present go. That experience—the lush years of Robin Lester—had left the Trinity faculty resentful toward any successor, and certainly unprepared for one of Berrisford's ilk. They reacted badly, in ways that on the merits and in retrospect are hard to credit. Yet from the narrow trench they feared themselves in at the time, they reacted as educators alarmed and not irrationally. Lester and they together had put Trinity on the map as a highly desirable independent school in one of the world's fiercest markets for such education. They had good reason to be confident, proud even. More's the pity then that they had not confidence enough to grant Berrisford a fuller hearing or at least to have given him the fairer shake of a little more time.

What Berrisford saw as returning the school to better business practices and looking its financial weaknesses square in the eye, the teachers interpreted as betrayal, a threat to their living, even to their way of life. They did not wait out even his first full year to say so. It has become part of the lore of the school from that period: their "no-confidence" vote on Berrisford's leadership, taken at a special faculty meeting on March 11, 1988. It was not that literally, for there was no binding mechanism whereby faculty might thus pass judgment on a head of school, who served not them but the board. But it had devastating political effect. The faculty sensed they were strong, the head weak. They were right, and they pounced.[18]

Their letter was signed by the five members of the Faculty Representative Committee (Richard Blumenthal, Carole Brighton, Carole France, Sandy Kaplan, and Joe Scavone), whose role was to represent faculty views on salaries and benefits. On this occasion they served as conduit for much else, purporting to summarize the meeting and suggest something of its temperature. The issues included communication, trust, managerial style, morale, lack of due process, and "an educational philosophy that seems at variance with what most people had thought of as Trinity School." All staffs complain about their bosses, but this was no routine whining. They wrote a statement then and there, took a vote (sixty-eight in favor, none opposed, one abstention), and told their representatives to tell it to the board.[19] If there were any moderates in the room, they lost out in the editing: "We believe an emergency situation exists that will affect the educational life of our school for years to come. Therefore, the faculty of Trinity School regretfully reports that we question the competence, education philosophy, and credibility of the present headmaster. Although we sympathize with him as a person, we lack confidence in his ability to lead this school." (If there had been a prudent editor in the crowd, "school" might have been struck for "faculty.") The committee's letter reporting this went to the trustees three days later, duly carbon-copied to Berrisford.[20]

Nor was that all. Teachers talk, children listen, parents get anxious. It is hard to determine now just how much the faculty actively stirred up the parents, but stirred up they became.[21] Two days after the faculty fired their salvo, the executive board of the Parents' Association fired off its own. This was a larger group of signatories (twenty-seven mothers, including three joint husband/wives), and they sounded, compared to the faculty, more earnest than angry. "We understand that all organizations must constantly reexamine their goals and means of attaining them . . . and that there are many styles of leadership and do not believe that our concerns represent an overreaction to a change from one to the other." The disclaimer is not wholly convincing. Of course, the parents seemed to say, we are all grown-ups who know how imperfectly the world works (even the faculty had offered a lame "we sympathize with him [Berrisford] as a person"), but soft issues conveyed a hard agenda. They spoke of the "clouded atmosphere" that had settled over the school, presumably in contrast to the sunshine of the previous administration. They fretted over the leadership's "lack of receptivity and responsiveness." And they explicitly allied themselves with the dissident teachers: Parents were "increasingly concerned to hear the expression of similar feelings from members of the school's outstanding and loyal faculty."[22] The adjectives were important: This was a united front. In their letter, the faculty had reciprocated, citing "deep dissatisfaction" with Berrisford among present and prospective parents, and claiming adverse effect on admissions and downward trends in fund raising (none of which can be documented).

Consequences, parents said, already looked dire. Otherwise loyal Trinity families were talking about removing their children to other schools. Prospective ones were thinking twice before applying. At colleges interviewing Trinity students, comments were surfacing that all was not well with "one of the premier independent schools in America." Reputation was threatened. So to the fateful verb: Parents "demand the immediate attention of the Board and of the Headmaster."[23] What is clear is that none of this was meant as a mere shot across the headmaster's bow. It was carefully aimed and meant to sink him. It did, if slowly. That trouble lurked was of course known, to some trustees at least, before the faculty threw down its marker in March.[24] The board's behavior subsequently revealed caution, then frustration, then concession masked as compromise.

The board wasted no time responding, promptly meeting with faculty representatives and separately with Berrisford. The executive committee solicited further faculty views, interviewed the three principals, the assistant principal of the upper school, the dean of faculty and the chaplain and *individually* sixty-three faculty and staff members. They also talked to other parents. Within four weeks they thought they had distilled the problem(s) or at least categorized them: Berrisford's lack of communication effectiveness, his lack of leadership tactics and personal style, and perceived differences between his educational ideas and those of the faculty.[25]

Though they had had an earful, the trustees decided first, and quickly, to support Berrisford. They also took some responsibility, resolving to monitor the situation actively and to try to remediate some of the headmaster's alleged weaknesses. This was honest, well-intentioned, and fruitless. They met frequently. Trustee and parent Richard Foster, a senior partner at McKinsey & Company, offered consulting services pro bono in an attempt to help mediate the need, as Berrisford had identified it, for greater operating efficiency, with the faculty's anxieties about educational philosophy and management style.[26] Flurries of meetings, among themselves and with other school constituents, busied the board thenceforth through the remainder of Berrisford's tenure. In terms of its owns peaks and valleys, probably nothing had occupied the board so intensively at least since the decision to build the Hawley Wing/Trinity House and the controversies that surrounded that, nearly twenty years before. Such activism was educational. More board members probably learned more about the day-to-day operations of Trinity than they ever anticipated or probably wanted to know, as they crisscrossed the line between governance of the school and its management. With no choice, Berrisford, whom they had hired to manage it and who apparently gave no thought to giving up quickly, accepted their help whether at heart he wanted it or not. He tried to keep his balance and was no pushover. At the end of that first fateful year, which he wryly described as having been "packed with incident," he tried to shift the focus to actual operations.[27]

That picture was, from some altitude at least, bright enough. College admissions were strong. Admissions to Trinity were, too, slightly stronger in the Lower School than at the ninth grade. (There was then a general demographic dip that touched other private schools in the city as well, and, though it is unproven supposition, weakness in ninth-grade admissions could have had a connection with Trinity's internal turmoil in which Upper School teachers were prominent.) Sports and community service programs were healthy. There had been change in the dress code, a thankless tangle ever since the admission of girls and perceptions of a "double standard" that discriminated against boys. Rules for girls got some tightening up, while for the first time Trinity boys were allowed to come to school without coats and ties. Upper School parents generally approved, though some Lower School ones thought the school's image had suffered. At least a constant source of friction between teachers and students was removed, surely a positive outcome.[28] "I can understand the concern about image," Berrisford wrote, "although I have to hope that people do not measure the quality of Trinity's education by how close the school holds to the 'preppie' look."[29]

Business and financial affairs, he reported, were at last beginning to get the attention they demanded, though it was just such attention to "efficiency" that so riled the faculty. Plans for a regularized yet "supportive" system of faculty evaluation were set in motion. Decision making was streamlined, as day-to-day administration devolved entirely to the Principal of the Upper School (Suellyn Preston) with overall responsibility and an assistant (history teacher Bill Major) who concentrated on ninth and tenth grades; to the Principal of the of the Upper Middle School (Jim Iredell); and to the Principal of the Lower and Lower Middle schools, for the moment under the direction of Emily Scharf. In place of the old omnibus School Advisory Committee, Berrisford instituted two smaller groups with more specific responsibilities. The Curriculum Committee, composed of division principals and academic department heads, was to become responsible for curriculum quality and coordination and was chaired by a Director of Studies, a new position first filled by English teacher Carol France and charged with evaluation and supervision of the curriculum in the Upper and Upper Middle schools. The other new position, Dean of Students (Tom Ramsey), chaired the Committee on Student Life, which was to look after everything

outside the curriculum, focusing on opening up opportunities and recon-
ciling conflicts. Principals, in every case, bore ultimate responsibility for
everything that happened at their level.[30]

While Berrisford knew the ground was shaky, the board anxious and uncertain, the faculty unreconciled to his program if not his very presence, he
saw these tribulations perhaps in larger context than any of them.[31] Trinity
required administrative fixing and above all financial shoring up. Such
changes and the disciplines entailed would, he figured, have been unsettling
anywhere at that time. Schooling was at the forefront of public debate, with
schools being called upon to do ever more and more. He cited Harvard
president Derek Bok's summons to attend to the inculcation of moral values
in young people, and arguments that the day-to-day experience of school
life may prove to be as significant as the subjects taught. Berrisford recognized the declining relative advantage of private schools like Trinity, where
graduation no long automatically conferred admission to the most prestigious colleges, as students from other backgrounds exerted their claims to
such places. Trinity's job was growing tougher than ever, and doing it well
required harder, smarter work. We imagine him choosing his words carefully: "Relying on good intentions and a friendly disposition will not be
enough."[32] And we can imagine exactly to whom he directed them.

Not the best coaching, however, could solve the problem. Berrisford
shared with Lester's predecessor Richard Garten a disadvantageous exterior.
Suave and polished, he often appeared dismissive and arrogant, capable of
leaving behind from even the most cursory interactions a cloud of ill will.
His was, in the end, a case of the right man at the right time with the right
policies but in the wrong place. Nor could any amount of delay, board attention, and consultation probably have won over the Trinity faculty.

By this time Trinity faculty enjoyed both intellectual and political power
that gave Trinity a scholarly aura unusual in secondary schools and that
made it a challenge to handle. Trinity teachers were a concentrated subset
of the sort of individuals attracted to independent schools generally. Well-
trained and serious about teaching, some of them intensely serious about
the subjects they taught, they were bright people who had weighed the superior teaching environment of selective independent schools against the
higher salaries of the public system and opted for careers, typically long and
faithful ones, in independent education. Long tenure made them feel secure
and also made them expensive, as salaries rose with seniority, and retire-

ment benefits extended obligations into the future. Trinity's faculty was not tenured in fact, but the spirit of tenure was palpable among them. Trinity teachers knew best what they taught and how they taught it and cared not for the judgment of others about it. Though Trinity was large enough that its faculty was organized formally under division principals and academic department heads, its predominant dynamic was horizontal, not vertical. Accountability to authority was low. Politics abounded. Neither as individuals nor as a group did it respond well to directions from administrators. It was not easily led.

This is what Berrisford had the temerity to attempt, in the form of improving operating efficiency and evaluating professional performance. He believed in good people, but also in good procedures. From the outside and in retrospect it is difficult to see any of his proposed "reforms" as anything but prudent ideas for how to make a good thing better, which some employees might have accepted if not welcomed. Trinity's faculty could not. Lester, the old history teacher at heart, had flattered his way into the graces of these talented men and women who, rightly or wrongly, identified Trinity with themselves. Berrisford did not, and his proposals for change, however incremental in fact, looked to the faculty apocalyptic. Some trustees probably sensed a storm from the start. "The faculty was headstrong," remembered trustee parent Martha Watts, "and Berrisford had a mandate to get a grip on them."[33] Or so he thought.

Berrisford managed to accomplish not a little of what he had been charged to do. By his departure, he had corralled costs and returned the corporation to the black. He set important things in motion, including faculty evaluation, curriculum review, long-range planning.[34] Much of his abrasive ambition to tighten up management of the school would in fact be accomplished more fully by his successor. Berrisford's regrets are not recorded, but the record of his subsequent success as head of the Chinese International School in Hong Kong suggests he picked himself up and carried on quite nicely. Upon departure from Trinity, he measured his accomplishment against a warning expressed in the report of the last NAIS visiting committee that examined Trinity in 1981. The examiners had expressed concern for what seemed to be "a feeling within the faculty that things are going so well that little more needs to be done . . . a certain smugness that could be the school's biggest danger." Berrisford recognized this and tried to change it, with partial success: "Elements of it remain, but many are now willing to recognize that there are other, perhaps better, ways to handle some issues and teach some material—the Trinity way may not always be the best way."[35]

Berrisford's ultimate fate highlights an important truth about the evolution of Trinity School. By the time he arrived, Trinity was no longer, and never again would be, led by a traditional "strong," that is, independent *and* authoritarian headmaster. Rather, the school's scale and complexity and the need to align multiple, diverse constituencies demanded a different approach to leadership. It also illustrates just how touchy independent schools can be about their top leadership. Such headships demand an unusual mix of talents. Because they are jobs that entail, fundamentally, the nurturing of the young, which means managing the bright people who teach them and winning and keeping of the trust of parents, they call for exceptional levels of communicativeness and sympathy. Heads of schools like Trinity are neither civil servants, as are public system principals, nor are they the fund raisers dressed as Ph.D.'s that many leaders in higher education have become. Personalism matters in this setting and in part defines competence. The Trinity faculty was not incorrect, in this sense, when they accused Berrisford of incompetence.

Interpretations of Berrisford's tenure still vary. Board president and parent at the time, lawyer Barbara Robinson would ascribe this ragged chapter mainly to Berrisford's aloof style and to poor preparation, on the board's part, for the transition. Hiring faculty member John Hanly as interim head against the advice of search-firm counsel, she believed, looking back, sent the wrong signal to the faculty that nothing much would change.[36] When Berrisford, a veteran school administrator who for twenty years had been used to being in charge, appeared and attempted quickly to take hold, it was a shock. Another trustee and parent at the time, real estate lawyer Eugene Pinover, who joined the board the year Berrisford arrived, described the problem more broadly as a case of comprehensive misperceptions, which the faculty's and parents' complaints about "communication" probably echoed. "It was a very troubled period, the school was running in the red, the endowment was miniscule, and the community was deeply fractured, as the student and parent body had changed over the preceding decade moving from all boys to coed, from an Episcopal school to a mixed environment, ratcheting-up of the focus on college admissions and achievement in the parents' minds. The pressure was being turned up by an economically higher powered parent body who had very high expectations for their sons and daughters, which flowed back into the school." Pinover believed that the board was still more traditional than the evolving school community, and the community rebelled at the appearance of a throwback to an English schoolmaster.[37]

Appearances can deceive, however, and an argument can be made that Berrisford was in fact every bit the modernizer and agent of change that Lester was, only that what he proposed to change was now the larger, more complex, more achievement-driven school that was in part Lester's legacy. This Trinity now needed to be managed and secured. Everyone agrees, however, that it was probably the long shadow of the Robin Lester years that Berrisford could not have escaped, at least not without more help or without more careful preparation of the scene. Perhaps no one could have. Recalled one young teacher who arrived at Trinity in 1989 and watched the Berrisford melodrama unfold from relatively neutral ground: "After Lester, Mahatma Ghandi could have come in here and his robes wouldn't have been clean enough."[38] In a school with a different, less domineering faculty, there might have been a less rancorous result, but Trinity's faculty, while hardly blameless, was the product of its own laizzez-faire history. For alleged offenses against it, Berrisford was, as he himself put it to fellow administrator and friend Suellyn Preston Scull, "turfed out."[39]

LEADER AS LISTENER

Not all at once, however. It was four years, start to finish, before Berrisford was gone, suggesting no unseemly rush to judgment. Actually, he had but one independent year (his first, at least up until March), followed by two effectively on probation, and the fourth (1990–91) a negotiated closure arranged to avoid another interim head, to give time to find a successor, and to keep political peace on the board.[40] The search that identified Henry Clay Moses, his successor, was cochaired by trustees Blaine V. "Finn" Fogg, a corporate lawyer, and Martha Watts, a parent and Harvard Ph.D. in romance languages, and was professional and consultative, open to faculty, students, and parents. It was Berrisford, however, who had first brought Moses, dean of freshmen at Harvard, to Trinity on several occasions to speak to Trinity students on the transition from high school to college life. Earlier, he had invited him to Harvard Westlake in Los Angeles, Berrisford's previous school. The two men liked each other.[41] Moses was, however, something of the dark horse compared to the other three finalists, all experienced administrators at the secondary level and one the headmaster of a prestigious independent day school in the Midwest somewhat smaller than Trinity but with three times the endowment. Moses had spent the previous twelve years in higher education, albeit at the beginning stages of it at Harvard, supervising academic performance and discipline as well as the living conditions of 1,600 seventeen- to nineteen-year-olds and a staff of 140. He was Princeton undergraduate with a doctorate in American literature from Cornell.[42] He had no independent secondary school history (he attended New Rochelle High School) and no experience at all with early childhood education, other than his one daughter's and four sons', since his own. He was a Presbyterian, divorced and remarried to Mary Sarah Holland. He was fifty in 1990.

What Moses did have, in addition to the cache of experience and strong references at Harvard[43] (which did not fail to impress an Ivy League college admissions-anxious Trinity), were good ears and a mind that was not made up about the job ahead.[44] Moreover, he not only had such qualities, but he was seen to have them. For trustees, the transition from Berrisford to whoever came next could hardly have been more fraught.[45] Trinity could ill afford another error in picking its top leader. It was perhaps, however, learning how to look. Not everything can be read on the resumé. Berrisford's could not have looked more perfect. Lester's had had some big holes, though he indisputably brought to the Trinity of that time the lift it sorely needed and energized it by force of personality alone. Nor had Moses done this sort of work, literally, before. In particular, the record revealed nothing about his fund-raising capability. He came across strongly as "a real educator, passionate about teaching and intellectually very acute."[46] He was "cordial, interested, smart."[47] Yet he was a risk.

From his standpoint, so was Trinity, and not just in comparison with his post at Harvard. He was being offered a job at which the incumbent had struggled publicly. Moses's success would depend on securing the right relations with the board while sustaining a level of deliberateness and communicativeness in dealing with the full community that would exceed anything he had needed in Cambridge. Certainly it was a fresh challenge. He took it up at first gently, as suited the political moment.[48]

It could be that his lack of primary/secondary school experience may have been in his favor in that he had no previous model to which he might have been tempted to make Trinity conform. He had some ideas but not a lot of baggage: "I consider myself someone who doesn't have theories about secondary school." He was interested in the "wholeness and design" of the curriculum, traditional faculty territory. Faculties, he said, must feel "well-led and believed-in." Leading this one would be an "an immensely complicated thing." Careful about saying much about issues he might address, he did not fail to pick up on the suspiciousness between faculty and administration that had marked the Berrisford years: "People don't feel talked to very much. . . . Someone should be listening hard and trusted to be listening hard, and then make decisions." To start, Moses had lofty if not very specific aims. He wanted "to live and work in a community where people are trusted by one another."[49] That alone, at Trinity just then, was a fairly tall order.

Arriving, Moses listened to everybody but kept his own public pronouncements modest. "Until I'm taught, I can't claim to understand." With no experience of lower or middle schools except as a long-ago student and current parent, he needed to do a lot of exploring there especially. He was careful everywhere. He recognized that the central tension at the school—the disjuncture between Trinity's financial wherewithal and its educational habits and ambitions—had not yet been resolved. In a breath, he could speak soft phrases about Trinity's need to be "a whole place," and cryptic ones about Trinity's continuing "rough financial times."[50] A year on, however, Moses was ready to report publicly on what he was about prospectively. It was a daunting list and mature agenda that would not much change for the eighteen years he remained headmaster.[51] Fulfilling it took hard work and endless learning, from Moses and many others. It entailed issues of governance, finance, and management; of teaching and learning; and of the justification for what Trinity did and its goals in doing so.

GOVERNANCE AND FINANCE

One consequence of Berrisford's departure was unprecedented board activism in not just governing the school but managing it. Governing meant primarily responsibility for the financial health of the institution through monitoring of budgets and through fundraising, and prudent investment and property management. Additionally, the board governed through oversight of the professionals hired to administer the organization's day-to-day operations. (Specifically, the by-laws then in effect enumerated the board's duties in two categories, the first to include review of the school's mission and strategic plan, setting general guidelines for admission and graduation, appointment and supervision of the head of school, and general procedures for appointment, promotion, and dismissal of other staff. The second category went to all matters to do with getting money and monitoring its expenditure: the review of policies for managing the school's business office, responsibility for all physical facilities, approval of the annual budget including setting tuition and the general level of faculty and staff salaries, raising funds for operations, maintenance and endowment, receiving gifts and managing the investment of endowment, and, of course, securing the yearly audit. Of the board members aboard when Moses was hired, nine were alumni, fifteen were current parents, and eleven were parents of graduates. Their professional backgrounds included law, finance, education, business, real estate, printing, management consulting, architecture, religion, and publishing.[52] They worked through seven permanent standing committees: executive, development, education, facilities, finance and investment, personnel policy, and nominating.[53]

During Berrisford's tenure, the board took a more active role. There were visitations directly with faculty and parents and much executive committee interaction with the headmaster and senior administrative staff. Berrisford may have remained in the chief executive role for the school (the board president was chief executive of the corporation), but after his first nine months he was on a shortened leash. As Moses and the board got to know one another in an operating context, the expansion of board mission and impact became apparent.[54] In Moses's word, board committee activity "exfoliated" in the 1990s, which was one way to give trustees the eyes and ears they needed into school life yet generally keep them on the right side of the governance/management line. Increasingly, aims and expectations got written down. Committees got their own mission statements, which focused activity and prevented wandering. In the three years prior to 1991, the full board had worked with the faculty on restating the school's general mission, then a tangled work in progress that would continue in deep earnest under Moses. It also monitored implementation of the long-range plan.

Probably most important was the ratcheting up of its oversight of the school's business management.[55] The finance committee had begun to meet monthly with the goal of consistently balanced budgets and improvement in the school's cash flow and repayment to the endowment over a five-year period of a decade's borrowings against it. Enlargement of endowment also got fresh attention, with trustees' own level of giving up substantially in two years, and hiring of fund-raising counsel to advise on a new capital campaign, "long overdue." Funds for plant maintenance were increased to more reasonable levels (3 percent of annual budget), and a space-needs master plan, though needing revision, was put in place. In the early 1990s, the board acted to acquire the two brownstones adjacent to the 139 building for possible expansion.[56]

The board also became aware of the need for better communication between itself and the school's various constituencies. It had taken no small part of the blame for the Berrisford mess, an experience no trustee wished to repeat. It established fall and spring meetings with the parent body, including a presentation focused on finances. It had an annual meeting with the faculty. It restructured its standing committees to work more effectively and invited nontrustees (parents and faculty) onto some of them. Ad hoc committees, on diversity and religion, for instance, were established. The executive committee set biweekly meetings with the head, and undertook his formal evaluation, asking him first to write a self-evaluation. Their conclusions were transmitted back to the head by the president of the board. Trustees also began to evaluate themselves. Seventy-five percent that year actually did.[57]

This board awakening of sorts occurred first as Trinity trustees tried to damp down a crisis, and then as they learned to work with a new head, who himself had not worked directly for a board before. To Moses as he began to get his legs under him, what was by one reckoning a heightened awareness of the tenets of good trusteeship could look like hyperactivity, even occasional trespass onto management's ground. By the end of the 1980s, as Moses saw it, "the board was trying to run the school in a vacuum." Defining that line between governance and management, and building respect for it, became a central theme in his management of Trinity. He was fortunate to have allies among leading trustees like John Arnhold and Benjamin Shute who understood and respected it, too.[58]

Gradually, Moses and the board built a solid, pragmatic relationship, something helped along by his own growth in the job. The board saw to it that Moses, the soft-spoken Harvard academic who could talk endlessly about teaching and learning but knew virtually nothing about raising money, got professional coaching on how to pitch Trinity's cause. In time, he became very good at it. He also got the help he needed, in the office, to manage money and see that it kept coming in.

Business manager Joan Dannenberg had an M.B.A. from Columbia and an old boss at Time, Inc. who knew the search firm that had identified Berrisford. Berrisford had brought her to Trinity in January 1988, a lasting legacy. In Dannenberg's own estimation, she spent three "hellish" first years until Moses was aboard with the mandate and the talent to manage. She had arrived amid threats of staff unionization, troubles with tenants at Trinity House, soft enrollment, and the handicap of a boss himself soon on probation.[59] Moses and treasurer John Arnhold praised her from the very start for correcting financial management problems identified in previous audits, and they relied on her increasingly.[60] In 1998 Moses changed her title to chief financial officer to better reflect her abilities and responsibilities. An English teacher, Moses was careful with words, and these were not inflationary.[61]

Trinity had had no development office at all until the late 1970s, when parent Susan Ulin, as president of the Parents' Association an ex officio trustee, took on the job as if by default. "We looked around the board table one meeting, and I was the only one left who didn't have a job," Ulin recalled of how she began.[62] Robin Lester had just arrived, and with endowment of only $1 million, Trinity was in dire need of development help. It was the start of a slow progress, as Ulin and her next two successors, Lynn Giusio and Gretta Estey, with help from alumnus Steven Cobb, gradually increased consciousness among parents and alums of the importance of continuous fund raising, the "endless campaigns" of annual giving. When Myles Amend arrived, toward the end of 2001, he inherited an office with good plans and people, but at a moment when everyone felt the need for a breather after the capital campaign to finance the middle school (see later description). Amend came with a background both in schools and in institutional development in New York City.[63] He was impressed by the clarity of Trinity's sense of mission just then newly restated, but believed breathers were not affordable. He thought Trinity suffered most from "inadequate expectations," and he commenced a focused giving program combined with relentless efforts to educate the school community about Trinity's financial needs and priorities. The school's annual report became a key communications tool, detailing Trinity's financial condition much better than peer schools and explaining what the numbers meant.

Everything pointed to making the budget process and all the school's finances more transparent. "Over the next year or two," Moses said at the outset, "we must bring principals and department heads more fully into priority-setting and budget making. The eventual goal is to insure that each person in the school with responsibility for supervision has a sufficient sense of history and enough current information to make wise recommendations on programs and budget."[64] Procedures were put in place for identifying and winnowing program priorities against available funds, or if funds were not available from recurring sources then addressing ways to find them elsewhere. A base of improved day-to-day and year-to-year operating procedures gave confidence needed for larger fund-raising campaigns and investment management goals, which then followed in their wake. It was important to know Trinity could manage what it raised.

In 1992, the school again took hold of its financial future as it had not done since the decision to double its size with building the Hawley Wing over twenty years before. This was made possible against the backdrop within Trinity of perceived stable and capable executive leadership and newly energetic trustees. It occurred in the context of competitive worries that Trinity, whose tuition was reaching record heights and was at the top end of its league, would fall behind in physical facilities.

BUILDING

This background is important. Massive and bold as the Hawley Wing project had been in its time, it had been fundamentally opportunistic. The school then had decided to take advantage of West Side Redevelopment and public funding sources to acquire land along Columbus Avenue on favorable terms and erect its first truly new purpose-built facility since the 139 building had gone up in the 1890s. It did this to the end of staying in Manhattan and specifically on the Upper West Side, when that was hardly an obvious choice. The idea was bold and risky, and it worked. Aesthetics aside, the big new building worked too: It gave Trinity, particularly the Upper School, facilities that were the envy of other Manhattan private schools at the time, and it gave Trinity in the Robin Lester era the big stage it needed to declare itself a high-performance independent school. The Hawley Wing was not, however, part of a plan for the whole school and in fact may have precipitated a period of neglect of its lower and middle components. Twenty years later, wear and tear on the 139 building, which was home to the Lower School, was adding up, while the awkward accommodation of middle-school-aged children hither and thither in this building and that echoed the awkwardness of early adolescence itself. "Lower" and "Upper" Middle School, designations as much convenience- and space- as pedagogy-driven, never had been convincing and by the 1990s constituted a big hole in the notion of Trinity as a "whole" school.

Planning to fill it preceded Moses, but it was a long process that came to fruition slowly. In 1987, Trinity had explored the potential of another big real estate development project, centering on a residential air-rights tower project on the site of the 1950s gym, fronting on 91st Street in between the Annex and the Hawley Wing. As in that earlier project, Trinity would utilize the lower floors of the new tower for much-needed new classrooms, athletic facilities, and offices. This second vertical expansion plan was tabled a year later. During the same period, the two brownstones at 149 and 151 West 91st Street became available, and wishing to seize a rare opportunity to acquire contiguous property, the board authorized their purchase, which was finalized in October 1988, though the buildings were not fully vacated and available for use for another two and a half years.[65]

Space planning slowed down during the headmaster search, but by the spring of 1991 the thought was to demolish the brownstones and erect a new 12,000- to 23,000-square-foot structure on their site. Architects at Buttrick White & Burtis also looked at using portions of the headmaster's house to improve the layout of the new building and reviewed means for creating a unified middle school. Architects then proposed, in addition to demolishing the brownstones, demolishing the 1950s gym and constructing another new facility there. When this seemed beyond the scope of the then in-motion capital campaign, the architects were told to concentrate on centralizing the Lower School in some rendition of the headmaster's house and the brownstones, but still to propose regarding additional athletic space and means to a unified Middle School. It was thought that in the process the headmaster's house too might be razed, though the facade of the landmark building would have to be preserved. At that point, Moses named a ten-member in-school architecture committee representing the administration and the three school divisions. The faculty wanted the biggest possible building footprint to allow optimal room layouts, and four options were then presented ranging in cost from $5 million to $13 million. At first they picked one that would only have concentrated the Lower School in new construction, with a gym in the space where the brownstones had been, and locating the Middle School entirely in the 139 building.[66]

Plans evolve, and the one that in fact was realized would leave the Lower School where it was (and leave the brownstones standing and in time handsomely recycled into offices) but unify the Middle School in a new building on the site of the 1950s gym, fittingly in between the lower school and the Hawley wing. These particular plans, however, are of historical interest as much for the arguments justifying them, as they are as blueprints for what happened: not just the what, but the why. They reveal an institution sorting through its hoped-for future, near the point where will and wherewithal met to achieve it. Chaired by Martha Watts, the committee laid out the reasons that Trinity needed to raise the money that would eventually fix its middle and thence its whole.

Primarily, they argued, Trinity must build because it was "educationally right." Space defines and limits teaching methods and learning opportunities, and advocates of more experiential learning particularly called for more of it. A new gym would free up space for more practices and enable a systematic schoolwide fitness program and a better after school program, plus it would make possible more equitable attention to athletics for girls. New classroom space would get the seventh and eighth grades out of the Hawley Wing (designed for a school with enrollment of 750, since grown to over 900), where experience had shown they were lost among high schoolers, and reduce by 25 percent the student population there. More space generally makes possible more flexible scheduling, double periods, more elective classes at better times, less fragmented school days, a more congenial atmosphere. However it finally got parsed, the upshot was three unified school divisions. Unity brought a heightened sense of place and belonging, especially important in early adolescence.

There were other reasons also to make the push that all this would require. Raising the school's profile was central. Better facilities, it was said, were an important tool in attracting and retaining superior faculty, and in competing for qualified paying students. Better facilities also supported the still evolving goal of increased diversity, in that flexible classrooms invited different pedagogies accommodating different learning styles. At the highest level, it enhanced "Trinity's values" in no small part through larger and more shared spaces. One Upper School teacher on the architecture committee had commented: "There are lot of things we can't do because we don't know each other."[67] At the most basic level, it would make old buildings safer and begin to address issues of handicapped access, which were growing increasingly problematic. With the Annex and the 139 buildings about to mark their centennials, their renovation could be regarded as a 100-year birthday present.

All added up, the plan would enable the whole school to operate more smoothly. The school had studied its space problems for five years with remarkable consistency of conclusions, through a change of administration, new faculty, constantly rotating board membership, and two architectural firms. They knew what they wanted and needed.[68]

Delay, moreover, would be costly, and could throw Trinity several years behind the pack. By rough count, New York City's independent schools were then spending upward of $75 million on ongoing improvement projects: Spence, $7.2 million; Chapin, $8 million. Dalton was in a capital campaign to raise $27 million for a new gym and other capital improvements. Market competition, not growth, was the driver, as they quoted to themselves from *The New York Times*: "With a few exceptions [Trinity was not one of them] the schools are not creating new space to expand enrollment nor are they anticipating a rush of applicants. Rather they are upgrading to meet the changing needs of their students and putting money into more sophisticated science labs, expanded room for computer studies, new gymnasiums, larger cafeterias and libraries and more spacious and comfortable work areas for teachers. Competition for students plays a major role in the decision to modernize."[69] Expectations were changing, it is tempting to say, extravagantly. "Up-to-date-ness," however, is relative. In the 1890s, the 139 building had been touted for just that, with its modern ventilation system and a real gym, and so the new gym of the 1950s with the nice new locker rooms and shiny showers, and so the Hawley Wing in the late 1960s with its auditorium/theater/chapel and expansive cafeteria. What was different by the 1990s was the competitive element, the external challenge to change.

By the end of the 1995–96 academic year, plans at last settled out for how Trinity would respond and build. A new building would rise on the site of the 1950s gym, designed to address multiple concerns. It would house two new gyms, one on the third floor and one in the basement, which would mark a significant upgrade in overall athletic facilities. But centrally, it would contain two floors of new classrooms that would permit consolidation of grades five through eight in one physical location, creating at last a unified Middle School. The new space would also relieve pressure on both Lower and Upper schools, enabling better use of those spaces.[70] The building, designed by Harry Buttrick of Buttrick White & Burtis, with its own street number, 115, would open in 1998 and be a striking addition to West 91st Street. It symbolized the distance Trinity and the neighborhood had traveled since building of the fortress-like Hawley wing. It was brick and light limestone, with a bell tower (a clever solution to disguise mechanicals) and a graceful pitched roof. The first two floors were filled with windows, thirty of them, most of three casements each, on the street side alone, plus grand ones in the gym space above.[71] An almost all glass, three-story hyphen connected with the Annex on the west, whose faded Victorian formality it complemented but did not imitate. To the east, 115 even took some of the modernist chill off the Hawley Wing, with its grudging heavy-eyebrowed second-floor slits of windows. This new Trinity Middle School was a rare architectural accomplishment: a middling style and scaled building that not only met its prescribed functional needs but mediated the buildings around it.[72]

The unifying symbolism of that style mattered at this point in Trinity's history, as the campaign to pay for it was dubbed, inclusively, the "Campaign for Trinity." The building itself cost some $16 million, and was financed through a combination of current campaign and bonded debt, approximately half and half. The idea, advanced by trustee Daniel Brodsky and managed by treasurer Glenn Greenberg and Joan Dannenberg, was to ask alums and current users to pay now but enable future users to pay later.[73] The campaign for the building, at this writing Trinity's last major brick-and-mortar undertaking, brought forth substantial givers. There were thirty-four gifts of $100,000 to $250,000, nineteen between $250,000 and $500,000. In the then largest ever single gift in the school's history, the Lauder family made a lead gift, donating $1 million in support of the building, and the campaign soon saw two other comparable gifts, from Scott W. Bates, class of 1935 and scholarship boy for all of his four years at Trinity, and his wife Natalie Leighton Bates. An anonymous donor gave $2 million, another first.[74]

The campaign aimed for $20 million and reached its goal in June 1998, with over 1000 donors.[75] Its scale and its success hinted at the potential power of the Trinity giving base. The new building was its most visible immediate achievement. Increased endowment, for faculty support and student financial aid, was its second but not secondary aim. In 1993, Trinity's endowment stood at $6 million. The Campaign for Trinity, prudent management, and the market brought it to nearly $19 million in 1998. This was the decisive starting point of steady growth in an area long neglected. Trinity measured its position relative to other competing schools in terms of endowment per student. In 1995, it ranked fifth out of seven, at $12,600, which absolute number, however, was much closer to the bottom ($4,400) than to the top ($45,500).[76]

Slim endowment put upward pressure on prices. A key element in each year's budgeting process was determining the amount by which tuition needed to increase. Between 1984 and 1995, it rose by between 3.75 and 9.6 percent per year. Over the same period, faculty salaries rose between 5 and 10.4 percent per year, student financial aid between 0.62 and 26.5 percent per year.[77] Despite efforts to control costs and still deliver new programs, such as language instruction in the Lower School, and improve others, the pattern of raising tuition year after year at rates above the general cost of living was ominous. The comparatively small endowment and in turn the endowment's relatively low contribution to school operations (Trinity observed a spending policy of 5 percent of average market value over the previous twelve quarters) reduced budgetary flexibility and hobbled planning.

Trustees and senior administration ever since would bear down hard on the issue of increasing endowment income and relieving pressure on tuition and fees. Professionalization of the development office under Amend, and reinvigoration of the alumni base under Benjamin Shute, '54, orchestrated both consistently successful annual fund drives and strategic giving to keep endowment growing.[78] It was a relentless task, however. Trinity had started late, and it was hard to catch up and keep pace with other top schools. By 2001–02, Trinity had more money but so did everyone else, and of course everything cost more. Its critical endowment per-student position, then up to $24,000, remained stuck in the bottom third of the pool, which then topped out (at Brearley) at $90,000.[79] By 2005–06, the board still reported Trinity's sources of income "perpetually under strain," its then $41 million endowment converting to a per student ranking still third from the bottom. The problem was not eased by the fact that only just over half of Trinity's endowment was wholly unrestricted, which limited endowment income that could be used to supplement annual operating costs. Other schools, with endowments far less restricted, enjoyed far greater spending flexibility.[80]

Anxiety about endowment was not unique to Trinity and would only increase in urgency. To Andrew Brownstein, board president in 2007, it bespoke the stubborn fact that education, as practiced in independent fee-charging schools like Trinity, was a unique industry with little or no capacity to offset natural expense increases with operating efficiencies.[81] It had been and always would be about people, who were expensive, on the job and in-

creasingly in retirement after they left it. Flurries of talk about "mechaniza-
tion in the classroom" heard in the 1960s and 1970s (but never at Trinity)
died away quickly enough. No one yet has figured out how to school children without teachers. "Technology," to which Trinity belatedly would devote substantial resources starting in the 1990s, was seen as a curricular en-
hancement, not an efficiency tool. Berrisford had boldly told Trinity teachers
they needed to teach more children in a classroom and thus make a then
wobbly Trinity "more efficient," but that was about as far at it went. Good
business administration practices, as Trinity at last put in place in the 1990s,
could manage costs, but that was about as far as they went. Thus, endowment remained Trinity's greatest need as it began its fourth century.[82]

IN CLASS

The students who today are the direct beneficiaries of all this grown-up
work are a clever bunch. A visitor senses it early.[83] Overheard in a sixth-
grade science class, as the author introduced himself before the teacher arrived: "You're writing the history of Trinity? Wow, we're a really old school
aren't we? That's cool. Will we be in it?" The boys and girls are comfortable
with visitors. This bunch was studying magnetism—the "how do you turn
an ordinary nail into a magnet experiment" that even this nonscientist visitor knew the answer to. They gave prepared presentations, and with a little
prompting dutifully cleaned up bits of copper wire and colored insulation
from their worktables before leaving for their next class.

Howard Warren's Lower School science classes meet somewhere up on
top of the old building in what seems like the attic. Here they build bridges,
drop but do not break eggs, grow vertical urban gardens, and on field trips
go prospecting in landfills and then make "commercials" from old ads in
LIFE that document what they have found, putting things now unfamiliar
into context. Among their more high-value finds from New York's material
past—the remnant of a lady's garter belt. Nobody in the class apparently had
a clue what this was. Lesson: If you dig in the past, be prepared for surprises.
So Warren explains how science, in this instance science as industrial archaeology, helps us understand social studies. In a closet in his attic, Warren keeps, unopened, a special treasure: a fifty-year-old unearthed can of
Ballantine's Light Lager—and a church key (as mysterious to students as the
garter belt), in case of emergency.

In a second-grade class doing math, the fifty-something teacher jokes about the words now applied to numbers and that didn't used to be: "We used to call it 'carrying' and 'borrowing'—now it's called 'trading.'" It is, after all, New York. "Don't call out; raise your hand" punctuates question time. In a third-grade gym class, while they are stretching their quadriceps, students count to ten in Spanish, and then count again in French.

In the fifth grade, Trinity students can sometimes be found strewn about the Lower School library (which started life back in the 1890s as the chapel), working up a project on the Middle Ages—knights, seneschals, manors, and all that, though nowadays not much is said about damsels in distress—learning about research: "Do five cards with one fact/big thought per card . . . You're not supposed to write it out word for word . . ." Boys clump with boys, girls with girls, last innocence. Long-time Lower School librarian and children's book author Sue Hipkins has worked up a display of several decades worth of Newbery Prize winners. The eye of an observer of a certain age, over forty, say, goes quickly to Robert McCloskey's classic *Make Way for Ducklings*.

Of course, teaching and learning means that not just students learn but teachers, too. An eighth-grade algebra class, where the subject was simple quadratic equations, illustrates. The procedure is cemented in the memory, like Latin declensions . . . *us, i, o, um, o* . . . Factor it out using all those parentheses, set to zero and solve for *x*, or something like that. The students then do this, some more confidently than others, but the process seemed to be getting across. And then, some innocent asks: "Why are they called quadratics?" Up front, a pause. Teacher: "I don't know." As the other adult in the room and fearing the question would come next to him, the visitor wishes he could crawl under his notebook. But the teacher is poised and does not take advantage. He is also a valuable item: the teacher who doesn't know everything and knows what he doesn't know.

Some teachers are visitors. Keith Ward, canon of Christ Church, Oxford, came to Trinity in 2004 as theologian in residence. In Upper School morning assemblies, Ward went through polished paces in talks about rational thought, moral responsibility, the soul, Thomas Aquinas, God. Trinity has a small fund to support this sort of thing, and it attracts top talent. One can read Ward's work—*Pascal's Fire: Scientific Faith and Religious Understanding; Re-thinking Christianity*—anytime. So can Trinity students; his books are just upstairs in the library. It is face to face, however, that he wins them: few shuffles, absolutely no talking. The hour is early, and one or two Trinity

Upper Schoolers may still doze. Yet attentiveness can never be completely faked, and as Ward commanded it, Trinity students offered it. For all his sophistication, Ward's unpretentious moral earnestness touched these teens. Bored adolescents show it, and these were not they.

A few school-days clichés, though, pass down through the decades, impervious to editing. Even at Trinity, some won't give up. One has to be the teaching in ninth-grade English of J. D. Salinger's *Catcher in the Rye*, a book that strikes some observers as a seriously overrated and overtaught piece of writing, eternally "age appropriate" though it seems to be. But that is one of the endearing things about education, for parents, anyway: seeing their children read and wrestle with some of the same, sometimes mediocre, books that they suffered through years ago. Not that *Catcher* is not well taught here, which is more important, anyway. Strong teaching trumps even marginal subject matter. The young English teacher in this instance was a strong one, and her students knew it. Bruner might have smiled.

Trinity today gets its pick of smart students anxious for the privilege to attend. Yet it is a New York pick, and not therefore utterly unprovincial. In eleventh-grade American history, a teacher tries to liven up a rather ordinary review session on the coming of the Civil War with a musical interlude and draws solid historical meaning from it. Apologizing up front and explaining that he hoped no one would be offended, he plays a recording of "Dixie." He explained its roots in the culture of minstrelsy, and how it was once regarded in North and South. Offended, however? Even at this moment in history when the culture could not be touchier to deemed offensiveness in speech or ethnic reference, it turned out that the teacher need not have worried. Only two or three students even recognized the tune.

There are strong teachers, and then there are masters. The old-fashioned word persists curiously even today in some prep-school settings—less at Trinity than at some others, though the idea behind the word is intact. (In 1927, Lawrence Cole had hired Bruner to Trinity's "mastership" in English.) "Schoolmaster" was how William Huddleston called and thought about himself. Today the official term is the gender-neutral "head," though "headmaster" is tough to slough off completely. The head, in addition to many of the duties of a chief executive, still teaches and formally heads all the other teachers. One catches a whiff of *Tom Brown* and boys-alone, but the word "master" fits in with today's inclusive Trinity, where it embraces two related meanings. Masters knew their subject: the content they taught. (Many Trinity faculty today have "master's" degrees, a significant number doctorates.) Masters also mastered their classes, commanding students' respect, even awe, because of what they knew and their ability to pass it on. Many of them (particularly but less and less exclusively in the Upper School) still are men, many women. Many would be as uncomfortable with the old-fashioned title "schoolmaster" ("schoolmistress") as with the newfangled one of "educator" and prefer modestly just to think of themselves as teachers. Yet examples abound of mastership at Trinity, however they call it.

In an eighth-grade history class, veteran Middle School teacher Ann Johnson discusses Chinese pottery and politics. The occasion was review, the sort of marching through material in class that "might" show up on the test. The drill, the anxiety, the dynamic are timeless. The teacher reveals so much but no more. The students press and are gently rebuffed. Of course there is never enough time. Dismissal approaches. Trinity students being what they are—anxious to do well, amply endowed with the mental equipment to do well, depressed when they don't—ask if they can come by for extra help. Or is it hints, advantage? Who knows? All of these? And the master—who is female in this case—welcomes them to come by indeed, but with a warning. "*Before* coming to see me, give yourself time to think."

Math master Elisabeth Ruedy, teaching students four years farther on, juniors and seniors, cautions her charges not much differently: "When you come to see me, don't just say 'I need help'; be sure you've done the review work and come with a concrete question." *These* are the ones, she explains afterward, who are the "wonderful students." Not the best students necessarily, but the ones who have got hold of the process, who have learned the job of learning, math or anything else. That, in her book, defines the contract between teacher and student. She works. They work. Schooling doesn't work any other way.

"I interpret silence as 'no,' not as deep thought!" she teaches them for a nervous laugh. "Mobilize your neocortex! You won't have your calculator on the test!" she adds without a smile. "And remember, this is a *math* class: 'I don't teach tricks, I teach mathematicians.'" And what do mathematicians do? She rolls on. "They think what hasn't been thought before." Bringing up the big gun, she paraphrases Goethe: "You're only thinking when that which you are thinking can't really be thought about." Not much response to that one: The students are in a swirl. They have had enough and are ready to go. Anyway, the high never stands without the low, as this particular master well knows, and so to a closing moment of charm and truth: "Remember: Don't be so sophisticated that you can't do the simple things anymore; it's very annoying."

Of course these are not mathematicians she is teaching, at least not yet; they are just high school students, who before that were Middle and Lower Schoolers in all likelihood right here at Trinity—"survivors," in school argot. By the time they hit twelfth grade and the mind turns to college and other grown-up matters, they will have had lots of opportunity to connect the dots: vertically down the years of their own growth here; horizontally across the subjects they have been taught here, subjects that others learned long before them. And despite some exotic-sounding electives, these remain pretty much bread-and-butter subjects to which Trinity boys from long ago would not have been utter strangers. This is what theologian Keith Ward, back in chapel but this time addressing Middle Schoolers, meant when he told them: "That's what we come to school to do: to learn how others have seen the world, and to get enough of the right tools ourselves to be able to add to it something of each individual's own unique vision now."

THE PROGRAM

Since the 1990s, the teaching and learning whereby this sort of schooling occurred at Trinity evolved in some ways that were unique to the school's different divisions and in others that were common to them all. Berrisford appointed Midwesterner Rosemary Milliman principal of the lower school in 1989, to a tenure it turned out far longer than his but in its early years nearly as contentious.[84] Milliman was from Minnesota via the Dwight School in New York City and arrived to find kindergartners taking standardized tests separated off in individual carrels and a Lower School where "classroom doors were closed" and a curriculum organized by discipline "just like high school."[85] Workbooks that would not have been unfamiliar to a grown-up with memories of 1950s school days abounded; teachers worked hard and taught well, but often in isolation. Student report cards were mechanical and lacked detail. Resignation of three kindergarten teachers gave her an early opportunity to build from the ground up with new hires: Giuliana de Winter, Pat Manchester, Rick Parbst, and Howard Warren. Milliman instituted grade-level teams starting and working up from kindergarten, and subject by subject, first social studies, then language arts, and then math, she set out to refurbish the curriculum less on the model of a single recipe (as she characterized the top-down pedagogy she inherited) but in the manner of a menu. This did not mean, of course, electives for first graders, but it did acknowledge that not all first or fourth graders learned in exactly the same ways or at the same rates, very bright though most of Trinity's were. The elementary grades in this respect were emphatically unlike high school and college, driven as they tended to be by the need to master bodies of knowledge. "Every lower school in America," Milliman asserted, "teaches the same things. The difference lies in how they teach it." She focused on the instrumentalities of learning that enabled content. More and more at Trinity's Lower School this came to mean varieties of cooperative teaching and learning, a theory-based pedagogy that by traditional Trinity lights sounded touchy-feely but that had straightforward commonsense consequences if applied consistently. Teachers might think of themselves solely as fonts of wisdom and purveyors of content, which in fact they were. They might in addition see themselves as one part (the lead part) of a teaching and learning process where, properly encouraged and guided, children also learned from one another. When this happened, classrooms opened up, became more cheerful, child-like places, yet without teachers sacrificing authority. They also became more efficient as more was taught and more learned.

It was not an approach for everyone. It demanded change, and there were good teachers who gradually stepped aside to make way for it. Major turnover occurred five years into Milliman's tenure, and, with Moses's backing, the reform of the lower school along cooperative child-centered lines continued. It extended to cooperation at the faculty level, too, as teachers were encouraged and sometimes pushed to learn about and embrace all manner of "best practice." By the 1990s, academic research related to instruction of young children, and not anecdotal but hard science to do with how the young brain functions in taking up and processing new information, "was light years ahead of what it used to be." Dyslexia and disorders related to attention and concentration yielded to new understanding. Keep up, Lower School teachers were admonished, veterans and rookies alike.[86] Naturally, younger teachers were poised more easily for change and sometimes wondered why it came slowly. Senior teachers sometimes appeared to hold back. It was the political challenge of administrative leadership to reconcile the two orders of talent and to blend energy with experience. As this happened, the Lower School witnessed a renaissance of professionalism that parents noticed and respected.

The curriculum began to flow through the grade levels with enhanced connectivity.[87] The central assumption of kindergarten was that learning at this early age took on meaning and had lasting effect when it was based on a child's experiences. At Trinity, kindergarten taught both measurable academic skills and aimed for less tangible goals: commitment to a task and developing respect for others. Academically, language arts focused on the four language skills of listening, speaking, writing, and reading. First graders in language arts learned about reading as a source of both information and pleasure, through both whole language and language experience and formal work in phonics and word recognition. The writing program complemented reading, as a child's first reading experience often came from being able to read his or her own words. First graders kept journals and diaries and wrote letters, learning about their own thinking and how to make their thoughts accessible to others. Second graders moved on to make choices about what they read and to understand writing as a thinking tool. In the context of their own writing, the curriculum introduced concepts of grammar, punctuation, and organizational skills. Spelling lists and dictation reinforced correct spelling. Second graders also moved on to cursive handwriting in their second semester. Third graders stepped up to reading literature, selections from novels and biographies chosen for good writing, engaging themes, and diversity of characters and settings. In writing they were assigned personal and expository tasks, and wrote about their own discoveries and scenes in literature. Both personal voice and mechanics were emphasized; spelling, punctuation, and sentence structure were taught throughout the year. The fourth-grade student found an increased emphasis on inferential thinking, the ability to place ideas in sequence, to draw conclusions, to make predictions, and to support an argument with details drawn from a text. Fourth-grade writers moved from sentences, to writing paragraphs with topic and supporting sentences. Everyone became deft at using the computer in composing and revising.

In math, kindergartners used everyday objects to learn concepts of numbers, classification, measurement, and place values, while exercises in making connections and recognizing patterns were designed to develop logical thinking needed for problem solving. First graders began each day with a look at the calendar, counting the days spent in school, and using it as a resource in a variety of mathematical concepts. Children typically worked in small cooperative groups to solve problems in written addition and subtraction, counting and grouping, place values and simple geometrical puzzles. Games reinforced concepts, moving students carefully from the concrete to the abstract world of working with paper and pencil. Second graders moved on to double-digit addition and subtraction, a more advanced number sense, and problem-solving strategies. Graphing skills were introduced to illustrate concepts visually, while electronic calculators were introduced as a problem-solving tool. The third-grade curriculum emphasized more problem solving, the facts of the four operations, and introduced students to subjects to be mastered later, including geometry, probability, and the addition of like fractions. Everywhere, both oral and written expression of thinking were encouraged. Fourth graders worked with both commercial and teacher-made materials that reinforced the importance of math. Addition and subtraction were practiced out to five digits, multiplication and division out to two. Standard and metric measurement were introduced, as were additional concepts in geometry, including identification of plane and solids figures, naming and drawing angles, congruence and symmetry.

Social studies for lower schoolers began in kindergarten with a look at basic needs for food and clothing as relevant to five- and six-year-olds. Field trips to an orchard or a pumpkin patch generated comparisons of the weight of produce, an interview with a farm manager, even a cooking project. Food study also led to an awareness of environmental influences and differing physical and cultural characteristics. First graders moved on to look at animal habitats and human habitats and homes, using the school community and neighborhood as foci. They considered various types of shelter and considered how different types of structures express physical and cultural needs. Second grade brought geography together with history in the study of Northeast Woodland Indians such as Lenape and Iroquois and other Native American tribes. Third grade shifted to study New York City and the period of immigration known as "The Great Wave" as a pathway into an appreciation of the city's multi-ethnic heritage. Study of immigration prompted study of families, with students writing their own immigration diaries in which they created a character who went through the entire immigration process. The circle widened further in fourth grade to include the study of world cultures, starting with Japan as a reference point and emphasizing the perspectives of history, anthropology, and archaeology. By the end of the year students applied their understanding of the common elements of cultures to a study of Ancient Egypt. Map and globe studies were continuous.

Each student planned, presented, and defended a final research project. Science through all levels was presented through a variety of learning experiences, including hands-on laboratory investigations, class discussions, and cooperative learning groups, as students were impressed with the importance of science and its methods in solving problems of effectively and ethically. Kindergartners studied seeds. First graders classified mammals, birds, fish, reptiles, amphibians, and insects and studied the properties of water and the ecology of a tide pool. Grade two scientists germinated seeds, while dealing with magnetism and electricity and building and using simple machines. Third graders had a laboratory period, recording their findings in writing and talking about results with others. Science and social studies merged in microscopy, where students participated in a bloodless forensic investigation to document an immigrant's history by investigating a suitcase full of personal effects; in ecology, where students looked at packaging practices of toy manufacturers and created their own biodegradable package sound enough to cushion an egg in a fifty-foot fall; and in bridge building, where students learned about tension, stress, opposing forces, balance, and symmetry, replicating actual New York City bridges and considering why particular designs had been used. Fourth graders, capable of working more independently, had double lab periods and a core curriculum centered on the New York City shoreline, which entailed collecting sea life from Jamaica Bay, studying it in class in a 125–gallon saltwater aquarium—and then returning specimens to nature unharmed.

Third and fourth graders also experienced French and Spanish, when they were still unselfconscious about trying out new sounds. Everyone from kindergarten on worked with computers, which combined in fourth grade basic word processing with the old-fashioned skill of touch typing. The art curriculum aimed at a sustained studio experience and sought to instill appreciation of art as necessity, not privilege. City parks and street scenes became subjects for painting projects, while artistic skills were extended to other academic experiences, for example, in creating paper models of Elmer and the dragon when reading *My Father's Dragon*. A ceramics, woodworking, and sculpture component taught three-dimensional media and likewise complemented grade-level social studies, language arts, and science curricula. Music in the lower school was seen as an academic discipline equal to any other, and afforded children as they progressed through the program increasing mastery of pitch, rhythm, and score reading. Weekly chapel meetings provided a special venue for sharing solo and ensemble accomplishments and demonstrating music as communication. The school's library, once upon a time its chapel and probably the most comforting and welcoming space anywhere at Trinity, constituted one of the largest elementary school collections in New York with some 25,000 volumes and was arranged with the needs of young children in mind. Every Lower School class came to the library once a week for a scheduled class where librarians talked about reading activities and supervised reading-aloud sessions. Grades three and four received a formal library skills course and introduction to basic techniques of research. Physical education aimed at exercise but also at enhancing social skills and building conceptual knowledge of movement and sports. Students played in the gym, in the pool, and on the turf, by fourth grade working their way up to activities in track and field, lacrosse, soccer, wrestling, softball, and dance. Everyone learned safety and good sportsmanship.

Parents could read about all this in elaborate curriculum guides and observe some of it on school visits. The content could seem daunting and by past standards was. Nothing was an add-on; everything was central. From it, however, their children reaped the even more central experience of learning how to learn. This was the harvest of what Milliman meant by cooperative teaching technique and best practice, and it was what readied small children to move up to Middle School.

Through the 1990s and early 2000s, Trinity's Middle School remained a work in progress. Anxiousness about how and where to handle Trinity's young adolescents reached back to the time of the Hawley Wing expansion, which placed the older half of them in the high school, which was not successful, leaving the younger ones not quite clear of the lower school. Completion in 1998 of the dedicated Middle School building at 115 West 91st Street answered the where question, if not quite the how. Trinity tracked the development of the middle school movement of the late 1970s and early 1980s, which saw a move away from open classrooms back to more structured settings and which had identified the middle school years as a time of blossoming capabilities that required unique nurturing. Middle schoolers were not just smaller high school students, though into the 1990s at Trinity fifth graders took final exams just like seniors, and neither fifth nor sixth graders had home rooms. Today they have homeroom time both in the morning and in the afternoon. Such basic structures were important for transitioning from the self-contained classrooms of lower school, to the interdependence of fifth and sixth grade, and slowly toward independence in seventh and eighth.

The Middle School was the product of some of Trinity's most accomplished teachers and of four administrators. Emily Scharf had worked hard at the beginning to implant the notion of a dedicated middle school curriculum. Jane Rosen established an advisory system that would become central to both the academic and social experiences of middle school. Beverly Anderson cemented five–six and seven–eight into one within one physical plant, which at last created a self-conscious and self-contained teaching and learning unit.

Dianne Stewart-Garrett, who became principal in 2004, built on this heritage, creating or in some cases resurrecting new leadership opportunities for faculty to help shape school agendas: a child study team, a curriculum committee, and a deans's group to help even out disciplinary matters. A faculty diversity committee was started from scratch, along with a faculty technology committee, a community service committee, and a "sunshine" committee—"hokey," admitted Garrett, but with the important job of keeping everyone happy, fed, and cared for, physically and spiritually. Garrett acknowledged the power of what she had walked into and claimed only to have honed it to a happier level of performance.[88] "If Diane happens to be absent one day, other than people calling to ask me if I'm okay, the ship sails." She liked to liken the Middle School faculty to world-class musicians who just needed a conductor who could hear them. She heard perfectionists of uncompromising high standards, which may have kept things a shade too ascetic. When Garrett arrived, first as a one-year interim, there was no art on the walls and there was talk of a curatorial committee to determine what might qualify. Today art and color abound: "It's a middle school, not a university; obviously we needed a standard, but just get the work up!"

The trend was to disperse participation and responsibility for school life through the faculty, to bring to the surface latent talents. An example was the course called "Life Skills," the Middle School euphemism for sex education, which had grown beyond mechanics to embrace more broadly human sexuality education and decision making, alcohol and drug use, Internet safety, street safety, a whole tool kit for navigating adolescence. As opposed to being taught just by the health teacher, it was taught by a dozen Middle School faculty volunteers who received extra stipends and in-service training to develop a curriculum from the ground up. Students loved being taught it by their math or science or French teacher. The regular curriculum too was better aligned with the help of new hires, starting with English, then history, including the use of documents and city museums and other outside resources, then the sciences and math. Math was the only academic program in the Middle School that was tracked, a historical vestige that raised an interesting challenge as the students moved up to the Middle School from a Lower School newly committed to diversifying its population. As this happened and Trinity broadened its admissions net from, say, the top 2 to the top 10 percent of the city, it also became necessary to broaden support for children asked to manage a curriculum in the Middle School that was on average a year to a year and a half above grade level. Trinity had always had children with diverse learning needs, but the fostering of other types of diversity as a general policy aim (see later discussion) did increase their critical mass and posed new challenges for teachers. This echoed Trinity's welcoming sibling policy and pride in being a "family school," though not all siblings were created equal. Trinity's faculty beyond any doubt was excellent at teaching very smart students. It became better at teaching some among them who learned in slightly different ways. So the Middle School math program was retooled, with math enrichment for the "brilliant ones" at one end and plain fifth-grade math for fifth graders at the other and everything in between. In history, a teacher who once used a text that one parent remembered himself having had as a freshman at Oxford was persuaded to use, for a text, something slightly less daunting.[89]

Though soundly invested with its own integrity, Middle School also inevitably implied transition to something else. Eighth graders were pretty much expected "to hit the ground running," and every one met in January of that year with Upper School principal Mark Simpson to help ease the next big step. Students entering Trinity's final four grades were presumed to have learned how to learn and headed into new classes thick with content.[90]

The Upper School curriculum maintained through the early 21st century an unwavering traditional core, but with increasing embellishments. Seminar, or at least group discussion, probably edged out lecture as a dominant teaching style, but Trinity teachers varied widely in how they chose to go about their business and were afforded wide freedom to do so. For graduation, Trinity required a straightforward set of accomplishments: four years of English, three of math, biology plus one year of a second laboratory science, three years of history, three to four years of a foreign language, two semesters in the arts, one of religion, and four years of athletics. Since 1986, when principal John Hanly became interim head of the school, the Upper School had three subsequent principals: science teacher Suellyn Preston Scull, history teacher Bill Major, and English teacher Mark Simpson. Each supervised a heavily credentialed and experienced faculty nearly universally spoken of by students as the hardest of teachers and closest of counselors. Explained one sophomore who admitted finding Trinity a struggle: "They won't let you slack."[91]

They taught content, on the assumption that students by the time they reached ninth grade, whether survivors or newcomers, were ready for sustained and serious intellectual work.[92] It was relentless. The English program required students to read at least five books over each summer and in class to develop the ear for great literature, sampling in ninth grade Steinbeck's *Of Mice and Men*, in tenth Willa Cather's *My Antonia*, in eleventh Dickens's *Great Expectations*. Seniors had choices within sets of requirements and might find themselves ranging from *Twelfth Night* to Wright's *Native Son*, from the novels of Jane Austen to Jewish-American literature to Joyce's *Ulysses*, from Baldwin's *Go Tell It on the Mountain*, to Ishiguro's *The Remains of the Day*. With close reading went endless writing of academic essays, and forays into fiction and poetry. The history department taught students to study the past through both the narrative of events and their interpretation. From ninth grade on, students were tutored in the use of primary sources as the building blocks of historical understanding. Through junior year, course offerings were straightforward: "Crisis and Change," which introduced freshman to the emergence of modern Europe, and more recently included its early collision with Islam; for sophomores, Modern European History from the seventeenth century, and more recently including the challenges associated with globalization; juniors studied American history from pre-Columbian times to the present. Again, seniors chose from a number of topical electives, from a high interdisciplinary offering dubbed "Understanding Gotham" that combined urban and local history, architecture, economics, and politics. "Dispatches from the Twenty-first Century" toured the itinerary of global challenges from immigration, to financial and biotechnological revolutions, to the role of women in international development. "The History of the Palestinian–Israeli Conflict" looked at a current trouble spot historically. "American Pleasures" considered the rise in the twentieth century of leisure and mass consumption framed by theorists like Theodor Adorno and Raymond Williams, but it could be fun, too, with Macy's, Times Square, and Coney Island employed as primary sources. In the home of the Yankees and the Mets, "Baseball and Society: A Social History of the Sport" spoke for itself. Trinity's math teachers ranged over material that met dual needs, of students requiring basic skills for daily living in a technological age, to those whose futures held careers that would demand more highly developed skills, from first-year algebra to advanced placement calculus. The science department similarly taught both how the method of science—observation, critical analysis, experiment—itself worked, and how the tools of science explained the physical and natural world. From earthworm dissection in freshman biology through controlled explosion of a hydrogen-filled Trinity-blue balloon in junior chemistry on homecoming day, to advanced physics and "Cutting-Edge Issues in Biology and Chemistry" where seniors studied acid rain and global warming, Trinity presented science as the door to problem solving and a tool for decision making.

Classics combined history with language and was offered in related spirit, with Latin and Greek approached neither as abstract linguistic systems nor as mere exercise for developing mental discipline, though they were this, but as instruments for understanding great cultures and literatures and the importance of ancient Greece and Rome to the heritage of Western civilization. Latin progressed from essentials for ninth graders to work preparing for Advanced Placement exams and then Trinity's unique Vergil Academy, in which students read a book of the *Aeneid* in tutorial for public examination by university faculty. Three years of classical Greek (more for those qualified) rewarded students, as classics teacher Donald Connor straightforwardly put it, with the ability to read some of the classic literature of classical civilization unmediated, in their original tongue.[93] Modern language instruction, in French, Spanish, and since 2005 Mandarin, aimed to develop concurrent skills in listening, speaking, reading, and writing to a level of proficiency enabling both communication in a variety of settings and, as with classics, to open the door to reading literary texts in their originals. A commonality of many Trinity courses was to address student needs on several levels at once. Languages taught language, plus history and culture. The computer science department first taught basic task-oriented applications essential to using the ubiquitous tool: word processing, databases, spreadsheets, computer graphics. It also taught programming and logic, from basic structures through MicroWorlds and on to the JAVA programming language, which prepared students for computer science Advanced Placement exams.

Arts offerings for Trinity Upper Schoolers ranged widely, but within a structure that aimed to use the creative process to heighten aesthetic awareness and sharpen critical thinking and analytic capabilities. Art history courses introduced students to the study of visual art through an inquiry-based approach rooted in close observation and analogous to the close reading practiced in English courses. Most works studied were housed in New York City museums and could be experienced firsthand. Students wrote analyses of works observed or created their own originals based on works studied. Advanced courses explored non-Western as well as Western art and addressed the role of art in broad historical context, for instance, changing definitions of beauty, the nature of modernity, the relation of art and architecture to urban development. Opportunities in the studio reinforced thinking about art with making it, from drawing and painting to ceramics, printmaking, and photography. The performing arts taught drama, from acting to set design and play production. Music taught basic theory and an array of choral and instrumental opportunities for performance. In dance class, students learned movement concepts, performance techniques, and choreography.

The teaching of religion, if dated from the first mandates of the SPG, was the oldest subject at Trinity. By the twenty-first century, with the chaplaincy and the department of religion and ethics no longer coterminous (see below, "Faith, Doubt, Settlement"), the subject was approached both as an academic discipline providing literacy in different worldviews, and as an encouragement to young people to locate their own ethical and religious identities. A "World Religions" course surveyed indigenous religion as a worldview based on tradition, Confucianism as a worldview based on reflection and experience, and Islam as a worldview based on inspired revelation as presented in a sacred text. There were courses about faith and doubt in literature where reading ranged from Allen Ginsberg to T. S. Eliot, on great moral exemplars and sacred literature, on religion in America, which visited issues like abortion, prayer in public schools, and stem-cell research, and on business and professional ethics in the contemporary workplace.

Close up it could look daunting, and students, who were the ones in a position to know best, confirmed it. Few whined, and most appeared to under-

stand their rare good fortune in being able, one way or another, just to attend. "I feel like I need to do everything I can while I'm here," reported one
sophomore. "I know it's all about getting ready for college, but it's so great to
be here every day."[94] From higher up, Henry Moses toward the end of his
headmastership framed such thoughts to justify all teaching and learning at
Trinity. At the 2007 baccalaureate service, held at Trinity Church, he spoke
on St. Paul's faith/hope/charity text in First Corinthians. Moses reminded
graduates why all that context, in subjects ancient and modern, was offered
and endured at Trinity: "We have taught you to read and to speak so you will
not become a mere clanging cymbal. We have taught you math and science
so that you can begin to plumb the mysteries of nature and the physical universe. And we have taught you history so that you will have a hint of
prophecy."[95] Successful college admissions (see below) and distinguished
later lives and careers suggested the power of such high hopes joined to hard
work.

CULTURES AND COMMUNITY

Beneath and behind both life at Trinity as students and teachers experienced it day to day, and the experience of trustees and administrators who
governed and managed it, lay questions about training up the young that
would not keep still. This was not always so. Through long decades of the
nineteenth century and well into the twentieth, Trinity's why's and where-
fore's had seemed fixed and self-evident, its world sometimes worlds apart
from what went on around it. Those days of isolation, even freedom, ended
in the 1970s. Since then, Trinity engaged the world beyond itself, indeed invited it in, endlessly examining itself in the process. The mood of introspec-
tion fit and in part flowed from the restless mind of Henry Moses.

No theme fretted it quite so much as diversity. The subject bids caution
from the start. As it filled the public discourse by the end of the twentieth
century, diversity had come to carry a heavy load of meaning and was code
for a range of attitudes, from those who saw in it a progressive social model
based on multiculturalism and advancing equality, to others who saw a
specter of guilt-driven identity politics of group entitlement at odds with individualism and assimilation. Its history at Trinity was not long, at least not
self-consciously so. The word, if not quite the idea, is absent from Trinity
vocabulary nearly to the 1970s.

The idea had crept in earlier, first in the context of race.[96] With the early rumblings of the civil rights movement, headmaster Hugh Riddleberger in the late 1950s had worried about finding some qualified "colored" boys to attend, and indeed a few non-white faces began to appear in class photographs. When Richard Garten in the early 1970s used the word diversity, it was with reference to diversity of talents among largely white boys, emphatically not diversity of groups. Robin Lester was more liberal but was not terribly deliberate. Prep for Prep, which he pioneered, might however be seen in the light of racial uplift, reaching out, and diversity building. By the early 1990s, the subject was in the air with students themselves talking about it, if not yet with quite with the right vocabulary.[97] Christopher Berrisford certainly understood that diversity had become one of the givens of the educational world and spoke of it with all the correct phrases, though he had short time at Trinity to act on them. If the enemy of diversity is homogeneity, then it was coeducation in the 1970s that most dramatically broke the old mold, though coeducation too had come to Trinity with less than pure motives: The Hawley Wing was big and needed to be filled up, Trinity families had daughters as well as sons to educate, girls would "civilize" if complicate the old place, which seemed to most everybody a fair trade-off. Beyond that, diversity as policy waited upon other leadership.

It came quickly and relentlessly with Henry Moses, though the stage in part was already set. The Long Range Plan of 1990 had mentioned, if not highlighted, diversity as a goal both in faculty recruitment and in the student body. Racial diversity was what then was meant, and there had been some progress: three times more "students of color" (as the phrase became to identify nonwhites), sixteen out of fifty-seven, entered the kindergarten class in 1992 than in any previous year.[98] Over five years, 1989–90 to 1993–94, enrollment of students of color school-wide rose from 125 to 157, or 14 to 17 percent.[99] Success in racial diversity recruitment was tied to financial aid, it then being the experience that most minority families could not afford Trinity unassisted, to perceptions about how welcoming Trinity was to nonwhites, and to multicultural curriculum content. There were faculty workshops to sensitize and train teachers to work with a newly diverse student body and a train of assemblies and chapels on topics related to diversity.[100] Denise Philpotts, a dean, was appointed Multicultural Coordinator. Faculty recruitment depended on convincing applicants from a small and much sought-after talent pool that Trinity was serious about diversifying the teaching staff. This would prove difficult. For seventeen openings, in 1993–94, five hires were minorities, not a small percentage, but in the larger scheme where perception was critical, a small number.[101]

The issue of identification by group, or the classification of individuals into groups, was both central to achieving greater racial diversity and a touchy subject. In admissions, Trinity did not ask candidate families to identify themselves by race or ethnicity, but of course it met all such families face to face. The school acted on that experience according to its own goals and reported "what we think we know."[102] It used categories prescribed by the National Association for Independent Schools. In the mid-1990s these were "African American," for black American citizens of African and/or Caribbean ancestry; "Latino/Hispanic," for American citizens of Puerto Rican, Cuban, Mexican, Dominican, or Latin American ancestry; "Asian American," for citizens with ancestries tying them to China, Japan, Korea, India, Philippines, Thailand, Cambodia, Laos, Vietnam, and the Pacific Islands; and "American Indian," for those of American Indian, Eskimo, or Aleut ancestry.[103] The board's committee on diversity in 1997 emphasized the continuing challenge: "We have heard from parents and students of color that the school's limited success in diversifying the faculty has created a highly visible issue. We need minority faculty members to serve as mentors for students of color, to provide examples of successful teachers to the community as a whole, to provide increased sensitivity for the community and to serve as a resource for the community on minority issues."[104]

Moses thought, talked, and wrote about it all ceaselessly, his leadership nothing if not earnest, he himself often frustrated. "Certainly we should give one another room to disagree even about our priorities as a school," he mused to the board in 1998, "but I believe we should have a strong consensus in support of the goal of increasing racial diversity." Pretty clearly by then there was consensus, but Moses still wondered why real progress was so slow, and "why we all don't see it as an urgent matter."[105] Sometimes it was even necessary to backtrack and reaffirm aspects of diversity thought to be taken for granted. This occurred in the mid-1990s, in response to an advertising campaign by select girls' schools, particularly Emma Willard, on behalf of single-sex schooling that implicitly challenged coeducation. Moses used the event to prompt Trinity into articulating again the virtues of coeducation for itself. Slightly more than a year after graduation of the first Trinity class that had been coeducational from kindergarten, he formed a new advisory committee on coeducation to advise on what to do next and how to shape the school's continuing commitment in this area. Girls' progress had been impressive: high numbers in advanced math and science courses, girls in significant leadership positions, girls being vocal and persuasive in and out of class. But was it enough? Were faculty yet good enough in recognizing how gender differences and similarities shaped a young person's education? What sorts of pedagogical, social, and political experimentation was there still room for at Trinity? While "lots of different sorts" was probably his own answer, Moses could be cautious too and worried about how "to distinguish what is critical for Trinity from what is merely trendy."[106]

The most explicit and comprehensive data as to who exactly Trinity had become partially as a consequence of diversity policy dates to a survey conducted by Kane, Parsons & Associates, with data collected in 1999.[107] It revealed both a Trinity where ambitions for diversity had clearly had some effect, and a school of some striking contrasts. Trinity students in fact came from highly educated families and affluent ones. Most (this the one finding that could be said not to have changed much since well before mid-twentieth century), 80 percent, lived on the Upper East and Upper West Sides and divided nearly equally. Thirty-eight percent of the fathers worked in business or finance and 20 percent were lawyers. Other professions included communications/journalism, medicine, and education. Nine of ten mothers worked too, most often, 21 percent, in business and finance. Thirteen percent of mothers were homemaker/student/retired, and 2 percent of the fathers. Seventy-three percent of fathers and 65 percent of mothers held advanced degrees. Overwhelming majorities owned computers and had access to the Internet. Mothers and fathers were present in most homes, 80 percent were original two-parent households. (The survey did not query the presence of same-sex couples.). Most were white or partly so: 89 percent reporting at least one white parent. Other racial or ethnic groups reported were Asians 9 percent, African American 4 percent, Latino/Hispanic 3 percent, others 1 percent. All minority groups contained above-average proportions of families who did not live on either the Upper West or East Sides. There were considerably more families who reported multiple religions. Fifty-three percent had at least one parent who was Jewish (this figure rose to 65 for East Siders), 36 percent had one who was Roman Catholic (this figure rose to 46 for West Siders), 22 percent had at least one who was Protestant (Episcopalians were not identified separately). Buddhists numbered 3 percent, Greek Orthodox and Hindus 1 percent each, others 9 percent. Nor were Muslims identified separately. Sixty-two percent belonged to some church or synagogue (73 percent on the East Side and 70 percent among Jewish families).

Evidence of wealth and prominence was straightforward. Median family income was $333,000 and was above $500,000 for East Siders. Three-quarters of Trinity families owned their own home, and nearly half owned a second one. Nearly a third owned "valuable art." Majorities of parents sat on foundation/not-for-profit boards. A third of the fathers were corporate directors. Close to a third of those earning over $500,000 were trustees of educational institutions. Twenty-seven percent had at least two children at Trinity.

For many, the financial requirements of attending Trinity were not onerous. More than half and more than a third of East and West Siders, respectively, assessed their circumstances as above average compared to other Trinity families. At the other extreme, about a third said their finances were below the Trinity average. Just over half of all Trinity families said that tuition was not a concern. Just over a quarter "managed" but not with much discretionary income left over. A fifth said that paying tuition was difficult and required sacrifices; 49 percent said so in the under $200,000 income bracket. Within that bracket, 46 percent of families received financial aid, which most found adequate. Only 10 percent of families who did not receive financial aid advocated a tuition reduction. More than a quarter of those in the lowest ($200,000) income group thought the school should charge less. (Financial aid was not correlated with race or ethnicity.)

The meaning of and the motives for diversity at Trinity evolved. Whether it led slightly or tracked tightly, Trinity reflected its New York City context. Initial concerns at least about the appearance of racial integration sprang from the civil rights movement in the 1960s. Coeducation in the 1970s echoed the fall of all-male bastions everywhere in education then and was also driven by the market and new school capacity (the Hawley Wing). Both Robin Lester and Christopher Berrisford had spoken sincerely about the value of diversity, but they had agendas and problems that busied them with other priorities. Henry Moses chose to make diversity a centerpiece of life at Trinity, and with his endless pushing and shoving and conversation, diversity in the 1990s and early 2000s evolved into something that transcended older meanings.

Moses chose to make it a distinct leadership issue, which was not without risk. The larger national conversation about diversity could be contentious. For progressives, diversity signified realization of America's long-delayed promise of equality for all, and policies of affirmative action and multiculturalism (in school, the seeking out of minority faculty, for instance, and developing multicultural curriculum that reinforced diversity in the classroom) were the chief tools toward achieving it. For conservatives, diversity signified a troubling tendency to categorize people by group and grievance, which only corroded community. Dissent from the consensus of where Trinity needed to be on this particular front in the culture wars was probably never great, however. This was, after all, the late twentieth and early twenty-first centuries in Manhattan (and the Upper West Side of it at that), one of the most politically and socially liberal places anywhere. Those who may have had second thoughts either wrote private letters to the headmaster or just stayed quiet and kept their own counsel with their own children, contenting themselves with the school's academic brilliance and putting up with the rest.

Under Moses's leadership, Trinity was nothing if not forthright in talking about diversity of all orders, all up and down the school. In 1999 and 2001, the school magazine, *Trinity Per Saecula*, published a two-part series on Trinity and diversity—"the buzzword with a thousand faces"—that examined aims and performance and invited opinions about how the school was doing.[108]

The school did not track, formally, religion, economic class, or sexual orientation. Author Kevin Ramsey interviewed widely among students, faculty, and administrators and drew conclusions largely in keeping with the survey, a year later, of Trinity families. The school was divided nearly equally between Christians and Jews, with from time to time a few Muslim, Hindu, and Buddhist students. Most felt that Trinity was a school for the "very wealthy and the very poor." The only middle-class contingent, so went the joke, was the faculty. The school did report students according to racial categories stipulated by independent school monitoring agencies: roughly 80 percent of Trinity was Caucasian, and the next highest percentages in all three divisions were Asian Americans, African Americans, and Latino/Hispanics, respectively. This was widely at variance with the racial diversity of Manhattan schoolchildren at large, only a quarter of whom were white.

Students talked eagerly, often asking to be quoted by name, in print.[109] An African American middle schooler commented that still most everybody seemed Caucasian. Another middle schooler reported coming to Trinity with "no idea what Jewish people did" but soon learning a lot. From a middle schooler of East Indian descent: "If Trinity had more diversity, then the pressure on students who look different would be more evenly divided between a lot of students instead of just one." Another, however, saw fewer differences between groups than some made out: "Of my best friends, one is Spanish, one is Filipino, and one is Indian, and we act totally the same way and we're totally the same person . . . I don't think that we need to spend so much time analyzing the differences between different races and different groups and different people, we should just try to enjoy each other for who we are." In the Upper School, members of the Asian Appreciation Club said it was hard to deny that there was a majority of white upper-class students at Trinity, but that Asians moved easily among them: "I think I'm different just as every person is different. I feel different but not alienated." Members of the Black Affairs Club had other views: "Having more than one black person in your grade at Trinity is pretty amazing," from one. "There's a lack of knowledge of anything outside of their [white] community," observed another, also linking up two kinds of diversity: "Race goes along with economic diversity at Trinity. A lot of what I need to talk about are family situations that are related to economics." Another, "In diversifying the school they need to bring in students of color who are of a higher economic class. There are a lot of assumptions here that all black and Hispanic kinds are poor." Another pled for respect for individualism beyond stereotypes: "We were discussing if *Huckleberry Finn* was a racist book or not, and everyone turned to me and said, 'What do you think?' Well, I do think it's a racist book, but not every other black person thinks that. What I say does not reflect the views of the entire community." From members of the Gay–Straight Alliance came bitterness and optimism. "Everyone wants to be politically correct, so they may not want to act homophobic, but they have to be indirect about it. So people will joke around with their friends and say things like 'You're so gay.'" Some were not shy: "The sex ed classes I took earlier this year were just the same old crap. They don't teach you how to make a dental dam out of a condom, or the risks of sexual activity other than heterosexual sex, and it's all so tiresome." Others took heart that while it was "the kids who have the problem," administrators and faculty were "great." On the impact of the recent coming out of art teacher William Shipley (then a twenty-year Trinity veteran): "It shows that they are perfectly normal people, are very sensitive people, who can contribute in a positive way to the community, and I think Mr. Shipley shows that."[110] From Speak Up!, a club that focused on gender issues, students suggested that real coeducation, after thirty years, still had some way to go. Did boys control the Trinity social scene?: "Totally." It was not just the parties either: "I can't tell you how often it is that we will be in the 'swamp' and see some guy slap a girl's behind. It happens all the time. And the girls are not going to make a fuss because if they do, then they're immediately identified as 'the bitch.'" Every year on senior retreat, Moses asked each senior to write him a letter about their Trinity experience. One young woman of Speak Up!: "I wrote to him about how good Trinity is academically. I love it. I think that the teachers have been really great and I've had a stellar education here, but socially there have been so many problems. The cliques at Trinity are very complicated. I'm really looking forward to going to college and being as far away from Trinity as possible." The argument roiled on, and students sometimes pulled back from the nearly inevitable emphasis in diversity policy on characteristics (like color) amenable to counting. "When the subject comes up," declared one equally vehement senior in 2008, "I think we worry way too much about numbers. What about diversity of passions and interests? That's what makes Trinity diverse."[111]

JUSTICE

For a senior like the one worried about cliques, in particular one who had spent the full thirteen years on West 91st Street, that was not an unhealthy attitude and probably less an indictment of Trinity than it sounded. Indeed, all such testimony remains to a degree subjective, the views of bright adolescents with a sharp eye for problems all around them and ever anxious about where they themselves fit in. Less subjective was the question that all the surveys, the statistics, and the anecdotes danced around and that remained unanswered. Granting diversity's virtue, how much was enough? How much diversity was required in order to be diverse? It is a question that attaches to most policy initiatives in most organizations—how to know when the goal is reached—but one that with diversity policy, the ever unreachable, receding target, may prove unanswerable. This was not a trouble unique to Trinity, which shadowed the country's pursuit of the same goal on a vast scale and at a pace that showed no signs of letting up soon.

For the great long middle of its history, from the late nineteenth century until sometime past the middle of the twentieth, the United States as a matter of cultural aspiration saw itself as an upwardly mobile, middle-class nation capable of, indeed requiring, assimilation of women and men in great variety. By the end of the twentieth century this self-image had attenuated. If not quite yet edged out, it was being given a good run by a competing aspiration of diversity and inclusiveness that required adherence to multiculturalism. Once upon a time, through the 1950s, Trinity had looked like that other America or at least a northeastern, New York City slice of it: blazers and ties, white boys alone who came from middle-class families where dad went to the office and mom stayed home. By the early 2000s, Trinity had committed itself to look like a wholly different America, and a different New York, both of which, some said, needed to look a lot more like the larger world. In that context, diversity was compelling for reasons of utility—"To be able deal with the world," as board president Andrew Brownstein distilled it in 2007, "students should be exposed to an environment as reflective of the world as possible; everybody benefits."[112] Diversity was not however compelling for utility alone.

For many among the generation of American intellectuals who grew up professionally amid the civil rights movement and other movements for social change in the 1960s and 1970s, the importance of social justice loomed large. It did for Henry Moses, who pondered it at Trinity by means of a favorite story, the parable of the Good Samaritan—"in our school, the paradigmatic story of service to others."[113] Trinity, like just about all private schools then, called upon students to perform community service: making sandwiches in a soup kitchen, running a penny drive for UNICEF, collecting cast-off winter coats for the Salvation Army, reading aloud to senior citizens in a center across the street, or traveling with a teacher across the world to volunteer in a Saigon veterans' hospital. The projects were impressive, but what of how students perceived their motives?

Most saw participation in service or affirmative action programs as an obligation or a debt inherent in privilege: "I and my family have been so fortunate, the world has given me so much, I want to give something back," or "black people have been shut out of places like this school for so long that we should throw open our doors and welcome them in order to right that past wrong." But neither privilege nor restitution was what the parable taught. Both motives made the recipients of service into objects of largesse, which could further antagonism between groups and, Moses worried, "shut down the conversation." In the Bible story, the experience of being beaten and robbed had wrenched the traveler on the road to Jericho out of his ordinary life and rendered him an outsider to the world that was familiar to him. The first two wayfarers to encounter him were insiders, and they passed by. The third was the Samaritan. Samaritans were by law and social practice outsiders, but it was this man who interrupted his journey, crossed over and helped. What were his motives? Jesus' spare telling does not say, but might not, wondered Moses and others before him, the Samaritan have been moved to mercy by "the resemblance between himself and the victim of the robbery as outsiders"? If so, then his service arose from neither privilege nor restitution but from empathy, the acknowledgment of shared humanity, from the flash of recognition that the man in the ditch "is me." Empathy erased noblesse and did justice, and justice, Moses believed, was central to teaching students about citizenship.

Both affirmative action and community service at Trinity presumed outreach, and so connected to the parable. Community service encompassed any effort by students or others in the school community "to help others." Affirmative action, while not to be confused at Trinity with government-mandated programs, was, Moses wrote, "to be understood frankly as purposeful social engineering for the good of education." They were school policies that constituted deliberate, planned disruptions of ordinary business and comfortable routines, like the unnamed traveler's falling among thieves and then the Samaritan's decision to help. The test of both policies lay with who benefited. The beneficiary should not be one (or several) disadvantaged groups. The purpose was neither to import the disadvantaged within its walls in order to share privilege with them, nor for the privileged to learn from poor about how the other half lives. Trinity strove to become more pluralistic through affirmative action and service so that students might learn empathy from one another and from others in preparing for citizenship.

As Moses put it in 1999, justice at Trinity meant "advancing the accessibility of the school to an ever widening group of New Yorkers."[114] Justice justified diversity, but did not make it happen. On one particular aspect of diversity, socioeconomic diversity/social and economic class, it proved especially thorny as the school pursued diversity by recruiting from groups that were historically (though not exclusively) poor, at the same time that the price for attending Trinity approached levels prohibitive (upper school tuition crested the $30,000 mark in 2008) for all but the very well-to-do. What had originated as a school for the poor (some quite aspiring poor to be sure) in the eighteenth century, and had become a school for the middle class in the nineteenth and twentieth centuries, had, by the late twentieth century become a school of the rich, if not for them, plus a few of the poor, but one without much middle. If a central tenet of diversity was that different groups, or simply "difference," has something unique to contribute and is to be respected and encouraged for that contribution, then what was Trinity missing out on as it became a "barbell" school?[115]

Like most independent schools, Trinity had four categories of families relative to ability to pay: the poor who could pay next to nothing, some who could pay something, those who could pay all, and those who could pay all plus pay for some others.[116] Thinness in the second category created the barbell. In 2005, the board appointed a special task force on financial aid to focus on how best to keep Trinity a reasonable prospect for middle-class families.[117] Probably nowhere else was the challenge of social and economic class more vexing than in New York City, itself so polarized economically. The city had boomed in the 1990s and become a vastly more attractive place for families to live, though an ever a more expensive one. Families who might once routinely have left for the suburbs and patronized public schools there stayed on in a city where the public schools were not an option and so swelled the waiting lists of Trinity and its competitors. Many were professional and prosperous, but not by New York standards rich, and so financial aid dilemmas increased.[118]

How to give more to the middle, yet not take from the bottom? Why was the claim of the middle important anyway, aside from its clamor in the market? Was one of the "undesirable changes in the character of the school,"[119] consequent upon the dearth of middle-income students, the decline of community between rich children and poor children alone? Might not more "middle" mitigate between the disparate worlds of those families with very much and those with very little? It was a work in progress and a hard one. The board defined middle income in a New York City context, as those families needing some but not all financial aid in order to attend (tuition in 2007–2008 was $29,000 in the lower and middle schools, $30,120 in the upper school, plus fees). While on first analysis at least the situation looked not as dire as some perceived,[120] the fundamental anxiety persisted. In the 2006–07 budget, new partial tuition awards were earmarked for four entering ninth graders, specifically to help diversify the class economically, "adding students from less commonly represented neighborhoods, and adding parents from less commonly represented professions."[121]

MISSION

Challenges so daunting demanded that Trinity's people be able to talk about what they did and strove to do, among themselves and to others. To Moses that meant writing things down, or at least using writing to sort things through, winnow ideas, connect policy to philosophy.[122] Doing more meant more deliberateness in doing so—and inevitably deeper thickets of paper and electronic communication. Given its 300–year pedigree, Trinity had a written statement of purpose far older than most schools in New York City or anywhere else in America. Or at least it had a founding doctrine, decreed from London long ago by the Society for the Propagation of the Gospel in Foreign Parts, that its pupils be taught to read, to believe and live as Christians, to be instructed in the Anglican catechism, to write plainly and legibly, and to be taught enough arithmetic and spelling to fit them for useful employment.[123] The modesty and narrowness of that charge fit the place for several decades past American independence. Even as Trinity retooled itself in the 1830s and 1840s as a different sort of Episcopal school, one for boys alone bound for college and business, nothing much more was deemed necessary to say. True, there were occasionally robust visions of the future—"Eton on the Hudson," it was declared on Trinity's 150th anniversary in 1859—but the school was in general quiet about itself. Modestly endowed, not expensive to run, and un-beset by the worlds outside itself, it could afford to be. Through long years of Episcopal ascendancy and then slow decline, nothing much more was said. Trinity was what it was, for those who knew, who largely also knew each other.

The need to represent, even project, Trinity's aims and purpose to those outside and perhaps looking to come in, as well as to have a written standard against which to test its own actions day to day, dates from more recent history and the shedding under Robin Lester of the old Episcopal cocoon and emergence as an independent school in a competitive market. The school's first self-conscious mission statement, from the 1980s, was a collection of not unpredictable themes common to many good independent schools. It spoke of "intellectual interaction" among students and teachers as the heart of Trinity and stated explicitly that small class size was essential to achieving this aim (sacred ground where Berrisford had threatened to trespass). It spoke of the need for balance and a body/mind/spirit education, the importance of ethics and service to others, the value both of tradition and of taking risks in order to grow. There was a sentence on the importance of diversity, compassion, and respect in the school community.[124]

While admiring the intent, Moses disliked the words from the start. The entirely new version of what Trinity was about, which the school published in 2000, was a highly consultative and very different set of words that had percolated through many constituencies during the 1990s. It was highly intentional. Above all it strove for inclusiveness, in keeping with Moses' anxieties about justice.[125]

Though he did not like to think of it thus, "Our Idea of Excellence," as the new statement was called, attempted to explain a high purpose. No longer, however, was high purpose seen to demarcate, to set apart, the small close community of teaching and learning that Trinity had been for centuries, but rather to integrate a diverse Trinity within and beyond itself. The document was well written and had four parts. "Our Vocation" spoke of the centrality of teaching and learning conceived as "the conversation between student and teacher" and expressed the obligation not to challenge minds and bodies alone but to teach respect for others and joyful giving. "Our Obligation" spoke of preparing the individual for the world, by supplying tools for inquiry and self-expression and, through the commitment to diversity, teaching young people "how to be colleagues and friends so they can act out of respect and love." "Our Promise" promised to engage Trinity with worlds other than its own, through service to neighbors, exploring the city of New York, and learning its ways and history: "We will embody and celebrate its diversity." "Our Means" enlisted the old motto, *Labore et virtute*, hard work and moral excellence, to the future task of pursuing "the promise and joy of Trinity School."

"Our Idea of Excellence" reached far beyond the usual performance-related notions of an overused word ("excellence") and into moral as well as academic territory. As it happened, the document was finalized in the wake of the killings at Columbine High School in Colorado, a tragedy that Moses said should prompt Trinity to ponder anew "what sort of community we are and what sort we might aspire to be." At a variety of forums, faculty and board meetings, the Parents' Association, chapels, could be heard the repeated questioning theme of "what care we owe one another."[126] The larger tragedy of the attacks of September 11, 2001, evoked similar reflectiveness. Trinity needed "to step off the usual paths in order to pay attention to a world that was suddenly hard to understand," and then, in 2003, to face "the question of how best to incorporate the fact of the war in Iraq into daily school life."[127]

These were demanding times, for which Trinity's mission, as articulated in the early 2000s, and its capabilities appeared well matched. Though ambitious, its sense of mission parsed basically into two strong and simple themes: preparation and present experience. What, when they come to Trinity, should students get that equips them for their next lives (preparation)? And how, when they come to Trinity, should students live their lives each day, as if perhaps there were no next ones (present experience)? The shock of outside events and heightened sense of danger—"safety and security have become virtually permanent agenda items on the docket of the administration"[128]—focused minds on the preciousness of each school day, not just how teachers and students taught and learned from and with one another, but how they lived those hours spent in company.

Preparation reduced into two parts of its own. First was preparation for college. New York City was filled with anxious, ambitious, and highly competitive people, some of them Trinity parents. For the children of some of them, preparation for college began the day they entered Trinity, whether in kindergarten or in ninth grade. Trinity had routinely been sending all of its seniors off to college since the 1950s at least, but in a different competitive context that today's. Then, a smaller number of high school graduates competed for the slots at good colleges, and colleges often shopped for students by virtue of their high school labels. Good northeastern prep schools, like Trinity, fed good northeastern colleges, particularly the Ivies. By the mid-1990s, two things occurred that raised temperatures in the college admission process and so the experience of preparing for it.[129] After a small dip in the college-going demographic in the 1980s, demand again surged while the supply of college places grew little. At the same time, colleges turned themselves into highly sophisticated marketers. For decades, high school students and counselors had learned about colleges by reading their catalogues and the *College Board Handbook*; until 1995, Columbia University (from whose admissions office came Trinity's current director of college counseling) did not even have a web site. Today, high schools and high school students are barraged with information—and advertising. The surge in student population coupled with the ease of electronic outreach created a hyper-competitive admissions environment. This raised the anxieties of students, who then applied to more and more schools, making the matter worse. There was a silver lining, however, at least at Trinity, where the tightening down of the Ivies and other schools deemed most highly "selective" afforded counselors the opportunity to educate Trinity students and their families in a broader universe of possibilities. Currently some 30 to 35 percent of Trinity graduates attend schools outside the Northeast.

Trinity's college counseling process started formally in the second semester of the junior year, and it took as a primary challenge to turn down the volume and filter the noise on a subject for which the public appetite was huge and not always discerning.[130] It included family conferences, role playing that turned students into mock college admissions committees, and hours spent one-on-one between counselors and individual students. The result was a continuing high-end, but also more diverse, list of schools where Trinity students went and where they did well. Such lists were, frankly, a high school's most visible report card, and achieving them was not without danger. The sad consequence of intense meritocracy in college admissions, believed Lawrence Momo, Trinity's director of college counseling for fourteen years, was fear or at least aversion to risk. Just at the moment when young adults should be most open to risk, experiment, simply attempting new things, many worried that they dare not and that one false move now would alter long lives to come. This may have exaggerated, and Trinity juniors and seniors were probably no more stressed and anxious about college than bright adolescents elsewhere, also raised from the cradle on high-calorie diets of parental expectation. Still, the path of admission to college had become an undeniably public rite of passage and an increasingly fraught one. Trinity's college counselors faced the dual challenge of making the process effective and of helping students and families bring to it some sense of proportion.

Preparation for college, for what literally came next, existed in uneasy tension with a second sort of preparation, as Moses thought of it. Could Trinity prepare students for life long after college? Could it both equip bright college-bound adolescents with the tools of continuing academic performance and mold them for citizenship? Some things transcended how smart one was. Elite schools like Trinity had long talked, boasted even, of how they prepared students for "leadership," and indeed some students were destined to become leaders. All, however, were responsible at least for participating, for taking their place around the table of adult life in a diverse democracy or just a diverse world. Could one speak (perhaps in languages other than English)? Could one listen? Could one persuade? Could one compromise? Could one do good in a world filled with bad? "The question of whether we are simply preparing our young people to be admitted to elite colleges and universities or developing good, curious, committed people" would in the future become an agenda item as pressing as and more profound than anything to do with safety and security.[131]

It is tempting to say that the first, the academic aspect of preparation was the easy part. Trinity's consistently stellar college admissions performance certainly suggested that Trinity teachers knew how to go about that part of their business. Of course, it was not easy, as any of them would attest: Subject matter did not sit still as once it had, and each student each year presented unique challenges and opportunities. Good teaching in a supercharged setting like Trinity was terribly hard and wearing, as much so as any doctoring or lawyering at the highest levels of those and other elite professions, but was hardly rewarding financially (at Trinity's 300th anniversary, teachers' salaries ranged from $48,000 to $105,000 per year, well below what Trinity's board defined as "middle class" for Trinity parents). Teaching is of course utterly rewarding in other ways, which is why great teachers teach at Trinity and elsewhere. But at least teaching is in some sense measurable: Look at evaluations, look at test scores, look at college admissions, or best ask students who the great teachers are. They always know. There were fewer measures for the other aspect of preparation—for citizenship—and, preparation for the future completely aside, for the quality life at Trinity now.

FAITH, DOUBT, SETTLEMENT

In the daily life of today's diverse multicultural Trinity, the hope that students would experience a degree of comradeship miles beyond the old-time notions of just learning to "get along" with others, and would be taught to render service to others not from noblesse or guilt or other obligation but from empathy, rested upon distinct moral intention. So, it was no surprise to find that "Our Idea of Excellence" spoke plainly of matters that could be interpreted as related to, even rooted in religion (in organized branches of which even in secular twenty-first century New York City over 60 percent of Trinity families claimed membership) or at least spirituality.[132] In addition to challenging minds and training bodies, it spoke of enlarging students' spiritual lives. It spoke of showing students how to act out of love. It admonished them to serve their neighbors as themselves and pursue moral excellence. It bade them be joyful.

Indeed, what had made a new statement of mission necessary at all was the end of the old mission, as for two and a half centuries it had related to the church. By the last decade of the twentieth century, that church/school relationship had grown awkward. This was in part a consequence of Trinity's growth and success as an independent school in the years after the expansion that came with the Hawley Wing and the return of coeducation. With a renowned faculty, new plant, and after 1975 genial new leadership, Trinity attracted, without trying, new diversity in the form of a steady stream of affluent Jewish families eager for academically superior, non-parochial education for both their sons and daughters. Trinity did not ask and certainly did not count, but anecdotal evidence suggests that many Jews found Trinity attractive for its unusual mix of secular and sacred: Certainly not a "church" school, it yet claimed moral anchorage in one of the world's great religions. It was a place known for its seriousness about serious things. By the century's end, Jewish families would constitute a slight majority of Trinity families.

They brought talent, energy, uncompromising high standards and expectations. Few found the expense of a Trinity education an obstacle. They were ideal constituents. It is also possible that the Jewish influx into Trinity stirred resentment. Anti-Semitism may be too strong a term: New York was not Warsaw, but a proudly progressive city and home to one of the most vibrant and comfortably assimilated Jewish communities in the world. It was probably less the strength of the Jews than the insecurity of the Episcopalians that caused the appearance of a problem. Robin Lester had arrived at a troubled Trinity in 1975, and one of the troubles he sensed was the relationship with Trinity Church. He set about shoring it up through his own relationship with its then also new rector, Robert Ray Parks. The two could hardly have been more different: Lester a Midwestern progressive Presbyterian, Parks a conservative Southerner. Parks had two sons at Trinity, however, and a professional interest in schools.[133] Ex officio, he came to school board meetings and took part. The Episcopal church (of which Trinity Church was the single wealthiest parish) was then in turmoil of its own over the ordination of women to the priesthood, approved in 1976, and comprehensive liturgical (some said theological) revisionism that led to replacement of its historic Book of Common Prayer with more modern rites in 1979. Religious practice at Trinity School in these years had also become attenuated, forms lacking functions. Lester and Parks agreed that one way to forestall secularization of the teaching of religion at Trinity was to combine the post of head of the religion department with the school chaplaincy. Parks convinced the vestry of Trinity Church to underwrite the strategy with a restricted endowment of $500,000, stipulating that the posts be amalgamated and that the incumbent be, naturally, an Episcopal priest. Dan Heischman became the first to serve under the arrangement, and thence under Lester an assistant headmaster and dean of admissions.[134]

Cement for embattled Episcopalians? Defense against Jewishness at Trinity? Both? Last ditch for "heritage"? Lester (who himself would convert to Episcopalianism) claimed nothing but warm relations with Trinity's Jewish constituents: "I was saved by Jews on the board any number of times over social issues; we had an inclusive operation."[135] He tended to the church relationship in other, symbolic, ways too, returning Trinity's commencement exercises to Trinity Church and its history-laden setting at Broadway and Wall Street. For Trinity's 275th anniversary year, 1984–85, he arranged with Mayor Ed Koch to join him in leading Trinity's faculty and students in a walk from St. Paul's Chapel to Trinity Church for graduation exercises. Koch closed down the three blocks of Broadway for the occasion, and everyone had a grand time. "If you didn't think you had a part of this Manhattan rock," Lester liked to tell departing seniors, "well, you do now. This is your school and your history." If it was history with a religious tinge, it was not enough apparently to put off Jews or other non-Christians. Discovery that Trinity Church early in its history had donated land for a Jewish cemetery was the sort of historical footnote that could be useful as Lester and Parks strove to put forth a new more progressive image of church and school: "This is not the standoffish old Trinity Church. This is a church that is dynamic and serves all the people."[136]

That was true enough, as Trinity Church and the larger Episcopal church in these years opened themselves wide to new social currents and made inclusion and social justice themes equal to salvation. Whatever its original motivation, however, the conditioned $500,000 that came to Trinity School from Trinity Church to endow the chaplaincy came in time to look more like an impediment, as the school wrestled with the conflict implicit be-

tween its heritage and its commitment to diversity (the fact of a school population that was less than half Christian and far less Episcopalian than that).
Certainly it looked so to Henry Moses, who studied harder on the problem
of religion at Trinity than anyone probably since the days when SPG
churchmen had commanded memorization of the Anglican catechism in
their schools and that everyone be taught "to believe and live as Christians."

From Trinity's formal statements on religion, which began to appear
early in Moses's tenure, the word "Christian" (and "God" or "gods") was absent. Trinity had long talked about religion by not talking about it, at least
not as policy. It taught courses in religious history and it had chapel, actually two of them, both adorned with crosses, and compulsory chapel services. The cross also adorned the school crest, and the iron gratings on the
new street-level windows that had been punched into the Hawley Wing in
the 1990s. And of course there was the name itself, "Trinity," with its reference to that most central and difficult doctrine of Christianity. The need to
understand religion amid diversity put pressure on this heritage. Conversation began and continues about how to think and what to do about it.

One solution would have been to jettison religion and let Trinity become
wholly secular or at least, through neglect, let heritage dwindle into quaint-
ness. It might be said that this was occurring anyway as Trinity, New York,
and America appeared to secularize after mid-century.[137] Certainly not all
Trinity students from families of Christian or Jewish heritage were obser-
vant Christians and Jews. Yet by the end of the century, religion or some
would say, in America, religiosity, would stage a remarkable comeback in
private lives and the public square. The attacks of September 11 and the long
wars that followed, couched as they often were in terms of cultural, even civ-
ilizational conflict rooted in religion, forced attention as never before onto
matters of faith and different faith traditions. Allegedly secular New Yorkers thought as seriously about these things as any Texas evangelical, and
some of the ways they thought about them were reflected in the ways that
Trinity ultimately handled it.

While only the second leader of Trinity not to be an Anglican, Moses was
a believer, a Presbyterian of liberal leanings, and just forgetting about religion at Trinity was not an option. One of the things he believed in was that
religion and education could be made to mix fruitfully outside parochial
settings, and that the life of the spirit, which Trinity from time immemorial
had claimed to nurture, needed nurturing as much in the twenty-first cen-

tury as in the eighteenth. Trinity was a school, not a church, and a school that had lately put high premium on the idea of "difference" in its community, including difference in (or indeed indifference to) religion. Trinity strove to make itself a reflection of a diverse world, locally and globally, and to prepare young people to walk in it. The answer was never to claim too much for any one faith, but to claim much for all of them, for all of them were invited and welcomed at Trinity.

It was tricky though, chiefly because of the legacy of a founding faith. That faith, Episcopalianism, was itself opening up in these same years, to an extent that made it in some respects unrecognizable to an older generation. By the time Trinity opted for diversity and social justice, so had the church; there was no doctrinal conflict. Still, learning how to "do religion" in a pluralist school community—learning how not to offend or exclude, without reducing rich and ancient faiths to twaddle—took some working out. It was a very long legacy. Trinity had offered instruction in religion since its beginning. By the 1990s, its department of religion offered courses about the Bible, theology, religious history, comparative religions, religion in literature, and ethics. The educational goal, as then articulated, was to explain "the important role religious belief and values have played in history, literature and philosophy." Beyond formal teaching and learning, religion at Trinity also comprised "celebration, meditation and invitation to prayer."[138]

The school neither boasted about nor disguised its long association, "in varying degrees," with Trinity Church, Wall Street, the fact of the endowed chaplaincy, and that the church's rector was also a school trustee. But the connection was described in words notable mainly for their faintness. The connection was said still to impose an obligation to honor "Trinity's rich traditions and historical ties to the Episcopal Church." Maybe, but there seemed little heart in it. The energy had shifted to now, as could be read in the verbs: "We are committed to religious diversity in what is read, sung, and spoken; we strive for balance among the traditions of the school and those of our families, students and teachers. We continually seek forms of celebration that achieve that balance. . . . Trinity aspires to foster respect for the beliefs and traditions of every individual in the community; diversity of belief and its attendant values of tolerance and understanding help to shape all of our practices."[139]

It was a heavy load, hard indeed to balance, and there was considerable thrashing about as the school tried to get a new grip. Moses for a time even mused about removing the great wooden cross from the front wall of the main school chapel in the Hawley Wing, consecrated space mostly put to secular uses as Trinity's primary auditorium and theater.[140] It was not, however, an issue for symbolism alone.

"A school aspiring to the good," Trinity by the 2000s had a mission that promised, in context of much else, to enlarge its students' spiritual lives "and lead them to do right." Shy as it may have become of the word "God" (or even "gods," let alone "Jesus" or "Jehovah"), not so with moral purpose. The words they in time settled upon to represent religion at Trinity finely finessed the matters of founding faith and the reality of pluralism.[141] This was not Moses's work alone. Chapel councils of students, senior staff, faculty, the board's committee on religion and diversity, the board itself, all thought, talked, wrote, and revised. In particular, Timothy L. Morehouse, chaplain since 2004, helped craft Trinity's twenty-first-century approach to the sacred. Brought up a Presbyterian, Morehouse was a young Episcopal priest with an academic bent who had come to Trinity at first to teach in the religion department, and then at Moses's behest took on the chaplaincy. One of the things that had drawn him to Anglicanism also helped him see how religion might work at Trinity.

Anglicanism is an unusual branch of Christianity, intensely secular in its historic origins, neither (or both) quite Protestant nor quite fully Catholic but a "middle way" known less for its doctrinal rigor than for its rigorous spiritual method. From its famous "three-legged stool" of scripture, tradition, and reason, as Thomas Hooker set it forth in the sixteenth century, derived such notions of authority as it would collectively admit, and in company of which it derived compromise and lurched along, if not ahead. Rejecting both the magisterium of Rome and the Biblical certainties of Geneva, it was not the faith for everyone, but something about it fit the temper of twenty-first century, post-Christian Trinity better than most others.

Chiefly applicable to Trinity, as Morehouse saw it, was the Anglican aptitude for conversation, for reasoning with the others.[142] Christian theology aside, its habit of thinking was not foreign to the search for and transmission of knowledge as it occurred or should occur in good schools, at the heart of education: What do the sources say? How have others, who came before, thought about this problem? What can our own reason and intelligence contribute to the solution? Sprung notoriously and expediently from dynastic necessity in the reign of Henry VIII, Anglicanism proved itself in the next generation as midwife to the political and religious compromise known as the Elizabethan Settlement: worship (publicly at least) in conformity to this common prayer book, decreed Henry's daughter Elizabeth, who, beyond that, would look no further into men's souls.[143]

This was also the problem at Trinity, as prickly in its way and time on issues of religion and tolerance as the Elizabethans were in theirs. Theirs, moreover, was a mere bipolar world, the only players Protestants of multiple stripes and Catholics. Trinity's twenty-first-century world was multi-polar, as illustrated in the community gathered around its table—in old Prayer Book language, "all sorts and conditions of men," in today's idiom, "diversity." As it evolved through four centuries since Elizabeth, Anglicanism also proved its aptitude as a big-tent religion, embracing across many cultures a gamut of the faithful, from high churchmen to evangelicals, from those who loved the Bible best to those who loved the beauty. Trinity needed a big spiritual tent, too, one that would embrace all sorts of believers and seekers and include the faithless who believed nothing at all.

So Morehouse and Moses struggled to turn what might have been a troubling legacy into a useful tradition. Both found the relationship with Trinity Church, at least as it had been construed by a previous administration, an impediment. What Robin Lester had seen as an arrangement to reaffirm (Christian?) religion at Trinity—church endowment of the chaplaincy and stipulation that the chaplain also head the department of religion—Moses regarded with suspicion. Eventually he ended it.[144] It fuzzed the border between church and school and had about it a last whiff of privilege. It was important that, around Trinity's table, none be hosts, none guests. By what presumption anyway, in an academic department of religion in an independent school that taught about many faiths, did a Christian and only a Christian lead? That the chaplaincy would remain exclusive Anglican territory was left alone, embedded anyway in the by-laws and an acceptable nod, if not quite a salute, to history.

Early twenty-first-century Trinity required all students to take three courses in religion between grades 5 and 12, and weekly attendance at chapel was required of all students and faculty. Such requirements and other rituals with spiritual reference (religious holiday observances, matriculation and baccalaureate services held at Trinity Church, a school prayer, the crosses) constituted a common practice, analogous to liturgy, in which Trinity found unity in lieu of common doctrine. Within such practice, diversity could be mined for the values that united rather than divided the community. Students' and faculty's diverse religious and philosophical convictions themselves became instruments for learning and teaching one another about "the wisdom in the religious traditions of the world." At the most philosophical level, religion commanded historic place in the conversation about "what it means to be human." At the most practical level, the study of world religions and their ethical and artistic expression was "essential for effective citizenship in an increasingly complex and challenging world."[145]

It misleads to describe the story of religion in Trinity's most recent past as an instance of retreat, or mere accommodation to the increasing secularism of the times and the place. While this may have been so for the 1960s and 1970s, by the 1990s and early 2000s the school faced the different challenge of accommodating religion's resurgence, and not one religion alone but a diversity of them.[146] It was at this point that Trinity carved out for itself an odd but tenable position. In no way did it describe itself any longer as a "Christian" school. Yet it continued to describe itself and without hypocrisy[147] as an "Episcopal" school, filled largely with non-Christian students, and governed by a board whose leadership often as not was Jewish. Episcopalianism, both historically and as it was evolving in these same years, stood out if not as a superior brand of faith at least as a superior facilitator in welcoming conversation and argument about faith and, for that matter, about doubt. It was why, as Morehouse liked to say, "Episcopalians can do schools better than other denominations," at least those schools committed to pluralism.[148] It is true that for believers of a more orthodox temper, of which there probably still were a few at Trinity, this position looked indeed like a retreat. For most of the community, however, it looked like a fair enough place to be, a kind of "settlement" that permitted, indeed encouraged, the community to treat seriously the life of the spirit in times that were extraordinarily sensitive to slights of any kind, but that prohibited in speculative matters of belief resort to any authority that might be perceived to exclude.

CHAPELS AND STATE OCCASIONS

Continuing use in Upper School chapel services of the Book of Common Prayer—not the Bible but a book filled with the Hebrew and Christian testaments, arranged in a particular way—bespoke this settlement and Trinity's stance toward faiths other than the Judeo/Christian ones. Today small numbers of Muslims, Hindus, and Buddhists also sit in chapel on those same hard, scuffed-up wooden pews. The Prayer Book supplied "basic forms" that anchored against the drift toward subjectivism, yet were loose enough to encompass even agnosticism and atheism and enable everyone to "feel at home and in fact own the institution of chapel." It was an approach that demanded balance among faith traditions and that aimed not for certainty but for "resonance," among differing but often similar "sacred texts, prayers, ritual, music, dance, ethical perspective and stories." What had made the Book of Common Prayer revolutionary at its origins in the sixteenth century—forms written down to be prayed publicly "in common" for the sake of peace in a community overwrought with religion, but that left the rest to private conscience—remained Trinity's approach in the twenty-first.[149]

In 2007, Henry Moses mused aloud to architects and others about how to make Trinity's barn-like chapel/auditorium/theater feel more like a "sacred space."[150] Chaplain Tim Morehouse monitored the program that filled it, week by week. Diligent to keep the chapel experience sacred but never sectarian, he strove to avoid a past tendency toward chapels that were watered-down "little church services" and instead guided students in learning to use well a time deliberately structured for reflection.[151] Students in Upper and Middle schools participated in planning chapel agendas with maturity sometimes beyond their years.

All Trinity chapels were unique, some joyful. Leonard Leaman was a science teacher in Trinity's Middle School for many years, and in summers worked at Camp Winaco in the Maine woods. He died suddenly in the summer of 2007. That autumn, just before Thanksgiving, the school held a memorial service in chapel to honor him. To an outsider, the size of the crowd said he had been popular and for a long time: Current students to middle-aged alums filled the pews at seven o'clock on a weekday evening for a program that lasted nearly two hours. For the prelude, fine arts teachers Steven Rochen, violin, and Mary Evelyn Bruce, piano, played Kreisler's *Liebeslied* (love song). Senior Chloe Zale sang Brahms's *Erinnerung* (remembrance). They read from the Bible (Psalm 8) and poetry by Maya Angelou. Chaplain Morehouse offered prayers and invited testimony. Colleagues talked first: then-acting head Suellyn Preston Scull, Middle School principal Diane Stewart-Garrett, former Lower and Middle School principal Emily Scharf, friend and fellow camper Howard Childs. Some spoke from prepared remarks, others not. Happy reminiscence abounded: of Leaman's famous "boy, have I got a lab for you" greeting at the start of class, of the covey of quail he kept in "Quailsville" on the fourth floor of the 139 building, of the boa constrictor that escaped, of his fascination with the night sky and tales of lying with students on Trinity's Turf to teach them firsthand the constellations or catch a glimpse of Halley's Comet.[152]

Education today is beset by measurement, and Trinity, filled as it is with bright people anxious for successful outcomes, is no exception. One measure of education lies not, however, with what it sets forth, but with what it leaves behind. Len Leaman's life as a teacher illustrated this. Student Finn Freymann, with a shock of dark hair, wearing khakis and a purple sweater and not much taller than the podium, approached with no notes. For three or four minutes he held forth like Lincoln, with confidence and startling poise. Nor was this a senior but a sixth grader, yet old enough to be veteran already of dozens of Trinity chapels, where all sorts and conditions of men and women, girls and boys, week after week, year after year, talk and listen. The experience accumulates. That November evening the collective experience of Trinity chapel stood, in the body of a schoolboy, before all those who had come together to remember a teacher. At twelve, one's life is filled with future, and the past is short. What the boy remembered from his past was something Leaman had left behind in it: "You'd always walk out of his room with a smile on your face." In silence, the chapel smiled with him. "I only had him one year," the boy ended, "but it seems like I always knew him." So apparently had they all. It was a great deal, for certain sure, for a teacher to have left behind.[153]

Henry ("Hank" to all who knew him) Moses, Trinity's twenty-seventh headmaster and a teacher, too, died suddenly on April 16, 2008, from complications following heart transplant surgery.[154] He had earlier announced his retirement, effective at the end of the school's 300th anniversary year in 2009, and the search process to find his permanent successor was under way at the time of his death.[155] Moses's premature passing cast a cloud over Trinity just as graduation time approached; indeed, Moses's son William Holland was a member of the class of 2008. Trinity marked Moses's loss, in the words of Upper School principal Mark Simpson, with the ritual of "a state occasion."[156] The memorial service was held at Temple Emanu-El on Fifth Avenue and 65th Street, a fitting venue for the remembrance of a man of deep ecumenical convictions and the head of a school called "Trinity" the majority of whose students were Jewish. Temple Emanu-El is also large, seating over 2,500, and Hank Moses filled the house.

Magnificence, however, is not a Trinity trait, and though Temple Emanu-El is magnificent sacred space, it was, when filled with Trinity people, transformed into chapel. For all his Trinity career, Moses had wrestled to find right representations for the sacred in a pluralist setting, and he was in the end best remembered using the forms that for years had helped thousands of Trinity boys and girls, teachers and staff, approach the same hard questions. Moses's memorial, though grander, and science teacher Leonard Leaman's were much the same. There were readings from texts, remembrances from those who were closest, music by school musicians, a time for prayer, a blessing. In this instance, Moses's two sons, Laurence Holland '05, and William Holland '08, side by side from the pulpit prayed responsively the school prayer, worn copies of which they pulled from their wallets, after the custom of their father. The prayer's remarkable final petition speaks of furthering, in school from generation to generation, the "capacity for gallant living." It was a favored phrase of Hank Moses and a great deal, for certain sure, to have left behind.

CHARITY

How far should a school's responsibility reach from academics into life? The answer, at Trinity in 2009, is quite far. Henry Moses thought that citizenship as well as scholarship lay at the core of the school's purpose, that together they formed one purpose, and that by doing a superior job with citizenship Trinity could distinguish itself in the market and finesse the charge of elitism. He entertained the more radical possibility, too, that indeed the only justification in a modern democracy for such elite schools as Trinity was civic, and not in the old presumptive leadership-training sense either but in the progressive sense of training citizens, for America and the world.[157] Its commitment to diversity expressed this responsibility to the extent that the benefit of diversity transcended academic experience and changed lives for the good. The experience of creation, teach both Bible and biology, is richest in its variety, and so with women and men, boys and girls, in school.

Perhaps it had always been so. Diversity is not a word that had much meaning at Trinity until fairly recent times. But other words for the same idea did have. For Moses and many others at Trinity at the eve of the school's fourth century, diversity was only the modern answer to an old question of what care, anywhere two or three are gathered together, do we owe one another? Trinity's mission put it plainly: We owe respect and "love."[158] For the first century of its history, Trinity had employed another word for this idea in its very name, which then also stated its mission: the "Charity" School of Trinity Church.

That world is afar off, dim and dissimilar from our own, except in this. Charity meant and means giving, not from obligation but from goodwill, empathy, love. We have scant means to peer very far into motives so long ago but to pronounce them mixed, as they are now. History is clearer about what happened then and what happens now. The old charity school taught literacy, numeracy, and Christianity to the poor, in order to lift them up. At Trinity today, where they still teach literacy and numeracy and the life of the spirit, it is believed that diversity uplifts everyone, rich and poor alike and even some in the middle. If so, then Trinity keeps faith, whatever they call it.

Notes

1. See Francis J. Sypher, "Mr. C. Bruner-Smith," *Trinity Per Saecula*, Fall 2001. The family did not use "Jr.," and Bruner himself later added the hyphen.

2. Following: "The Memoirs of C. Bruner-Smith Over the Past Sixty Years," May 1992 (Memoir); and Bruner-Smith interview, November 13, 1992, Trinity School Archives (TSA). "I learned more in a few months of actual teaching than I had from all the theoretical textbook material and lecture courses I had been exposed to as a student" (Memoir, 2).

3. It is uncertain how well French knew Cole, but apparently they were acquainted. Bruner remembers that French visited Trinity for graduation in 1928, the end of Bruner's first year there, and Cole seated him as an "honored guest" on the platform.

4. "A good servant, a good cook and a good housekeeper" (Memoir, 49).

5. "It was a source of satisfaction," remembered ever-charitable Bruner, "when I learned somewhat later that he had independent means and owned a townhouse in Greenwich Village so I had not put a poor, struggling teacher out on the street" (Memoir, 4).

6. Interview, 2.

7. Memoir, 21.

8. Memoir, 17.

9. The contrast between these two, like the contrast between Cole and his predecessor, illustrates a transitional dynamic that would be repeated for the rest of the century whenever Trinity changed leadership.

10. Interview, 24, 27.

11. Interview, 28.

12. "I have contended for years that we teach youngsters to throw, bat and kick a ball but don't teach them to stand and walk well" (Memoir, 16).

13. For the school's 150th anniversary, on the eve of the Civil War in 1859, a Columbia divinity professor framed Trinity's story in frankly religious—"The fear of the Lord is the beginning of knowledge" (Proverbs i:7)—terms, florid with high and holy purpose especially apt just then, he thought, when New York City and the nation needed leaders, leaders who needed to come from God-fearing schools like Trinity. In 1925, trustees growing anxious over the school's finances commissioned a legal history to look into how the endowment was being used, and offered a careful conclusion that probably too much of it was being used and that the old charity model so beloved by then-headmaster Cole was past the end of its useful life. In 1947 and ten years after retirement, Cole himself gave it a brief go on the occasion of the 250th anniversary of Trinity Church, which relationship, as the old-time churchman he was, Cole was apt to

venerate more than a little. In 1963, Trinity entered the dissertation literature, when Edward Stewart Moffat submitted his orderly account of Trinity through the 1950s, for a Columbia Ph.D. in political science. Bruner condensed 290 or so years of the story into a few pages of the alumni magazine, *Trinity Per Saecula*, in 1995 and 1996, and more fully considered the twentieth-century school in his own manuscript memoirs. In 2001, another lawyer (and Trinity parent) Wolcott B. Dunham, Jr., explored some of Trinity's nineteenth-century legal history starting with the school's incorporation in 1806 as an entity separate from its namesake parish. Another dissertation in progress, by Kathryn Bordonaro, examines William Huddleston's years as schoolmaster.

14. Appointed head in 1991, Moses announced his resignation in 2007 effective with the school's 300th anniversary in 2009. When Moses suffered a heart attack in October 2007, the board named Associate Head Suellyn Preston Scull as Interim Head pending selection of Moses's permanent successor. Following complications of heart transplant surgery, Moses died on April 16, 2008. See chapter 8.

15. Henry Moses, remarks at Trinity Alumni Day, May 15, 2004.

16. See chapter 8.

CHAPTER 2: WILLIAM HUDDLESTON'S SCHOOL (14–37)

1. John Nichols memorandum, Trinity School Archives, October 12, 2000.

2. For instance: Carl Bridenbaugh, *Vexed and Troubled Englishmen* (New York, 1968); Bernard Bailyn, *The Peopling of British North America* (New York, 1986); and Trevor Astin, ed., *Crisis in Europe, 1560–1660* (London, 1965), especially chapters 2 and 3: E. J. Hobsbawm, "Crisis of the Seventeenth Century," and H. R. Trevor-Roper, "The General Crisis of the Seventeenth Century."

3. Early biographical details from Kathryn Bordonaro, dissertation in progress, on William Huddleston's tenure at the Charity School (Bordonaro); John Nichols, research memoranda, 2000 and 2002 (Nichols); and Edward Stewart Moffat, "Trinity School, New York City: 1709–1959," dissertation, Columbia University, 1963 (Moffat).

4. Lawrence Stone, "Social Mobility in England, 1500–1700," *Past and Present*, 33 (1966); Jack P. Greene, *Pursuits of Happiness: Social Development of Early Modern British Colonies* (Chapel Hill, 1988); Bailyn, *Peopling*.

5. See Virginia Anderson, *New England's Generation: The Great Migration and the Formation of Society and Culture in the Seventeenth Century* (New York, 1991).

6. Bordonaro, 17.

7. See Elizabeth Blackmar, *Manhattan for Rent, 1785–1850* (New York, 1989).

8. Bordonaro details his transactions, 18–33.

9. Some of the numbers from the mid-1690s—parcels with price tags in the hundreds of pounds—look large enough to wonder whether Huddleston had brought capital with him from England. If so, he must have judged land the best way to put it to work in New York. For Huddleston's wealth relative to other New Yorkers of the time, see Thomas J. Archdeacon, *New York City, 1664–1710: Conquest and Change* (Ithaca, 1976).

10. See Herbert Johnson, "English Statutes in Colonial New York," *New York History* 58 (1977).

11. Nichols, 2002, p. 2.

12. Jacob Leisler was a German-born New York trader, who seized Fort James in May 1689 and effectively took control of New York upon the flight of Francis Nicholson in June. Lieutenant of Edmund Andros, governor of the short-lived Dominion of New England, which was to include New York, Nicholson was rumored to be involved in a recusant plot centering on Governor Thomas Dongan, an Irish Catholic. Leisler proclaimed for William and Mary, formed a committee of public safety, and called an assembly. Fresh outbreak of war between England and France heightened anxiety for the Protestant cause (French and Indians burned Schenectady in February 1690). The Lords of Trade appointed a new governor, Henry Sloughter, delayed by shipwreck until March 1691 and preceded to New York by Major Robert Ingoldesby. When Leisler refused to surrender the fort to Ingoldesby, hostilities broke out in March just two days before Sloughter finally arrived. Leisler then gave up, but with his lieutenant, Jacob Milborne, Leisler was hanged in May.

13. See Richard Pointer, *Protestant Pluralism in the New York Experience: A Study of Eighteenth-Century Diversity* (Bloomington, 1988); Patricia U. Bonomi, *Under the Cope of Heaven: Religion, Society and Politics in Colonial New York* (New York, 1986); and John Webb Pratt, *Religion, Politics and Diversity: The Church-State Theme in New York History* (Ithaca, 1967).

14. Edwin G. Burrows and Mike Wallace, *Gotham: A History of New York City to 1898* (New York, 2000), 103.

15. "State support according to local option" was how historian Michael Kammen described the solution in pluralistic New York [Michael Kammen, *Colonial New York: A History* (New York, 1975), 221].

16. Kammen, 216ff.

17. Lawrence Cremin, *American Education: The Colonial Experience, 1607–1783* (New York, 1970), 338ff; John Calam, *Parsons and Pedagogues: The SPG Adventure in American Education* (New York, 1971); Daniel D. O'Connor, *Three Centuries of Mission: The United Society for the Propagation of the Gospel, 1701–2000* (London, 2000); and William W. Kemp, *The Support of Schools in Colonial New York by the Society for the Propagation of the Gospel in Foreign Parts* (New York, 1913).

18. The SPG would carry on the good fight after American independence in other equally vast parts of the world still to come under British dominion.

19. New York was probably the scene of the SPG's most ambitious efforts, from missionaries to charity schooling to its role in the founding of King's College [Columbia] in 1754. See Cremin, *Colonial Experience*, 344–45; Kemp, *Support of Schools*.

20. Neau actually requested that the Assembly decree that there could be no connection between a slave's legal status as a bondsman and his embrace of Christianity (Kammen, *Colonial New York*, 225).

21. SPG files, Library of Congress [LC], vol. 10, p. 203.

22. Wrote Huddleston to London in July 1708 about the competition: "Mr. Andrew Clark teaches Latin . . . and hath 33 scholars and receives for each of them as much a quarter as I and others do; Mr. Cornelius Lodge hath about 20 scholars; Mr. John

Shiphens 28 scholars; Mr. John Bashford 8 scholars and I have about 30 and no more since these new masters taught people here being fond of novelties, to that by this account you may see that there are but 119 boys taught by all the five masters whereas I have heretofore for several years (as may appear by my testimonials heretofore presented to the Venerable Society) taught sixty boys myself, and I am certain with as much satisfaction to the parents as is now given, and as many boys appear in the Church as now generally do; I have nothing to charge any of the Gentlemen with but that they are all ingenious diligent and good men, but I am humbly of opinion that only two masters whom if there were a right understanding might live well of their business and would be sufficient to discharge all that duty which now the five masters spend their time upon and can but live very poorly thereon" [SPG files (LC), vol. 4, letter 53].

23. SPG files [LC], vol. 13, letter 174. On Huddleston's teaching before 1709 see Nichols, 2000.

24. To Jonathan Postlethwaite, Master of St. Paul's Free School and his supporter in London, Huddleston wrote October 9, 1706: "I am informed by a line from said Mr. Chamberlayne [SPG secretary] that the society hath been pleased to make me a Present of Ten pounds in Money: and as much more in books to be Distributed amongst my Scholars which when received shall as tis my duty return them my humble thanks. I shall always persist by the Grace of God discharge my Duty in the station which it hath pleased the Almighty to place me in but if that Hon'ble Bord were thoroughly acquainted with the Service I have done for the Church in Trayning up Dissenting Children to be true Sons of her, I am safisfyed their bounty would have extended further towards me; and that they wou'd freely have allowed me an annual pension. . . . Before I conclude I make bold to acquaint you if the Hon'ble society would send over some common Prayer books in Dutch and French. They would conduce very much to the bringing over these people to the Church; for I find nothing makes them averse to the Church, but their Ignorance of the Excellency of her Service" (SPG files, vol. 3, letter 8; vol. 4, letter 7).

25. SPG files, vol. 2 letters 130, 132.

26. Huddleston lost no time in pressing for more—and nagged ever after for money. Writing in July 1710: "I humbly desire that the Venerable Society of their great wisdom goodness and charity will be pleased to consider that forty boys are a great number to teach and will take up most part of my time, and therefore make no doubt but for my pains and trouble they will be graciously pleased to allow me such suitable yearly encouragement as may enable me to discharge that duty with chearfulness, having now only eight boys left that pays me." And the books he had been promised had not yet come: "[S]o I hope you will be pleased to move for more, for reason that most of the parents of those 40 boys now under my care by the Society's direction are so miserable poor that they are not able to provide them Books that's necessary" [SPG files (LC), vol. 5, letter 63]. Writing in February 1717: "My certificates of the discharge of my duty have been so ample that if all America would subscribe with me except some gentlemen out of Pity, more than ordinary charity would appear for me; all my applications will be

rendered fruitless; however since the meanest of Creatures by Constant Endeavor and Address sometimes finds acceptance, I shall not yet remain without hope" [SPG files, vol. 12, p. 260).

27. Trinity Church Vestry Minutes (TVM), February 2, 1707.

28. Bernard Bailyn, *Education in the Forming of American Society* (New York, 1960), 14.

29. Lawrence Cremin, *Traditions of American Education* (New York, 1977), 134.

30. Cremin, *Colonial Experience*, 20–21. The text is William Heard Kilpatrick, *The Dutch Schools of New Netherland and Colonial New York* (Washington, D.C., 1912).

31. Kammen, *Colonial New York*, 200ff.

32. SPG files, vol. 7, p. 232.

33. Or so it is reasonable to infer. He clearly took very nearly only paying students before the SPG grants started, and nothing in the grants directed him to cease taking them afterward. Presumably as valuable to him financially afterward as before, paying students must have remained in his classes if not on the SPG rosters. Nichols makes the argument that, when viewed in this paying context, the SPG grant money amounted to financial aid for forty designated students (Nichols, 2000, p. 6). Pleading for additional support, Huddleston wrote: "Having a wife and seven Children to maintain, it must needs be believed that £10 per annum will scarcely find us dry bread tho' most of my time is taken up in the discharge of that duty [to teach forty charity students]." Most, but not all. SPG files, vol. 8, p. 123.

34. SPG files, vol. 8, p. 326.

35. Wrote Huddleston to London, September 26, 1713: "I am still doing my duty in teaching the poor boyes of this city as by a Certificate herewith sent may appear which I entreate you to communicate to the Venerable Society, and in my behalf please to pray them to consider the hardship I am under, for the city will not allow me anything toward my support on that acct. so that I am reduced to extream want having a numerous family. I am heartily thankfull for their continuing my salary as before; but Hope that ye will be pleased to consider my condition and augment it; I have been now four years in the Service, and have drawn three bills of Exchange for £10 each set of Bills, two of which came back protested; but understand that one of them is since paid; but that which I last drew payable to one Mr. Headman a Merchant here I am told is not paid, which with submission I think is very hard. If you would be so kind to joyn with my friends, the Rev. Mr. Postlethwaite and Mr. Evans who I am sure will appear for me, to move for some relief for me it would be an act of very great charity to the poor under my care and also to him who is, Your obliged humble servant Wm Huddleston" (SPG files, vol. 9, p. 97).

36. New York Mayor Caleb Heathcote certified the list to the SPG, reporting that he had frequently visited the school and "found the same number of boys actually under his care" being instructed in "the English tongue, the Church Catechism, the English Liturgy and singing of Psalms with writing and arithmetick of which several are already put out to trades" (SPG files, vol. 9, pp. 179–80). The first list of "Poor Boyes":

John Lawrence Sen	John Blanchead	Thomas Kilmaster
John Baptist	John Sackett	Richard Sackett
Henry Stanton	John Deffore	John Hitchcock
Francis Warne	William Golding	John Wood
Francis Revoa	John Kilmaster	Peter Germine
John Rogers	Elisha Thebond	Job Thebond
John Martin	Robert Provoost	Stanley Holmes
Henry Lowerere	John Lowerere	Wm. Lowerere
John Cox	Thomas Cox	Jacob Cox
Edward Barnes	Israel Chaddock	Benjamin Moor
James Toy	Edward Tudor	James Jamison
George Fielding	Wm. Fielding	John Bant
Daniel Dunscomb	John Dunscomb	Samuel Dunscomb
John Boroughs		

SPG files, vol. 9, pp. 179–80.

37. SPG files, vol. 10, p. 266.

38. It is possible he was detained there for debt; whether or not, he certainly seemed to be having a hard time: "That your excellencys Petitioner at the time he received those poor boys into his School had at least £100 per annum for teaching other children of the City who paid him Quarterly but on the receiving of the poor, the other immediately left him, and being allowed only Ten pounds per annum by the Society, and only Thirty pounds of that in almost five years being paid your poor petitioner is reduced to extream want and even to confinement in the City Hall, and may it please your Excellency had not the Rev'd. Mr. Vesey collect the charity of some few good people, I and numerous family must have unavoidably Perished the last winter." From Huddleston to General Francis Nicholson, May 11, 1714 (SPG files, vol. 9, p. 213; vol. 10, p. 165; vol. 12, p. 408); also Callam, *Parsons*, 105.

39. SPG files, vol. 16, p. 261.

40. SPG files, vol. 17, p. 324; TVM, February 17, 1723.

41. Cremin, *Colonial Experience*, chapter 11, "Missions and Encounter."

42. Ibid., 551–56.

43. SPG files, vol. 10, pp. 165–67, 200ff.

44. See Kenneth A. Lockridge, *Literacy in Colonial New England* (New York, 1974); Lawrence Stone, *Past and Present* (London, 1981); Harvey J. Graff, *Legacies of Literacy* (Bloomington, 1987); Cremin, *Colonial Experience*, 546ff.

45. SPG files, A Collection of Papers, "Instructions for School-masters," 1706:
    I. That they well consider the End for which they are employ'd by the Society, viz. The instructing and disposing Children to believe and live as Christians.
    II. In order to this End, that they teach them to read truly and distinctly, that they may be capable of reading the Holy Scriptures, and other pious and useful Books, for informing their understandings and regulating their Manners.
    III. That they instruct them thoroughly in the Church-Catechism; teach them first to read it distinctly and exactly, then to learn it perfectly by heart;

endeavouring to make them understand the Sense and Meaning of it, by the Help of such Expositons, as the Society shall send over.

IV. That they teach them to Write a plain and legible Hand, in order to the fitting them for useful Employments; with as much Arithmetick, as shall be necessary to the same Purpose.

V. That they be industrious, and give constant Attendance at proper School-Hours.

VI. That they daily use, Morning and Evening, the Prayers composed for their Use in this Collection with their Scholars in the School, and teach them the Prayers and Graces composed for their Use at Home.

VII. That they oblige their Scholars to be constant at Church on the Lord's-Day, Morning and Afternoon, and at all other Times of Publick Worship; that they cause them to carry their Bibles and Prayer Books with them, instructing them how to use them there, and how to demean themselves in the several parts of worship; that they be there present with them, taking Care for their reverent and decent Behaviour, and examine them afterwards, as to what they have heard and learn'd.

VIII. That when any of their Scholars are fit for it, they recommend them to the Minister of the Parish, to be be publickly Catechized in the Church.

IX. That they take especial care of their Manners, both in their Schools, and out of them; warning them seriously of those Vices to which Children are most liable; teaching them to abhor Lying and Falsehood, and to avoid all Sorts of Evil-speaking; to love Truth and Honesty, to be Modest, Gentle, Well-behave'd, Just and Affable, and Courteous to all, their Companions; respectful to their Superiors, particularly towards all that minister in holy Things, and especially to the Minister of their Parish; and all this from a Sense and Fear of Almighty God; endeavouring to bring them in their tender Years to the Sense of Religion, which may render it the constant Principle of their Lives and Actions.

X. That they shall use all kind and gentle Methods in the Government of their Scholars, that they may be lov'd, as well as fear'd by them; and that when Correction is necessary, they make the Children to understand, that it is given them out of Kindness, for their Good, bringing them to a Sense of their Fault, as well as of their Punishment.

XI. That they frequently consult with the Minister of the Parish, in which they dwell, about the Methods of managing their Schools, and be ready to be advised by him.

XII. That they do, in their whole Conversation, shew themselves Examples of Piety and Virtue to their Scholars, and to all, with whom they shall converse.

XIII. That they be ready, as they have Opportunity, to teach and instruct the *Indians* and *Negroes*, and their children.

XIV. That they send to the Secretary of the Society, once in every six months, an Account of the State of their respective Schools, the numbers of their Scholars, with the Methods and Success of their Teaching.

46. Calam, *Parsons*, 120–22.

47. Cremin, *Colonial Experience*, 548ff.

48. Moffat, 21.

49. Seldom did he follow the reporting guidelines to the letter as laid out in the SPG's "Noticia Scholastica; or an Account to be sent every Six Months to the Society by each Schoolmaster, concerning the State of their respective Schools.

1. Attendance daily given.

2. Number of Children taught in the school.

3. Number of Children baptized in the Church of England.

4. Number of Indian and Negro Children.

5. Number of Children of Dissenting Parents.

6. Other Schools in or near the Place.

7. Of what denomination.

8. Other Employments of the Schoolmaster.

The account to be attested by the Missionary (if any upon the Spot) and by some of the Principal Inhabitants." What looked demanding on paper could be loose in administration. He was never called on it.

50. Bordonaro, 23.

51. Ian Green, *The Christian's ABC: Catechisms and Catechizing in England, 1530–1740* (Oxford, 1996), 161–64, 194–95, also *Print and Protestantism in Early Modern England* (Oxford, 2000); William Davies, *Teaching Reading in Early England* (London, 1973). Catechisms were best-sellers of the age. One subtitle, from John Boughton's *God and Man* (1623), would make good blurb copy today: "A Treatise catechistical, wherein the saving knowledge of God and man is plainly, and briefly declared, whereby such as are ignorant may be helped, to hear sermons with profit, to read the Bible or other books with judgement, to receive the Lord's Supper with comfort, to discern between truth and error with understanding, and to give an answer to their minister, or any other that shall ask them a reason of their faith,with readiness. Collected out of sacred scriptures, and the most orthodox and best approved divines ancient and modern, for the good of such as desire to be made wise to salvation and heirs of eternal life." Even pithier was John Boyes's catechism also from the early seventeenth century: "In forty questions and answers, containing principles necessary to be known for holy hearing, blessed believing, powerful praying, right receiving, well doing and dying, and life everlasting." Who, asks catechism historian Green, could resist such an offer?

52. TVM, August 21, 1709.

53. His bill for 1716: 50 primers, 25 Psalters and a quarto Common Prayer, for £1/8s (SPG files, vol. 11, p. 356).

54. Through the early modern period "writing largely remained a craft and a skill, often highly valued but not taught conjointly or sequentially with reading. It was a skill distinct from reading, in part because parchment and quills made it difficult. Similarly, the traditional emphasis on the spoken word caused reading to be linked more often with speaking" (Graff, *Legacies of Literacy*, 34–35).

55. TVM, August 10, 1747.

56. Moffat, 34.

57. Patricia C. Cohen, *A Calculating People: The Spread of Numeracy in Early America* (Chicago, 1982).

58. Bernard Bailyn, noting a decisive change in the nature of apprenticeship in seventeenth- and eighteenth-century America, hinted at in the terms of indentures whose requirement for formal schooling in addition to vocational training sent apprentices to Huddleston's school. "[T]here took place a reduction in the personal, non-vocational obligations that bound master and servant and a transfer of general educational functions to external agencies. With increasing frequency masters assigned their apprentices to teachers for instruction in rudimentary literacy and in whatever other non-vocational matters they had contracted to teach." Evening school, which mushroomed in the eighteenth century, represented the institutionalization of this trend, but clearly charity schools like Huddleston's also stood ready to serve (*Education in the Forming of American Society*, 31–33).

59. New-York Historical Society, "Indentures of Apprentices, 1718–1727, pp. 144, 149, February 1 and May 29, 1721.

60. Bordonaro, 14–20.

61. And it was at home, it is important to remember, that most colonial children received basic literacy and numeracy training, if they received it at all. Cremin calculated that there were two to seven schoolmasters in New York City in any one year during the first third of the eighteenth century. If each taught as many as fifty students, never more than 350 boys and girls would have been in school in a given year out of a childhood-age population of 1,300 to 2,100. Moreover, the English Charity School was not exclusively English. Its students included Dutch children from families that continued to worship in their own church but who did not otherwise resist encroaching English ways. The English did not need anglicanization; other ethnic groups did, and some found a pathway to it at Huddleston's school.

62. For helpful context see Joyce Goodfriend, *Before the Melting Pot: Society and Culture in New York City, 1664–1730* (Princeton, 1992).

63. Bailyn, *Education*, 21.

64. Cremin, *National Experience*, 544ff.

65. Cremin, *Traditions*, 34ff.

66. SPG files, Abstract of the Proceedings, 1711/1712, p. 48.

CHAPTER 3: THE EIGHTEENTH CENTURY:
PIOUS AND PRACTICAL LEARNING (38–63)

1. *SPG Journal*, vol. 4, p. 295.

2. SPG Letterbook A, 17, pp. 247, 312.

3. TVM, I, pp. 149–50.

4. SPG Journal V, p. 136. Except for the money bits, there was not much to distinguish son's reports from father's for deference to a patron who valued piety alongside performance: "I thought it my duty for the better satisfaction of our Benefactors to Signifie the Names of the poor Boys which I have now Actuall under my care. Since I

have been in this Service I have done my Utmost Endeavour to promote the pious de-signe of the Honorable Society and shall ever Pray that Almighty God may reward them and you with the good things of this world and the next" (May 11, 1725).

5. SPG, A 23, p. 375.

6. TVM, I, p. 161; *SPG Journal* V, p. 325.

7. SPG, B, vol. 1, p. 155.

8. Here we know he was wrong, since at any time in the 1720s the school's roll con-tained pupils from six to sixteen years of age, though of course Mrs. Huddleston sup-posedly was involved only with minding the girls. Campbell did not let go easily, how-ever, and in a "Supplement to the said Vindication" published several months later steamed on: "How basely Mr. Vesey has behaved towards Mrs. Huddleston is very well known, for he obliged her to take out the Society's bounty in good from hucksters and shopkeepers with whom Mr. Vesey dealt, to the prejudice and loss of the said Mrs. Huddleston, at least a third of the money. He has employed her son Huddleston to write out his merchants accompts for several years, and sometimes till the ringing of the last bell on Sundays, neither has he paid her, or her son, for his pains and troubles to this day; On the contrary, it was by his interest that she was disappointed of the school, which she was ten times more qualified to teach than Mr. Noxon."

9. TVM, I, January 21, 1731; *SPG Journal* V, p. 325.

10. TVM, I, pp. 168, 177.

11. TVM, I, p. 161; there is a genealogy in the New York Public Library that tells us this much of the Noxon family but not much more, and the connection with Trinity's "Thomas" is insecure. If it is the right family, then he would have been about the same age cohort as Huddleston and so in his seventies when he got the job. See Moffat, 41.

12. "Ordered that the Rector & Church Warden or one of them with Mr. John Roade, Mr. Duane, Mr. McEvers, Mr. Augustus Jay & Mr. Moore or any three of them be a Committee to visit the society's school in this City and to give proper certificates and directions relating thereto and to take care that the pious design of the Society be complied with" (TVM, I, p. 164).

13. SPG, Letter-book A, 24, p. 165.

14. See William Kemp, *Support of Schools in Colonial New York by the Society for the Propagation of the Gospel in Foreign Parts* (New York, 1913).

15. Morgan Dix, *History of the Parish of Trinity Church* (New York, 1898).

16. *SPG Journal* IX, p. 133.

17. SPG Letter-book B, 11, p. 117.

18. TVM, May 8, 1754; March 11, 1756; May 25, 1758; September 13, 1759; October 30, 1760; November 12, 1762; March 20, 1764; December 23, 1766; December 15, 1767; De-cember 19, 1768; January 11, 1769; November 15, 1770.

19. Not all bequests noted specific amounts. About £4,000 came in during Hildreth's term. TVM, I, 154, 214, 268, 272, 287, 285, 291, 195, 310, 337, 345, 384, 446, 455, 520.

20. A typical order: "Resolved that the Reverend Doctor Auchmuty and the other Gentlemen of the clergy belonging to the church be requested to preach Charity Ser-mons to make a collection for the benefit of the Charity School under the direction of

this corporation and that the Rector and church wardens do appoint the different days for that purpose giving notice thereof to the several congregations the several Sundays preceeding their Preaching the same" (TVM, November 6, 1769).

21. "On Sunday next in the Forenoon, a Charity Sermon will be preached at Trinity Church by the Reverend Mr. Barclay; and on the Sunday following in the Afternoon, a Charity Sermon will also be preached St. George's Chapel, at both which a Collection will be made towards cloathing the Charity-Scholars" (*New York Mercury*, January 3, 1757, cited in Kemp, 104).

22. On the twenty-fourth Sunday after Trinity 1760, Rector Henry Barclay preached on Galatians vi: 9–10: "Let us not be weary in well-doing: for in due Season we shall reap if we faint not. As we have therefore opportunity let us do good to all men especially unto them that are of the household of faith." It took him ten pages to get there, but he did adapt St. Paul's admonition to the cause of the charity school: "Surely I may again venture to recommend to your Beneficence one of the most noble objects of Christian charity. I mean the children here before you. Children the most endearing part of mankind, those whom we naturally find a tenderness for, and the sight of whose wants, miseries and sufferings do naturally move our compassion. Christian children members of God's family and of the household of faith, such as our Blessed Redeemer could not endure should be kept from him, but embrac'd them in his arms, and laid his hands upon them and blessed them. These children He in the tenderest manner again recommends to your care. He requires that you endeavour to the utmost of you're ability to preserve them from the contagion of an Evil and corrupt world, that ye bring them up in the nurture and admonition of the Lord, that ye dispense to their use a portion of that wealth entrusted to your hands, as good and faithful stewards. That you thus honor the Lord the Great Creator and absolute proprietor of all things with your substance, and devote some portion of the first fruits of your increase to this excellent purpose. And greater honor you cannot possibly do unto him than to endeavour that his divine image originally stamped upon man be not utterly effaced but that it be restored to its original beauty and luster on these, who for want of your friendly and pious assistance must in all probability have remained under the tyranny of Satan, but are now by your charity put into the state of arising to the true and saving knowledge of God and Jesus Christ."

Then the flattery: "These children who by the loss of indigence of their parents, were destitute of the necessaries of Life and exposed to the rigor and severity of the winter, are now by your Beneficence comfortably cloathed, and enjoy great privilege of a virtuous and Christian education, to the unspeakable benefit not only of the children themselves but also to the publick peace, safety and happiness of the community of which they are members. For it must be confessed that the extirpating of ignorance and idleness, of dishonesty and impiety and the promoting of knowledge, industry, probity and piety and all kinds of virtue is the best method of promoting the peace and happiness of society. This is the design of the charity now recommended."

Then the evidence: "The happy influence whereof has been already visible in several youths that have been educated in this school, whose behaviour is a credit to it. [He did not name names.] Some being useful tradesmen, others faithful apprentices to merchants and mechanics, others qualified to enter the service of either as opportunity arises. The school is very regularly and punctually attended by the master, frequently visited by a committee of the vestry. The scholars publickly examined, and it may with justice be said that they make as good proficiency in general as any children of like age and standing."

He reported additional money was needed because twenty more children were being taught than "first stipulated and upon account of the much greater expense of living at present. Firewood, paper and other necessaries make an additional expense. We have indeed great reason to bless God, who continues to raise up friends to the design, who by considerable legacys have laid a good foundation for a fund, which we hope will in time be sufficient to convert this school into an hospital for feeding as well as cloathing poor orphans and helpless children. [Nothing more was heard of this.] May God raise up many such benefactors and may their memory be blessed by the latest posterity. In the meantime my brethren you must permit us to depend upon your voluntary annual contributions, and blessed be God we have no reason to doubt, but that they will always prove sufficient as they have hitherto done; for we have great reason to bless God on your account that we have not only at all times found amongst you a readiness to assist in promoting this blessed work, but your contributions have always exceeded those of the former year." The piety sounds dated, not the psychology (Barclay Sermons, Trinity Parish Archives).

23. A "play-tragedy" called "The Orphan," and a comedy called "The Committee, or the Faithful Irishman." New-York Historical Society Collections, 1870, pp. 156, 182–83.

24. TVM, I, p. 250, April 15, 1748.

25. *Ibid.*, May 3, 1748.

26. SPG Letter-book B, 16, p. 54, November 6, 1748.

27. Morgan Dix, *History of the Parish of Trinity Church in the City of New York*, I, 226ff. His portrait hangs in the museum of Trinity Church.

28. *Ibid.*, p. 55. The vestry directed "that Col. Robinson (Churchwarden) furnish and pay such moneys as shall be necessary (over and above the subscriptions) for carrying on and compleating the building of the Public School" (TVM, I, p. 254).

29. SPG Letter-book B, 18, p. 100, April 6, 1750.

30. Morgan Dix, *History of the Parish of Trinity Church*, I, p. 252. The scene depicting the fire in the schoolhouse leaping across to the church steeple is commemorated in silver on a bowl by A. Bancker in the Metropolitan Museum of Art. It is inscribed, directly: "This Hapen'd, Feb'y 23, 1749/50."

31. TVM, I, April 18, 1768.

32. TVM, I, p. 398. The numbers would support the supposition that there was another schoolhouse. Three times in 1768, the Trinity vestry voted a total of £2,100 for work on "the parsonage and the schoolhouse," an amount that should easily have covered the renovations to the second schoolhouse, cost of a "temporary" schoolhouse, and of a third "permanent" one (TVM, April 22, July 7, November 7).

33. See Edwin G. Burrows and Mike Wallace, *Gotham: A History of New York City to 1898* (New York, 1999), 167–72.

34. *Ibid.*, 176–77.

35. See Morgan Dix, *History of the Parish of Trinity Church*, I, p. 472, Appendix 3: "Queen Anne's Grant," and II, Appendix 9: "A History of the Title to King's Farm and the Litigation Thereon," 293ff. The thence-ever-after greatly remarked wealth of Trinity Church, originating in the form of land once a farm, foreshadows, even mocks, Trinity School's similar good-fortune-turned-missed-fortune at the end of the eighteenth century with bequest of other Manhattan farmland also destined to be priceless but whose value to the school strangely slip away.

36. Robert A. McCaughey, *Stand Columbia: A History of Columbia University in the City of New York, 1754–2004* (New York, 2003), 20.

37. SPG Letter-book B, 3, p. 156.

38. *Gotham*, 220–21.

39. *Ibid.*, 232.

40. *Ibid.*, 242.

41. George Washington, who watched the spectacle from Harlem Heights, was not above taking rueful satisfaction: "Providence, or some good honest fellow, has done more for us than we were disposed to do for ourselves" (*ibid.*).

42. SPG Letter-book B, 3, p. 171, October 6, 1776.

43. TVM, I, pp. 397–98.

44. SPG Letter-book B, 2, p. 71, May 10, 1777.

45. SPG Letter-book B, 2, p. 71.

46. "A good man of unblemished moral character, of steady Loyalty, a good English scholar, writes a fair hand, is well skilled in Church Music, and has an excellent voice. He has taught psalmody in this city for some years, and we instrumental in improving many Members of the congregation in that part of Divine Worship" (Inglis to SPG).

47. TVM, I, April 11, 1780, p. 414.

48. He later lived in Hartford as a teacher and choirmaster (Moffat, 63).

49. SPG secretary William Morrice wrote to Inglis, August 6, 1782: "I must confess to you, that had it [the request of the £15 allowance] not been pressed by yourself, I don't think the Society would have adopted the measure so readily. Many members were of opinion, that so considerable a place did not want that assistance, and that it had been too long allowed by the Society. Something of this you will perceive in the Resolution of the Board 'That the salary be allowed in consideration of the present unsettled state of affairs but that inquiry be made into the annual emoluments of the schoolmaster, exclusive of the Society's bounty, as it appears extraordinary that any assistance should be wanting to support a school at New York.' You will be so kind therefore as to give me some satisfaction on these points. Be assured of this, that the Society are always disposed to do everything in their power for the promoting of religion, and in the distribution of their benevolence would wish always to have it place where it is absolutely necessary, and where it can be of most effective use" (TVM, I, p. 428).

50. *Ibid.*, April 15, 1782 through February 21, 1783.

51. Moffat, 65. Inglis's likeness too hangs in the Trinity Church museum.

52. Of similar vintage were the charity schools of the Dutch and the Jews. See Henry

W. Dunshee, *History of the School of the Reformed Protestant Dutch Church in the City of New York, 1633–1883* (New York, 1883) and David and Tamar de sola Pool, *An Old Truth in the New World: Portrait of Shearith Israel, 1654–1954* (New York, 1955).

53. Jackson Turner Main, *The Social Structure of Revolutionary America* (Princeton, 1965), 278; Carl F. Kaestle, *Evolution of an Urban School System, 1750–1850* (Cambridge, 1973), 3–5.

54. Between mid-century and outbreak of the Revolution, perhaps 200 New York men (no women) attended college, or about 5 percent of the age group, with 120 attending King's, two Yale, and none Harvard or William & Mary.

55. Kaestle, 41ff.

56. Lawrence Cremin, *American Education: The National Experience, 1783–1876* (New York, 1980); Diane Ravitch, *The Great School Wars: New York City, 1805–1973* (New York, 1974)

57. Quintilian on the "Comparative Merits of Private and Public Instruction": "The future orator whose life is to be spent in great assemblies and in the blaze of public life, become accustomed from his earliest years to face men unabashed and not grow pale by living in solitude." Plato thought public was better too. Cited in Kaestle, 16.

58. TVM, I, p. 254.

59. Given high inflation and Wood's large family, the vestry again relented on this point, and the practice was the norm. Most New York schoolmasters taught in more than one venue, or did something else in addition to teaching.

60. The name migrated about during Wood's tenure, with the school being referred to as the "free School, "the first charity school," the "Episcopal Charity School," and the "Protestant Episcopal Charity School." With independence, American Anglicans changed their name, too, if not their spots; "Episcopal" or "Protestant Episcopal" replaced "Church/Church of England/Anglican" usages.

61. Following, see Samuel S. Randall, *History of the Common School System of the State of New York* (New York, 1871); and Elsie G. Hobson, *Educational Legislation and Administration in the State of New York, 1777–1850* (Chicago, 1918).

62. New York County's share came out to £1,888, which meant a local property-tax match of £944.

63. Moffat, 81; Kaestle, 60ff.

64. The first—"Thou shalt love the Lord thy God with all thy heart, soul, and mind"—was the job of worship and prayer.

65. The indenture describing the arrangement is dated June 21, 1800 (TVM). The purpose of the school, as reiterated, remained as in SPG days "to train the children of the indigent members of the said Church in the paths of virtue and piety and instruct them in the elements of useful learning and render them profitable members of the society to which they belong."

66. The others: orphans and other poor children of other denominations.

67. Trinity settled on the school designated property in addition to the schoolhouse and a fund for its annual expenditure. The property consisted of land "bounded on the south by rector Street in length 172 feet—by Greenwich Street on the west 108 feet 10

inches—by Lots No. 27 and No. 3 on the North and by Lumber Street on the East, including the Charity School House and Grounds now appropriated to its use." This property then yielded an income of £67 per year "and at the expiration of the present leases will be of infinitely more value." The fund consisted of bonds and mortgages valued at £8,610, which at 7 percent yielded £602. "It is the opinion of the committee that the above mentioned premises should be granted in fee to the trustees of the said Episcopal Charity School which the committee hope will be forever reserved and the income applied to its use. The preceding appropriations with the addition of revenue arising from the annual charity Sermons [anticipated at £150] and other contingencies which the trustees aforesaid must eventually receive will certainly en able them to meet all the present wants and probably in future furnish them with the means of extending its beneficent influence." Average annual expenses for the school were £700, against this total provision of £820 (TVM, II, June 13, 1800).

It wasn't quite enough, however. Less than a year later, and working in dollars, the church had to top things up. The take from charity sermons was slipping, and the church substituted rents from more land and a $1,000 note from the Bank of New York: "the committee are of opinion if this aid be afforded the institution, no further assistance will be required of this corporation so long as the institution is conducted on its present establishment" (March 9, 1801).

68. "The present charity school is founded for the common benefit of all the Episcopalians of the City, it is governed by its own Trustees, and not by Trinity Church, it is therefore expected that annual collections will be made in all the churches towards the support of this school; and should others be necessary that they be founded on the same cooperative principle." So there (TVM, April 14, 1808).

CHAPTER 4: NINETEENTH-CENTURY INCARNATION:
CHARITY TO EPISCOPAL SCHOOL (64–114)

1. Edwin G. Burrows and Mike Wallace, *Gotham: A History of New York City to 1898* (New York: Oxford University Press, 1999).

2. See Robert H. Bremner, *From the Depths: The Discovery of Poverty in the United States* (New York: New York University Press, 1956); Robert Ernst, *Immigrant Life in New York City, 1825–1863* (New York: King's Crown Press, 1949); and Raymond A. Mohl, *Poverty in New York, 1783–1825* (New York: Oxford University Press, 1971).

3. Hence the theme of Allan Stanley Horlick, *Country Boys and Merchant Princes: The Social Control of Young Men in New York* (Lewisburg, Pa.: Bucknell University Press, 1975).

4. See Sean Wilentz, *Chants Democratic: New York City and the Rise of the American Working Class, 1788–1850* (New York: Oxford University Press, 1984), *passim*.

5. Interpretation shaped here by Diane Ravitch, *The Great School Wars: A History of the New York City Public Schools* (Baltimore: Johns Hopkins University Press, 1974).

6. Where arguably it reached back to the 1640s and the first laws that directed towns to establish elementary schools and was reiterated after the Revolution, when New England pioneered tax-supported district schools.

7. See chapter 3.

8. Ravitch, *Great School Wars*, p. 6.

9. Sydney V. James, *A People Among Peoples: Quaker Benevolence in Eighteenth Century America* (Cambridge, Mass.: Harvard University Press, 1963); A. Emerson Palmer, *The New York Public School* (New York, 1905); and Carl F. Kaestle, *The Evolution of an Urban School System: New York City, 1750–1850* (Cambridge, Mass.: Harvard University Press, 1973), 82. One of the society's original patrons, Mathew Clarkson, was president of the Bank of New York and a parishioner of Trinity Church, a lone Episcopalian among Friends.

10. Ravitch, *Great School Wars*, p. 10. See also William O. Bourne, *History of the Public School Society of the City of New York* (New York: W. Wood, 1870); and William W. Cutler, "Philosophy, Philanthropy and Public Education: A Social History of the New York Public School Society, 1805–1853" (Ph.D. dissertation, Cornell University, 1960).

11. The sensibility of a "waning elite," see Michael B. Katz, *The Irony of Early School Reform: Educational Innovation in Mid-Nineteenth Century Massachusetts* (Cambridge, Mass.: Harvard University Press, 1968) and Kaestle, *Evolution*, which saw in tax-supported public schooling means to control as well as uplift the lower classes.

12. Kaestle, *Evolution*, 8ff.

13. The system is described and illustrated briefly in *Centuries of Childhood in New York: A Celebration on the Occasion of the 275th Anniversary of Trinity School* (New York: New York Historical Society and Trinity School, 1985), 23–24.

14. See Carl F. Kaestle, ed., *Joseph Lancaster and the Monitorial School Movement: A Documentary History* (New York: Teachers College Press, 1973).

15. Kaestle, 82–83; Bourne, *Public School Society*, 36ff.

16. The Female Association continued to operate in parallel with the Free School Society and at first used the same building but a separate room. It was absorbed in the then Public School Society in 1845, though class segregation by sex, at parents' insistence, continued for many years. Land for the second Free School Society school building, at Hudson and Christopher streets, was donated by Trinity Church (Bourne, *Public School Society*, 22ff.

17. Board of Trustees minutes, January 12, 1808; Jean Parker Waterbury, *A History of Collegiate School, 1638–1963* (New York: Clarkson N. Potter, Inc., 1965), 73–81.

18. Board of Trustee minutes, November 2 and 16, 1808, Trinity School Archive. The "School Committee" minutes from these years, as referenced in Edward Moffat's dissertation from which this discussion draws, are missing (Edward Stewart Moffat, Trinity School, New York City, 1709–1959, Ph.D diss., Columbia University, 1963).

19. See David Salmon, ed., *The Practical Parts of Lancaster's* Improvements *and Bell's* Experiment (Cambridge: Cambridge University Press, 1932).

20. Lancaster and Bell ended up hating one another, though in the beginning Lancaster admitted, after a manner, his indebtedness to Bell. Bell's *Experiment* came into his hands in 1800, and in the first edition of his own *Improvements* Lancaster wrote: "I ought not to close my account without acknowledging the obligation I lie under to Dr. Bell of the Male Asylum at Madras, who so nobly gave up is time and liberal salary,

that he might perfect that institution, which flourished greatly under his fostering care. He published a tract in 1798. . . . From this publication I have adopted several useful *hints*; I beg leave to recommend it to the attentive perusal of the friends of education and of youth. . . . I much regret that I was not acquainted with the beauty of his system till somewhat advanced in my plan; if I had known it, it would have saved me much trouble and some retrograde movements. As a confirmation of the goodness of Dr. Bell's plan, I have succeeded with one nearly similar in a school attended by more than 300 children." (Bell claimed he could educate a thousand children with one teacher and the assistance of monitors.) Salmon, *Practical Parts*, xxiii. It could be, and probably was, that both men happened on the same ideas more or less at the same time. For teachers facing more students than they could handle, some version or other of a monitorial system was only common sense.

21. There was another book—the "Black Book"—kept of disciplinary infringements. Despite the dark title, it was a jury of good boys who Bell said should best "try" culprits: "It is essential to the wellbeing of the school that its rewards and punishments, which are left to discretion and circumstances, be administered with equal and distributive justice. It is not to be forgotten that temperate and judicious correction is more effectual than that which is intemperate and severe; that praise, encouragement, and favour, are to be tried before dispraise, shame, and disgrace; confinement between school hours, and on holidays and play-days, which your teachers enable you to inflict, is to preferred to corporal punishment; and even solitary confinement to severe flagellation" (Bell's *Experiment*, chapter 5, Salmon, 76).

22. *Experiment*, chapters 8 and 9.

23. See Henry James Burgess, *Enterprise in Education: The Story of the Work of the Established Church in the Education of the People prior to 1870* (London, 1958), 27ff.

24. Both Lancaster and Bell had big visions of social consequences. Bell: "The advantages of this system, in its political, moral, and religious tendency; in its economy of labour, time, expense and punishment; in the facilities and satisfaction it affords to the master and the scholar; can only be ascertained by trial and experience, and can scarcely be comprehended or credited by those who have not witnessed its powers and marvelous effects. Like the steam engine, or spinning machinery, it diminished labour and multiplies work, but in a degree which does not admit of the same limits, and scarcely of the same calculation as they do. For, unlike mechanical powers, this intellectual and moral engine, the more work it has to perform, the greater is the facility and expedition with which it is performed, and the greater is the degree of perfection to which it is carried." Cited in Denis Lawton and Peter Gordon, *A History of Western Educational Ideas* (London: Woburn Press, 2002), "Industrialism, Nationalism and the Cult of Efficiency," 117.

25. Into their considerations probably also figured, though the connection is not explicit, the decision also in 1821 to abandon the school's limited but costly boarding program, thus reducing yearly expenses by a quarter, to around $3,000 (Board of Trustees minutes, January 19 and May 21, 1821).

26. Burrows and Wallace, *Gotham*, 374.

27. Board of Trustees minutes, December 1821; Powell Mills Dawley, *The Story of the General Theological Seminary: A Sesquicentennial History, 1817–1967* (New York: Oxford University Press, 1969).

28. Board of Trustees minutes, February 10, 1824.

29. The source of that funding was not without humor given the society's appeal, which stressed the need to save New York's poor children from "the contagion of bad example" and from becoming "pests to society."

30. Summarizing the arguments: "A Circular to the Friends of the Education of the Poor in the City of New York on the Subject of a Bill now before the Legislature, Relative to the Distribution of the Common School Fund," New York, 1824; Moffatt diss., 90ff.; Kaestle, *Evolution*, 85ff.

31. Again, De Witt Clinton took the nonsectarian side: "The obtrusion of Charity Schools on our System has done much evil. I was opposed to it from the start—but how to get rid of it is difficult." Kaestle, *Evolution*, 86, and Charles J. Mahoney, *The Relation of the State to Religious Education in Early New York, 1633–1825* (Washington, D.C.: Catholic University Press, 1941).

32. Of all New York state jurisdictions, New York City was the last to provide for the maintenance of schools from a real estate levy, relying up to then solely on the common school fund, matching city grants and private philanthropy (Ravitch, *Great School Wars*, 24).

33. Ravitch, *Great School Wars*, esp. chapters 4–8.

34. Wilentz, *Chants Democratic*; Burrows and Wallace, *Gotham*, chapter 31.

35. Other adjectives could and did in different times and places apply. In the United States in the second half of the twentieth century, private schools increasingly styled themselves as "independent" schools. In Britain and Europe, public schools (in the American sense) were "state" schools.

36. Collegiate reached the same conclusion as Trinity. See Waterbury, *Collegiate School*, 86.

37. Laws of New York, April 16, 1827; Charter, Trinity School Archives.

38. Trustee Minutes, May 1832.

39. On schooling and mobility, see Kaestle, 94ff.

40. Visitor's Report of John McVickar to Board of Trustees, November 1832.

41. Board of Trustees minutes, December 21, 1826; Moffat, 107. For the curricula of the New England academies, see Theodore R. Sizer, ed., *The Age of the Academies* (New York: New York Bureau of Publications, Teachers College, Columbia University, 1964).

42. Certainly this was trustee John McVickar's interest later in the decade. See later discussion and also Moffat, 113.

43. Trustee Minutes, May 21, 1838, Trinity School Archive.

44. Robert A. McCaughey, *Stand Columbia: A History of Columbia University in the City of New York, 1754–2004* (New York: Columbia University Press, 2003), chapter 3, esp. 80–87.

45. Moffat summaries, unannotated, 133.

46. Moffat dwells on them, 86 and 130ff.

47. Trustee Minutes, May 1830, 1832.

48. Moffat, 131

49. Trustee Minutes, May 1836 and May 1837, Trinity School Archive.

50. Burrows and Wallace, *Gotham*, chapters 36–37, esp. 613–21.

51. The documentary trail to Morris is very faint. According to records in the archive of the Episcopal Diocese of New York at the Cathedral of St. John the Divine, Morris was ordained a deacon in Rensselaerville, New York, in 1835 and a priest the following year. We thank Wayne Kempton, archivist of the Diocese, for his assistance in tracking down Morris and other Trinity School masters.

52. Trustee Minutes, May 1827.

53. On McVickar's life and career, see John Brett Langstaff, *The Enterprising Life: John McVickar, 1787–1868* (New York: St. Martin's Press, 1961). This volume, alas, says very little about McVickar's relationship with Trinity School but see pp. 31–32. McVickar was a perennially unsuccessful candidate for the presidency of Columbia. See McCaughey, *Stand Columbia*, 89–92 and 95. On his Jacksonian political views, see Wilentz, *Chants Democratic*, 277–78, and Paul Keith Conkin, *Prophets of Prosperity: America's First Political Economists* (Bloomington: University of Indiana Press, 1980), 111–15.

54. Moffat, diss., 138–39 and 314. The provision in the 1806 charter became an issue again during attempts to sell Baker Farm. See later discussion.

55. Trustee minutes, February 2, 1852.

56. "Rules in regard to Benefices," Plan of School, 1841. Such records have not survived in the TS Archive.

57. Nowhere is there explanation for the difference. Older boys, more clothes?

58. Taken from the "Plan of School," 1841, as close as we can come to the start of the new arrangements (TS Archives). Any alteration in the plan required approval of the Corporation of Trinity Church. In the nineteenth century, it did not change much.

59. George Messiter, *History of the Choir and Music of Trinity Church, New York from its Organization to the Year 1897* (New York: Edwin S. Gorham, 1906), 42; Moffat, 140–43.

60. Minutes, May 22, 1858.

61. Collegiate was one such: see Waterbury, *History of Collegiate School*, 91–92.

62. Burrows and Wallace, Gotham, 459, 655; Roy Rosenzweig and Elizabeth Blackmar, *The Park and the People: A History of Central Park* (Ithaca: Cornell University Press, 1992), 27. St. John's Church was torn down in 1918–19. Today the site is near the exit of the Holland Tunnel.

63. The nearest Trinity Church chapel of ease was Trinity Chapel on 25th Street, west of Broadway.

64. Trustee minutes, May 1, 1857, and May 22, 1858.

65. Allan Nevins and Milton Halsey Thomas, eds., *The Diary of George Templeton Strong*, Vol. 2, *The Turbulent Fifties, 1850–1859* (New York: Macmillan, 1952), entry for November 14, 1859.

66. Quotations in this paragraph and the next come from "One Hundred and Fiftieth Anniversary of Trinity School" leaflet, Trinity Church Archive.

67. On Morris, see Neil Grauer, "The Six Who Built Hopkins," *Johns Hopkins Magazine* (April 2000), online edition, accessed April 25, 2006. On his appointment, see Trustee minutes, June 5, 1857. This early faculty included Robert Holden (an alumnus), first teacher of classics; W. M. Ferris, second teacher; P. E. Farnsworth, third in English; Charles Bradbury, fourth in math; a "Monsieur" l'Oeust who taught French; and James Johnson, in music (School Committee minutes, 1859).

68. James Elliott Lindsley, *This Planted Vine: A Narrative History of the Episcopal Diocese of New York* (New York: Harper & Row, 1984), 191–92.

69. Burrows and Wallace, *Gotham*, 869, 887–99, esp. 895. See also Leslie M. Harris, *In the Shadow of Slavery: African Americans in New York City, 1626–1863* (Chicago: University of Chicago Press, 2003), chapter 9.

70. *Supra*, n. 61.

71. Moffat, diss., 153, quoting *Acta Diurna*, January 1899, 26–27.

72. Moffat, diss., 159–160; obituary, *New York Times*, March 13, 1901; records of Holden's ordinations at the Diocese of New York archives.

73. Based on an estimate of an average of twenty-five to thirty *new* students arriving each year. The number was higher in certain periods—the 1820s and 1830s, for example—but also lower for long stretches. Complicating the estimate is the fact that we simply do not know how many students attended for part of a year or who attended off and on over several years.

74. Moffat, diss., 145; *Ephemerida*, November 1891.

75. Langstaff, *The Enterprising Life*, 389–90.

76. Sam Davis Elliott, ed., *Doctor Quintard, Chaplain C.S.A. and Second Bishop of Tennessee: The Memoir and Civil War Diary of Charles Todd Quintard* (Baton Rouge: Louisiana State University Press, 2003), 9–10. Some of Bishop Quintard's writings are available on online at http://anglicanhistory.org/usa/ctquintard (accessed April 25, 2006).

77. Maury Klein, *The Life and Legend of E. H. Harriman* (Chapel Hill: University of North Carolina Press, 2000), 29–32. Klein mistakes Harriman's age at the start of his Trinity years—ten, not twelve, and also errs in saying that Harriman spent only two years at the school and that his parents scraped together the funds to pay for it. See also *Centuries of Childhood in New York City*, 29–30. Harriman's sons Averill and Roland co-founded Harriman & Co., a private bank that merged with another in 1931 to form Brown Brothers Harriman & Co. Averill Harriman later served as governor of New York and unsuccessfully pursued nomination for president as a Democrat. Toward the end of his long life, he was a leading U.S. diplomat.

78. "Torrens Law Fixes Title," *New York Times*, July 17, 1921, 84.

79. See sketch legal history of the Charity School of Trinity Church and the New York Protestant Episcopal Public School, Jackson Fuller Nash & Brophy, 1925 (Trinity Church archives). Also Record of deeds of New York Protestant Episcopal School property (Trinity School archives).

80. Trustee minutes, March 19, 1855, March 10, 1856, and March 23, 1857.

81. *Diary*, II, May 11, 1857.

82. *Diary*, April 3, 1859.

83. *Diary*, II, April 12, 1859.

84. *Diary*, II, April 19, 1859. Also Strong report to Trustees, April 9, 1859.

85. *Diary*, Vol. III, *The Civil War, 1860–1865* (New York: Macmillan, 1952), November 15, 1860.

86. See *The People v. The Rector etc of Trinity Church et al*, 22 New York 44 (1860), and *In re Trustees of the New York Protestant Episcopal Public School . . .* 31 New York 574 (1864), which involved the provision in the Baker will whereby after devising all his real estate in life estates to a number of persons, the remainder went to the governor in fee simple, in trust, to receive rents and apply them to the education of charity scholars of the charity school under the care of Trinity Church. The court held that the devise to the governor and all future governors was extinguished by the 1806 Act and that the remainder was duly vested in the school corporation. Assessments remained a thorn, however. See *In re Petition of New York Protestant Episcopal Public School to Vacate Certain Assessment for Sewers*, 47 New York 556 (1872), where the school fought payment of assessments on property in Yorkville imposed by the Croton Aqueduct Board. See Wolcott B. Dunham, Jr., "Legal History of the Trinity School in the 19th Century," 2002 (Trinity School Archives).

87. Trustee Minutes, May 1865 (Trinity School Archives). The new address under a different numbering system was 467 Eighth Avenue. Moffat, diss., 161, has a brief description of the building.

88. Trustee Minutes, December 12, 1866; May 1, 1870; May 7, 1877, (Trinity School Archives).

89. Trinity financial records, 1880s (TS Archives). There was a converging trend, however: In 1866, downtown rents were about $7,000, the Baker Farm $300. In 1875 downtown was $9,000, the Farm about $6,000; in 1883 the spread was $13,000 and $8,000.

90. Annual statement of accounts, 1885, and minutes (Trinity School archives).

91. The location was also described as 1477 or 1521 Broadway.

92. Attendance was a serious matter, a boy's admission to Trinity a privilege not a right: "The Rector wishes to impress upon Parents the importance of a careful scrutiny of these reports. An abstract of them is periodically laid before the Trustees, and their attention is specially called to the regularity or irregularity of each boy's attendance. It is the fixed resolution of the Board not to suffer any boy to continue to share in the bounty of the school, who does not, by his conduct, diligence and punctuality, show that he and his parents appreciate and are anxious to retain the advantages of his position." Report of M. McGeachy from June 1859 (Trinity School Archives).

93. Trinity School notice, undated but from Holden's tenure [1863–1890].

94. Trinity School Archives Student Registers, 1850s through 1890s.

95. Trinity School Archives

96. Moffat, diss., 167 reported record, now lost, of a conversation (undated) between a long-retired Stevenson and Miss Martha Wadsworth of Trinity School. In 1963, two Trinity boys interviewed Stevenson in a Vermont nursing home "to help him celebrate

his one hundredth birthday" (*Alumni Bulletin*, December 1963). Stevenson memorabilia including religion exercise books was contained in a school time capsule opened in 1966.

97. George Stevenson religious notebooks (Trinity School Archives).

98. For Butler's career, see. McCaughey, *Stand Columbia*, esp. chapter 7; and Allan S. Horlick, *Patricians, Professors, and Public Schools: the Origins of Modern Educational Thought in America* (New York, E. J. Brill, 1994), chapter 5.

99. Cremin, *The Transformation of the School*, and Ravitch, *Great School Wars*.

100. Secretary [William Eigenbrodt] to board, May 3, 1886 (Trinity School Archives).

101. Trustee Minutes, May 2, 1887 (Trinity School Archives).

102. On the development of the Upper West Side, see Francis J. Sypher, Jr., *St. Agnes Chapel of the Parish of Trinity Church in the City of New York 1892–1943* (New York: Trinity Church, 2002), chapter 1; Peter Salwen, *Upper West Side Story: A History and Guide* (New York: Abbeville Press, 1989), *passim*; also chapter 5 of this volume. For the location of the cathedral, see Lindsley, *This Planted Vine*, 203–204; on Columbia's move, see McCaughey, *Stand Columbia*, 205–208.

103. Trustee Minutes, May 6, 1894.

104. Trustee Minutes, May 6, 1889 (TS Archive); Moffat, 194.

105. Trustee Minutes, May 5, 1890 (Trinity School Archives).

106. Trustee Minutes, May 5, 1890 (Trinity School Archives).

107. Trustee Minutes, November 3, 1890, and February 2, 1891 (Trinity School Archives).

108. On Ulmann, see Moffat, 175–76; ordination records at the diocesan archive, Episcopal Diocese of New York.

109. Information in this and next paragraph is drawn from the previously named publications, which are also summarized in Moffat, 181–87 and 189–94.

110. Quoted in "Trinity School to Move," *The New York Times*, February 12, 1893, 17.

111. McCaughey, *Stand Columbia!*, chapter 5, and references there cited to contemporaneous developments at Harvard, University of Chicago, Cornell, Johns Hopkins, and other pioneering institutions.

112. The course in 1893: Prima: Religion, Greek, Latin, English, French, Geography, History, Mathematics; Secunda: Religion, Chemistry, German, Physics, English, Algebra, Trigonometry; Tertia: Religion, History, German, Geography, Greek, Latin, French, Arithmetic; Quarta: Religion, English, Latin, German, English, History, Geography, Arithmetic; Qunita: Religion, English, Latin, German, Arithmetic, Geography, History; Sexta: Religion, Arithmetic, History, Spelling, Language (Annual examinations schedule, Trinity School Archives).

113. "Two Methods in Teaching," *New York Times*, April 11, 1897, 7.

114. *Ephemerida*, October 1891, ff.

115. The literature on this topic is vast. A place to begin is with Jon H. Roberts, *Darwinism and the Divine in America: Protestant Intellectuals and Organic Evolution* (Madison: University of Wisconsin Press, 1988).

116. And so, a few years before Ulmann, George Stevenson had recited his St. Paul in the original tongue.

117. *Acta Diurna*, February 1893, ff.

118. He also understood something about the temptations of chronological snobbery. "Every generation has labored under the mistake that it had reached the zenith of knowledge and has considered its conclusions and reasoning final and *all correct*, until the succeeding generation took a step upward and forward. . . . Now our own generation is sadly afflicted with that peculiar kind of myopia which persuades a man that he has reached the top-most round of the ladder and that there is nothing above him and beyond him. This assumption puffs him up with pride and when he actually meets with a fact which defies his tethered reason and transcends his knowledge he throws it overboard, and in this summary way gets rid of it. Would it not be far better to grant that there may be a higher, a divine knowledge according of which, if we could only acquire it, any miracle could be as easily explained as the simplest chemical experiment? To believe that there may be a divine power which can raise the dead as easily as the feeble hand of the mechanic can raise the hundred ton trip hammer."

119. For Butler's career, see Robert A. McCaughey, *Stand Columbia: A History of Columbia University in the City of New York, 1754–2004* (New York: Columbia University Press, 2004), esp. chapter 7; and Allan S. Horlick, *Patricians, Professors, and Public Schools: The Origins of Modern Educational Thought in America* (New York, E. J. Brill, 1994), chapter 5.

120. Cremin, *The Transformation of the School*, and Ravitch, *School Wars*.

121. Wrote New Yorker and American political historian Richard Hofstadter of the radicalism of the reformers: "They were not content to say that the realities of American social life had made it necessary to compromise with the ideal of education as the development of formal learning and intellectual capacity. Instead, they militantly proclaimed that such education was archaic and futile and the noblest end of a truly democratic system of education was to meet the child's immediate interests by offering him a series of immediate utilities" [*Anti-Intellectualism in American Life* (New York, 1962), 328].

122. Ravitch, *Wars*, 170.

123. *Ibid.*, 171.

124. *Acta Diurna*, April/May 1893.

125. First records of such activities are found in *Acta Diurna*, 1892–93, and are recounted in Moffatt.

126. *New York Times*, February 12, 1893, 17.

127. *Acta Diurna*, March 1895.

CHAPTER 5: EPISCOPAL TWILIGHT (115–151)

1. *Trinity School Yearbook*, 1920–21, 11.

2. *New York Times*, December 4, 2005.

3. Following, yearbooks and memoir of Clarence Bruner Smith, *Over the Past 60 Years*, May 1992.

4. His thesis was published as *The Basis of Early Christian Theism*, Columbia University Contributions to Philosophy, Psychology and Education, 1898 (*Who's Who, 1937–38*).

5. *Who's Who*, 1910s–1930s.

6. Memoir, 8.

7. Memoir, 17.

8. Moffat, 207. Sources cited there of faculty meeting notes and Ulmann record books no longer extant.

9. These events must have hit Ulmann hard. His next job was clearly a lesser one (assistant principal of the Callison School), and he then left teaching altogether and returned to parish work as assistant rector of St. Augustine's, Croton-on-Hudson.

10. *Trinity School Yearbooks*, 1903ff.

11. St. Agatha, Trinity's sister school established in 1898 and operated as part of the same corporation, was marginally smaller, over the same years enrolling 110 (1903), 214 (1912), 256 (1919), 268 (1926), 264 (1931), and 207 (1936). See later discussion.

12. *Trinity School Yearbooks*, 1903ff.

13. *Trinity School Yearbooks*, 1903ff.

14. It is speculation, but plausible that Ulmann's departure owed something to this change.

15. See Robert A. MCaugthey, *Stand, Columbia* (New York, 2004), 277ff.

16. *Trinity School Yearbook*, 1913–14.

17. Moffat, p. 233.

18. *Acta Diurna*, June 1904.

19. *Ibid.*

20. Trinity Catalog, 1920–21.

21. Steven Cobb, class of 1936, came to Trinity in 1924 and ate a lot of it. Interview, December 9, 2006.

22. *Acta Diurna*, 1909–1925 (Trinity School Archives).

23. *Acta Diurna*, June 1918.

24. Steven Cobb, interview, December 9, 2006.

25. *Acta Diurna*, June 1919.

26. *Ibid.*

27. *Acta Diurna*, June 1909.

28. Trinity School dramatics bulletin, 1923.

29. Trinity School dramatics bulletin, 1919.

30. *Acta Diurna*, June 1919, from *New York Evening Sun*, February 7, 1919.

31. Clear records here begin in 1910, but are not sustained year by year.

32. *Acta Diurna* senior class listings, June issues, 1910ff.

33. *Ibid.*

34. *Ibid.*

35. Trinity School, 1937–1938, Directory (Trinity School Archives).

36. *Acta Diurna*, 1906–31.

37. *Acta Diurna*, 1918.

38. Source history: Francis J. Sypher, Jr., "St. Agnes Chapel, 1892–1943," Trinity Church, 2002.

39. See "St. Agnes Chapel Day School, *The Message*, Trinity Church New York, Ascension 1919. (There is no primary record of this.)

40. Sypher, 81.

41. *Ibid.*, 83.

42. Nor did St. Agnes feel the cold wind alone: Trinity Chapel at Madison Square and St. Augustine's Chapel on East Houston also were destined to go.

43. See Ira Rosenwaike, *Population History of New York City* (Syracuse, 1972), 90–130, for the period 1900–1940.

44. Sypher, 93ff.

45. St. Agatha 1940–41 Yearbook, Diocese of New York Archives.

46. *Ibid.*

47. Kevin D. Ramsey, "St. Agatha Day School for Girls," *Trinity Per Saecula*, 1998; St. Agatha Archives, Episcopal Diocese of New York. Toward the end of its life, in an effort to boost enrollment, St. Agatha's added a secretarial course and even admitted boys to the first four grades.

48. NYPES "Income received from Investments," chart, Episcopal Diocese of New York archives.

49. Following: Trinity School financial reports, Trinity Church archives.

50. "Trinity School/St. Agatha's School Annual Student Enrolments," chart, Episcopal Diocese of New York archives.

51. *Trinity School Year Book*, 1920–21.

52. Trinity School financial reports, Trinity Church archives.

53. Auditors' report to Board of Trustees, NPEPS, October 26, 1938, Trinity Church archives.

54. Lawrence Cole to School Committee, June 16, 1936, Diocese of New York archives.

55. Auditors' Report to the Board, October 26, 1938.

56. Chapel services were daily at both schools and there is no record of provision for students being excused and sitting out.

57. For comparisons see Moffat, 238. Trinity's listed fees, before subventions, were below those of Berkeley, Collegiate, Cutler, and Allen-Stevenson.

58. Discussion informed by Ravitch, *The Great School Wars*, 161ff.

59. *Ibid.*, 210ff.

60. *Ibid.*, 229.

61. *Ibid.*, 238.

62. Financial records, Trinity Church archives.

63. Cole to school committee, June 16, 1936, Diocese of New York archives.

CHAPTER 6: MANAGING FOR THE MIDDLE (152–195)

1. Dann biographical note, *Trinity School Yearbook* for 1944 (Trinity School Archives).

2. "Yearbook" was the term long used for what later would be deemed a school cat-alog and should not be confused with the student-produced and -centered yearly me-mentoes of school life that would become common later.

3. *Trinity School Yearbook*, 1938–39.

4. *Trinity School Yearbooks*, 1937–38ff, 9 (Trinity School Archives).

5. Bruner-Smith memoir; Broward Craig interview, December 2002; John Beebe interview, October 2003.

6. *Trinity School Yearbook*, 1938–39. There is no hard data on the presence of Jews or Catholics in this period. The presumption is that if there, it was slight.

7. Viz., Edie and George of "Georgeds, Inc.," who ran the school bus service: "Lim-ousine-cars: $2.50 per hour . . . Busses: starting at $15 per day."

8. M. E. Dann letter book (Trinity School Archives). Surely the oddest note came from Lois Reese Cooper, 230 Park Avenue (March 31, 1937), a self-described "artist of sorts" who had seen Dann's photograph in the *Herald-Tribune* and found that it bore "the most startling resemblance to a very dear friend of mine, lost some time since." She asked Dann for a better quality copy that she wished to retouch "to bring out the like-ness." She sounded smitten by memory: "The other man had much heavier eyebrows, which were inclined to lift a bit at the outer corners and 'beetle' across the nose; his forehead was at once narrower, more concave and not so high as yours, with the hair less full on top and longer at the temples. Cheeks somewhat thinner, with the bones more prominent, although that may only seem so from a white newspaper print. The nose, mouth and eyes are perfect, especially the slight narrowing of the eyes and the somewhat quizzical expression around the faintly smiling mouth. I think you are a bit younger; this picture looks to be of a man around 28 or 30 years, where my friend was nearly 40 when I lost him." In closing, she enclosed a snapshot of herself, "which may tell you better than I can, that I am just a homely person who once lost a good friend, and who has no design in writing you other than appears here." Who knows? Her pho-tograph is missing, and there is no record that Dann replied.

9. "Headmaster," not "rector," was the term used.

10. Fleming to Dann, April 27, 1936 (Trinity School Archives).

11. Relevant file "Headmaster, M.E. Dann, 1937–1955" (Trinity School Archives).

12. Dann to Erskine, July 29, 1935 (Trinity School Archives).

13. Erskine to Dann, June 12, 1935 (Trinity School Archives).

14. Erskine to Dann, July 26, 1935 (Trinity School Archives).

15. Erskine to Dann, April 22, 1936 (Trinity School Archives). In the same letter, Ers-kine referred to "the plan you spoke of" but told Dann there was little chance of "its going through in the form in which it was presented by you. I'll explain after I return from the South." This could have been a reprimand to an over-eager new broom, but "the plan" remains a mystery.

16. Dann to Erskine, June 15, 1936; Erskine to Dann, September 17, 1936 (Trinity School Archives).

17. Dann to Fleming, October 24, 1939; Fleming to Dann, October 27, 1939 (Trinity School Archives).

18. On January 8, Erskine responded to Dann about matters involving more effi- cient cooperation with St. Agatha School, adding a hand-written postscript: "Dr. Cole has resigned. He will probably tell you—until then it's a secret, I suppose."

19. Erskine to Dann, January 8, 1937 (Trinity School Archives).

20. Dann to Erskine, January 29, 1937 (Trinity School Archives).

21. Dann to Erskine, October 1, 1937 (Trinity School Archives).

22. Dann to C. Aubrey Nicklas, February 21, 1940 (Trinity School Archives).

23. Dann to William G. Brady, Jr., June 14, 1943 (Trinity School Archives).

24. Description 1950, "Treasurer's Office" (Trinity School Archives). Hawley gradu- ated from Trinity in 1886 and served for many years as trustee. He led an exciting life, making early record-breaking balloon flights (the most famous, in 1910, from St. Louis to Lake St. John, Quebec, which proved the superiority of rubber over cotton balloons), as an organizer of the Lafayette Escadrille during World War I, and as a founder of the Automobile Club of America. His will named Dann and Milo Gates, Dean of the Cathedral of St. John the Divine, executors, and the bequest to Trinity then valued at some $330,000 was stipulated for the establishment of a fund for "the Encouragement of Student Effort for Students at Trinity School for Boys." The executors were author- ized to award seventeen prizes annually, of $250 each to students of Trinity and St. Agatha (*Trinity Times*, February 23, March 9, 1938). The fund would figure more grandly into Trinity's future in the 1960s when it became the basis for nearly doubling the size of the school. See chapter 7.

25. Financial Records, 1944–59 (Trinity School Archives).

26. Following drawn from Francis J. Sypher, *St. Agnes Chapel of the Parish of Trinity Church in the City of New York, 1892–1943* (New York: Parish of Trinity Church, 2002).

27. The nave measured 167 feet, the transepts 108 feet, a magnificent campanile with at the time the largest swinging peal of bells in the country, plus two pipe organs.

28. Bellinger died shortly before Easter, 1943, three months before the chapel shut down (Sypher, 98).

29. *New York Herald Tribune* and *New York Times*, November 23, 1942, cited in Sypher, 96.

30. Undated clipping (lost); see Sypher, 104.

31. John Erskine, *Memory of Certain Persons* (Philadelphia: J. B. Lippincott, 1947), 220, cited in Sypher, 101.

32. Dated March 15, 1944. A grant from the Charles Hayden Foundation supplied the money (*New York Times*, March 18, 1944).

33. See chapter 5.

34. See Kevin D. Ramsey, "1998 Marks the 100th Anniversary of the Founding of St. Agatha Day School for Girls," *Trinity Per Saecula*, Spring 1998.

35. Cited in Ramsey, 1998.

36. Record of this exists from but one—the Pawling—side. See Troupe Noonan, *The Pride of Fighting Gentlemen: Trinity–Pawling at 100* (2006); and correspondence be- tween Pawling trustees John D. Burnham of Philadelphia and Wesley M. Oler of New York City, May 1939–February 1940 (Trinity-Pawling Archives).

37. Interview recorded by Allison Hall Whipple, Trinity-Pawling Class of 1976, April 30, 1976 (Trinity-Pawling Archives).

38. Wesley M. Oler to John D. Burnham, June 1, 1939 (Trinity-Pauling Archives).

39. Oler to Burnham, February 8, 1940 (Trinity-Pauling Archives).

40. Oler to Burnham, January 31, 1940 (Trinity-Pauling Archives).

41. *Ibid.*

42. Bill Goralski, class of 1948 and a boarder from Connecticut, left a memoir of the experience: *Away from Avon . . . for Awhile* (1990).

43. Dann interview, April 30, 1976; *New York Tribune*, August 16, 1946. Pawling's historian, Troupe Noonan, records an incident from years later to illustrate Dann's conviction that Trinity-Pawling really dated from 1947, not 1907. During a renovation of the library in the 1960s, Dann approved removal of marble tablets given by the classes of 1916 and 1917, recording the names of each year's senior prefect through 1942. An echo of the destruction of the mosaic floors at St. Agnes Chapel, also on Dann's watch, the tablets were crushed and used as fill around the campus (Noonan, *Pride of Fighting Gentleman*, 96).

44. Opinion was divided, however. Remembered long-time Trinity Upper School principal Clarence Bruner-Smith: "Academically, it never touched Trinity in New York" (Bruner-Smith interview, 1992). John McPhee's *New Yorker* profile of Boyden became *The Headmaster: Frank L. Boyden of Deerfield* (New York: FSG, 1966).

45. Dann interview.

46. Dann married, briefly, in 1940 but the union was annulled.

47. Until the end: When Dann died in 1987, it was in a road accident as he attempted a U-turn from the shoulder of Route 22 near Pawling and drove his Chevrolet into the path of a dump truck ("Accident Takes Life of Former Trinity-Pawling Headmaster," clipping in Trinity-Pauling Archives).

48. Senior partner at White & Case.

49. A civil engineer and chairman of the Board of Hudson and Manhattan Railroad, Carleton gave $450,000 in the early 1950s for the gymnasium that bears his name. In his will, Trinity-Pawling got another $500,000 (Columbia School of Mines $6.5 million). Trinity got nothing (Bruner-Smith interview, 1992).

50. While Trinity permanently reintegrated girls in the 1970s, Trinity-Pawling brought in day girls as a temporary expedient to boost enrollment and revenue, then returned to boys alone in 1981, with the last girl graduating in 1985. Its contemporary marketing material emphasizes the returning acceptability of single-sex education as one answer to discrimination against boys. The dress code is still blazers and ties. See www.trinitypawling.org.

51. Asked years later whether Trinity-Pawling fulfilled the ambition of keeping boys from going on to boarding schools, Clarence Bruner-Smith replied: "No. It was a complete failure to do so, since the school academically never approached the Trinity School here in New York" (Bruner-Smith interview, 1992).

52. Too nicely for some. At the time of the dissolution, Trinity conveyed Trinity-

Pawling's buildings, a physical plant valued at $16 million, for $600,000. "A tragedy," to partisan Bruner-Smith. Also Noonan, *Pride of Fighting Gentleman*, 146.

53. Bruner-Smith interview.

54. Bruner-Smith interview, 1992. It is interesting that Trinity's great Chips figure, Bruner-Smith, had a soft spot for Dann, a man so outwardly different from himself. Eulogizing at Dann's memorial service in 1987: "Then there was the Matthew Dann that not everyone knew. When he learned of a family problem with a youngster, or of a boy whom circumstance had deprived of an opportunity to get a good education, he would spare nothing in an attempt to help—even to the point of taking the individual into his own house—even to accepting the responsibility of being a foster parent. There are those here today who called him 'Dad.'" (The two were Bruce Huffine of Stamford and Christopher Doyle of New York City, Dann's wards for eight years whom he guided through Trinity-Pawling and college. See clipping "Accident takes life of former Trinity-Pawling headmaster," Trinity-Pauling Archives.)

55. Trinity reacted slowly to this fact, but then decisively. See chapter 7.

56. See Diane Ravitch, *The Great School Wars: A History of the New York City Public Schools* (Baltimore, 1974), 233ff., and *Left Back: A Century of Battles Over School Reform* (New York, 2000), on the beginnings of dissidence; also Lawrence Cremin, *The Transformation of the School* (New York, 1961).

57. *Essays of E. B. White* (New York, 1977), 119.

58. A euphemism that meant "not quite ready for college," perhaps requiring a year of "post-grad" at another prep school.

59. Trinity School yearbooks (catalogues), 1940–1955.

60. *Ibid.*

61. Education Records Bureau Tests, Reports to Matthew E. Dann, November 3, 1943; October 25, 1946, Trinity School Archives.

62. The earliest surviving application form dates from 1962.

63. Trinity School Yearbook, 1938–39, 1949–50 (Trinity School Archives).

64. *Ibid.* A standardized admissions test for boys entering above the fourth grade was instituted in 1956–57. "As a result of this program, we expect to make many less errors in judging the quality of the students whom we are considering" (Report of the Headmaster to trustees, February 1, 1956, Trinity School Archives).

65. A generation older than Bruner-Smith, Langford came to Trinity in 1903, the same year as Cole, and stayed on for fifty-two years, to the end of Dann's administration. The Chips figure to the boys in the Lower School, he had degrees from Oneonta State Normal College and Columbia and had taught at a small school in Greenwich and the New Rochelle public schools before coming to Trinity. On his retirement, the Upper School boys in charge of the *Trinity Times* wrote sagely about the value of good beginnings: "Mr. Langford tried, with much success, to lay the ground work of good citizenship and honorable living. Faithfully guiding the development of mind and character of boys in the Lower School, he has aided their climb up the educational ladder and influenced their later life." His boys included Humphrey Bogart and Tru-

man Capote, and for years, after commencement, he was known to have dinner with the same alum who had graduated from the Lower School just as Langford had been starting out. "One of the greatest pleasures I have found," he summed up, "is to have worked under and with two wonderful headmasters—Dr. Lawrence T. Cole and Dr. Matthew E. Dann" (*Trinity Times*, October 15, 1955).

66. Moffat, 249.

67. Dann to Clarence Bruner-Smith, May 26, 1937 (Trinity School Archives).

68. Dann to Bertrand Bartram, May 26, 1937 (Trinity School Archives).

69. "I think you know of my happiness in having you associated with me in the new work of Trinity School," Dann finished up, "and it gives me much satisfaction to know that I can rely upon you as we go forward together" (*ibid.*).

70. Dann to Simpson, June 26, 1939 (Trinity School Archives). Dann to Hall, June 19, 1939.

71. Dann to Bruner-Smith, June 6, 1942 (Trinity School Archives).

72. Dann to Bartram, May 26, 1937.

73. Dann to Bartram, May 26, 1937.

74. Thomas K. Brown III to Dann, March 16, 1941; Dann to Brown, July 1, 1941; Brown to Dann, July 5, 1941.

75. Dann to Judson C. Loomis, April 18, 1945; Loomis to Dann, June 24, 1945; Dann to Loomis, July 2, 1945 (Trinity School Archives).

76. Dann to Charles D. Walker, April 22, 1947 (Trinity School Archives).

77. Memorial to Sidney Aylmer Small, no date (Trinity School Archives).

78. Record #3811, stamped "confidential" (Trinity School Archives).

79. *Trinity School Yearbooks*, 1944–1959 (Trinity School Archives).

80. These, class of 1944.

81. Craig went on to Harvard, Beebe to Princeton. As grown-ups, both men had accomplished careers in business, and not all of their time was spent in New York (Craig was lawyer and executive, Beebe an investment banker in Chicago). In retirement, both landed in Virginia, Craig in Charlottesville, Beebe in Richmond.

82. Broward Craig interview, December 5, 2002.

83. John Beebe interview, October 6, 2003.

84. *Trinity School Yearbooks*, 1944–58 (Trinity School Archives). Note that these are "yearbooks" as they have since become known, produced by senior students, not the older catalogues that technically went by that name.

85. Yearbook, 1953.

86. Rogers Peet at 600 and 479 Fifth Avenue and Warren at Broadway were Trinity's official outfitters for blazers and caps. "New Old School Ties" (blue and gold stripes) the school sold itself through the Trinity Exchange, large and small sizes $1.25 (*Trinity Times*, May 25, 1955).

87. In 1937–38: $250 (grades 1–3), 300 (grades 4 and 5), 350 (grade 6–8), 400 (high school). In 1949–50: $350, 400, 450, and 475, respectively. In 1955–56: $450, 550, 575, 600 (forms 1 and 2), and 650 (forms 3–6). In 1959–60: $500 (grades 1–2), 650 (grades 3–5), 700 (grades 6–8), and 800 (forms 3–6). Source: Catalogues, 1937–60.

88. Salaries were seniority, experience, and market based. Maigi, who earned the least that year, had come to Trinity only the year before, in 1951. But so had Lawrence Wilson, who taught industrial arts and got paid $3,000. There was no significant differential between Lower and Upper schools.

89. Report to Board of Trustees, November 12, 1952 (Trinity School Archives). And there were those who thought Dann probably resented it. Bruner-Smith years later said Dann believed "you paid faculty what you had to" (Bruner-Smith Memoir).

90. Report to Board of Trustees, February 1, 1956

91. Report to Board of Trustees, November 6, 1957 (Trinity School Archives).

92. *Trinity Times*, 2007.

93. Who, naturally, thought themselves underappreciated: "The football. basketball and baseball teams are surrounded with an aura of glory. The respected legislators of the Student Council are universally loved and admired. Even the tennis team is not without honor. But where in the Hall of Fame is the little band of intrepid men who work their fingers to the bone producing that monument to scholastic journalism through whose thrilling pages the heroic exploits of all the others are brought to a breathless public? It is, then to these unsung heroes that we dedicate the following dramatic epic-the men of THE TRINITY TIMES" (November 10, 1943).

94. *Trinity Times*, October 27, 1943.

95. *Trinity Times*, November 10, 1943.

96. *Trinity Times*, November 24, 1943.

97. *Trinity Times*, November 10, 1943.

98. "Almighty Father, we commend to Thee our brothers, the men of Trinity who are now enrolled in the armed forces of our country. May their service to the Cause be cheerfully given, intelligently carried out, and effectively completed. In days of weariness let their hearts be uplifted by warm memories of school days. Do Thou help them be at their best in times of stress and strain, courageous in action, gallant in defeat, and well-poised in victory. Strengthen us all in our devotion to the truth that shall make us free, and in good time grant peace, O Lord, to our land, in the name of Thy Son, the Prince of Peace, Jesus Christ our Lord. Amen" (*Trinity Times*, November 24, 1943).

99. Yearbook, 1945.

100. *Trinity Times*, April 19, 1944.

101. *Trinity Times*, November 11, 1954.

102. *Trinity Times*, October 25, 1950.

103. *Trinity Times*, December 19, 1950. Trinity drew up emergency defense plans early in 1951 to protect the student body in the even of air raid or fire. "Trinity Practices First Bomb Drills: Recently, in tune with the overall defense effort of the City of New York, Trinity has been testing various Atomic Bomb drills. In the classroom a Take Cover Drill has been used under the expert supervision of Mr. Ballentine and Mr. Langford" (February 14, 1951).

104. *Trinity Times*, February 14, 1951.

105. *Trinity Times*, October 15, 1953.

106. *Trinity Times*, December 16, 1953.

107. *Trinity Times*, November 25, 1953.

108. *Trinity Times*, April 21, 1954.

109. Yearbook, 1954.

110. A questionnaire was circulated to determine what was needed: "to retain the ties between the graduates and the school itself, and to strengthen the connections and friendships that were formed in the days when we were schoolboys, by arranging gatherings where we can renew our acquaintances" (*Trinity Alumni News*, April, 1938, Trinity School Archives).

111. *Ibid.*

112. Following recorded 1954.

113. Dwight Eisenhower to Hugh Riddleberger, March 24, 1959 (Trinity School Archives).

114. Nelson Rockefeller to Hugh Riddleberger, April 24, 1959 (Trinity School Archives).

115. There was also a letter from Vice-President Richard Nixon (soon to engage Khrushchev in the "kitchen debate") that talked of the importance of education to "the struggle for world peace" and to maintaining "the highest standard of living of any country in the world" (Nixon to Hugh Riddleberger, October 6, 1958; Trinity School Archives).

116. *Suprême of Fresh Fruit Lucullus, Prime Ribs of Beef Anniversaire, Champs-Elysée Potatoes, Bibescot Glace Waldorf.* . . . Robert A. W. Carleton, '00, toastmaster, greetings from board president and Trinity Church rector John Heuss, Matt Dann, Hugh Riddleberger, and Otto Kinzel, '28, president of the alums, speech by Grayson Kirk, president of Columbia. Music by the Trinity School Band, Glee Club, and Leo Dryer and his Orchestra.

117. "Spirit of Life, counselor of men, let they presence in our midst make this school a fountain of wholesome activity and true knowledge. To its trustees, grand ripe wisdom. To its teachers, gifts of leadership, and to its students, a questioning spirit; that soundness of learning, loftiness of character, and capacity for gallant living may be furthered in this place from generation to generation, through Jesus Christ our Lord."

118. 250th Anniversary Fund brochure (Trinity School Archives).

119. "A Time for Rededication: Trinity School from 1709 to 1959" booklet (Trinity School Archives).

120. *Alumni Bulletin*, 1959.

CHAPTER 7: DIVIDING LINE(S) (196–260)

1. As New Yorkers and others witnessed in the three-part exhibition mounted in 2007, "Robert Moses and the Modern City," consisting of "Remaking the Metropolis" at the Museum of the City of New York, which examined his efforts to revitalize the center city; "The Road to Recreation" at the Queens Museum of Art, which explored parks, parkways, beaches, and pools, and "Slum Clearance and the Superblock Solution" at Columbia University's Wallach Art Gallery, which considered residential

urban renewal. Also see the accompanying catalogue, Hillary Ballon and Kenneth T. Jackson, eds., *Robert Moses and the Modern City: The Transformation of New York* (New York: W. W. Norton & Company, 2007). On the reputation of Caro's great book, see Michael Powell, "A Tale of Two Cities," *The New York Times*, May 6, 2007.

2. Peter Salwen, *Upper West Side Story: A History and Guide* (New York, 1989), 271ff.

3. There is no record that Moses noticed the episode.

4. Controversial, high-handed, undemocratic as he was, Moses liked playgrounds and had an undeniable romantic streak. On why he spent life as he did (and he did not die a rich man): "It is partly sheer stubbornness. Certainly there are no material rewards comparable to those which can be expected from similar devotion to private work. I made up my mind long ago to get my reward from tangible [built] accomplishments, from the dogwood, the tulip, the chrysanthemum, the curving parkway, the spiderwork of suspension bridges, the reclaimed waterfront, the demolition of slums, the crack of a baseball bat, and the shouting of children in playgrounds." Cited in *Robert Moses and the Modern City*.

5. West Side chronicler Salwen recounts the story of how it got started, with Nelson Rockefeller and William Zeckendorf looking for some profit out of the area and their wives, at a canasta game, suggesting why not "build a cultural center" (*Upper West Side Story*, 272).

6. "It was the worst slum in New York, and you call it a 'neighborhood.' *Christ*, you could never have *been* there!" The neighborhood did enjoy one last hurrah as the set for the movie production of *West Side Story* (*ibid.*).

7. The city tried hard he said to be sensitive to the interest of displaced tenants to give them all the help it could, but, commented Moses with characteristic directness, "we cannot give everyone and his lawyers what they want." Audience applause. Cited in *Robert Moses and the Modern City*

8. *Ibid.*

9. "West Side: A Summary of the Final Plan," New York Housing and Development Board, 1959 (Trinity School Archives).

10. *Ibid.*, 2.

11. *Ibid.*, 11.

12. *Ibid.*, 10. Critically, designations would change however. See later section, "Lester and the Community."

13. *Ibid.*, 12.

14. On Mitchell-Lama see Caro, *The Power Broker*; and Joel Schwartz, *The New York Approach: Robert Moses, Urban Liberals, and Redevelopment of the Inner City* (Columbus: Ohio State University Press, 1993).

15. Clarence Bruner-Smith Memoir.

16. Richard Garten interview, December 12, 2002; *The New York Times*, February 23, 1964.

17. See Glover Johnson to E. G. Picken, VP New York Bank for Savings, October 1, 1965 (Trinity School Archives).

18. Following architectural, legal, and financial concepts of the plan drawn from

Eliot Lumbard report to Trinity Trustees, December 11, 1964, and memorandum of special counsel Demov & Morris to Trinity board of trustees, November 1965: "Site #24, West Side Urban Renewal Title I Area Combined School and Housing Project" (Trinity School Archives).

19. Richard Garten to Bernard Guenther, November 23, 1964.

20. "Air rights" projects were and would remain controversial. In a project like Trinity's the concept was benign: The "air" above to be developed was just that, so much air. This was not the case everywhere. The Old Penn Station was destroyed in the context of air rights, Grand Central Terminal nearly so.

21. Glover Johnson to Milton Mollen, Chairman Housing and Redevelopment Board of New York, February 9, 1965 (Trinity School Archives).

22. Glover Johnson to Richard Garten, February 9, 1965 (Trinity School Archives).

23. Eliot Lumbard memorandum to board, October 20, 1966 (Trinity School Archives).

24. *Ibid.*

25. Glover Johnson (treasurer New York Protestant Episcopal Public School) to E. G. Picken, Vice President New York Bank for Savings (holder of Trinity's then current mortgage of $300,000), October 1, 1965 (Trinity School Archives).

26. *New York Law Journal*, October 5, 1965. This summarizes. The clause read: "provided that no investment shall be made in real estate, loans or mortgages or any participating shares or interest therein." Lumbard argued, successfully, that the answer was to see that the Hawley money be used only for school building construction and "not for any purpose related to the potential housing. Thus there is no 'investment' in real estate; indeed, money used for school construction would not be an 'investment'" (Eliot H. Lumbard to Glover Johnson, January 25, 1965, Trinity School Archives).

27. Johnson to Picken, October 1, 1965.

28. Trinity Fund booklet "A Commitment to Superior Education in an Urban Environment" [1968] (Trinity School Archives).

29. Wallis B. Dunckel '18, Chairman of Trinity Fund, to John V. Butler, D.D., Rector of Trinity Church, January 16, 1967 (Trinity School Archives).

30. Dunckel to Butler, February 3, 1967 (Trinity School Archives), with thanks: "The generosity of the grant itself will go a long way to help us attain our goal, but I think it is also fair to say that without it, our campaign for funds could not be pursued."

31. Or to which the administration said they were committed.

32. See press releases and brochure 1968, Trinity School Archives record 3897. The campaign was headed by Wallis Dunckel '18, Glover Johnson '19, Margaret Liebling, immediate past president of the parents' organization, Frederic W. Frost '28, president of the alumni association, and Disque D. Deane, chairman of the leadership gift committee.

33. It gave over one page and two paragraphs to history, including small images of the first Trinity Church where the school held its first classes, the 1754 building where King's College held its first classes, and the "present" 1894 building, from an architect's

rendering in the commemorative booklet at its cornerstone laying. In the left foreground, a horse and buggy perhaps conveyed a subliminal message in 1968.

34. "A Commitment to Superior Education in an Urban Environment"; also "The Trinity Fund Report," May 22, 1968.

35. Hugh Riddleberger to Howard Craig, April 5, 1957 (Trinity School Archives).

36. Richard Garten report April 1968, Minutes, May 1, 1968.

37. "Trinity's Young Impresssionists Report," Trinity Fund Report, May 22, 1968.

38. *Trinity Times*, October 5, 1966.

39. I.e., Edward Stewart Moffat's, 1959 Columbia University Ph.D. dissertation, "Trinity School, New York City, 1709–1959."

40. *Trinity Perspective*, Spring 1969. *Perspective* was a short-lived publication begun in the winter of 1968–69, meant to provide a single publication for all of Trinity's constituents, boys, teachers, trustees, alums, parents, and friends.

41. Garten to Board, January 1970.

42. Interview report by H. E. Batchelder, April 13, 1966. Trustee, and chairman of the building committee, Howard R. Craig said the same thing, in the negative, when assessing the giving potential of Trinity parents: "Potential not very great except in few cases of present parents. There are a great many young, middle and low income families involved in Trinity. They are saving to put sonny through college when Trinity graduates him." Interview report to H. E. Batchelder, April 25, 1966 (Trinity School Archives).

43. Trinity Fund Prospects, 1971–72, Record 3906 (Trinity School Archives).

44. *Ibid.*

45. *Trinity School Alumni News*, May 1975.

46. *Trinity School Alumni News*, May 1975.

47. "Retrospects and Prospects," *Perspective*, Spring 1969.

48. *Ibid.*

49. And these were not trifling. When the Hawley wing opened in December 1969 it was to the accompaniment of still incomplete financing due to protracted difficulties with the city, and still imcomplete furnishings. See Garten to Board, January 1970, November 1970.

50. Standing Committee Trinity School, June 4, 1968.

51. Actual increases thus (for the year 1969–70): grade 1, $995 to $1,250; grades 2 and 3. $1,250 to $1,450; grades 4, 5, and 6, $1,375 to $1,600; grades 7 and 8, $1,490 to $1,700; grades 9 through 12, $1,600 to $1,800 (Board Minutes November 6, 1968).

52. Garten to Board, April 1968.

53. Trinity Times, February 7, 1969

54. Report to Board, October 1968.

55. *Ibid.*

56. *Trinity Times*, February 7, 1969: "Marijuana: Dr. Louria Discusses Problem." Louria was a doctor at the Cornell Medical Center who thought that in small doses marijuana was less hazardous than alcohol: "In the long run it is a less dangerous drug.

But what we are being asked by society is an entirely different question. It is whether to alcohol we should add marijuana. And I have always said that we should not add any more intoxicants to an already intoxicated society."

57. Report to Board, October 1969.

58. Report to Board, May 1969.

59. Report to Board, January 1969. There were other instances of moral slovenliness, including a wave of thefts and vandalism culminating in destruction of the school candy machine by a group of students and witnessed by many more. "Indefensible Acts," as the school paper condemned it, but perhaps there was something to worry about (*Trinity Times*, November 27, 1968).

60. "The 'why' of chapel at Trinity is also the why of life and being. Chapel is where we ask the big questions; it is not where we give or get all or sometimes any of the answers, but it is that oasis in all our busy variegated lives where we pause and address the large questions" (Robin Lester in *Upper School Handbook*, 1984–85).

61. The stipulation about footwear would have struck Dann or Cole as extremely odd.

62. *Ibid.*

63. Board minutes, November 6, 1968. At the same meeting, Dann, who was still on the board and headmaster of Trinity-Pawling, reported discussions with Lowell Thomas to gift his estate (real estate) to Trinity-Pawling and establish there a coordinate girls' school. (This did not occur, but Trinity-Pawling did add girls, if only as an expedient to boost tuition revenue, and later reverted to all boys, as it remains today.

64. *Trinity Times*, October 10, 1968.

65. *Trinity Times*, February 7, 1969.

66. Report to Board, October 15, 1970.

67. Board Minutes, February 3, 1971.

68. *The New York Times*, February 12, 1971.

69. Report to Board, October 1971.

70. "Another Male Bastion Falls, *The New York Times*, November 2, 1971.

71. *Trinity Times*, February 24, 1971.

72. It was a time of falling inhibitions in expression: "The other day a friend wailed to me, 'How can we expect sports when we haven't even got a locker room? There are hundreds of nude little kids in there, and the boys' locker room is empty! I thought we were moved to prevent that! And to top it all off, the damn white box in the bathroom is empty, honey!'" (*Trinity Times*, November 1, 1974).

73. "Women in Trinity," *Trinity Times*, November 1, 1974.

74. *Ibid.*

75. *Ibid.* Smith was having fun: "But how many unknown violets are wasting their fragrances on the desert air? First of all, girls, please pay attention to the changes in fashion around you, and let's begin by showing some style and chic as befits the brightest and best young ladies of Manhattan!" Another writer, senior Caroline Franklin (class of 1975) and something of a feminist, would not have taken the tease. Do you

think girls will ever become equal to boys at Trinity? "There's no way that women will regress enough to be equal to men."

76. Such was long-time master Clarence Bruner-Smith's view (Bruner-Smith interview, November 13, 1992).

77. Garten and the older faction of the board had let the Pawling situation drift. Dann may have been the chief impediment here. He had built himself a nice house on exclusive Quaker Hill near the school, which he treated like "a fiefdom." To Garten's successor, Robin Lester, Pawling made no sense at all, and he pushed to get rid of it (Lester interview, August 20, 2007).

78. *Trinity Insider*, October 1971.

79. Garten once told long-time English teacher John Hanly that it hurt him that people thought he was stiff and difficult to approach. "Everyone lived in mortal fear of him," remembered Hanly whose respect for Garten increased after he himself had served as a headmaster (of the Pingree School in New Jersey in the 1980s and 1990s) (John Hanly interview, October 30, 2002).

80. *Trinity Times*, March 17, 1971.

81. *Trinity Times*, March 17, 1971.

82. *Trinity Times*, June 5, 1975.

83. "The Dress Code," May 31, 1974. In 1975, Lord & Taylor Boys' Shop still advertised itself in the *Trinity Times* as "home of your official school blazer" (May 13, 1975).

84. Much to worry about: "In a time when so many draft-eligible males are anxious to avoid service in Vietnam . . ."; "The problems of bad housing and insufficient government response to poverty conditions on the Upper West Side has come into acute focus in recent weeks . . ."; "How would you feel if you were in a room with all of the other students members of another race?"

85. *Trinity Times*, February 3, 1971.

86. *Trinity Times*, February 22, 1974

87. The same issue of the paper that reported the chaplain's incendiary reported a Parents' Day where the biggest gripe was "it's so cold in the classrooms!" Most moms and dads, it seemed, liked what they saw and heard for themselves, unfiltered by their sons and daughters: "Enjoying my visit"; "Getting a feeling of the school environment"; "Fascinating"; "Love it."

88. Report to Board, May 1974.

89. Memorandum to executive committee members from board chairman Otto Kinzel, October 7, 1974.

90. The others: Broward Craig (chairman), E. Virgil Conway, Michael Fribourg, Eliot Lumbard, and Dr. Edward Lorenze. Special Meeting of the Standing Committee, October 31, 1974.

91. Broward Craig interview, December 5, 2002.

92. Board minutes, November 13, 1974.

93. *Trinity Times*, November 2, 1973; Garten interview.

94. He landed at a lesser place, the Gulf Stream School, a small school in Florida

whence he retired. Of Trinity, he said he left "with strongly mixed feelings . . . that of regret-regret at leaving my native city, 'my' school with all that it has meant, and all the associations my family and I have enjoyed" (*Alumni News*, May 1975).

95. *Ibid.*

96. Board minutes, February 26, 1975.

97. *Ibid.*

98. *Ibid.*

99. Standing Committee minutes, April 24, 1975; *Trinity Times*, October 3, 1974.

100. "Misunderstandings," *Trinity Times*, June 3, 1975. Some of the ill-feeling leaked to the larger press. "Some upperclassmen interviewed criticized Mr. Garten's last years at the school, noting that 16 teachers left Trinity last June. . . . Mr. Garten responded to criticism of the rate of teacher turnover by saying that his attitude toward 'faculty stability' had changed. He said he now believed it was best to have 'a core of veterans and a changing stream of newcomers'" (*The New York Times*, October 6, 1974).

101. "A New Era," *Trinity Times*, September 19, 1975.

102. Lester interview, August 20, 2007.

103. *Trinity Times*, May 14, 1976.

104. "There is going to be a dress code and as long as we have one it should be logical. Jeans are incongruous with a tie and jacket." At the threat of another blue-jeans-day protest, he said, "Students aren't going to get anywhere" (*Ibid.*).

105. *Alumni News*, May 1975.

106. The school sold it that September for $56,400, of which $25,000 went to renovating the brownstone for the Lesters. Executive committee minutes, September 24, 1975.

107. Report to board, May 1975.

108. Lester to Board, March 7, 1977.

109. Lester to Board, May 5, 1977.

110. Report to board, October 9, 1976.

111. Executive committee minutes, April 25, 1977.

112. Lester to Board, May 5, 1977.

113. Summary report of *The Psychology of Sex Differences* by E. E. Maccoby and C. H. Jacklin of Stanford University, and other current literature, March 9, 1977.

114. See Report to Trinity School Committee, December 1978, by John H. Jones and Gerald N. La Grange.

115. It hadn't, but this apparently was an echo of the original decision to admit girls to the upper school in 1971, when some who were there then were sure that the faculty had not been consulted, "and this clearly caused a great deal of unhappiness and frustration, signs of which are still evident" (*Ibid.*, 5). English teacher John Hanly recalled how the faculty "found one day in their mailboxes a questionnaire dealing with upteen aspects of Trinity School and one question, something like question 77 out of 100, was 'would you be in favor of Trinity accepting girls?' A few months later we were told we were" (John Hanly interview, October 30, 2002).

116. "On Coeducation," *Trinity Times*, November 10, 1978.

117. Consulted: Brearley, Chapin, Riverdale, Horace Mann, Collegiate, Dalton, Columbia Grammer, St. David's, Allen-Stevenson, and Town schools.

118. In that still pre-Title IX era, however, the phrase "equal opportunity" does not appear.

119. The current plumbing arrangement ("Ladies" in the east stairwell between first and second floors, "Boys" between second and third and third and fourth) would not meet city code; 139, where the Lower School was and would remain, was a weary old building: "The toilet rooms are clean and serviceable, but they cannot be characterized as attractive or modern. The present arrangement must also be awkward for female teachers and the young boys of the Lower School: one kindergarten group has to use these stairwell facilities."

120. Report, 31.

121. See Robin Lester to Board, "The Co-ed Issue," January 1979.

122. Richard Garten interview, December 13, 2002.

123. "Popular," as in "popular girl/popular boy," is one of the clichés of high school life and usually refers to boys and girls who not only are, thanks to personality, well liked but who also need to be. As with teenagers, so sometimes with headmasters.

124. Robin Lester interview, December 13, 2002.

125. Trinity School Faculty Salary Scale Guidelines, March 11, 1976. Lester saw the A.B.D. slot as an innovation: "ABDs already know everything there is to know about their fields and make fine teachers. Who cares if they've finished some narrow dissertation, which tells you nothing about their teaching ability" (Lester interview, August 20, 2007).

126. Lester to Board, May 5, 1977.

127. Lester interview, August 20, 2007.

128. Lester to Board, January 1979.

129. Lester to Board, October 1978.

130. Lester to Board, April 29, 1978.

131. *Ibid.*

132. Quoted in Lester to Board, April 29, 1978.

133. Lester to Board, October 1978.

134. *Ibid.*

135. John Hanly interview, October 30, 2002.

136. Wry Englishman Hanly looked back on his relationship with Lester this way: "Robin and I complemented one another. He was great with parents and making people feel good, and I was great at making them feel bad. It worked out very well" (*ibid.*).

137. Lester to Board, May 21, 1979.

138. *Alumni News*, Fall 1978.

139. Lester to Board, October 1978.

140. "Recent History of Trinity," Statement to Faculty, February 15, 1978, in report to board March 9, 1978.

141. Seventy-six percent (192 out of 254) responded. On religion: 45 percent identi-

fied themselves as members of a Christian denomination but the most checked single religion was Judaism (26 percent); 14 percent checked Episcopalian; 48 percent said they believed in God; asked separately if they believed in a "creative force" 65 percent said yes. On ethics: 82 percent said they had cheated on a quiz, one in five on exams; cheating rose with grade level and boys and girls seemed evenly prone; when overlain with believe-in-God questions, the faithful and the faithless also cheated about evenly; over 50 percent said they had stolen from stores. On drugs: experimentation at least was widespread, 95 percent claiming alcohol use, 72 percent marijuana; 68 percent said they drank for relaxation, 28 percent for social demands, 1 percent admitted dependency; twice as many thought alcohol dangerous as they did marijuana; 29 percent of seniors admitted trying cocaine and LSD; two tenth graders said they had sampled heroin; usage rose with grade level and boys indulged more heavily than girls. On sex: 88 percent said they approved of premarital sex; 75 percent said they had engaged in petting with members of the opposite sex; 49 percent claimed to have engaged in sex with members of the opposite sex, with boys busier than girls; there were no questions about birth control or disease but there were about masturbation, which seemed prevalent, again more so among boys, and homosexuality, which seemed less so, though 30 percent admitted curiosity and six students admitted to have "engaged in homosexual activity" (*Trinity Times*, April 7, 1976). In a follow-up riff on the subject, students read: "Heterosexuality Rampant Among Trinity Faculty: Extensive investigation by the *Times* has uncovered an alarming amount of heterosexuality among the school faculty. Many teachers have been confirmed heterosexuals for a considerable length of time. These so called 'straights' often find themselves misunderstood and out of place in New York society . . ." (*Trinity Times*, May 14, 1976).

142. *Ibid.* Also see Lester's op-ed piece aimed at the professoriate: "Professor, Teach," *New York Times*, March 5, 1979.

143. Report to Board, October 25, 1979.

144. Garten was the last headmaster to sit on the board and experience its ambiance firsthand. He recalled, wistfully, one-sentence treasurer's reports, followed by desultory reports of the two headmasters (by seniority). Nothing unpleasant ever was allowed to surface in meetings: "It was wonderful." Afterward, Garten and board president Glover Johnson often repaired to the Downtown Association, nearby to Johnson's offices, for a long lunch over Scotch highballs and dry martinis (Richard Garten interview, December 13, 2002). Lester, of a different temperament, thought the board then was run by "some real fat heads." Lester recalled his amazement when board president Otto Kinzel told him during his job interview: "I'm going to be your boss, but I want you to know that when somebody complains to me about that school, I just tell them to go to hell." Meetings started at 5:00. At 6:00, Kinzel rapped on the arm of his chair with his signet ring, pronouncing "The ice is melting: do I hear a motion to adjourn?" (Lester interview, December 10, 2002).

145. Trinity School Yearbook, 1955–56; board list, 1975 (Trinity School Archives).

146. See discussion in Board Minutes, June 5 and September 9, 1975.

147. Board minutes, November 6, 1975.

148. There was also reference to the changes facilitating severance of Trinity-Pawling, "if such action were deemed advisable or desirable by the Corporation in the future." It soon was.

149. Minutes of Ad Hoc Committee to Revise the Charter and By-laws of The Trinity Episcopal Schools Corporation, September 16, 1975. The detail: Everyone resigned January 8, 1976, pending Board of Regents approval of the revised charter. Classes I (Alumni and Parents' Association presidents) and Class II (Historic Trustees) were automatically reconstituted as such on Regents approval. Class III (term trustees) were selected by lot as members of A, B, or C groups to serve one, two, or three terms, respectively and were assured of re-election to additional three-year terms. Members of groups A, B, and C would serve four, five, or six years and then had to retire for at least one year (C. E. Doyle, secretary, to O. Kinzel, president, January 8, 1976).

150. Board Minutes, November 17, 1975.

151. In 1977 Trinity mailed applications to 1,130 prospective students and interviewed 527 for some 100 spaces in K–11. The record became repetitious: That year Lester reported "we have been inundated with extremely impressive boys and girls [in grade 9]. We simply do not have the room for all the bright youngsters who would like to do their high school here. . . . An important point about this group of incoming students is that they come from not only our normal K–8 feeder schools. Students from Brearley, Dalton, Columbia Prep, United Nations, Riverdale, Spence, Birch-Wathen and Friends are trying to transfer to Trinity. Many well-qualified students linger wistfully on our waiting lists. They simply do not want to be told there is no room" (Report to Board, May 5, 1977). Five years later: "Last year the number of candidates was so overwhelming we had to close applications to Kindergarten and Grade One in November" (Lester to Trinity Community, August 1982). Getting in was easier for brothers and sisters: "All other things being equal, we give preference to our sibling applicants. Over the last few years, we have accepted a larger proportion of sibling applicants than any other category." Substantially: In 1983–84, Trinity took in 65 percent of all sibling applicants, about 15–18 percent of all others (Lester to Board, January 19, 1984).

152. Cited in Lester to Board memorandum, January 16, 1984, "Long Range Financial Planning."

153. Report to Board, October 25, 1979.

154. Report to Board, January 20, 1977.

155. In 1983 Lester invited his headmaster counterpart at the Westminster School in London, John Rae, for a visit. Rae stayed three weeks and taught Lester's senior history seminar. He was struck throughout by the similarity of the two institutions, both old traditional boys' schools turned coed, with high standards and top teachers, whose students are "affluent, urban, intelligent children." The key word—"affluent"—was a long way from deserving. Lester did not demur (*Alumni News*, Spring 1983, reprinted from *The New York Times*, February 26, 1983).

156. Porter–Sargent red guides.

157. Following Memorandum, Lester to Board, January 16, 1984; financials.

158. *Ibid.*

159. See Capital Campaign Outline, June 21, 1979 (Trinity School Archives).

160. "Local Residents Speak Out on Trinity's Role in Neighborhood," *Trinity Times*, March 5, 1969.

161. "Trinity's most dangerous and upsetting problem is street crime. . . . Matt Miller, a seventh grader, was approached by a youth on his way to school last Thursday. Witnessing the crime, one of the student's parents grabbed the suspect and attempted to disarm him from his lockblade knife. During the struggle, Lyle Redelinghuys, Head of the History Department at Trinity, rushed to the aid of the parent. The two men disarmed the youth and dragged him up 91st Street to Amsterdam Avenue. There the police soon met the men and arrested the suspect" (*Trinity Times*, October 17, 1975).

162. Following: Report to Trinity Board of Trustees, December 11, 1964; 387 F. Supp. 1044, 1054 (Southern District of New York 1974); *Strycker's Bay Neighborhood Council, Inc. v. Roland N. Karlen et al.* US 62 L Ed 2d 433, 100 Supreme Court, January 7, 1980; and David B. Wescoe, "Urban Conflict: Trinity School and The West Side Urban Renewal Plan," Columbia University Law School paper, December 1977.

163. "Mayor Lindsay decided in 1970 to run for President and his key liberal constituencies were the poor and the black. Assemblyman Blumenthal, whose district embraced the West Side Urban Renewal Area, decided in 1970 to run for Mayor and his key liberal constituencies were the poor and the black. State Senator Ohrenstein and City Councilman Weiss follow his requested lead. Manhattan Borough President Sutton, a black, also decided in 1970 to run for Mayor and that he should do all things to emphasize his central constituencies of the poor and the black" (cited in Wescoe, 5).

164. CONTINUE president in the late 1970s Eugene Halpern: "We're an irate gang of middle-class and working-class people who have been stomped on, and now we're stomping back." See Fergus M. Bordewich, "West Side Story: From Gang Fights to Class War," *New York Magazine*, June 5, 1978.

165. It became regular fare for the *Trinity Times*, viz., "The Community and the Courts . . .Mr. Lumbard to Lead Housing Suit . . . Trinity Suit Incurs Wrath of Neighbors and State Senator . . . Merchants and Residents Favor Mixed Rent Housing," January 27, 1972.

166. Lumbard thought this fatuous and that Trinity, with money at risk, had the high ground: "It wasn't a matter in the abstract of are we for the poor or not for the poor. We entered the deal-and this is very important-many years ago under the assumption that the real estate values surrounding this area would be maintained. Trinity undertook a long-term mortgage commitment of twenty years. It couldn't walk away from that. So once we signed on, we had a stake in the quality of the neighborhood" (Lumbard interview, November 13, 1992).

167. *Otero v. New York City Housing Authority*, 484 F. 2d 122 (2nd Circuit, 1973), where the court held the city was "obligated to take affirmative steps to promote racial integration even though this in some instances may not operate to the immediate advantage of some non-white persons."

168. Thought Trinity counsel Eugene Morris: "The argument on tipping is the same

whether you call it low income or racial. The distinction between the two is totally phony" (cited in Wescoe, 13).

169. After Trinity had withdrawn, the case reached the U.S. Supreme Court, which on writ of certiorari reversed, eight to one, the lower court's decision in favor on the plaintiff (by then CONTINUE) on the environmental issues. Thurgood Marshall dissented, arguing that certiorari dismissal was not appropriate and that HUD's own revised environmental impact statement "raised enough valid questions about the potential social and environmental impacts involved" to negate the significance of delay and mandate "ameliorative measures" (US 62 L Ed 2d 439).

170. *New York Times*, July 25, 1975.

171. *New York Times*, January 17, 1975; also *New York Post*, January 16, 1975. The student press weighed in, too, opposing the action: *Trinity Times*, February 6, 1975

172. An example of a homemade flier appearing in Trinity's neighborhood (and probably at St. John the Divine), signed "Coalition to Save the West Side: DEMONSTRATE: Tuesday January 11, 139 W. 91st Street: Demand that Trinity School drop it's [sic] federal court suit to stop low rent housing on Site 30. Since 1971, Trinity School has held up construction of low rent housing on Side 30 of the West Side Urban Development Area by going into Federal court to claim that low-income people are undesirable. In his November 15, 1974 decision US District Court Judge Irving Ben Cooper rejected Trinity's argument that low-income persons tend to induce 'neighborhood deterioration' and said: 'One cannot accept a propensity toward anti-social behavior with low-income families.' But although Trinity's racist and anti-low-income people argument lost out in Federal court, Trinity could still prevent construction on Site 30 by appealing the decision and keeping the case in the courts for months or years. WE DEMAND THAT TRINITY DROP ITS SUIT AND NOT APPEAL THE NOVEMBER 15 DECISION" (Trinity School Archives).

173. Lester interview, August 20, 2007.

174. The move may have been principled, but it involved little sacrifice: "We weren't roughing it in anyway; that was a great house" (Lester interview, December 10, 2002).

175. The fight over community use of the pool was a long one. In the summer of 1972, seventy-five protesters from the Strycker's Bay Neigborhood Council picketed outside Trinity with placards like "Trinity Lives in Luxierie [*sic*] while the Poor Live in MISERY." The Council argued that the new Trinity was a public building because it had been built with a "tax abatement, public funds and a Mitchell–Lama mortgage subsidy." Lumbard shot back that only the House, not the school, had thus benefited. To the demand that the neighbors swim along with Trinity, board president Glover Johnson, arguing expense of insurance and staffing issues, responded "no" (*Trinity Times*, October 6, 1972).

176. "I have a kind of radical background. I mean it's not really Marxist but I've been an active Democrat, a precinct captain in Chicago under Mayor Daley and on the Democratic central committee here in New York" (*Ibid.*).

177. Lumbard interview, November 13, 1992.

178. Lester to Board, May 21, 1979, January 29, 1980; "Innovative Program Prepares Minority Pupils for Prep School," *The New York Times*, December 2, 1979.

179. *Alumni News*, Fall 1979.

180. Garten to Board, October 1968.

181. Lester to Board, January 12, 1978.

182. "Forgotten New Yorkers Get Taste of Holiday," *The New York Times*, November 25, 1977. Also "Feasting with Gramps," *The Westsider*, December 1, 1977; "Kids Aid Seniors," *Wisdoms Child: New York's Free Weekly Paper*, November 29, 1977.

183. Board minutes, February 26, 1975.

184. Lester interview, August 20, 2007.

185. Board minutes, February 26, 1975.

186. Lester interview, December 10, 2002

187. After short headmasterships at University High School in San Francisco, Chicago Latin, and the Blake School in Minneapolis, Lester ended his career as he had begun, as a history teacher in Chicago (at Francis W. Parker, unlike Trinity or Latin famous as a progressive school).

188. Trinity admissions booklet, n.d., ca. 1983–85.

189. See photograph, *ibid*.

190. Lester interview, December 10, 2002.

CHAPTER 8: ELITE EDUCATION IN A DEMOCRATIC SOCIETY (261–326)

1. Lester certainly "did it" as far as the faculty and students were concerned, and after years of institutional aloofness he reconnected school to community. He did not do it in the department of finance. "I was never comfortable with finances," Lester remembered years later-nor did he ever claim such at the time (Lester interview, August 2007).

2. *Trinity Today*, 1985.

3. *Ibid*.

4. The Pingree School in New Jersey.

5. That he was also, at the time of his hiring, divorced and single seems to have been no obstacle.

6. John Hanley interview, October 30, 2002.

7. *Ibid.*, 1988

8. Berrisford died in 1998 in Hong Kong. Neither personal papers nor interviews survive.

9. Berrisford to Board, November 1987.

10. "I make no apologies for emphasizing evaluation; it is the foundation of a sound educational system. Indeed the accreditation committee which visited Trinity in 1981 specifically enjoined the school to institute formal evaluation procedures. When every one gets used to the process, I foresee much creative interaction, some of which has already begun. Within a few years, I expect that Trinity teachers will be writing self-evaluations, which is the most effective and interesting way to develop a teacher. I have been told that some faculty members are concerned that any evaluation system could be used unfairly to discontinue an experienced teacher. Actually, the opposite is true;

good evaluation is a protection against arbitrary judgment" (Berrisford to Board, October 4, 1989, Headmaster's Files).

11. *Ibid.*; NAIS documents.

12. Berrisford to Board, November 1987.

13. *Ibid.*

14. June Hilton, long-time director of admissions in the Lower School, remembered that under Lester admissions policy, fantastically, had not been linked to budget at all, and that spending was routinely conducted in a vacuum from any budget (June Hilton conversation, November 13, 2007).

15. Berrisford to Board, May 19, 1988. On Ryan's departure, Berrisford reported delicately: "In order to assess more accurately how we allocate our resources, I began last September to take a closer look at our budget and financial statements. As we began this review, John Ryan decided, after 15 years of devoted service to Trinity School, that he would like to move out of the city and thus he resigned his position here." Dannenberg took over July 1, 1988, and remains at this writing Trinity's chief financial officer (CFO). See Joan Dannenberg interview, October 31, 2007.

16. Berrisford to Board, January 1988.

17. Annual reports; financials from office of Chief Financial Officer.

18. See correspondence, Board of Trustees special meeting, March 18, 1988, Headmaster's Files.

19. The faculty then totaled over 120. Faculty Representative meetings, however, were voluntary, and sixty-nine was a higher than usual attendance.

20. Faculty Representative Committee to Barbara Paul Robinson [board president], March 14, 1988, Headmaster's Files. What escapes the record of that meeting was criticism of the board that hired Berrisford. "What," one surmises some teacher saying, "could they have been thinking?"

21. Barbara Robinson, then parent and board president, interview, November 2, 2007.

22. Executive Board Parents' Association to Board of Trustees, March 16, 1988, Headmaster's Files. There were specific complaints, too: "Issues as important as the selling of air rights over our buildings, or the loss of several senior administrators and faculty, or the changing of dress codes, or changes in student counseling and support services, are communicated late, inadequately, or not at all."

23. *Ibid.*

24. Officers: Barbara Paul Robinson, president and parent; Douglas T. Tansill, vice-president, alum, '56; Marvin Deckoff, treasurer; Martha Watts, secretary, parent; Stephen Kaufman, assistant secretary. Trustees: Terry L. Andreas; John P. Arnhold, alum '71; J. Robert Ave; D. Broward Craig, alum '46; David H. Feinberg; Richard N. Foster, parent; Vartan Gregorian, parent; Jordan L. Gruzen; Edwin A Heard, alum '44; S. Lloyd Kaufman, Jr., alum '64; Evelyn Lauder, parent; Edward J. Lorenze, alum '40; Daniel P. Matthews, rector, Trinity Church ex officio; Carl A. Morse; Rupert Murdoch, parent; Charles S. Olton; Kathryn Piper; Richard Seaver; Carolyn Smith; Marlene Turner, parent.

25. Board minutes, April 7, 1988.

26. *Ibid.*, also January 25, 1990. In April 1988 Board President Robinson sent trustees an article from *Newsweek* (April 25, 1988) on "Management for the 1990s," which quoted Foster, a prominent authority on innovative organizations: "The ideal manager of the future will combine cost-consciousness with creativity and a new ingredient, caring. McKinsey & Co. director Richard N. Foster stresses that the last two of the three c's are linked: firms with high morale will usually be the most innovative. The 90s, Foster says, will pit 'attackers—those who try to make money by changing the order of things—[against] defenders, those who protect the status quo.' And morale, he adds, is important to the attacker—the innovator. He is 'often more powerful than he appears, because he is more motivated.'" Added a stressed Robinson in a PS: "I thought you might be interested in the enclosed *Newsweek* article quoting Dick Foster. We are all looking forward to his help in connection with improving our own morale!" (Robinson to Board, April 21, 1988, Headmaster's Files).

27. Berrisford to Board, May 19, 1988, Headmaster's Files.

28. Remembered then Upper School principal Suellyn Preston Scull, who was instrumental in the dress change: "The faculty wouldn't buy into the old dress code, and fighting it just wasn't worth it."

29. *Ibid.*

30. *Ibid.*

31. Not every trustee was uncertain. Board president Robinson remembered Rupert Murdoch, whose daughter then attended Trinity, as a steadying influence but of decided views. At one board meeting the media mogul reportedly slammed the table and, on the subject of faculty "demands," pronounced: "The pressmen cannot be allowed to run the paper!" (Barbara Robinson interview, November 2, 2007). Also Benjamin Shute, trustee, interview, October 31, 2007.

32. *Ibid.*

33. Martha Watts interview, October 29, 2007.

34. As laid out in 1990, a five-year multipronged plan laid out seven goals intended to influence policy: "1) to provide an academic program which develops clear thinking, a love of learning and intellectual curiosity in all its students; 2) to maintain the school in a strong financial position; 3) to attract, support and retain outstanding teachers through an effective compensation system and attractive working conditions; 4) to maintain the highest standards for admission while achieving a rich mix of talents and backgrounds; 5) to maintain and improve the plant and facilities to make it possible to achieve the academic, athletic and extracurricular goals of the school; 6) to address consciously moral and ethical issues at all grade levels, both within and outside the formal academic program; 7) to encourage both students and faculty members to be full, effective and responsible participants in all aspects of the school's life, and especially to engender qualities of leadership in students" (April 12, 1990, Headmaster's Files).

35. Berrisford to Board, May 9, 1991, Headmaster's Files.

36. Barbara Robinson, interview, November 2, 2007.

37. Eugene Pinover, interview, October 30, 2007.

38. Howard Warren, conversation with author, December 17, 2007, by permission.

39. Suellyn Preston Scull, conversation, October 2007. Memory of the Berrisford episode lived long in Trinity's collective memory, particularly with regard to the faculty's reputation for contentiousness. Not everyone, however, found that remarkable. Mark Simpson, who was hired from the outside (Trinity and New York) as principal of the Upper School in 2003, heard much in the hiring process of Trinity's "querulous faculty." "So how," he mused, "did that distinguish them from any other faculty?"

40. Eugene Pinover, interview, October 30, 2007; resignation letter, Berrisford to Board president Douglas Tansill, March 14, 1990; Tansill to "the Trinity Family," March 15, 1990, Headmaster's Files.

41. Moses owed Berrisford a debt not just for the introduction: He had the advantage of coming after him, not Robin Lester. About Berrisford's fate Moses later commented: "The contrast [with Lester] killed him" (Henry Moses, interview, October 3, 2007).

42. John R. Johnson, Saint Louis Country Day School, *Trinity Times*, November 15, 1990.

43. Including Trinity alums who knew him in Cambridge: "Everyone here likes him a lot. He'll make a great headmaster" (Douglas Kaden, Trinity '90, *Trinity Times*, February 14, 1991).

44. Board visitors looked closely at the quality of Moses's Harvard performance and testimony of his strength in "supervising people" (Benjamin Shute, alumnus '54, trustee, interview, October 31, 2007).

45. Eugene Pinover, interview, October 30, 2007; Martha Watts, interview, October 29, 2007.

46. Martha Watts, interview, October 29, 2007.

47. Marlene Turner (Trustee and Parents' Association president), interview, October 29, 2007.

48. Moses took up the job in July 1991. Remembered trustee and search committee member Eugene Pinover, Moses looked above all like a peacemaker, but "it was a slow dance" (Pinover, interview, October 30, 2007).

49. *Trinity Times*, December 14, 1990.

50. *Trinity Times*, February 14, 1991. Trinity's operating budget the year Moses was hired was modestly in the black, some $200,000 on revenues of $11.7 million. Of those revenues, however, over $10 million derived from tuition and fees, $1 million from annual giving, and only $266,000 dividends and interest (endowment) (1991 Annual Report).

51. "To promote coherence in the curriculum and fairness and consistency in decision-making; to clarify and create policies and procedures while reviewing fundamental processes, such as student discipline and contract decisions; to begin to develop a clear sense of shared priorities and to develop programs and budgets that support them; to continue to increase racial and ethnic diversity, and to continue to find ways to nurture the spiritual life of the school" (1992 Annual Report).

52. See "Role of Governing Body" attachment to Henry Moses to Board October 3, 1991, Headmaster's Files.

53. By-Laws of Trinity Episcopal School Corporation, 1993. Trustees were to be at least nineteen years old but less than seventy, they were to number from fifty to thirty, and no sitting headmaster was eligible to serve. The rector of Trinity Church and current presidents of the Parents' and Alumni associations sat ex officio. Trustees could serve two consecutive three-year terms, and a third after a one-year hiatus.

54. "I've begun to visit with you in your own lairs. Stand by for a call. These times are very useful for me: I learn how you got to the Board and what you think some of the important issues for the Board and School are. Thanks in advance" (Moses to Board, October 3, 1991, Headmaster's Files).

55. Moses tells the story of how shortly after his arrival, there was "on the table" a plan to replace the artificial grass covering on the school's playing field, known as "the turf." It was to cost over $300,000, which the new headmaster was baffled to find nowhere in any budget. "That was typical: they just sort of found it" (Moses, interview, October 3, 2007).

56. Eugene Pinover, interview, October 30, 2007.

57. "Role of Governing Body" document, *passim*.

58. Henry Moses, interview, October 3, 2007.

59. Joan Dannenberg interview, October 31, 2007.

60. Board minutes, October 3, 1991.

61. Board minutes, October 22, 1998.

62. Susan Ulin, interview, November 1, 2007.

63. A history teacher and development director in schools in New York, high school principal in Florida, and director of development at the Museum of the City of New York (Myles Amend, interview, December 19, 2007).

64. Moses to Board, October 31, 1991, Headmaster's Files.

65. Eugene Pinover, interview, October 30, 2007.

66. See Report of the Planning Committee to Board, June 11, 1992, Headmaster's Files.

67. *Ibid.*

68. Eugene Pinover, board secretary, to Board, June 11, 1992 (Headmaster's Files).

69. "Private Schools Turn to Reconstruction," *The New York Times*, October 13, 1991.

70. Augustus K. Oliver, board president, in Annual Report 1995–96.

71. The Hawley Wing as first built had none at all at street level. Windows were added only in the 1990s.

72. In addition, as part of the building program, three floors of the Annex were renovated to create new performing arts classrooms, a computer laboratory, and athletics faculty offices. The fourth floor of the 139 building was renovated for the Lower School, and a new photography laboratory was built in the Upper School.

73. President's report, Annual Report 1996–97; Joan Dannenberg to Board, January 19, 1996, memorandum discussing tax-exempt bond financing, Headmaster's Files; Eugene Pinover, interview, October 30, 2007.

74. Annual Report 1997–98.

75. *Ibid.*

76. Schools surveyed: Brearley, Collegiate, Dalton, Ethical Culture, Horace Mann, and Riverdale (John Howard, treasurer, report to Board, January 18, 1996, Headmaster's Files).

77. Howard to Board, January 18, 1995; Augustus Oliver, president, to parents, April 12, 1995, Headmaster's Files.

78. In fiscal 2001–02, the first year the Development Office tracked annual pledge activity (not just gifts received), 100 percent of trustees gave an average of $11,600; 84 percent of parents averaged $2,100; 19 percent of alumni averaged $740 (Trinity Fund–Comparative Analysis, May 31, 2002). See "The Case for Endowment at Trinity," Annual Report 1998–99.

79. Annual Report 2001–02.

80. Annual Report 2005–06. During the five years ending 2005–06, endowment and other long-term investments provided on average 6.9 percent of Trinity's total income.

81. Andrew Brownstein, interview, October 31, 2007.

82. It was possible to debate the utility of endowment versus a pay-as-you-go model of finance: peg prices high enough to cover costs plus a cushion and pray the market would not soften (as seemed a remote but not impossible prospect for Trinity in the New York City of the early 2000s). Such an approach of course would collide with other goals. See diversity discussion later in this chapter.

83. Following, author's class visits, 2004, 2007.

84. When Berrisford went, Milliman feared with some reason that she would be next. "Soldier on," Berrisford advised, wisely it turned out for her (Rosemary Milliman, interview, October 30, 2007).

85. Following, Rosemary Milliman, interviews October 30, 2007, and January 9, 2008.

86. Milliman interview, January 9, 2008.

87. Following, Lower School curriculum guides.

88. Diane Stewart-Garrett, interview, January 9, 2008.

89. *Ibid.*

90. *Ibid.*

91. Seminar with seven upper school students, January 10, 2008.

92. This was true, if sometimes unevenly. An Upper School "achievement center" staffed by full-time learning specialists provided additional boosts as needed, in reading, writing, and math skills critical to academic success in the classroom.

93. Conversation with Donald Connor, November 2007.

94. Seminar with seven upper school students, January 10, 2008.

95. Henry Moses, baccalaureate address, 2007.

96. From the Cole era, Trinity appears to have enrolled, randomly, a few students who might have been said to represent a sort of diversity-one or two Jewish boys, a few with Hispanic surnames, and of course non-Episcopalian Christians. Their presence, however, went wholly unremarked and, one supposes (there are no records), may well have been limited had numbers ever threatened the Episcopal character of the school.

97. "Varying Opinions on Diversification," *Trinity Times*, December 14, 1990.

98. Moses to Board, Implementation of Long Range Plan (1990), October 21, 1993, Headmaster's Files.

99. Admissions Office report, September 20, 1993, Headmaster's Files.

100. Long Range Plan Implementation, *passim*.

101. Chart, Minority Faculty/Staff Recruitment for 1993–94, Headmaster's Files.

102. Moses to Board, December 7, 1995.

103. *Ibid.*

104. Diversity committee to Board, April 11, 1997, Headmaster's Files.

105. "Notes for an Essay on Diversity," Moses to Board, December 2, 1998.

106. Headmaster's column, Annual Report 1995.

107. Following from Survey of Trinity School Parents: Report of Findings," April 2000, Headmaster's Files.

108. Following, Kevin D. Ramsey, "A Diverse Community," *Trinity Per Saecula*, Fall 1999 and Summer 2001.

109. In what may have been a reflection of a yet imperfect state of affairs and work yet to do, author Kevin Ramsey decided not to identify any students regardless of their requests: "to protect them from attacks by some members of the Trinity community" (*ibid.*, Summer 2001, p. 12).

110. Not yet so, apparently, for students: "I don't know anyone who has come out as being gay at Trinity and I don't think I ever will, because this is not an environment in which someone would feel comfortable to come out. If anyone ever did, he or she would be ostracized by every person in the school."

111. Seminar with seven Upper School students, January 10, 2008.

112. Andrew Brownstein, interview, October 31, 2007. Brownstein also noted that the challenge of being able to do very much was very large, because Trinity had so few open spots.

113. Following, Henry Moses, "Justice Project: Community Service and Affirmative Action," draft August 5, 2007; "Membership and Competition," draft September 27, 2007. Moses to author, October 2007.

114. Annual Report 1999.

115. Some students demurred at the image so fretted over by their elders. A diverse group of Trinity Upper Schoolers interviewed in 2008 uniformly dismissed the barbell anxiety, or at least the perception of it in daily school life. "Trinity is more middle class than a lot of people think, and nobody puts anybody down because your family might have more money than someone else's" (seminar with seven Upper Schoolers, January 10, 2008).

116. Andrew Brownstein, board president, interview, October 31, 2007.

117. Annual Report 2005.

118. Benjamin Shute, Jr., trustee, interview, October 31, 2007.

119. Annual Report 2006.

120. In 2005–06, 17 percent of families receiving aid paid more than 50 percent of their tuition themselves; 44 percent paid over one-quarter (Annual Report 2006).

121. *Ibid.*

122. Pointing in his office to a long shelf of binders containing seventeen years of memos, chapel talks, board reports, speeches to alums and parents, Moses the headmaster and the English teacher said: "There are times when I think the most significant thing I've done here has been to attempt to write Trinity into existence" (Moses interview, October 3, 2007).

123. See chapter 2.

124. See Annual Report 1988.

125. See "Our Idea of Excellence," Annual Report 2000. The document was prepared in context of the self-study required for Trinity's ten-year recertification by the NYSAIS, but one suspects would have happened anyway. Not long after, Trinity—Moses, the board, the faculty—attempted to discern the challenges likely to confront twenty-first century students and how they would affect what went on at Trinity now and how Trinity might have to change. They could not be accused of shirking big issues, including: changing demographics that would place whites in the minority, a world where "whiteness" is not the norm; the individualization and privatization of leisure and pleasure that would reduce a sense of community; the coming world citizenship and changing assumptions about the creation and distribution of wealth; continuing political and cultural tensions between the coasts and the heartland; the rising velocity particularly of information technology and attendant questions of access and ethical use; the withering of traditional means of cultural expression and the need to develop new notions of literacy. "What," wondered Moses," will the twenty-first century hammer us with next?" (Henry Moses to Senior Staff, draft, "Educating Students for the Twenty-first Century," February 1, 2001, Headmaster's Files; Moses, interview, October 3, 2007).

126. Moses letter, Annual Report 2000.

127. Moses letters, Annual Reports 2002, 2003.

128. Annual Report 2003.

129. Following, Lawrence Momo and Liz Pleshette, director/associate directors of college counseling at Trinity, interview, December 20, 2007.

130. See, for example, The Wall Street Journal, November 30, 2007, "How to Get Into Harvard," which ranked Trinity seventh out of forty high schools (fourth in New York City, after Collegiate, Brearley, and Chapin) for their success rates in getting students into eight highly selective colleges: Harvard, Princeton, MIT, Williams, Pomona, Swarthmore, the University of Chicago, and Johns Hopkins. The narrowly based and cursory survey (the article was, however, the most read in the paper for that day) ignored the broader college universe. "Of course, college placement is only one measure of a high school's success, and varies from year to year. Many high schools emphasized to us that they strive to find the right match for each student, not the college with the most cachet." Indeed.

131. Moses and John P. Arnhold, board president, letter, Annual Report 2001.

132. See earlier discussion of survey.

133. Robert Ray Parks interview, November 17, 2004.

134. Later after he had left Trinity, when there were complaints about the restrictive-

ness of the arrangement, Lester defended it: "It was Episcopalian money. People have given it to Trinity Church, so why shouldn't they have it? If it were a [Jewish] temple, and they had that same stipulation, I wouldn't feel called upon to question it; it's the ball game" (Robin Lester, interview, December 10, 2002).

135. *Ibid.*

136. Lester interview, *ibid.*

137. See Charles Taylor, *A Secular Age* (2007).

138. "Religion at Trinity" document, 1994, Headmaster's Files.

139. *Ibid.*

140. Many protested, and not Christians alone, at such tampering with "Trinity's traditions," and the cross stayed.

141. Henry C. Moses and Timothy L. Morehouse, "A Letter on Religion at Trinity," April 26, 2007.

142. Timothy L. Morehouse, interview, October 5, 2007.

143. Full political emancipation of Catholics and other nonconformists in England waited many more years, until the late nineteenth century.

144. Daniel Matthews, Rector of Trinity Church, to Henry Moses, June 30, 2003; Henry Moses to Board of Trustees, October 3, 2003, Headmaster's Files.

145. "A Letter on Religion."

146. Timothy Morehouse, interview. In the early 2000s, religion's return and the weakness of secularization, for good or ill, were often remarked in context of resurgent conflict between Muslim cultures and the West, but not exclusively. See English philosopher John Gray, "How Futile has been our Faith in Exorcising Religion," *Financial Times*, June 29, 2007; also Gray, *Black Mass: Apocalyptic Religion and the Death of Utopia* (2007). The entire culture wars phenomenon that reshaped modern American political life from the 1980s onward posited competing moral visions rooted in religion that were extremely difficult to mediate. For example, James Davison Hunter, *Culture Wars: The Struggle to Define America* (1991); Robert N. Bellah, *Uncivil Religion* (1987); Peter L. Berger, *The War Over the Family* (1984); Alasdair MacIntyre, *After Virtue* (1984).

147. Trinity is not a parochial school and since 1969 operates under no supervisory arrangement with Trinity Church or any other parish. It is a member of the National Association of Independent Schools and of the National Association of Episcopal Schools, whose director at this writing was the Rev. Dan Heischman, former Trinity chaplain.

148. Timothy Morehouse, interview.

149. "A Letter on Religion."

150. Chapel renovation meetings, January–October, 2007. Both Trinity chapels were renovated by 2009, with crosses remaining.

151. Timothy Morehouse, interview.

152. Emily Scharf told of seeing it, with Leaman, on the beach: "Len drove, picking up assorted friends and my entire family, including my sister-in-law who was visiting from France. He took us to Jones Beach, which is dark and scary and cold in the middle of the night in winter. Just getting out of the car in the parking lot to look wasn't good

enough. Len urged us to plod through the sand to an ideal place near the water so that we could look up and appreciate Halley's Comet in all its glory. The only problem was that it was pouring rain" (Emily Scharf, memorial tribute to Len Leaman, November 14, 2007).

153. Notes on memorial service for Leonard Leaman, Trinity School Chapel, November 14, 2007.

154. *The New York Times*, April 19, 2008; *New York Sun*, April 17, 2008; *Trinity Times*, May 2, 2008.

155. Associate Head Suellyn Preston Scull was named Acting Head in November 2007 and appointed Interim Head for 2008–09 in May 2008.

156. *Trinity Times*, May 2, 2008.

157. Moses credited this view to former Trinity history teacher Maxine McClintock (Henry Moses, interview, October 3, 2007). To such a proposition many tuition-paying Trinity families might have demurred, arguing that private education operated in a market like many others, and what further justification was needed than supply meeting demand?

158. "Our Idea of Excellence."

Index